## ADVANCE PRAISE FOR PENNY E. STONE'S
### *365 QUICK, EASY AND INEXPENSIVE DINNER MENUS*

"Thank you, Penny! Your book makes creating an inspired dinner as easy as looking on the calendar. *365 Quick, Easy & Inexpensive Dinner Menus* is bound to be a best seller for people with great taste and little time."

—R.A. FORSTER,
USA Today top selling author
of *Keeping Counsel*

"There is no excuse for taking the family out to dinner at a fast food restaurant even though you may be tired and weary from a long day at work. Simply open the new cookbook by Penny E. Stone, turn to today's date and whip up the suggested menu. Most of the recipes can be made in less than one hour...While you are broiling, baking or sauteing sit a spell and read the delightful anecdotes sprinkled throughout the cookbook. If the kids are driving you nuts, check out the many offerings of things for kids to do in the kitchen— there are great ideas to keep little helpers busy. I especially enjoyed seeing the preparation and cooking times listed for each recipe."

—BETH LILLEY,
newspaper columnist, author and editor of the
forthcoming *Oklahoma* cookbook
in Golden West Publishers'
"Cooking Across America" series

"If you're like me, trying to decide what to make for dinner often takes longer than making the meal itself. Penny Stone's terrific new cookbook, *365 Quick, Easy & Inexpensive Dinner Menus,* solves that problem by offering an easy to prepare, healthy, delicious meal for every single day of the year. A fun, wonderful cook book that belongs in every kitchen."

—ARLENE S. USLANDER,
author of *That's What Grandmothers Are For*
and award winning columnist

"As a wife and mother who juggles domestic duties with running a home-based freelance business, Penny Stone's book, *365 Quick, Easy & Inexpensive Dinner Menus* is an answer to my prayers. Thanks, Penny, for making my life easier—you've put together a masterpiece of a cookbook. It's one I'll use every day for years to come!"

—BEV WALTON-PORTER,
Editor/Publisher, Scribe & Quill Freelance Services

"In her new cookbook, author Penny E. Stone offers a year's worth of menu suggestions and recipes as palatable as they are practical. So forget the raspberry salsa. The on-the-go cook will appreciate the easy-to-read collection of recipes that are affordable to make, but don't skimp on the taste. Now, if Stone could only run to the grocery store for me, too..."

—LINDA FERRIS,
editor of *Alexandria Times-Tribune*

"This delightful, fun-to-read book is packed with recipes that will become family favorites because of their taste and ease of preparation. A practical gift for newlyweds or families with children, *365 Quick, Easy and Inexpensive Dinner Menus* is sure to find a place of honor in any busy kitchen. In addition to the recipes, there are parenting and kitchen tips as well as ideas about how to celebrate special days of the year. A masterpiece!"

—GRACE WITWER HOUSHOLDER,
journalist and author of *The Funny Things
Kids Say Will Brighten Any Day*

# 365
## Quick, Easy
## & Inexpensive
# Dinner
# Menus

# 365
## Quick, Easy
## & Inexpensive
# Dinner
# Menus

## PENNY E. STONE

READON PUBLICATIONS INC.
CONCORD

CHAMPION PRESS, LTD.
BEVERLY HILLS, CALIFORNIA

Group discounts are available. For more information call (360) 576 9261.

Publisher's Cataloging-in-Publication
(Provided by Quality Books, Inc.)

Stone, Penny E.
     365 quick, easy & inexpensive dinner menus /
Penny E. Stone. — 1st ed.
     p. cm.
     Includes index.
     LCCN: 99-74645
     ISBN: 1-891400-33-9

     1. Dinners and dining. 2. Quick and easy cookery. 3. Menus. I. Title.

TX737.S76 2000          641.5'4
               QBI99-1606

This edition published in Canada.
Licensed by Readon Publications in agreement with Champion Press
8241 Keele Street, Units 9-10, Concord, Ontario L4K 1Z5
Tel: (905) 761-9666  Fax: (905) 761-1377  Toll Free: 1-800-401-9774
E-mail: readon@readon.com  Website: www.readon.com

10 9 8 7 6

Book and Cover Design by Kathy Campbell, Wildwood Studios.

This book is dedicated to my four "professional taste-testers:"

Craig, my loving husband

Loressa

Zachary-Taylor

and Kiersten,

who endured endless dinners of new dishes and permitted me to take time away from them to put this book in writing. You make my world complete and I love you each more than mere words can describe.

## Acknowledgments

There are several individuals whom I feel compelled to publicly recognize. Without their influence, help, advice, support and friendship, I would not have been able to complete this project.

My heart overflows with gratitude for my mother, Joyce E. James, who is responsible for teaching me how to cook in the first place. Loving appreciation goes to Marna S. Stone, my mother-in-law, for sharing her recipes, her kitchen, her advice and her son with me.

Special thanks goes to Brook Noel, my friend, mentor and editor; to Gina Wahl for her meticulous editing; to Jean Eastman for her continued support and encouragement; to John and Anne Belzer, my uncle and aunt; to Julia Pierce, Patrick and Becky Skinner, Kathy Garner and Dr. Cindy K. Taylor, for being my friends no matter what; and to my editors at Elwood Publishing Company for all their words of encouragement and support. A big thank you goes out to the staff at the Elwood City Library for their invaluable assistance.

*Psalm 51: 10-12*
*Philippians 4:13*

# Contents

*Unless stated otherwise, all recipes make 6 servings*

Please note: Unless specifically stated, each recipe in this book may use the following substitutions—

• use margarine instead of butter
• use 2%, 1%, ½% or whole milk in place of skim
• use plain yogurt in place of sour cream or vice versa

# January 1

*Family tradition mandates that each person must take at least one bite of cabbage on New Year's Day. By eating cabbage in one form or another, you seal your fate for having a blessed and prosperous new year. My family first tasted this Unique Coleslaw as guests of the Rev. Ron and Mary Becker of Elwood, Indiana. One bite and we were hooked—including our three children! Now Cabbage Rolls and this Unique Coleslaw are my traditional fare for New Year's Day.*

## CABBAGE ROLLS

*Prep. Time: 30 min. / Cook Time: 20-30 min.*

6 cups cooked instant rice
head of cabbage
½ to 1 lb. ground beef, ground turkey
    or ground sausage
1 quart stewed tomatoes
1 cup shredded cheddar cheese
salt and pepper to taste

Preheat oven to 350 degrees.

Cut and remove the stem and core of the cabbage. Peel off the outer leaves. You'll need one full leaf per serving. It's a good idea to peel off a few extra leaves just in case one tears when stuffing.

Cook cabbage leaves in a large pot of salted boiling water until just tender. Remove leaves.

Prepare instant rice according to package directions. Purée tomatoes and add to the rice. Crumble the meat into a pan of boiling water and boil until done. Drain off the greasy water and blot meat dry with a paper towel. Add meat to the rice mixture. Add salt and pepper to taste and mix all ingredients together.

Put ¼ cup rice mixture in the center of each tender cabbage leaf. Roll leaf and secure with either string or a toothpick. Place stuffed cabbage rolls in a 9 x 13 pan. After all the cabbage leaves have been stuffed, pour the rice mixture over the rolls and fill the pan. Top with shredded cheese and put into oven until cheese melts. Serve immediately.

## UNIQUE COLESLAW (FUMI SALAD)

*Prep. Time: 25 min. / Cook Time: 0*

1 lb. shredded cabbage
sunflower seeds
4-6 small green onions, chopped finely
1 pkg. Ramen™ noodles (buy a package of
    Chicken Flavored Ramen™ soup and save
    the chicken seasoning packet
    for something else)
DRESSING:
4 tablespoons sugar
2 teaspoons pepper
1 teaspoon salt
2 teaspoons Accent™
1 cup salad oil
8 tablespoons rice vinegar

Toss together the above, adding the sunflower seeds and raw-uncooked Ramen™ noodles (broken up). Shake dressing well and pour just enough on the salad to moisten and to taste. Serve immediately.

### Recipe for a Happy New Year
*Author Unknown*

Clean thoroughly 12 whole months
Divide into 365 parts: set aside, prepare as follows:

MIX WELL INTO EACH DAY:
1 part patience            1 part generosity
1 part work               1 part kindness
1 part courage            BLEND WITH:
ADD TO EACH DAY:          1 part prayer
1 part hope               1 part meditation
1 part faithfulness       1 good deed

*Season the mixture with a dash of good spirits, a sprinkle of fun, a pinch of play and a cup of good humor. Pour mixture into a vessel of love. Cook over radiant joy, garnish with a smile. Serve with quietness, unselfishness and cheer.*

# January 2

*January is observed as the National Soup Month. In celebration of this, try this heartwarming and filling Cheesy Potato Soup with Dumplings.*

## CHEESY POTATO SOUP WITH DUMPLINGS

*Prep. Time: 20 min. / Cook Time: 1 hour*

6-8 medium to large potatoes, peeled and cubed
2 stalks celery
1 small to medium onion, peeled and left whole
2 cups milk
1 tablespoon cornstarch*
1 small jar Cheese Whiz™
2 eggs
1-2 cups flour
salt and pepper to taste

Put potato cubes, celery sticks and whole onion in a large soup pan. Cover vegetables with water. Add a teaspoon of salt. Bring to a boil and cook until potatoes and vegetables are tender.

Remove celery and onion with about a cup of water and puree in blender. Return mixture to the potatoes. Add the milk and cheese. Stir over medium low heat until the cheese is completely melted. Turn the heat up to medium, stirring frequently to avoid scorching.

In a separate bowl, crack eggs and discard shells. Stir in flour with some salt and pepper until a thick dough forms. When soup begins to boil, drop dough into soup by teaspoons. The dumplings will float when they are cooked through. Cooking the dumplings through will take less than five minutes if they are dropped into boiling soup.

Dissolve cornstarch in ½ cup cold water and pour into soup. Continue heating until soup is at desired consistency. Reduce heat and serve with saltine crackers.

*Note: If there's an allergy to corn, baby food rice cereal may be substituted for the thickening agent. Use 2-3 cups of baby food cereal in place of the cornstarch.*

## EASY RICE PUDDING

*Prep. Time: 20 minutes / Cook Time: 15 minutes*

1 large box vanilla pudding mix
2 cups milk
2 cups cooked rice
1 teaspoon vanilla
¼ cup sugar

Prepare pudding according to the package directions. Cook rice. Combine all ingredients and heat thoroughly or microwave on medium high for five minutes. Stir frequently. Refrigerate until cool and then serve with vanilla wafers.

# January 3

*Did you know that Oleobutter was patented on this day back in 1871? And the drinking straw was patented in 1888? With these discoveries in mind, make tonight's dinner a celebration with broiled orange roughy*, baked potatoes, a tossed salad and an old-fashioned hand-dipped shake!*

## BROILED ORANGE ROUGHY

*Prep. Time: 5 min. / Cook Time: 8-12 minutes*

broiled orange roughy; enough for one filet
    each (*or perch, cod, whiting or any other
    raw fish that comes in fillets)
2 tablespoons melted butter
1-2 teaspoons concentrated lemon juice
    (depending upon taste)
salt and pepper to taste

Usually orange roughy is bought frozen from the deli meat counter. Let fish thaw and then put on a lightly greased baking sheet.

Mix melted butter and lemon juice together. Spread over each filet with a brush or spoon. Set oven temperature to broil and insert the baking sheet. After two minutes, pull out baking sheet and turn fillets over. Baste with lemon-butter. Re-insert in oven and broil until tender and flaky.

# OLD-FASHIONED MILKSHAKE

*Prep. Time: 10-15 minutes / Cook Time: 0*

3 scoops (per serving) of vanilla fat free frozen
   yogurt, fat free ice cream, iced milk
   or regular ice cream
1 cup milk
1 teaspoon vanilla
¼ cup chocolate syrup (optional)

Add all ingredients into a blender and mix thoroughly. Pour into large chilled glasses. Add a drinking straw so you can slurp up every last drop. Enjoy!

# January 4

*Today's dinner menu makes use of the blender. In my household, two out of the three kids are anti-vegetable and picky eaters. So I hide vegetables in my homemade soup and stew stock. Here is an easy made-from-scratch Chicken and Rice soup. By the way, it only seems appropriate to make use of the blender since today back in 1910 it was invented!*

## CHICKEN AND RICE SOUP

*Prep. Time: 20 minutes / Cook Time: 1 hour*

2 chicken leg quarters, skin removed
2 cloves garlic, peeled
2 medium onions
2 cups instant rice, cooked
4 stalks celery
2 carrots
salt and pepper to taste

In a large pot, cover the skinned chicken and all vegetables with water. Add ½ teaspoon salt. Cook over medium high heat until the chicken is cooked through and all the vegetables are tender. Remove the chicken, set aside and let cool. Remove pan from heat and let it cool for an hour or add a tray of ice cubes. (If vegetables and broth are too hot when they are put into the blender, it will crack the blender.) With a cup of liquid from the pan, place each of the vegetables into the blender and puree. It doesn't matter if you puree just the onions and then just the celery or if you puree a small amount of several at one time. Each time, pour the puree back into the soup pot. The pureed vegetables will naturally thicken and flavor your soup stock. Stir.

Pull the chicken off the bone in bite-sized pieces. Add to the soup stock. Reheat the soup to boiling and add 2 cups of instant rice. Cover pot with a lid and remove from heat. Let set for five minutes to allow the rice to cook. Add salt and pepper as desired. Serve immediately. (You may add more rice if desired. Keep in mind though, the more rice you add, the less soup liquid you will have.)

# CINNAMON PUDDING CAKE

*Prep. Time: 20 minutes / Cook Time: 45-60 minutes*

*In a small saucepan, bring the following to a boil and then remove from heat:*
2 cups brown sugar
1 tablespoon butter
1½ cups water
½ teaspoon ground cinnamon

*Combine the following in a mixing bowl:*
1 cup sugar
2½ cups flour
¼ cup unsweetened applesauce
2 teaspoons baking powder
1 cup milk
1 tablespoon cinnamon

Grease a 13"x9" cake pan and spread batter in pan. Batter will be thick. Pat down with hands if necessary. Pour brown sugar liquid over cake batter. Bake at 350 degrees until knife inserted comes out clean. Approximately 50 minutes. Serve warm or cooled with whipped topping or ice cream.

# January 5

*I guess if I had to pick one recipe as my signature recipe, it would have to be this one. It has been passed down on my mother's side of the family for generations and, to my knowledge, has never appeared in a cookbook before. It's easy to make and very filling. Because it is so filling, we have it at dinner time instead of at breakfast. But, of course, any leftovers make wonderful breakfasts, too!*

## SAUSAGE & EGG GRAVY OVER BISCUITS

*Prep. Time: 1-2 minutes / Cook Time: 20-30 minutes*

1 lb. mild pork sausage (may use any type of
  sausage your family likes)
6 eggs
2-3 cups milk
½ cup flour
2 tablespoons cornstarch
½ cup cold water
salt and pepper to taste

In a medium pan, crumble up the sausage and add enough water to cover the meat. Bring it to a boil and let meat cook until done. Drain off the water

Place cooked sausage in a large skillet. Turn the temperature to medium. Let the sausage reheat for a few minutes, then add eggs. Stir in order to break the yolks. While the eggs are still liquid add the flour and stir into the eggs. When the flour is completely dissolved, then pour in milk (enough to fill the skillet). Stir constantly until the milk is heated through and hot to the touch.

In a small bowl, add the cornstarch to some cold water. Stir the cornstarch until it is completely dissolved, breaking any clumps. Pour cornstarch water mixture into the skillet. Continue stirring until the milk changes consistency and becomes a gravy. Cook to the desired consistency. Stir constantly to prevent scorching. Serve immediately.

## HOMEMADE YEAST BISCUITS

*Prep. Time: 1 hour 15 min. / Cook Time: 10-15 min.*

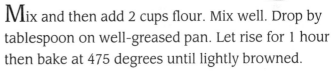

**Mix and let set for a few minutes:**
1 cup warm water
1 package dry yeast
¼ cup sugar

*Add:*
1 beaten egg
¼ cup melted butter

Mix and then add 2 cups flour. Mix well. Drop by tablespoon on well-greased pan. Let rise for 1 hour then bake at 475 degrees until lightly browned.

We enjoy this meal with a cup of hot tea as our beverage.

## KID BREAK!
### Edible Finger Paints

Mix up a box of vanilla instant pudding and divide it up into two to four smaller dishes. Use food coloring and color the pudding. Cover your kitchen table with waxed paper. You and your children can create wonderful designs and majestic artwork with the pudding on the waxed paper. When you're finished, lick your fingers and enjoy! Using the waxed paper makes clean up easy, too.

# January 6

*Sometimes it's nice to just sandwich it for dinner instead of cooking up a full meal. The following sandwich spreads go great with any leftover soup or stew.*

## TUNA SALAD SANDWICH SPREAD

*Prep. Time: 5 min. / Cook Time: 20 min.*

2 cans water-packed tuna, drained
¼ cup Miracle Whip™ Free
2 tablespoons sweet pickle relish
1 stalk celery, finely diced
2 boiled eggs, finely chopped
salt and pepper to taste

Mix all ingredients, then spread on bread, toast or buns.

## CHICKEN SALAD SANDWICH SPREAD

*Prep. Time: 15 min. / Cook Time: 1 hour*

2-3 cups cooked chicken,
    skin and bones removed
½ cup Miracle Whip™ Free
½ medium onion, diced
1 stalk celery, finely diced
salt and pepper to taste

Purée chicken in blender with ¼ cup water. Remove chicken and then mix all ingredients. Spread on bread, toast or buns.

## EGG SALAD SANDWICH SPREAD

*Prep. Time: 15 min. / Cook Time: 45 min.*

12 hard boiled eggs
½ cup Miracle Whip™ Free
¾ lb. bacon, fried until crisp
1 cup grated cheddar cheese
salt and pepper to taste

With a fork, mash up the boiled eggs in a bowl. Crumble bacon over eggs and add the Miracle Whip™. Stir until well blended. Add the cheese and seasonings, stir well. Spread on bread, toast or buns.

# January 7

*Go vegetarian with this great tasting homemade vegetable soup! Serve with homemade cornbread batter cakes.*

## VEGIE SOUP

*Prep Time: 20 min. / Cook Time: 1 hour*

Mix together in a large soup pan and heat until the bouillon has dissolved:
1 large can tomato juice*
2 beef bouillon cubes
2 cups water*
1 medium onion, finely chopped
2 teaspoons salt
¼ teaspoon pepper

Add your choice of the following vegetables and let soup cook until vegetables are tender:

| | |
|---|---|
| sliced carrots | cabbage, cut up |
| cubed potatoes | chopped broccoli |
| canned red beans | stewed tomatoes |
| diced celery | canned black-eyed peas |
| frozen or fresh sweet peas | diced zucchini |
| frozen or fresh corn | diced summer squash |

*More water and/or tomato juice may be required depending upon the desired consistency of your vegie soup. Some people like it more like a stew with less broth and others like it more like a soup.

# CORNBREAD CAKES

*Prep. Time: 5-10 min. / Cook Time: 3-8 min.*

1 cup yellow cornmeal
½ teaspoon baking soda
1 ¼ cups buttermilk
1 tablespoon butter, melted
1 teaspoon salt
1 egg, beaten

Mix cornmeal and salt together. Add egg then buttermilk. Beat until smooth. Drop a tablespoon of batter onto greased griddle or skillet. Brown on both sides. Serve immediately.

# CHOCOLATE BUNDT CAKE

*Prep. Time: 15 min. / Cook Time: 30-45 minutes*

1 chocolate cake mix
  (without pudding in the mix)
½ cup sour cream
1 small box chocolate or vanilla pudding
½ cup oil
4 eggs
½ cup water
1 small package chocolate chips

Mix all ingredients and pour into a greased and floured bundt cake pan. Bake at 350 degrees for 30 minutes or until done. Cool at least thirty minutes before removing from pan and serving.

# January 8

*Today kicks off National Pizza Week ! Homemade pizza is easy to make, far more nutritious, less fattening and better tasting than any pizza chain! It's also less expensive to make than to buy from a restaurant. Get the kids involved and let them top their own.*

*I will admit though, I cheat when it comes to the crust. Usually I go for the convenience section of the supermarket for my pizza crust. My family enjoys the taste of pizza made with the JIFF™ Pizza Crust mix, available in most baking aisles or next to the pizza items at the grocery store. We've also used Pillsbury's™ Pizza Crust in the refrigerated section. But if you want to make a homemade crust, the recipe is included here.*

# HOMEMADE PIZZA

*Prep Time: 20-30 min. / Cook Time: 30-45 min.*

2 boxes JIFF™ Pizza Crust mix
vegetable spray
1 can prepared pizza sauce

Your choice of toppings:
shredded Mozzarella cheese   pepperoni
cooked, crumbled sausage     mushrooms
shredded cheddar cheese      ham pieces
onion                        crushed pineapple
green pepper                 fresh tomatoes
Parmesan cheese              black olives
chives                       bacon, ground
                             beef, ground turkey
                             or chicken

Prepare the crust according to the package directions. Spray the pizza pan(s) with vegetable spray before spreading out the crust. Spray your hands in order to spread out the crust without having the dough stick to your hands. Bake crust in oven at 400 degrees for five minutes before adding toppings. Return topped pizza to the oven and bake until the cheese is melted and the edges of the crust are lightly browned.

Serve with a tossed salad and you've got yourself a meal!

# PIZZA DOUGH FOR 2 LARGE PIZZAS:

1 pkg. yeast
2 tablespoons oil
1 cup warm water
1 teaspoon salt
3 tablespoons sugar
3 cups all-purpose or bread flour

Dissolve yeast in warm water. Stir and let set for 5 minutes. Add sugar and stir. In a separate bowl, combine flour and salt. Add oil and yeast water. Knead dough until smooth and elastic. Spread out in greased pizza pans. Bake dough for about 5 minutes at 400 degrees before topping.

## FOOD FOR THOUGHT

- When it comes to eating, you can sometimes help yourself more by helping yourself less.

- A man achieves according to what he believes.

- Never do business with a woman who cheats herself while playing solitaire.

- Happiness adds and multiplies as we divide it with others.

- Time is nature's way of preventing everything from happening at once.

# January 9

*Baked pork chops, steam-fried potatoes and vegetable salad pizza makes a wonderful meal. Prepare the pizza first or early in the day.*

## VEGETABLE SALAD PIZZA

*Prep. Time: 45 min. - 1 hr. / Cook Time: 13-15 min.*

1 roll of prepared refrigerated biscuits
vegetable spray

Coat the pan with vegetable spray. Press each biscuit into pan, flattening it and making a crust. Bake at 400 degrees until lightly golden brown.

Mix together and spread over cooled crust:
1 (8 oz) package cream cheese, softened
½ cup Miracle Whip™ Free
2 tablespoons chopped fresh
   or minced dried onion
1 teaspoon dill seed or 2 teaspoons
   of dried chopped chives

Top with: Chopped carrots, celery, sweet peppers,

radishes, raw cauliflower, broccoli florets, olives, fresh mushrooms or whatever vegetables you prefer. Chop all vegetables quite small and spread evenly over the crust.

Refrigerate 2-6 hours before serving. Cut in small pieces to serve.

## BAKED PORK CHOPS

*Prep. Time: 20 min. / Cook Time: 30-40 min.*

1 pkg. Shake 'n' Bake™ for Pork
6-8 fresh pork chops
   (enough for one per person)

Prepare and bake pork chops according to package directions.

## STEAM-FRIED POTATOES

*Prep. Time: 20 min. / Cook Time: 50 min. - 1 hr.*

8-10 potatoes, peeled and sliced thin
2 cups water
1 tablespoon oil or bacon grease
2 small onions or 1 large, chopped fine
salt and pepper to taste

Coat the bottom of a large skillet with the oil or bacon grease. Add sliced potatoes until skillet is full. Add water. Cover potatoes with the onion, salt and pepper. Cover potatoes and let cook over medium high heat until tender. Remove lid and begin turning over potatoes, mixing in the onion. Continue cooking until all water evaporates and potatoes start sticking to the bottom of the pan. Let potatoes brown on the bottom before turning over with a spatula. Serve immediately.

# January 10

*Where's the Beef? Those immortal words were made famous on this day back in 1984 when Clara Peller appeared in a television commercial for Wendy's™. To commensurate, make your own all-beef patties for dinner, along with oven-baked potato wedges and a tossed salad.*

## BROILED ALL-BEEF PATTIES

*Prep. Time: 15 min. / Cook Time: 20-30 min.*

1 lb. ground beef
1 onion, finely diced
1 teaspoon salt
¼ teaspoon pepper
2 tablespoons steak sauce

Mix all ingredients together and form into patties. Place in the broiler pan and broil on each side until patties are cooked through. Serve on buns with your choice of condiments.

## HOMEMADE POTATO WEDGES

*Prep. Time: 15-20 min. / Cook Time: 45 minutes to 1 hour.*

6-8 potatoes, scrubbed clean.
   Leave skins intact.
3 tablespoons olive oil
vegetable spray
seasoned salt
grated Parmesan cheese

Line a large pan with aluminum foil. Cover the bottom of pan with olive oil. Cut potatoes into wedges and place wedges skin-side-down on a greased baking sheet. Spray wedges with vegetable spray and sprinkle with seasoned salt and grated Parmesan cheese. Bake for 45 minutes at 400 degrees. Check for tenderness. Wedges may need to bake an additional 15 minutes, depending upon how soft you like them.

# STRAWBERRY FLAN

*Prep. Time: 15 minutes / Cook Time: 30-45 minutes*

5 oz. butter, softened (lowfat works well)

For the Filling:
½ cup sugar
1 quart fresh strawberries, stems removed
2 eggs
1½ cups flour
¾ to 1 cup sugar
1½ teaspoons baking powder

Cream softened butter and sugar until light and fluffy. Beat in egg. Combine flour and baking powder; add to butter and egg mixture. In a greased pie pan or pastry dish, press the pastry dough into place covering the bottom and sides. Spread strawberries into dish. Sprinkle berries with sugar. Bake at 350 degrees for 25 to 30 minutes or until pastry is golden brown.

# January 11

*For a real change of pace, introduce your family to this super easy Crustless Quiche for your main entree. Serve with a complimentary Apple Raisin Salad and Sesame Bread sticks for a well-balanced meal.*

## CRUSTLESS QUICHE

*Prep. Time: 15 min. / Cook Time: 40-50 min.*

8 eggs
1 pkg. frozen chopped broccoli, cooked & drained
1 cup grated cheddar cheese
1 teaspoon salt
¼ teaspoon pepper
1 cup skim milk

Break eggs into a medium-sized bowl. Add milk and salt and pepper. Beat until well-mixed. Stir in broccoli and cheddar cheese. Pour into a greased pie pan or 8-inch round cake pan with at least 2-inch sides. Bake at 350 degrees until done, when a knife inserted in the center comes out clean.

# Apple Raisin Salad

*Prep. Time: 20-30 min.*

5-8 fresh apples (our favorites are the Royal
 Gala kind, but any will do)
1 cup raisins
½ cup Miracle Whip™ Free
1 stalk celery, finely diced
¼ cup sugar
1 tablespoon concentrated lemon juice

Core and chop apples into bite-sized chunks. Add
celery and raisins*. In a separate container, mix
together the Miracle Whip™, lemon juice and
sugar. Pour the Miracle Whip™ mixture over the
fruit and stir thoroughly. Refrigerate for at least an
hour before serving.

 *For chewy raisins, soak them in boiling hot
water for about five minutes and then drain on a
paper towel.

# Easy Sesame Bread sticks

*Prep. Time: 10-15 min. / Cook Time: 12-15 min.*

2 rolls of prepared refrigerated biscuits
butter-flavored vegetable spray
sesame seeds

Roll each biscuit into a bread stick and place on a
greased baking pan. Spray bread sticks with
butter-flavored vegetable spray. Sprinkle on
sesame seeds. Bake at 400 degrees until lightly
browned.

# January 12

*If you make a pot of Chili and then tire of eating bowl after
bowl, try using it on your next salad for a change of pace.
Both recipes follow:*

# Chili

*Prep. Time 30 min. / Cook Time: 1- 2 hours*

1 lb. ground beef, browned or boiled,
 drained and crumbled
1 medium onion, finely chopped
2 cups cooked elbow macaroni, optional
1 quart tomato juice
1 pint stewed tomatoes
2 15.5 oz. cans red beans
3 tablespoons chili powder,
 add more or less to taste
½ to 1 teaspoon cumin (start with the ½ teaspoon)
1 tablespoon salt, add more or less to taste
1 teaspoon garlic powder
2 teaspoons dried basil
2 teaspoons dried oregano
5-8 cups water, depending upon
 how soupy you want it

Combine all ingredients in a large pot. When
adding the stewed tomatoes, slice the tomatoes
with a knife into bite-sized chunks. Cook on
medium-to-low heat until heated through. Reduce
heat and let simmer for about an hour or longer.
Serve hot with crackers or peanut butter sandwiches. (I also like to add 1 tablespoon sour cream,
½ small chopped onion, ¼ cup shredded cheddar
cheese to my bowl. Yum!)

# Chili Salad

*Prep. Time: 15 minutes*

Prepare salad greens, green onion, tomatoes, etc.,
and add 1 cup of hot (temperature) Chili per salad
bowl. Add 1 tablespoon sour cream for the dressing. Sprinkle on ¼ to ½ cup shredded cheddar

cheese. Crumble up Nacho-flavored Doritoes™ or Corn Tostadas on top. Enjoy!

# BUTTERMILK PIE

*Prep. Time: 15 minutes / Cook Time: 1 hour 10-20 minutes*

1 9-inch pie crust, unbaked (not deep dish)
1¼ cup sugar
2 tablespoons sifted flour
3 eggs
1 teaspoon vanilla
¼ cup buttermilk
½ stick butter or margarine, melted

Mix ingredients together and pour into a 9-inch unbaked pie shell. Bake at 300 degrees for ten minutes, then reduce heat to 250 degrees and bake until golden brown-approximately 1 hour. The pie is done when a knife inserted in the center comes out clean. Let cool for 1 hour and then serve.

# January 13

*Credit for this recipe goes to Rachel Herring of Tipton, Indiana. I first discovered this incredible dish when she'd bring it to our church carry-in dinners. I hope you enjoy it as much as I do!*

# CHICKEN-DORITO™ CASSEROLE

*Prep. Time: 50 minutes / Cook Time: 30-40 minutes*

Chicken meat from 2-3 breasts and 2-3 thighs
    (cook chicken until just done, still very moist)
2 small or 1 large onion, chopped finely
    (sauté onion in water or cook
    in microwave until transparent)
1 can cream of mushroom soup
½ to ¾ lb. Lite Velveeta™
1 12 oz. can evaporated milk
Large bag of Nacho Doritos™
½ to 1 cup shredded cheddar cheese

In microwavable bowl, mix cooked onions, mushroom soup and milk. Heat until near boiling. Add Velveeta™, cut into small chunks. Heat in microwave, stirring frequently, until Velveeta™ melts. Mix well.

In casserole dish or pan: Layer Doritoes™, chunks of chicken, ½ of sauce, more Doritoes™, rest of chicken, last of sauce. Sprinkle with grated cheddar cheese. Bake at 350 degrees for 30 to 40 minutes.

# CREAM PUFFS

*Prep. Time: 40 minutes / Cook Time: 35-45 minutes*

Combine the following in a small saucepan, bring to a boil then reduce heat:

1 cup water
½ cup butter

Add the following and stir with a wooden spoon. Stir until the mixture leaves the sides of the pan:
1½ cups flour

Add the following, one at a time. Beat well after each egg is added.
4 eggs

Drop by tablespoonful on to ungreased cookie sheet and bake at 400 degrees for 20 minutes. Reduce temperature to 350 degrees and bake for 15 minutes or longer, until puffs are firm to the touch. Loosen them from the cookie sheet and cool on a wire rack.

Prepare 1 large box of vanilla pudding/pie filling according to the pie filling directions. When puffs are cool, use an icing tube and squeeze about one tablespoon of pudding into each pastry puff. Refrigerate for 1 hour and serve.

# January 14

*When my husband and I got married, I asked his mother for some of her family favorite recipes. Marna Stone gets the credit for this recipe. This Tuna Noodle Casserole is quick and easy to make and makes a satisfying dinner, too!*

## TUNA NOODLE CASSEROLE

*Prep. Time: 15 min. / Cook Time: 30 minutes*

1 tablespoon salt
3 quarts boiling water
1 bag noodles
1⅔ cups evaporated milk
2 cups shredded cheddar cheese
¼ teaspoon pepper
¼ cup chopped green onion
2 7oz. cans water-packed tuna, drained well
paprika for garnish

Add salt to boiling water. Gradually add noodles. Cook uncovered, stirring occasionally, until tender. Drain and rinse in cold water to stop the cooking.

Combine milk, cheese, pepper and onion. Cook over low heat, stirring frequently, until cheese melts. Arrange tuna and noodles in a greased 1½ quart shallow baking dish. Top with cheese sauce and sprinkle with paprika.

Bake at 350 degrees for 30 minutes.

## PUMPKIN PIE DESSERT

*Prep. Time: 20 minutes / Cook Time: 50 - 70 minutes*

Crust:
1 package yellow cake mix
¼ cup butter, unmelted
1 egg

Filling:
1 lb. solid packed pumpkin
2½ teaspoon pumpkin pie spice
¼ cup sugar

1 egg
½ cup milk

Topping:
1 cup (reserved) cake mix, dry
½ cup butter, melted
½ cup brown sugar
1 teaspoon cinnamon

Grease bottom only of a 13"x9" cake pan. Reserve 1 cup cake mix for topping. Combine remaining cake mix with butter and egg. Press into bottom of pan. Prepare filling—combine all ingredients and mix until smooth. Pour over crust. For topping, combine all ingredients and sprinkle over filling. Bake at 350 degrees for 45 to 50 minutes-or longer-until a knife inserted comes out clean. Serve with whipped topping.

## KID BREAK!

### Peanut Butter Claydough

PEANUT BUTTER CLAYDOUGH is quick and easy to make. In a large bowl combine **1 cup smooth peanut butter**, **1¼ cups powdered dry milk**, **1¼ cups powdered sugar** and **1 cup white corn syrup**. Mix all the ingredients and knead a little. Place the bowl in the refrigerator until mixture is chilled. Be careful though, leaving the claydough in the refrigerator too long will make it hard and unusable. For easy clean-up, cover your table with waxed paper during playtime. All kids love to play with claydough. The advantage to this kind is that it tastes like peanut butter fudge! When you're finished playing with the claydough you can either eat it or store in an airtight plastic bag.

# January 15

*Longing to make a great Ham 'n Beans recipe for my husband who loves it, I saught out this recipe from mom. Credit goes to Joyce James, Kokomo, Indiana, for not only her recipe, but also for her patience and skill in teaching me how to cook.*

## HAM 'N BEANS

*Prep. Time: About 20 minutes / Cook Time: 6-8 hours*

### SOAK METHOD

Wash 1 lb. soup beans and let them soak overnight in water. The next morning, rinse the beans again and put them in a large pan. Cover with enough water that you can dip your finger into it up to the first knuckle. Bring beans to a fast boil. When beans are boiling, transfer pan to the sink. Add 2 teaspoons baking soda and stir. Drain the beans in a colander and rinse.

Put beans in soup pot and cover with fresh water. Add 2 tablespoons vinegar, 1 tablespoon dried parsley flakes, 1 to 2 smoked hamhock(s), and desired amount of chopped (chunked) ham. Cook all day on medium heat (about 6 hours) or put in the crock pot and cook on high. Add salt when beans are ready to serve. *Tip: Never add salt to beans until you're ready to serve them. The salt will make the beans tough.*

**NO SOAK METHOD**—Wash 1 lb. beans, put in pan, cover with water and bring to a boil. Follow the same steps as in the Soak Method, except cook beans in a crock pot on high for 8 hours or longer.

## CORN BREAD

*Prep. Time: 10-15 minutes / Cook Time: 20-25 minutes*

1 cup yellow cornmeal
1 ½ cups all-purpose flour
¾ cup sugar
4 teaspoons baking powder
1 teaspoon salt
1 cup milk
2 eggs
¼ cup vegetable oil

Mix all ingredients and pour batter in muffin wrappers or a loaf pan. Bake at 425 degrees for 20-25 minutes. Serve warm from the oven. *Tip: Spray muffin wrappers with vegetable spray to prevent muffins from sticking to the papers.*

# January 16

*This quick and easy beef stroganoff recipe comes from my mother-in-law. Pick up a few extra round steaks when they go on sale and store them in the freezer for a quick dinner fix!*

## BEEF ROUND STEAK

*Prep. Time: 20 minutes / Cook Time: 90 minutes*

1 (2-3 lb.) round steak, trimmed of fat
1 can cream of mushroom soup
1 can cream of celery soup
1 can cream of chicken soup
2 teaspoons beef bouillon
2 cups sour cream
1 package noodles, cooked

Flour and brown round steak in a skillet with 1 tablespoon oil. Remove meat and put in baking dish. Mix together soups (do not add additional liquids) and beef bouillon and pour over the meat. Bake in oven at 350 degrees for 90 minutes. (The meat will be done in 60 minutes, but baking it longer will make it more tender.) Remove from oven and cut into pieces. Add 2 cups sour cream to soup mixture. Pour over cooked noodles. Serve immediately.

# CHEESY BROCCOLI

*Prep. Time: 5 minutes / Cook Time: 20 minutes*

1 pkg. frozen broccoli, chopped
5 American cheese slices
½ cup water

In a saucepan, place the block of frozen broccoli and water. Cover and cook on medium heat until broccoli is done. Drain off water. Remove pan from heat. Add cheese slices and replace lid on pan. Let set for another 5 minutes then serve.

# January 17

*My dad used to make an annual trek in the fall from Indiana up into Michigan to go Coho salmon fishing. This is an easy recipe where you can use either fresh or canned salmon.*

# SALMON PATTIES

*Prep. Time: 15-20 minutes / Cook Time: 25 minutes*

2 cups salmon, drained of all juices
¼ cup finely chopped onion
1 cup crushed saltine crackers
2 tablespoons minced parsley
2 eggs
1 tablespoon lemon juice
½ cup finely chopped celery

Combine all ingredients and mix well. Shape into about 12 small patties. Place on a lightly greased baking sheet and bake at 350 degrees for 25 minutes.

Craig enjoys his salmon patties with prepared cream of tomato soup poured over them. Prepare one can of condensed cream of tomato soup according to directions, using milk, and pour over patties when served. Personally, I like mine with a little bit of mustard.

# SKINNY BAKED MASHED POTATO CAKES

*Prep. Time: 45 minutes / Cook Time: 1 hour*

10-12 potatoes,
    peeled and cut into small pieces
½ cup skim milk
1 cup plain yogurt
3 tablespoons butter
1 clove garlic, diced
1 teaspoon chives
2 cups no fat small curd cottage cheese
½ teaspoon pepper
1 egg
2 teaspoons salt

Cook potatoes and garlic in salted water until tender. Drain off all water. Add yogurt, cottage cheese, egg, milk, butter, salt and pepper. Mash and whip into mashed potatoes. With a large spoon, dip out a large dollop of mashed potatoes on to a greased baking sheet. With hand, pat mounds down into a flat cake about 1-inch thick. Sprinkle chives on top of patties for garnish and seasoning. Bake for 30 minutes covered at 350 degrees and then uncover and continue to bake for another 30 minutes.

# EASY PEA SALAD

*Prep. Time: 15-20 minutes / Cook Time: 0*

1 head lettuce, chopped into bite size pieces
1 small onion, diced
2 cups shredded cheddar cheese
1 can sweet peas, drained
½ cup bacon bits
2 cups low-fat mayonnaise or Miracle Whip™ Free
¼ cup sugar or less

In a large bowl, mix together lettuce, onion, peas, bacon and cheese. In a separate bowl, mix together mayonnaise and sugar. Right before serving, add just enough of the sweetened mayonnaise to the vegetables to thoroughly coat. Serve immediately. Remaining sweetened mayonnaise may be stored in the refrigerator and used for another Easy Pea Salad recipe.

# LEMON CREAM DESSERT

*Prep. Time: 20 minutes Cool Time: 4 hours or longer*

**2 cups vanilla wafers, crumbled**
**½ cup Miracle Whip™ Free**
**12 oz. container Fat Free Cool Whip™**
**1-6oz. can frozen lemonade concentrate, thawed**

Mix together crumbled vanilla wafers and the Miracle Whip™. Press into a 8-to-9 inch pie pan. Bake for 10 minutes at 350 degrees. Remove from oven and let cool.

Combine thawed Cool Whip™ with thawed lemonade concentrate and mix together with a mixer on low speed. Spoon mixture over cooled crust. Freeze for 4 hours or until firm.

# January 18

*Today is Pooh Day! A. A. Milne, the author of the Winnie the Pooh stories was born on this day back in 1882. Since Pooh Bear loves honey, each of the following recipes contains a little bit of the sweet gooey stuff.*

# BROWN-SUGAR HONEY COATED HAM

**1 cup light brown sugar**
**¾ cup honey**
**½ cup water**
**1 can (regular, not diet) cola soda**
**1 boneless ham**

Remove wrappings from ham and place in a baking pan. Pour can of cola soda over ham and bake covered for 1 hour at 350 degrees. Remove from oven and drain. In a saucepan, combine light brown sugar, honey and water. Bring to a boil.

Pour over ham and cook for 15-20 minutes uncovered. Slice and serve immediately.

# HONEY-BEAR CARROTS

*Prep. Time: 20 minutes / Cook Time: 35-50 minutes*

*There is a story about how this recipe got its name. My father-in-law, Ray Stone, raises bees and robs the hives of their honey every year. He usually gives us our year's supply of honey. One year, because of the grandkids, he gave us a plastic honey-bear container filled with honey. I got caught by Loressa and Taylor using the Honey-Bear when making these carrots. This recipe has been called the Honey-Bear Carrots ever since. And they're my kids' favorite way to eat carrots!*

**6-8 fresh, raw carrots, peeled and sliced**
**1 cup water**
**1 cup light brown sugar**
**½ cup honey**
**2 tablespoons butter**
**½ teaspoon salt**

Slice carrots and put in a microwave-safe bowl. Add water. Sprinkle salt over carrots and stir. Add brown sugar, drizzle honey over brown sugar (don't stir!), and add butter in pats on top of the brown sugar. Place in microwave and cook on high for 20 minutes. Stir and cook for an additional 15 minutes on high. Stir again and check tenderness of carrots. Depending upon how tender your family likes their carrots, you may need to cook an additional 15 minutes on high. Stir before serving.

# FRESH BAKED SWEET POTATOES

*Prep. Time: 30 minutes / Cook Time: 30 minutes*

**3-4 large sweet potatoes**
**1 cup light brown sugar**
**large pan of water**
**½ cup honey**
**1 teaspoon salt**
**¼ cup butter, melted**
**1 bag miniature marshmallows**

Boil sweet potatoes in the large pan of salted water. Boil until potatoes are tender and the skins can be easily removed. Remove from water and peel. Cut potatoes into large pieces and place in a casserole dish. In a separate dish, mix together brown sugar, honey and butter. Drizzle over partially cooked sweet potatoes. Bake for 20 minutes at 350 degrees. Add miniature marshmallows and bake an additional 10 minutes or until marshmallows are melted and lightly browned.

# January 19
## ITALIAN BEAN SOUP

*Prep. Time: 20 minutes / Cook Time: 20-30 minutes*

1 lb. bulk sausage
1 small onion, chopped
1 clove garlic, minced
1 can light red beans, drained
1 can black beans, drained
1 can white or navy beans, drained
1 large (14½ oz.) can beef broth
1 teaspoon dried basil
2 tablespoons Parmesan cheese
1 can diced tomatoes with juice

In skillet cook sausage with onion and garlic until done. Drain off all grease. Combine all ingredients in soup pan. Add salt and pepper to taste. Heat and serve.

## HERB STICKS

*Prep. Time: 15 minutes / Cook Time: 10-15 minutes*

8 hot dog buns
¼ teaspoon dried parsley flakes
½ teaspoon garlic salt
½ cup melted butter (1 stick)
1 teaspoon crushed dried basil
Grated Parmesan cheese

Melt butter and add garlic salt, basil and parsley flakes. Mix together well. With a basting (small paint brush) brush, spread herbed butter over the inside of the buns. Sprinkle each bun with Parmesan cheese. Bake at 300 degrees until brown, about 10-15 minutes. Either discard herbed butter or refrigerate for use at another time.

## KID BREAK!

### How to Make Mosaics

MOSAICS are easy to make using common ingredients found in your kitchen. Have your child find a picture they like in a coloring book and tear the page out. Glue it on a piece of cardboard. Then set out a small dish of the following: red beans, navy beans, rice, various pasta shapes, unpopped popcorn, etc. Or you may want to use food coloring and color white rice. Colored rice can be used alone. Then using the various items (or colors of rice) fill in the spaces of the coloring picture with the art forms and all-purpose art glue. Small children should be carefully supervised to keep them from putting the glue in their mouths. Be generous with the glue—it will dry clear. The same thing can be done with egg shells crumbled into pieces, but using egg shells is a bit more difficult. Avoid using marshmallows, sugared items such as cereal, or anything that will draw ants or other unwanted critters.

# January 20

*Why buy the cans of condensed soup when this is so easy to make? Plus it tastes much better, too! We enjoy Homemade Chicken 'n' Noodle soup served with saltine crackers.*

## HOMEMADE CHICKEN 'N' NOODLE SOUP

*Prep. Time: about 45 minutes / Cook Time: 30 minutes*

1 chicken breast
1 chicken leg quarter
2 quarts water
2 tablespoons chicken bouillon granules
1 cup finely chopped celery OR large pieces*
1 cup finely chopped carrots OR large pieces*
½ teaspoon pepper
1 teaspoon salt
2 tablespoons parsley
2 cups dry noodles

Cook chicken in 2 quarts of water. Add chicken bouillon. Cook until chicken is done. (For a richer chicken broth, leave skin on chicken to cook.) When chicken is done, remove skin and discard. Debone chicken into bite-sized pieces. Return chicken to broth. Add all remaining ingredients except for the noodles. Cook on medium-low heat until celery and carrots are tender. If you have picky eaters that refuse to eat vegetables, remove the large pieces of celery and carrot with a cup of broth and puree in blender. Pour puree back into the broth. Add dry noodles and cook until noodles are done. Serve immediately.

## PEACH PIE

*Prep. Time: about 30 minutes / Cook Time: 40-50 minutes*

2 - 1 lb. cans sliced peaches (about 2½ cups)
½ cup sugar
2 tablespoons flour
dash salt
2 tablespoons butter
1 prepared 9-inch pie crust and top
dash cinnamon

Drain peaches, reserving ½ cup of the syrup. Combine sugar, flour, nutmeg and salt. Add reserved syrup. Cook stirring constantly until mixture thickens.

Add butter and then peaches. Pour into pie crust. Sprinkle lightly with cinnamon. Add pie top and pinch the top dough into the bottom dough. With a fork or knife, prick the pie top several times to allow steam and juices to escape. Bake at 400 degrees for 10 minutes. Reduce heat to 350 degrees and bake until golden brown which will be between 35-40 minutes. Remove from heat and cool before serving.

# January 21

*Did you know that today, back in 1967 the first microwave oven was invented? Here's a real easy dinner menu that can be done totally in the microwave.*

## MICROWAVE BAKED POTATOES

*Prep. Time: about 5 minutes / Cook Time: 25 minutes*

For each potato that you want to bake, wash it off and prick with a fork. Wrap each potato in a piece of paper toweling. To do one potato at a time, place potato in the center of the microwave oven. If you're doing more than one, arrange potatoes in a circle around the center of the oven. Bake on high for 15 minutes for one potato or 25 minutes for more than one. As soon as the microwave shuts off, wrap each potato individually in aluminum foil and set aside. The potatoes will finish their baking while wrapped in foil.

# SMOKED SAUSAGE SANDWICHES

*Prep. Time: about 5 minutes / Cook Time: 20 minutes*

After the potatoes come out of the microwave, cut the length of the smoked sausage to fit in a hot-dog bun. Prick the skins of the sausage and wrap them in paper towel. Microwave on high for 4-8 minutes and then remove from the oven. Let set for about 5 minutes before unwrapping them.

Unwrap the sausages and place one on each bun. Top with your favorite condiments or with warmed sauerkraut.

# SPINACH or MIXED GREENS

*Prep. Time: 15-20 minutes / Cook Time: 5 minutes*

While the sausages are in the microwave cooking, go ahead and fry up some bacon until it is crisp. Open a can of spinach or mixed greens and put them in to a microwave safe bowl. Crumble bacon over the greens and add 1 tablespoon of bacon grease. Stir well. Microwave on high for 3 to 5 minutes or until heated through. Serve immediately with a little salt and cider vinegar if desired.

# January 22

*If you're in a pinch for time and want to make a nourishing full-bodied soup, try putting together this Vegetable Cheese Soup. It goes together in just minutes and makes a wonderful meal all by itself! For an added treat, serve with homemade Pumpkin Bread.*

# VEGETABLE CHEESE SOUP

*Prep. Time: about 10 minutes / Cook Time: about 20-30 minutes*

4 slices bacon
1 10-oz. package frozen mixed vegetables
1 medium onion, chopped (about ½ cup)
½ cup water
1 can cream of potato soup
1 10¾ oz. can condensed tomato soup
1¼ cups skim milk
1 cup shredded American cheese
1 teaspoon Worcestershire sauce

In a 3-quart saucepan, cook bacon until crisp. Remove bacon; crumble and set aside. Drain off all grease. Add frozen mixed vegetables, chopped onion and water. Bring to boiling. Cover; reduce heat and simmer 10 to 12 minutes or until mixed vegetables are tender.

Stir in soups, milk, American Cheese and Worcestershire sauce. Cook and stir until soup is heated through and cheese has melted. To serve, top with the crumbled bacon and ladle into individual soup bowls. YUM!

# PUMPKIN BREAD

*Prep. Time: 10-15 minutes, / Cook Time: about 1 hour or a little longer*

1½ cups sugar
2 eggs
1¾ cups flour
½ teaspoon baking soda
½ teaspoon nutmeg
⅓ cup water
½ cup unsweetened applesauce
1 cup canned pumpkin
1 teaspoon baking powder
1 teaspoon salt
1 teaspoon cinnamon
1 teaspoon pumpkin pie spice
½ cup raisins (optional)

Add sugar to applesauce and then add eggs and pumpkin. Mix well. In a separate bowl, combine flour with spices. Slowly add spiced flour mixture alternately with the water and raisins to the pumpkin mixture. Mix well after each addition. Pour into two small or one large greased loaf pan(s). Bake at 350 degrees for 1 hour or until a knife inserted comes out clean. Let set for 10 minutes to cool before slicing.

# January 23

*Today is National Pie Day!!! What better to serve for dinner than an easy-to-make Chicken Pot Pie with Chocolate Pie Deluxe for dessert?*

## CHICKEN POT PIE

*Prep. Time: 45 minutes / Cook Time: 35-45 minutes*

1 can cream of chicken soup
1 can cream of potato soup
1 can skim milk
3-4 chicken breasts, cooked, skinned and deboned
2 cups frozen peas and carrots,
    cooked and drained
3-4 potatoes,
    peeled and cubed, cooked and drained
1 small to medium onion, diced finely
2 pkgs refrigerated biscuits
1 teaspoon salt
½ teaspoon pepper
½ teaspoon celery flakes
½ teaspoon parsley flakes

In a 13 x 9 casserole baking dish, combine soups with milk and seasonings. Break up chicken into bite-sized pieces and stir into soups. Add cooked peas and carrots, potatoes and the fresh onion. Bake at 400 degrees for 20 minutes. Remove casserole dish from oven and place prepared biscuits on top of the chicken and vegetable mixture. Cover entire dish with the biscuits. Return dish to oven, reduce heat to 350 degrees and bake until the biscuits are golden brown—about 20-25 minutes.

## CHOCOLATE PIE DELUXE

*Prep. Time: 20 minutes / Cook Time: 20 minutes*

1 9-inch prepared pie crust
1 large box (cook 'n' serve) chocolate
    pudding mix

4 cups skim milk
3 cups miniature marshmallows
1 cup milk chocolate chips
Fat Free Cool Whip™

Bake prepared pie crust in a 400 degree oven for 10 minutes. Remove from heat and let cool.

In a separate pan, combine pudding mix and milk and make according to the pie directions on the pudding box. When the pudding is thick and hot, stir in the marshmallows and chocolate chips. Stir until both are dissolved. Pour into baked 9-inch pie shell. Cover pie with plastic wrap and refrigerate for 2-3 hours or longer. When ready to serve, remove plastic wrap and garnish with the Cool Whip™.

# January 24

*Meatloaf is one of my family's favorite meals. If there is any meatloaf left over, use it for meatloaf sandwiches for the next day's lunch. I discovered the secret to really good home-made meatloaf is saltine crackers.*

## MEATLOAF DINNER

*Prep. Time: 30 minutes / Cook Time: 90 minutes*

2 lbs. ground beef
2 slices bread, the end pieces of a loaf
2 eggs
1 medium onion, finely chopped
⅓ cup finely chopped fresh green pepper
2 teaspoons salt
1 teaspoon pepper
½ cup ketchup
2 tablespoons steak sauce
1 tablespoon Worcestershire sauce
1½ to 2 full sleeves of salted saltine crackers
8-10 potatoes, peeled and left whole
6 carrots, peeled and cut into chunks
1 cup water
ketchup as desired

In a large bowl, combine ground beef with eggs, onion, green pepper, salt, pepper, ketchup, steak sauce and Worcestershire sauce. With both hands, knead the meat mixture until everything is thoroughly blended together. With the saltine crackers still in their sleeve, pound crackers until they are finely crumbled. Pour over the meat mixture and mix in. Form meatloaf into a large oval or divide into 6 smaller ovals. Place meatloaf in a large roasting pan. Place the ends of bread at each end of the meatloaf. (This is to help absorb some of the grease/fat from the meatloaf.) Surround meat with peeled whole potatoes and carrots. Add 1 cup of water to the pan. Pour ketchup over meat and vegetables as desired. Sprinkle with salt and pepper as desired. Cover baking pan and bake for 90 minutes in a 375 degree oven. If you form small loaves, reduce baking time to 60 minutes. Remove bread slices from meat and discard before serving.

## KID BREAK!
### Creative Snacks

SNACKS can be fun to make, too. Fluffer Nutter Sandwiches are a hit at our house. Spread your choice of peanut butter on one slice of bread and marshmallow cream on the other. Put the two together and enjoy a Fluffer Nutter! Peanut Butter is great as a dip for raw vegies, too. Use it for celery, carrots, and cauliflower. To go along with those Fluffer Nutter Sandwiches, you'll need something to wash them down.

Involve your kids in making magic potions to drink. Let each child pick his favorite flavor of Koolaid™ and make up a container of each. Then experiment with mixing the flavors together. You'll get not only unusual taste combinations, but you'll also give your kids an art lesson in mixing colors!

# January 25

*Ever walk down the supermarket aisle and see how many different brands and types of soups were on the shelves? Ever wonder why there are so many? Because soup is SOOO good! It's good for you, easy to make, filling and nutritious. If there's a vegetable that isn't your family's favorite, just substitute it for another one! It's almost impossible to make a bad pot of soup. Don't be afraid to experiment a bit.*

## HAMBURGER SOUP

*Prep. Time: 25 minutes / Cook Time: 2 hours or longer*

2 lbs. lean ground beef
2 teaspoons dried sweet basil
5¾ cups tomato juice
2 teaspoons dried crushed oregano
1 cup stewed tomatoes
2 tablespoons dried onion flakes
    OR 1 large fresh onion, finely chopped
2 cups chopped celery
1 cup sliced carrots
1 tablespoon Worcestershire sauce
2 cups green beans
2 teaspoons garlic powder
salt and pepper to taste

Cover crumbled ground beef with water and boil until hamburger is cooked through. Drain off all water. Add all the remaining ingredients and mix well. Cover the soup with a lid and bring to a boil. Stir thoroughly. Reduce heat and remove lid. Let simmer for 2 hours or longer on low heat. Serve with a generous supply of **Seasoned Oyster Crackers**, recipe below.

1½ cups oil
2 pkgs Original Ranch Salad Dressing mix
1 teaspoon dill weed
½ teaspoon lemon pepper
½ teaspoon garlic powder
32 oz. plain oyster crackers

Whisk together the first five ingredients. Pour over crackers, stirring to coat. Place on baking sheets and bake at 275 degrees for 15 to 20 minutes. Serve warm from the oven. For any leftover crackers, seal them in airtight closeable baggies and use them for a late-night snack.

# January 26

*My husband has fond memories of his mom fixing her Green Bean Stew for dinner. He says she always used home-canned green beans which made it taste even better. But this can be put together using the canned green beans available at the grocery store just fine.*

## GREEN BEAN STEW

*Prep. Time: 30-45 minutes / Cook Time: 1 hour or longer*

1-2 lbs. pork shoulder
4 cups green beans, drained
1 medium onion, chopped fine
½ fresh green pepper, chopped fine
2 tablespoons butter
5-8 potatoes, peeled and sliced
2 cups stewed tomatoes
salt and pepper to taste

Place pork in a pan of water and bring to a boil. Cook until meat is tender. In a separate skillet, melt butter and saute onion and green pepper until tender. When meat is tender, remove meat from water and let cool. Add sauteed onion and green pepper to pork water (stock). Add green beans and sliced potatoes and stewed tomatoes. Pull meat off bones and add to the pot of vegetables. Add salt and pepper to taste. Cook over low heat and let simmer for 1 hour or longer.

# January 27

## BAKED COD

*Prep. Time: 5 minutes / Cook Time: 45 minutes*

2 lb. cod fillets, thawed
4 tablespoons butter
salt
pepper
paprika

Melt butter and dip each piece of fish in butter. Sprinkle both sides with salt, pepper and paprika. Place in shallow baking dish and bake, uncovered, at 350° for 45 minutes or until fish flakes when forked. Serve with tartar sauce.

## ONION-GARLIC SLICED POTATOES

*Prep. Time: 20-30 minutes / Cook Time: 45 minutes to 1 hour*

6-8 medium potatoes, peeled and sliced
1 medium onion, sliced
2 tablespoons butter
garlic powder to taste
salt and pepper to taste

Line a cookie sheet with aluminum foil. Butter the foil. Thinly slice the potatoes and place them on foil. Top potatoes with onions and several dashes of garlic powder to taste. Sprinkle salt and pepper to taste. Fold aluminum foil over and bake at 375 degrees for 45 minutes or until potatoes are tender and golden brown.

# FRESH BROCCOLI AND TOMATO SALAD

*Prep. Time: 20 minutes / Cook Time: 0*

1 bunch fresh broccoli
1 carton cherry tomatoes, halved
6 slices crisp-cooked bacon, crumbled
1 bottle Green Goddess™ salad dressing
    by Seven Seas
Garlic powder to taste
Juice of ½ lemon

Cut broccoli into bite-sized florets. Toss broccoli, tomato halves and bacon in a large bowl. Combine the remaining ingredients, blending well. Add the dressing just before serving, being sure to coat the broccoli and tomatoes well. Garnish with garlic flavored croutons and serve immediately.

# January 28

*If you've got a busy day planned, throw together this Oven Beef Stew and let it cook all day while you're busy. Serve with thick slices of French bread or freshly baked refrigerator biscuits.*

## OVEN BEEF STEW

*Prep. Time: 15-20 minutes / Cook Time: 7-8 hours*

2 lbs. stew beef, cubed
6-8 medium potatoes, peeled and cubed
2 cups green beans
4 large carrots, sliced
2 cups peas
1 large onion, finely chopped
1 quart tomato juice
1 bay leaf
salt and pepper to taste
seasoned croutons

Combine all ingredients except the croutons in a 4-quart baking pan. Mix well. Cover with lid and bake at 250 degrees for 7 to 8 hours. Slow cooking at a low temperature will make the stew meat very tender. Top each serving with seasoned croutons. Enjoy!

# APPLESAUCE SPICE CAKE

*Prep. Time: 20 minutes / Cook Time: 45 minutes to 1 hour*

1½ cups water, divided
½ cup vegetable oil
1½ cups raisins
3 cups flour
2½ cups unsweetened applesauce
2 tablespoons cinnamon
½ teaspoon baking soda
3 eggs, beaten
2 tablespoons vanilla
2 cups sugar
2 teaspoons baking powder
vegetable spray

Combine 1 cup water and raisins in a small saucepan. Bring to a boil. Boil until water evaporates or is absorbed by raisins. Remove from heat. Watch carefully so raisins don't scorch.

In a large bowl, combine applesauce, eggs, sugar, oil and remaining ½ cup water with raisins. Sift together flour, cinnamon, baking powder and soda, adding gradually to applesauce mixture. Add vanilla. Stir after each addition.

Spoon batter into a 10-inch Bundt pan coated with cooking spray. Bake at 350 degrees for 40-45 minutes or until knife inserted comes out clean. Cool in pan for 10 minutes before removing from pan. Let cool and then serve.

# January 29

*Today is National Popcorn Day! Did you know that Indiana is one of the leading producers of popcorn? Treat your family to an unusual dessert, Cherry and Popcorn pie.*

## BAKED CHICKEN 'N' PASTA

*Prep. Time: 30 minutes / Cook Time: 30 minutes*

1 pkg spaghetti or other pasta
1 can cream of chicken soup
3-4 cooked chicken breasts, deskinned,
    deboned, and cut up into bite sized pieces
¼ cup melted butter
2 cups frozen peas, cooked and drained
Parmesan cheese

Cook pasta according to package directions. Drain. Mix cooked pasta with condensed soup, cooked peas and chicken. Melt butter in a separate pan and add cheese. Pour over the pasta mixture. Bake at 350 degrees for 20 minutes covered, then uncover and bake for 10 minutes longer. Serve immediately.

## CONFECTIONERS' POPCORN-CHERRY DESSERT

*Prep. Time: 20-30 minutes / Cook Time: 15 minutes*

4 cups popped popcorn (make sure popcorn
    is popped before measuring)
3 egg whites
½ cup sugar
1 can prepared cherry pie filling
2 cups Fat Free Cool Whip™

In an electric blender, process 1 cup of popcorn at a time until it is fine and crumbly. In a separate bowl, beat egg whites on high speed with an electric mixer until soft peaks form. Gradually add sugar, continuing to beat on high speed for two full

minutes. Fold in crushed popcorn. Spread in buttered pie pan. Bake at 350 degrees for 15 minutes. While crust is baking, fold together pie filling and the whipped topping. Pour into the cooled crust and chill until ready to serve. The crust will puff up and turn lightly browned when done.

# January 30

*When I was a child, our meals consisted of cooked hamburger in one form or another. I thought I knew every way to fix ground beef. But Craig's mom had this Hamburger Casserole recipe that I'd never tried before. I immediately fell in love with it.*

## HAMBURGER CASSEROLE

*Prep Time: 30-45 minutes / Cook Time: 30-45 minutes*

1 lb. hamburger or lean ground beef
1 medium onion, chopped fine
1 can condensed cream of tomato soup
1 tablespoon A-1 sauce™
1 can green beans, drained
3-5 medium potatoes (or 2 cups leftover
    mashed potatoes)
1 cup shredded cheddar cheese
salt and pepper to taste

In a large skillet, brown the hamburger and onion together. When meat is done and the onion is transparent, drain off all meat drippings. Peel potatoes and slice thin. Boil in salted water until tender. In a casserole dish, combine drained hamburger and onion with the green beans. Add can of tomato soup and the A-1 sauce™. Mix thoroughly. Drain potatoes. Add the cooked sliced potatoes or the mased potatoes to the casserole dish, or mash them first. Add salt and pepper to taste. Top with shredded cheese and bake at 350 degrees for 30 to 45 minutes, until heated through. Serve immediately.

# FRUIT COBBLER

*Prep. Time: 10-15 minutes / Cook Time: 40-50 minutes*

¼ cup butter, melted in casserole dish

In a separate bowl combine:

1 cup flour

2 teaspoons baking powder

1 teaspoon baking soda

1 cup sugar

¾ cup skim milk

Mix batter well until most of the lumps are removed. Pour batter over the butter, but DO NOT STIR.

Add desired fruit. Use either sweetened fresh fruit or a can of fruit or frozen fruit that is sweetened and thawed. Again, add fruit to the top of the batter and DO NOT STIR.

Bake at 400 degrees for 10 minutes then reduce heat to 350 degrees. Bake 20-30 minutes or longer until done. Sprinkle sugar over top as soon as the cobbler is removed from the oven. Serve warm with a dip of ice cream or cold.

# January 31

*What more fitting to end the month of January with than a Winter Pork Roast served with fresh vegetables. Plan ahead to make this dinner. The longer you can allow the pork roast to bake, the more tender the meat will be.*

# WINTER PORK ROAST

*Prep. Time: 20 minutes / Cook Time: 2-3 hours*

2 lb. pork roast

1 clove of garlic

1 large onion, sliced

6 medium potatoes

4 carrots, cut in 1-inch chunks

1 teaspoon salt

¼ teaspoon pepper

1 bay leaf

½ cup apple juice

Peel the garlic and rub the roast with it. Place meat in a deep baking pan or crock baking dish. Arrange vegetables over and around meat. Sprinkle seasonings on meat and vegetables. Drizzle with apple juice and then cover with a lid. Bake at 325 degrees for 2 to 3 hours or until meat is tender.

# BUTTERMILK BROWNIES

*Prep. Time: 30 minutes / Cook Time: 45 minutes*

1 cup butter

1 cup chopped nuts (optional)

½ cup cocoa

1 cup baby-food plums

4 cups confectioners' powdered sugar

2 cups flour

2 teaspoons vanilla extract

2 cups sugar

½ teaspoon baking soda

½ teaspoon salt

2 eggs

½ cup plus ⅓ cup buttermilk

Combine ½ cup butter with ¼ cup cocoa and 1 cup water in saucepan. Bring mixture to a boil, mixing well. In a separate bowl, combine flour, sugar and ½ teaspoon salt. Pour boiling mixture over dry ingredients. Add ½ cup buttermilk, eggs, baking soda, ½ cup babyfood plums and 1 teaspoon vanilla, mixing well. Pour into greased and floured jelly roll pan. Bake at 400 degrees for 20 minutes.

While brownies are baking, combine ¼ cup cocoa with ½ cup butter and ⅓ cup buttermilk in saucepan. Bring to a boil, blending well. Remove from heat and add remaining powdered sugar and 1 teaspoon vanilla. Mix until creamy. Frost brownies immediately upon removing from oven. Sprinkle chopped nuts on top for a garnish.

# COOKIES OF THE MONTH

## TRIPLE C COOKIES
### (CHEWY CHOCOLATE CHIP)

1¼ cup butter, softened

2 cups sugar

2 eggs

2 teaspoon vanilla

2 cups unsifted flour

¾ cup cocoa

1 teaspoon baking soda

½ teaspoon salt

2 cups white chocolate chips

Cream butter and sugar in large bowl. Add eggs and vanilla; blend well. Combine flour, cocoa, baking soda and salt—blend into creamed mixture. Stir in white chocolate chips. Drop by teaspoon onto a greased cookie sheet. Bake at 350º for 8 to 9 minutes. Do not over bake. Cookies will be soft. They will puff up during baking and then flatten upon cooling. Cool on cookie sheet until they're set, about 1 minute.

## BUTTERMILK COOKIES

2 cups sugar

1 cup butter

2 eggs

1 teaspoon vanilla

1 cup buttermilk

4 cups flour

1 teaspoon baking soda

½ teaspoon salt

Cream sugar and butter together and add the egg; beat well. Add baking soda to buttermilk before adding buttermilk to the creamed mixture. Gradually add the dry ingredients, beating after each addition. Drop by teaspoon on a greased cookie sheet. Sprinkle colored sugar on top of cookies. Bake at 350º for 10-12 minutes. Remove from oven BEFORE the edges start turning brown.

## NO BAKE OATMEAL DROPS

### CHOCOLATE VARIETY

2 cups sugar

½ cup butter, softened

½ cup milk

6 tablespoons cocoa

1 teaspoon vanilla

3 cups quick cooking oatmeal

### PEANUT BUTTER VARIETY

2 cups sugar

½ cup butter, softened

½ cup milk

½ cup peanut butter

1 teaspoon vanilla

3 cups quick cooking oatmeal

⅛ teaspoon salt

Combine sugar, butter and milk in a saucepan and bring to a boil. Add remaining ingredients and cook for 1 minute. Drop by teaspoon on lightly greased waxed paper.

Did you know that this particular month celebrates:
- Great American Pies Month?
- National Cherry Month?
- Potato Lovers Month?

With this in mind, I've tried to put together dinner menus using these particular items. Enjoy!

# February 1

## CHICKEN NOODLE CASSEROLE

*Prep. Time: 20 minutes / Cook Time: 20 minutes*

1 pkg. (1 lb./16 oz.) dried egg noodles,
   medium to wide width
2 cans condensed cream of chicken soup
1 can (de)boned chicken
1 can mixed vegetables
⅓ cup skim milk
3 tablespoons butter
Ritz™ or similar crackers

Prepare egg noodles according to package directions. Drain off water when noodles are tender. Add butter and toss noodles to evenly coat them. Drain liquid from chicken and mixed vegetables. Add all ingredients except for crackers and mix well. Pour into a buttered casserole dish. Top with crumbled cracker crumbs. Bake at 350 degrees for 20 minutes.

*When Craig and I first married, he was attending a small country church that met Sunday afternoons for their services. There was an elderly lady there, known by all as Aunt Edna. She made the best pies! I was fortunate enough to get her pie crust recipe before she passed away. This recipe will make either 12 pie shells or 6 covered pie shells.*

## AUNT EDNA'S PIE CRUST

*Prep. Time: 2 hours, give or take / Cook Time: 10 minutes to 55 minutes, depending upon filling*

12 cups all purpose flour
4 cups lard or one 2-lb. box
1⅓ cups water
4 teaspoons salt
4 tablespoons vinegar
4 eggs

Mix flour and salt together, cut in lard. In a separate bowl, mix eggs, water and vinegar. With your hand, create a well in the center of the flour mixture. Pour the egg mixture into the center of the well. Mix together with your hands. Roll out on a floured surface until dough is about ⅛ inch thick. Put a pie pan on the dough as a cutting guide. Cut dough with a table-knife about two inches larger than the pie pan. Invert pie pan and place dough in it. Push the dough down to conform with the pie pan. Crimp edges of dough between your thumb and index fingers. For a pudding type of pie, prick the bottom of the pie shell with a fork and bake shell at 400 degrees for 10 minutes or until lightly browned. If you're filling your pie with a fruit filling, do not prebake pie shell. Fill with fruit and add a topper. With your finger or a pastry brush, coat edges of pie shell with a little milk. Crimp the top layer of dough to the bottom layer. Prick the top layer of crust with a fork or knife to allow for steam to escape. Bake pie at 400 degrees until golden brown. Check after 25 minutes. Pie shells can be frozen, unbaked, after they are conformed to the pie pan.

# CHERRY-PEACH PIE

*Prep. Time: 15 minutes / Cook Time: 40-50 minutes*

¾ cup sugar

¼ cup flour

1 cup sour cherries, drained—reserve juice

2 cups sliced peaches, drained

¼ teaspoon almond extract

¼ cup cherry juice

3 tablespoons butter

Mix together sugar and flour. Sprinkle ⅓ of the mixture in the bottom of unbaked pie shell. In a separate bowl, combine fruit, almond extract and cherry juice. Mix thoroughly. Pour fruit mixture into the pie pastry. Sprinkle the remaining flour-sugar mixture over fruit. Dot with butter. Make a lattice top crust and flute edges. Bake at 400 degrees for 40 to 50 minutes. Let cool for at least 20 minutes before serving.

# February 2

*Did you know that when the day equals the month that it's considered to be a Party Party Day? Since this is the second day of the second month, it's Party Party Day! Make tonight's dinner a meal worth celebrating with the following recipes!*

# CHICKEN BROCCOLI DIVAN

*Prep. Time: 15 minutes Cooking Time: 20 minutes*

1½ lbs. broccoli spears, cooked and drained

2 cups cubed cooked chicken

1 can condensed cream of broccoli soup

1 can cream of chicken soup

2 cups processed American cheese cubes

⅓ cup skim milk

1 cup grated cheddar cheese

2 tablespoons crushed crackers

1 tablespoon butter, melted

In a 2-quart baking dish, arrange broccoli and chicken. In a separate bowl, combine soups, milk and American cheese. Microwave on high for 2 minutes and stir. Continue to microwave for 1 minute at a time until cheese cubes are melted. Pour soup and cheese mixture over broccoli and chicken. Sprinkle cheddar cheese over soup mixture. In a cup, combine bread crumbs and melted butter; sprinkle over cheese. Bake at 450 degrees for 20 minutes or until hot and bubbling.

# CHERRY NUT BREAD

*Prep. Time: 20-30 minutes / Cook Time: 1 hour, plus or minus*

1½ cups maraschino cherries, reserve juice

2 cups flour

1½ teaspoon baking powder

½ teaspoon salt

⅓ cup butter

¾ cup firmly packed brown sugar

2 eggs

1½ cups mashed ripe bananas

½ cup chopped macadamia nuts

Drain maraschino cherries, reserving 3 tablespoons juice. Cut cherries into pieces and set aside. Combine flour, baking powder and salt; set aside.

Combine butter, brown sugar, eggs and reserved cherry juice in a large mixing bowl. Mix on medium speed with an electric mixer until ingredients are thoroughly combined. Add flour mixture and mashed bananas alternately, beginning and ending with the flour mixture. Stir in drained cherries and nuts.

Spray a 9x5x3 baking pan with non-stick vegetable spray. Spread batter evenly in pan. Bake at 350 degrees for 1 hour, or until golden brown. When done, remove from pan and let cool before slicing.

## MAKE YOUR OWN VALENTINES!

*Project #1 I'm Nuts Over You, Valentine*

Brown Construction Paper
Black Permanent Marker
Hole Puncher
White or Red Ribbon, ⅛ inch wide
(thin Christmas ribbon is perfect)
Pink Plastic Wrap
Honey-roasted Peanuts or other nuts

Cut out a peanut-in-the-shell shape large enough to write I'm Nuts Over You, Valentine on the front. Let your child sign his/her name on the back. Hole punch the end and thread through a 6-8-inch length of ribbon.

With your scissors, split the pink plastic wrap in half before tearing it off of the dispenser. Tear off pieces that are near 5-inches x 5-inches. Let your child gather a small handful of nuts and place the nuts in the center of the plastic wrap. Gather the sides of the plastic wrap and twist, then tie the ribbon in place. Your Nutty Valentines are complete!

# February 3

*Because all of your ingredients are already prepared, this dinner menu goes together in no time. It's one I use when I just don't feel much like cooking, but yet still have to get something put on the table. It's filling and tastes good, so I can get away with cheating a little bit here and there.*

## CHEATER'S BEEF POT PIES

*Prep. Time: 5-10 minutes / Cook Time: 35-40 minutes*

2 (40 oz.) cans of prepared beef stew (such as Dinty Moore™ Beef Stew)
Prepared pie dough to make two 8-9 inch pies with a top crust
2 tablespoons grated Parmesan cheese

1 teaspoon dried parsley
½ teaspoon pepper
1 teaspoon dried minced onion

Heat oven to 375 degrees. In a large bowl combine beef stew, pepper and minced onion. Spoon stew into two prepared pie crusts. Top both with a pie crust top. Fold edges under and flute. Sprinkle both pies with parmesan cheese and parsley. Cut 2 or 3 slits in crust to allow steam to escape. Bake 35-40 minutes or until crust is golden brown and stew is thoroughly heated.

## CHOCOLATE CHEESE PIE

*Prep. Time: 25-30 minutes / Cook Time: 40-45 minutes*

2 pkgs (8 oz.) cream cheese, softened
½ cup sugar
3 eggs
1 cup semi-sweet chocolate chips
1 (9 inch) prepared chocolate or graham cracker crust
½ cup plain yogurt

Beat cream cheese with sugar using an electric mixer. Add eggs. Melt ½ cup chocolate chips in the microwave on medium heat for 2-3 minutes. Add melted chocolate to cream cheese mixture, beating until thick and smooth. Spread into pie shell. Bake at 350 degrees for 30-35 minutes or until firm in center. Chill 4 hours or overnight. Add topping before serving:

**Topping:**

Melt remaining ½ cup chocolate chips and combine with plain yogurt. Spread over top of pie. Chill until firm.

# February 4

*A very dear friend shared this recipe with me many years ago. Sue Howard of Winona Lake, Indiana, gave me her recipe for this Vegetable Lasagna. It's delicious served with home-made garlic toast.*

## VEGETABLE LASAGNA

*Prep. Time: 30 minutes / Cook Time: 45 minutes to 1 hour*

½ lb. sausage, optional
½ lb. ground pork, optional
1 onion, chopped fine
¾ to 1 cup green pepper, chopped
1 (8 oz.) can stewed tomatoes
2 (8 oz.) cans tomato sauce
½ cup fresh parsley, chopped
2 teaspoons crushed oregano
2 teaspoons crushed basil
1 teaspoon salt
2 cups lowfat cottage cheese
1 large zucchini or 1 large eggplant, sliced
2 cups grated mozzarella cheese

Cook meat, drain, add onion, green pepper and cook until tender. Add tomatoes, tomato sauce, ½ parsley, oregano, basil and salt. Heat to boiling, stirring occasionally, reduce heat and let simmer for 15 to 20 minutes.

In a separate container, mix together cottage cheese, egg and remaining parsley. In ungreased baking dish, spread thin layer of meat sauce. Layer zucchini (or eggplant), more sauce, cottage cheese mixture and mozzarella. Repeat pattern. Bake uncovered at 350 degrees for 45 minutes or until zucchini (or eggplant) is tender.

## HOME-MADE GARLIC TOAST

*Prep. Time: 15 minutes / Cook Time: 12-15 minutes*

2 slices of bread per person
½ cup soft-spread butter
1 teaspoon garlic powder
Parmesan cheese

Combine butter with garlic powder. Spread evenly over bread slices. Sprinkle Parmesan cheese over each slice. In an electric oven, place bread slices directly on oven rack and bake at 250 degrees for 10-12 minutes. If you have a gas oven, place bread on an ungreased baking sheet and bake 12-15 minutes in the center of oven. Serve hot from the oven.

# February 5

*Dinner time is my favorite time of the day. My husband comes home from work and the kids have had time to un-wind some from their day at school. It's a nice time for all of us to come together and share about our day. Keeping the meal simple helps me not to feel so pressured and I'm more relaxed and able to enjoy my family. Today's menu provides just the recipes for your Family Night around the table.*

## HAMBURGER STROGANOFF

*Prep. Time: 20-25 minutes / Cook Time: 15 minutes*

1 lb. lean ground beef
1 medium onion, chopped
1 tablespoon cornstarch
¼ cup cold water
1 teaspoon garlic powder
1 teaspoon salt
½ teaspoon black pepper
2 cans condensed cream of mushroom soup
1 pkg. (16 oz.) dried egg noodles
1 cup plain yogurt
dried, minced chives for garnish

In a large skillet, crumble up the ground beef and add the chopped onion. Cook until meat is done and the onion is transparent. Drain off all grease. Dissolve cornstarch in cold water and pour onto meat. Stir in garlic powder, salt, pepper and soups. Cook for five minutes, stirring constantly. Reduce heat to low and simmer for another 10 minutes.

Meanwhile, cook the noodles according to the package directions. Drain off water when noodles are tender.

Remove the meat mixture from heat and stir in sour cream. Serve over hot noodles.

## CHOCOLATE 'N' CHERRY DESSERT

*Prep. Time: 10 minutes / Cook Time: 0*

1 box instant chocolate pudding
2 cups cold skim milk
2 cups prepared cherry pie-filling

Prepare pudding according to directions, using the milk. Spoon pudding into dessert dishes. Top with cherry pie filling. Chill until ready to serve.

# February 6

*Today is officially known as the mid-winter's day. We're half way through the cold and flu season! I can't think of a better meal to celebrate the half-way mark than homemade Chicken Soup. You can throw this together and let it simmer all afternoon, filling your home with the aroma of soup or you can throw it together, heat through and serve immediately. Either way, it tastes wonderful!*

## CHICKEN SOUP

*Prep. Time: 20 minutes / Cook Time: 25 minutes to 2 hours, depending on vegetables used*

2 large cans prepared chicken broth
2 cups diced chicken meat (can use either canned deboned chicken or cooked fresh chicken, picked from the bone)
2 cups water
2 teaspoons salt
½ teaspoon pepper
1 medium onion, finely diced

2 stalks celery, finely diced
2 cups peas (use frozen peas if you plan to let cook for awhile; canned peas if you want to serve immediately)
6 potatoes, peeled and cubed (fresh if you let it cook; canned if you want to serve it immediately)
1 tablespoon butter

If you plan to serve soup immediately, saute celery and onion in butter until both are transparent and tender. Transfer celery and onion to soup pot. Add all the other ingredients, stirring well. If you're going to cook soup all day, just add celery and onion to the soup pot and don't saute anything. This will eliminate the need for any butter.

Cook over medium heat until potatoes are tender. Serve as soon as the potatoes are done or turn heat down to low and let soup simmer until you're ready to serve it.

## CHERRY-CHOCOLATE CAKE

*Prep. Time: 10-15 minutes / Cook Time: 30-45 minutes*

1 box chocolate cake mix
2 eggs
1 can prepared cherry pie filling

Combine all ingredients and mix well. Pour into a greased and floured cake pan. Bake according to the cake mix directions. Serve warm from the oven with a scoop of vanilla ice cream.

# February 7

*Your kids will think an alien has entered you when you set them down for tonight's dinner. Instead of a three-course meal, incorporate fruits and vegetables with starches and protein and serve as a snacker's delight meal. Keep these recipes handy for the next time it's your turn to do the entertaining for a party or get-together.*

Prepare a fresh vegetable tray with raw cauliflower, broccoli, carrots, celery, radishes, mushrooms, cucumber slices and cherry tomatoes. Arrange vegetables on a tray and garnish with kale and black olives. Serve with the following vegetable dips:

## DILL DIP

*Prep. Time: 10 minutes to mix together; let age overnight or for at least 6 hours before serving*

1 cup real mayonnaise
1 cup sour cream
2 tablespoons parsley
2 tablespoons minced onion
½ teaspoon garlic powder
2 teaspoons seasoned salt
2 teaspoons dill seed
2 teaspoons sesame seed (optional)

OR if you're concerned with fat and calorie content, you may substitute Fat Free Miracle Whip™ for the real mayonnaise and plain yogurt in place of the sour cream.

Combine all ingredients, stir well and let age in the refrigerator for at least 6 hours before serving. Best if left overnight.

## GINGER DIP

*Prep. Time: 10 minutes to mix together; let age overnight or for at least 6 hours before serving*

1 cup real mayonnaise
4 teaspoons soy sauce
1 teaspoon vinegar
1 teaspoon ground ginger
2 tablespoons minced onion

OR if you're concerned with fat and calorie content, you may substitute Fat Free Miracle Whip™ for the real mayonnaise and plain yogurt in place of the sour cream.

Combine all ingredients, stir well and let age in the refrigerator for at least 6 hours before serving. Best if left overnight.

## CREAMY SPINACH DIP

*Prep. Time: 10-15 minutes to mix together; let age overnight or for at least 6 hours before serving*

1 cup sour cream
1 cup real mayonnaise
½ teaspoon celery salt
½ teaspoon dill weed
¼ cup chopped green onions
3 cups frozen cut leaf spinach,
    thawed and well drained
8-oz. can water chestnuts,
    drained and finely chopped
3 tablespoons chopped red bell pepper
¼ teaspoon onion salt

OR if you're concerned with fat and calorie content, you may substitute Fat Free Miracle Whip™ for the real mayonnaise and plain yogurt in place of the sour cream.

Combine sour cream, mayonnaise and seasonings. Stir in onions, shredded spinach, water chestnuts and red pepper. Cover and refrigerate for at least 6 hours before serving. This dip is especially good when served with chunks of french bread.

Prepare a fruit tray using mandarin orange sections, pineapple chunks, maraschino cherries, red and green seedless grapes, fresh banana slices and apple wedges.

Sprinkle lemon juice over banana slices and apple wedges to prevent them from turning dark. Serve fruit with the following dips:

# ORANGE CREAM DIP

*Prep Time: 15 minutes*

1 cup whipping cream
1 (6-oz.) can frozen orange juice concentrate, thawed and undiluted
2 tablespoons chopped pecans, toasted

Beat whipping cream at medium speed of electric mixer until soft peaks form. Slowly add orange juice concentrate, and beat until firm peaks form. Pour into serving dish(s) and sprinkle pecans on top as a garnish.

# CHEESECAKE CREME DIP

*Prep. Time: 5 minutes*

2 (8-oz.) pkgs. cream cheese, softened
1 (13-oz) jar marshmallow creme

Combine the cream cheese with the marshmallow creme and beat until smooth.

# COOL FRUIT DIP

*Prep. Time: 5 minutes to mix together; 2 hours to chill*

1 (8-oz.) pkg. cream cheese
2 cups frozen non-dairy whipped topping
1 cup marshmallow creme

Mix all ingredients together with an electric mixer. Cover and refrigerate for at least 2 hours before serving.

# DEVILED EGGS

## JAMES STYLE *(Otherwise known as MY Way and HIS Way)*

1 doz. eggs, boiled
½ cup Miracle Whip™ or mayonnaise
1 teaspoon prepared mustard
3 tablespoons sweet pickle relish
1 stalk celery, finely chopped
paprika

## STONE STYLE

1 doz. eggs, boiled
½ cup Miracle Whip™ or mayonnaise
2 tablespoons juice from sweet pickles
salt and pepper
paprika

Crack and peel boiled eggs. Cut length-wise in half. Remove yolks and place in bowl. For either version, add all ingredients except for the paprika. Mix well. With a teaspoon, refill egg white halves with a mound of yolk mixture. Sprinkle with paprika for garnish. Serve immediately or refrigerate until ready to serve.

# LI'L SMOKIES

*Prep. Time: 10 minutes / Cook Time: 30-45 minutes*

1 pkg. Little Smokies sausages (may substitute with little hot dogs, or sliced smoked sausage or hot dogs)
2 cups regular Bar-B-Que sauce, any brand
½ cup ketchup
¼ cup light brown sugar
2 tablespoons grape jelly

Combine BBQ sauce with ketchup, brown sugar and grape jelly. Cook over low heat until brown sugar and grape jelly dissolve, stirring often. Add sausages (or hot dogs) and heat through. Simmer for 20-30 minutes to allow sausages to pick up the BBQ flavor.

# February 8

*Their mouths will be watering by the time you call them to the table tonight! Tell them you're having company and then set the table accordingly, using your best dishes. When just your immediate family is gathered 'round the table, tell them they are the very special company and you've prepared a special dinner just for them.*

## PORK ROAST

*Prep. Time: 10 minutes / Cook Time: 1½ hours*

3-4 lb pork roast
1 can cream of mushroom soup
1 can cream of celery soup
1 medium onion
½ cup water

Trim as much fat off pork roast as possible. Put meat in baking pan. In a separate container, combine soups and water. Mix together and then pour over meat, being sure to cover completely. Slice onion and cover meat with onion slices. Bake at 350 degrees for 90 minutes.

## RED 'N' ORANGE YAMS

*Prep. Time: 10 minutes / Cook Time: 30 minutes*

Canned yams or sweet potatoes
1 can prepared cherry pie filling

In a baking dish combine yams/sweet potatoes with cherry pie filling. Bake at 325 degrees for 30 minutes.

## FRIED APPLE RINGS

*Prep. Time: 20 minutes / Cook Time: 20-30 minutes*

6 tart cooking apples (Gala, Granny Smith, Jonathon, etc.)
½ cup butter
2 tablespoons brown sugar
½ teaspoon cinnamon
¼ cup granulated sugar

## MAKE YOUR OWN VALENTINES

*Project #2 You're Such a Sweet Heart*

Red and Pink Construction Paper
Black Permanent Marker
Hole Puncher
White or Red Ribbon, ⅛ inch wide
    (thin Christmas ribbon is perfect)
Pink Plastic Wrap
Cut-Out Sugar Cookie Recipe *(see page )*
Red Sugar or Multi-Colored Sprinkles
One large and one medium heart
    cookie-cutter

Help your child trace around the smaller heart cookie cutter and cut out hearts from the red and/or pink construction paper. On one side, write, You're Such a Sweet Heart. On the back, let your child write his/her own name. Together mix up the Sugar Cookie Recipe and using the large heart cookie cutter, cut out heart-shaped cookies. Bake according to directions. Let cool. Using a prepared frosting (white or pink), let your child frost the cookie and sprinkle on some red sugar or multi-colored sprinkles. Wrap each cookie in pink plastic wrap, twist at the top, and tie on the ribbon. Use the hole punch and punch a hole for the ribbon at the top of the heart and thread through the ribbon. Tie off. Your Sweet Heart Valentines are complete!

Cut ends from apples and slice into rings. Carefully cut the core out of each slice so you're left with a donut shape. In a large skillet, melt butter and stir in sugars and cinnamon. Add layer of apple slices and cook over medium heat, turning once. Serve warm, topped with pan juices.

# February 9

*If you make up a batch of Aunt Edna's pie crusts (see page 28), then you'll have half of tonight's dinner already prepared! If you opt not to make your own, you can always purchase prepared pie crusts in your refrigerated or freezer section at the grocery store.*

## TUNA POT PIE

*Prep. Time: 45 - 50 minutes / Cook Time: 45 to 50 minutes*

1 prepared pie crust in a 9" pie pan plus top crust
1 (12 oz.) can tuna, water packed, drained
1½ cups frozen peas, thawed and drained
½ cup chopped fresh onion
1 can cream of potato or cream of mushroom soup
1 teaspoon salt
½ teaspoon pepper
⅓ cup skim milk
½ teaspoon dried parsley
1 teaspoon dried celery flakes

In a separate bowl, combine tuna with remaining ingredients. Mix well. Pour tuna mixture into pie shell. Add a top crust to the pot pie; crimp edges to seal. Cut slits in top of crust to vent. Bake at 375 degrees for 45 to 50 minutes or until crust is golden brown.

## ICE CREAM CHOCOLATE ROLL

*Prep. Time: 20 minutes / Cook Time: 15 minutes*

### CAKE:

4 eggs, separated
1½ teaspoons vanilla
¼ cup cocoa
⅔ cup boiling water
1 cup sifted cake flour
1 teaspoon baking powder
⅛ teaspoon salt
½ cup granulated sugar

Beat egg yolks with vanilla. Blend cocoa with water; beat into egg yolk mixture. Sift flour with baking powder. Gradually add dry ingredients, mixing until smooth. Beat egg whites with salt until soft peaks form. Gradually add sugar, beating until stiff peaks form. With spatula, fold egg whites into chocolate mixture. Pour batter into greased and floured waxed paper-lined 10 by 15 inch jellyroll pan.

Bake at 325 degrees for 15 minutes. Run knife around edge. Turn hot cake onto cloth heavily dusted with powdered sugar. Remove waxed paper. Starting from narrow end, roll up cake with cloth and let cool.

When cake has cooled, roll cake back out and spread on softened chocolate (or vanilla) ice cream. Re-roll and freeze until solid. Slice and serve with chocolate syrup poured over each slice.

# February 10

*Today kicks off the national observance of Kraut and Frankfurter Week. As a kid, I never cared much for sauerkraut, but now I don't mind the taste too much. I made the mistake of assuming my kids wouldn't like it, so I never fixed it. But I was wrong! Encourage your children to try new foods, at least one bite. You'll both be amazed at what they may actually like!*

## KRAUT & FRANKFURTERS DINNER

*Prep. Time: 10 minutes / Cook Time: 25 minutes*

1 pkg. frankfurters (hot dogs) or sausages
2 cans prepared sauerkraut
6 potatoes, peeled
1 teaspoon salt
¼ teaspoon pepper

Add potatoes and sauerkraut, salt and pepper to soup pan. Bring to a boil, adding additional water if necessary to cover potatoes. When potatoes are tender, add hot dogs and heat through, serve immediately.

## PUMPKIN SPICE SHEET CAKE WITH CREAM CHEESE FROSTING

*Prep. Time: 20 minutes / Cook Time: 30-40 minutes*

CAKE:
2 cups granulated sugar
1 (16 oz.) can pumpkin
½ cup oil
½ cup unsweetened applesauce
4 eggs
2 cups flour
1 tablespoon baking soda
1 teaspoon ground cinnamon
1 teaspoon pumpkin pie spice
½ teaspoon salt

Combine sugar, pumpkin, oil, applesauce and eggs in large bowl; mix well. Add flour, baking soda, cinnamon, pumpkin pie spice and salt; mix until well blended. Pour into greased 9x13 inch cake pan. Bake 25 to 30 minutes or until a knife inserted in the center comes out clean.

FROSTING:
1 pkg. cream cheese (8 oz.)
¼ cup butter, softened
1 teaspoon vanilla
3 cups powdered sugar, sifted
1 tablespoon milk (plus a teaspoon or two, depending upon desired consistency)

Combine all frosting ingredients and mix well on low speed with an electric mixer. Spread over cooled cake. Garnish with crushed pecans if desired.

## KID BREAK!
### Make Your Own Valentines!

*Project #3 You're Beary Special, Valentine*

Brown Construction Paper
Black Permanent Marker
Hole Puncher
Transparent Tape
Individually Wrapped Suckers on a Stick
Large Teddy-Bear shaped Cookie Cutter

Help your child trace around the Teddy-Bear Cookie Cutter and cut out Teddy Bear shapes from the construction paper. In the center of the neck, where a necktie would go OR in the center of a paw, punch out a hole for the sucker stick. Write on the front of the bear, You're Beary Special, Valentine and let your child sign his/her name on the back. Then insert the sucker stick from the front side and tape into place on the back of the teddy bear. That's all there is to it!

# February 11

Although I do enjoy eating out at restaurants, I hate paying so much money when I can prepare the same thing at home for about a fourth of the cost. I like to keep French bread rolls and sliced roast beef in the freezer for a quick and easy meal—fast-food-style.

## FRENCH DIP ROAST BEEF SANDWICHES

*Prep. Time: 15 minutes / Cook Time: 20 minutes*

**1 to 2 French bread roll(s) per person**
**4-6 oz. sliced deli roast beef per person**
**1 packet Au Jus mix**
**1 packet brown gravy mix**
**2 cups water**

In a saucepan large enough to hold the roast beef, combine the Au Jus and brown bravy mixes; add two cups of cold water and whisk to mix. Heat and stir until mixes are dissolved. Add roast beef and let meat heat through. Remove meat from liquid and pile 4 to 6 oz. of meat on each sandwich bun. Pour the Au Jus/gravy mixture in small serving bowls (or dessert dishes) so those that desire to do so can dip their sandwiches.

Serve with mashed potatoes and fresh vegetables with dip.

# February 12

With a family of five, sometimes our schedules force us to be on-the-run. For this reason, I've developed some quick and in a hurry recipes that we use instead of driving through the nearest fast-food joint. By feeding my family something home-made, I can feed all five of us for less than a dollar per person. This computes into big savings if you have an active family like I do!

## PIZZA SANDWICHES TO GO

*Prep. Time: 10 minutes / Cook Time: 15-20 minutes, depending upon how many sandwiches you make*

**For each sandwich you will need:**
**2 slices bread**
**butter**
**1 tablespoon pizza sauce**
**1 tablespoon mozzarella cheese**
**2-3 slices pepperoni**

Spread butter on the outter sides of the bread, placing bread buttered-side down on a griddle. Top with pizza sauce and other ingredients. Butter a top slice of bread and place it on the sandwich, buttered-side facing up. Grill the sandwiches just as you do when you make toasted cheese sandwiches. Sandwiches are done when the cheese has melted and the buttered-sides of bread are lightly toasted.

Grab a can of soda or bottle of juice and you can be on your way!

## KID BREAK!

### MAKE YOUR OWN VALENTINES
*Project #4 — I Chew-z You, Valentine!*

Any Color of Construction Paper
Animal Shaped Cookie Cutters
Black Permanent Marker
Transparent Tape
Sticks of Gum OR Individually
   Wrapped Pieces of Salt-Water Taffy

Let your child trace around the animal shaped cookie cutters and cut out the shapes. On the front, with the permanent marker write, I Chew-z You, Valentine! Let your child write his/her name on the back. On the front, tape either a stick of gum or an individually wrapped piece of taffy. Presto!

# February 13

*In an effort to be more health-conscious, I've tried adapting some of my family's favorites into less fattening—calorie packed alternatives. That is how I came up with this Skinny Alfredo which my family loves. I hope your family enjoys it as well!*

## SKINNY ALFREDO

*Prep. Time: 20 minutes Cooking Time: 25 minutes*

1 (12 oz.) package uncooked fettucine noodles
3 tablespoons butter (diet variety works well)
1 tablespoon flour
½ cup skim milk (or 1 %)
½ cup Parmesan cheese
salt and pepper to taste
4 skinless, boneless chicken breasts, diced

Cook fettucine according to package directions, omitting the fat. Drain well. Place in a large bowl and keep warm. Boil or grill chicken breasts and then cut up meat and add it to the fettucine.

In another pan, melt butter and add flour. Stir until smooth. Cook for 3 to 4 minutes, stirring constantly. Gradually add milk. Turn heat up to medium and continue stirring until mixture is thick and bubbly. Reduce heat to low and stir in Parmesan cheese. Cook until cheese dissolves and mixture is smooth.

Pour sauce over fettucine and toss gently to coat.

Serve with a tossed salad and herb sticks or garlic bread.

# February 14

*We celebrate Valentine's day with a special dinner that every-one likes and at each person's place setting, there's a little Valentine waiting. The kids have received stuffed bears, trolls, packages of candy...always something little but nice. Craig and I usually exchange Valentine cards before we enjoy our meal. Not only is today Valentine's Day, but it's also the Na-tional Random Acts of Kindness Day. So while you're busy thinking of those you love, don't forget to stop and do a ran-dom act of kindness for someone you meet today.*

## CHICKEN CORDON BLEU

*Prep. Time: 30 minutes / Cook Time: 35-45 minutes*

6 skinned, deboned chicken breasts
3 slices (1 oz. per slice) cooked lean ham, cut in strips
3 slices (1 oz. per slice) Swiss cheese, cut in strips
1 egg, beaten
2 tablespoons all-purpose flour
vegetable spray
⅓ cup chopped onion
½ can cream of chicken soup, undiluted

Place chicken between 2 sheets of heavy duty plastic wrap and flatten to ¼-inch thickness, using a meat mallet or rolling pin. Place 2 strips of ham and cheese in center of each chicken breast half. Roll up length-wise and secure with wooden toothpicks.

Dip each chicken roll in egg and dredge in flour. Place chicken rolls, seam side down, in a shallow casserole dish coated with vegetable spray. Bake at 350 degrees for 20 minutes.

In a separate pan, combine onion and soup, stirring until well combined. Pour over chicken and continue to bake at 350 degrees for 15 minutes or until chicken is done.

## TWICE-BAKED POTATOES

*Prep. Time: 30 minutes / Cook Time: 20 minutes*

6 medium baking potatoes
½ cup milk
½ cup plain nonfat yogurt (may substitute sour cream if desired)
½ cup shredded cheddar cheese
1 teaspoon salt
½ teaspoon pepper
paprika

Wash potatoes and pat dry; prick each potato several times with a fork. Arrange potatoes end to end and one inch apart in a circle on paper towels in the microwave. Microwave on High for 15 minutes, turning and rearranging after 6 minutes. Let potatoes stand for five minutes before removing them from the microwave.

Cut potatoes in half, lengthwise. Scoop out pulp, leaving shells intact. Set shells aside. Mash potato pulp in a large bowl using a fork or potato masher. Add milk and yogurt and beat at low speed with an electric mixer until smooth. Add salt and pepper and mix thoroughly. Stuff each potato shell with mashed potato mixture. Top each with cheese and sprinkle with paprika. Bake at 350 degrees for 5 minutes or microwave on high for 30 seconds or until cheese melts.

## BROCCOLI IN CHEESE SAUCE

*Prep. Time: 15 minutes / Cook Time: 25 minutes*

1 pkg. frozen chopped broccoli
1 cup American cheese spread
    (such as Cheese Whiz™)
salt to taste
1 teaspoon butter
1 cup water

Cook broccoli in salted water with butter until done. Drain broccoli and put into a microwave safe bowl. Cover broccoli with cheese spread and microwave on high for 3 to 5 minutes. Serve immediately.

# February 15

*Isn't it interesting what moments our minds recall as special memories? I remember Craig preparing this dinner for me during our first year of marriage. He tried to make it so romantic, with fresh daisies on the table (my favorite flower!) and the two place settings perfectly set. It's a memory I'll always cherish.*

## KID BREAK!

MAKE YOUR OWN VALENTINES
*Project #5 — Sealed with a Kiss*

Juvenile Valentines
    that go into individual Envelopes
Bag of Hersey Kisses™
White Glue
Marker or Ink Pen

On the back of each Valentine, have your child write his/her name. Insert the Valentine in the envelope that is provided. On the front of the envelope, you write across the top, This is Sealed with a Kiss! On the back, help your child glue on a wrapped Hersey Kiss™ candy where the envelope seals. It can't get any easier than this!

## PEPPER STEAK

*Prep. Time: 30 minutes / Cook Time: 15 minutes*

2-3 fresh green bell peppers
1½ to 2 lbs. round steak
½ teaspoon Accent™ (this is a seasoning you can find
    at the grocery store in the herb/seasoning aisle)
1½ to 2 cups beef stock or bouillon
salt and pepper
3 tablespoons oil
2 tablespoons cornstarch
2 tablespoons soy sauce
½ teaspoon ground ginger
½ teaspoon garlic powder
cooked rice

Cut beef into ⅛-inch strips. Cut peppers into thin slices. In a small pan, mix cornstarch, Accent™, soy sauce and ½ cup water. Set aside.

Place oil, salt and pepper, ginger and garlic powder in hot skillet. Add beef, saute 3 minutes. Add peppers and stir well. Add all the ingredients except the starch mixture. Mix thoroughly. Cover and cook for 6 minutes, then add starch mixture, stirring constantly until juice thickens. Serve over cooked rice.

# February 16

*Did you know that today is National Slap a Cop Day? No, I'm not kidding! It really is! Or should I say, it has been called that ever since Zsa Zsa Gabor slapped a cop and got prosecuted for it. So invite your favorite cop over for dinner and give him a good pat on the back (instead of a slap)!*

## VEAL PARMIGIANA

*Prep. Time: 20-30 minutes / Cook Time: 20-30 minutes*

1 egg, beaten
½ teaspoon salt
¼ teaspoon pepper
1 cup crushed cracker crumbs
2 tablespoons Parmesan
1 to 2 lbs. veal cutlets
vegetable spray
1 (8 oz.) can tomato sauce
1 cup mozzarella cheese

Combine egg, salt and pepper; beat with wire whisk until blended. Combine crumbs and Parmesan cheese, stirring well. Dip veal into egg mixture and dredge in crumb mixture. Saute veal in large skillet that has been sprayed with the vegetable spray. Cook until golden brown. Transfer veal to a shallow baking dish. Pour tomato sauce over veal and top with grated mozzarella. Bake at 350 degrees for 20-30 minutes.

## LAYERED SALAD

*Prep. Time: 30 minutes to put together, overnight to age*

1 head lettuce
2-3 stalks celery
1 medium to large onion
¼ head cauliflower
1 pkg. frozen peas, cooked and drained
1 cup Miracle Whip™ Salad Dressing (Miracle Whip Free™ does not taste as good)
6-8 strips of bacon, fried crisp

In the bottom of a large bowl, put a layer of fresh lettuce broken into bite-sized pieces. Next, add a layer of finely diced celery. On top of the celery, add a layer of minced onion. For the next layer, add cauliflower, broken into tiny pieces. Top the cauliflower with the peas. Spread Miracle Whip™ Salad dressing over the peas. Seal the bowl with plastic wrap or a tight-fitting lid. Store overnight in the refrigerator. The next day when you're ready to serve, crumble up crisp bacon over the layer of Miracle Whip™ before tossing to mix and serve the salad.

## HEATH-BRICKLE BLONDE BROWNIES

*Prep. Time: 15-20 minutes / Cook Time: 30 minutes +/-*

1½ cup sifted all-purpose flour
2 teaspoons baking powder
½ teaspoon salt
½ cup butter
1 cup sugar
½ cup brown sugar
2 eggs
1 teaspoon vanilla
1 bag Heath Brickle (found in the grocery aisle along with the chocolate chips)

Sift flour, baking powder and salt together. Cream butter and add both sugars. Mix well. Add eggs and vanilla to butter/sugar mixture. Beat with an electric mixer on low speed until thoroughly mixed. Blend in dry ingredients. Stir in Heath Brickle. Spread over bottom of a well-greased 13"x9" baking pan. Bake at 350 degrees or until done.

When cooled, frost with chocolate frosting and cut into bars to serve.

# February 17

*Making up casseroles is much like mixing colors on a painter's pallet. At least that's how I approach it. Fortunately, I've been lucky in coming up with some great tasting dishes! If there's an ingredient listed that you don't have on hand or your family doesn't particularly care for—don't hesitate to substitute it with something similar.*

## CHEESY CHICKEN BROCCOLI CASSEROLE

*Prep. Time: 30 minutes / Cook Time: 45 minutes to 1 hour*

2 cups chicken meat, cooked, skinned and
    deboned, cut into pieces
1 pkg. frozen chopped broccoli,
    cooked and drained
1 can cheddar cheese soup
1 can cream of chicken soup
1 can evaporated milk
1½ cup grated cheddar cheese
2 cups cooked egg noodles

Mix together soups with milk. In a casserole dish, spread a layer of diced chicken. Cover chicken with broccoli. Sprinkle half of the grated cheese over the broccoli. Add a layer of the cooked noodles. Pour soup mixture over noodles. Top with remaining cheese. Bake at 300 degrees for 45 minutes to 1 hour.

## ANGEL FOOD CAKE

*Prep. Time: 20 minutes / Cook Time: 35-40 minutes*

1 cup sifted cake flour
¾ cup sugar
12 egg whites
1½ teaspoon cream of tartar
¼ teaspoon salt
1½ teaspoon vanilla
¾ cup sugar

Sift flour with sugar FOUR times. Yes, sift flour with sugar FOUR times. Then in a separate bowl, beat egg whites, cream of tartar, salt and vanilla on high with an electric mixer until egg whites are stiff enough to form soft peaks. Add remaining sugar to eggs only 2 tablespoons at a time, beating after each addition. Sift about ¼ of the flour over egg whites and fold in. Fold in remaining flour— adding each additions in fourths. Pour into an ungreased Angel Food cake pan. Bake at 375 degrees for 35 to 40 minutes.

# February 18

*February can be a dreary month with more grey skies than sunshine. Brighten up your mood by treating yourself. Whatever it is that always makes you feel good, do it for yourself! You deserve it.*

## STUFFED PORK TENDERLOIN

*Prep. Time: 45 minutes to 1 hour / Cook Time: 45 minutes to 1 hour*

2 lbs. whole pork tenderloin
½ cup chopped onion
2 cups coarsely crushed saltine cracker crumbs
1 cup dried fruit bits
½ cup apple juice
2 tablespoons chopped parsley
½ teaspoon salt
¼ teaspoon ground allspice
¼ cup apple jelly, melted
salt and pepper to taste

Cut tenderloin almost through lengthwise. Place meat between 2 pieces of plastic wrap and pound with a meat mallet until it is about ½-inch thick. Sprinkle with salt and pepper.

In a bowl, combine fruit bits, apple juice, parsley, salt and allspice. Add crushed cracker crumbs, toss until well combined. Spoon stuffing mixture on edge of meat and roll up; pinching ends to seal. Place meat seam side down, in a shallow pan. Roast in at 375 degrees for 30 to 35 minutes or until meat is no longer pink. Spoon jelly over top of meat the last 10 minutes of cooking time.

# COOKIES OF THE MONTH

## SOFT SUGAR COOKIES

1 cup shortening

2 cups sugar

2 eggs

1 cup sour cream

2 teaspoons vanilla

1 teaspoon salt

1 teaspoon baking soda

2 teaspoons baking powder sifted with enough flour to make a soft dough (about 5-6 cups flour)

Cream together shortening, sugar and eggs. Add remaining ingredients and mix well to form a soft dough. Roll out dough and cut in desired shapes. Sprinkle colored sugars on cut outs before baking. Place on a greased cookie sheet and bake at 350º for 8-12 minutes. Cookies are done when tops are fairly firm to touch.

## PEANUT BUTTER COOKIES

2 cups flour

1 teaspoon baking powder

¼ teaspoon salt

1 cup butter, softened

¾ cup brown sugar, firmly packed

½ cup sugar

½ teaspoon vanilla

1 egg

2 cups peanut butter chips

In small bowl, combine flour, baking powder and salt then set aside. In large bowl, cream butter with sugars and vanilla; beat at medium speed with an electric mixer until creamy. Add egg and beat well. Turn mixer to low speed and gradually add flour mixture. Stir in peanut butter chips. Drop by teaspoon onto ungreased cookie sheet. Bake at 375º for 7-9 minutes. Cool on cookie sheet for a couple of minutes before removing.

## TRADITIONAL CHOCOLATE CHIP COOKIES

1 cup plus 2 tablespoons flour

½ teaspoon baking soda

½ teaspoon salt

½ cup butter, softened

6 tablespoons sugar

6 tablespoons brown sugar, firmly packed

½ teaspoon vanilla

1 egg

1 cup semi-sweet chocolate chips

In small bowl, combine flour, baking soda and salt; then set aside. In large bowl, combine butter with both sugars and vanilla—beat until creamy. Add egg and blend well. Gradually add flour mixture, mixing well after each addition. Stir in chocolate chips. Drop by rounded teaspoon onto ungreased cookie sheet. Bake at 375º for 8-10 minutes.

# ZUCCHINI PATTIES

*Prep. Time: 25 minutes / Cook Time: 10-15 minutes*

2 cups grated fresh zucchini

2 cup grated cheddar cheese

4 cups (or more, depending upon consistency)
   crushed cracker crumbs

1 medium chopped onion

2 eggs

½ teaspoon salt

¼ teaspoon pepper

Mix all ingredients together and form into patties. Fry in skillet with either butter or bacon grease until golden brown on both sides. Serve immediately.

# SCALLOPED APPLES

*Prep. Time: 20-30 minutes / Cook Time: 45 minutes to 1 hour*

6 tart apples, peeled and sliced (such as Gala,
   Jonathon, Granny Smith, etc.)

1 cup sugar

½ teaspoon cinnamon

¼ teaspoon ground cloves

½ cup butter

1 can refrigerated biscuits

Toss apple slices with sugar and spices. In a greased shallow baking dish, layer apples below and on top of biscuits. Pour melted butter over contents and bake at 350 degrees for 45 minutes or until apple slices are tender and biscuits are browned. Serve warm as a side dish or with a scoop of vanilla ice cream for dessert.

# February 19

*My mother started training me in the kitchen when I was too young to really be of much help. Maybe that's why cooking has always been so easy for me—almost second to using common sense. I've tried to expose my three children to the art of cooking as well. Learning how to cook is just another basic necessity of life.*

# EASY STACKED DINNER

*Prep. Time: 30 minutes / Cook Time: 45 minutes or longer*

1 lb. lean ground beef or (leftover) lean roast

6 medium potatoes, peeled and sliced

3 large carrots, sliced

1 large onion, diced

1 medium green pepper, diced

1 can (16 oz.) whole tomatoes

¼ teaspoon pepper

¼ teaspoon dried basil

3 tablespoons A-1™ steak sauce

¼ cup Parmesan cheese

Crumble cooked hamburger (or diced roast) in a casserole dish. Layer potatoes, carrots, onion and green pepper. Pour tomatoes over the layers of beef and vegetables. Sprinkle the pepper, basil and Parmesan cheese over the tomatoes. Cover with a lid or aluminum foil and bake at 350 degrees for 45 minutes or until vegetables are tender. Serve hot from the oven.

## KITCHEN TIPS

• **Save those small plastic pill containers with snap-on lids. They're perfect vessels for salad dressing, ketchup or mustard in brown bag lunches. With them you'll never have soggy sandwiches or droopy salads again.**

• **Don't frost homemade cupcakes on top. Instead, split the cake and put the frosting inside to hold the halves together. This will prevent the frosting from sticking to the paper when packing a lunch.**

• **When baking, put all ingredients needed to the left of the mixing bowl; as you finish with each one, return the container to the cupboard. When the mixing is complete, your kitchen will be clean.**

• **Before sifting flour onto wax paper, always crease the paper down the center. This creates a handy pouring spout.**

# PECAN CAKE

*Prep. Time: 20 - 30 minutes / Cook Time: 30-45 minutes*

*In a saucepan, combine:*

2 cups brown sugar

2 tablespoons butter

1½ cups water

*Bring to a boil and let boil for three minutes. Turn off heat. In a bowl, combine:*

1 cup sugar

2 tablespoons shortening or butter

1 cup milk

2½ cups all-purpose flour

2 teaspoons baking powder

1 tablespoon ground cinnamon

1 cup crushed pecans

Grease a 13"x9" cake pan and spread batter in pan. Decorate with pecan halves if desired. Pour brown sugar liquid over cake batter—DO NOT STIR. Bake at 350 degrees until a knife inserted in the center comes out clean. The liquid will thicken and become a pudding on the bottom of the cake. Serve with ice cream or non-dairy whipped topping.

# February 20

*Sometimes in the hustle and bustle of every day life, we forget to slow down and enjoy one another. Make tonight's dinner special by creating a unique atmosphere that varies from the norm. Here are some easy suggestions: 1) Use your best dishes and a pretty centerpiece for the dinner table. 2) Eat your meal by candlelight with soft music playing in the background. 3) Tell everyone tonight's dinner requires formal attire. Have everyone wear their Sunday Best for dinner. 4) Spread a tablecloth on the floor and host an inside picnic.*

# HAM LOAF

*Prep. Time: 20-30 minutes / Cook Time: 90 minutes or longer*

1½ lb. ground ham

1½ lb. ground pork

1 lb. lean ground beef

3 eggs

1 cup milk

2 tablespoons prepared dry mustard

½ lb. cracker crumbs

pepper to taste

*Topping:*

1½ cups brown sugar

½ cup vinegar

½ cup water

whole cloves

Combine first 8 ingredients and form into two loaves. Place loaves in a roasting pan. In a saucepan, bring brown sugar, vinegar and water to a boil. Remove from heat and pour over ham loaves. Sprinkle whole cloves over the ham loaves for garnish. Bake at 350 degrees for 90 minutes or longer. Baste loaves with topping liquid every 15 minutes.

# OLD FASHIONED MACARONI AND CHEESE

*Prep. Time: 20 minutes / Cook Time: 20-30 minutes*

1 lb. spiral or elbow shaped macaroni, cooked and drained

1 can cream of chicken soup

1 cup American processed cheese (such as Cheese Whiz™)

4 slices American cheese

2 cups grated cheddar cheese

1 teaspoon salt

¼ teaspoon coarse black pepper

After cooking macaroni, rinse it in cold water to stop the cooking process. Let set to drain. Meanwhile, combine the soup and processed cheddar cheeses in the casserole dish. Add salt and pepper, mix well. Pour in the macaroni and stir to coat each piece well. Place cheese slices on top of macaroni, covering the entire top. Bake at 350 degrees for 20 minutes or until all cheeses have melted. Serve immediately.

# VEGETABLE FRITTERS

*Prep. Time: 30 minutes / Cook Time: 15 - 20 minutes*

1 ¼ cup whole wheat pastry flour or all-purpose flour

¼ cup cornmeal

½ teaspoon salt

2 tablespoons cornstarch

1 egg, lightly beaten

1 ¼ to 1 ½ cups water

2 ½ cups chopped vegetables such as onions, mushrooms, celery, green peppers, zucchini, broccoli, carrots, cauliflower, etc.

Mix flours, salt and cornstarch. Add water and egg to make a batter consistent with a pancake batter. Let batter set 20 minutes. While batter is setting, prepare vegetables.

## KITCHEN TRICKS

• TO PREVENT BROWN SUGAR FROM CLUMPING and turning hard, add a slice of bread to the bag or container and seal. The bread will absorb the moisture instead of the brown sugar and the brown sugar will remain soft and granulated as a result. When bread slice gets hard, discard and replace with a fresh slice of bread.

• DO YOU HAVE PROBLEMS WITH SALT CAKING IN THE SALT SHAKERS? Salt draws moisture so to prevent it from clumping, add a few grains of rice to each salt shaker. The rice is too large to come out of the holes when it's sprinkled, yet it works to draw out the moisture that would otherwise be absorbed by the salt.

• OUT OF CRACKER MEAL FOR COATING that fried chicken? Put saltine crackers in a baggie and seal. By using your fist, pound the crackers into a fine powder and use for your chicken coating mix.

Mix vegetables with batter and immerse by spoonfuls into hot oil. Oil should be at least 1 ½ inches deep. Fry for 3-5 minutes. Remove from oil and drain on brown paper sacks (paper towel leaves fritters soggy). Serve immediately.

# February 21

*Before you begin tonight's meal, take a few minutes just for yourself. Turn on your favorite music and fix a cup of your favorite beverage. Sit down, look around and savor the moment.*

# CHICKEN CACCIATORE

*Prep. Time: 30-45 minutes / Cook Time: 20-30 minutes*

2 tablespoons butter

2-3 lbs. chicken breast meat, skin removed and discarded

1 medium onion, chopped

1 stalk celery, diced

1 (26 oz.) can whole tomatoes, undrained and chopped

1 cup sliced fresh mushrooms

½ cup chopped fresh parsley

¼ cup chopped green pepper

1 teaspoon dried basil

1 teaspoon dried oregano

½ teaspoon salt

¼ teaspoon black pepper

cooked rice or noodles

Melt butter over low heat in a large skillet. Add chicken breasts and cook until meat is cooked through and lightly browned. Remove chicken from skillet and let cool. Chop chicken into pieces and set aside.

Add onion and celery to skillet. Saute in remaining butter until vegetables are tender. Return chopped chicken to skillet; add chopped tomatoes and juice and remaining ingredients. Cover and simmer for 20 minutes. Serve hot over hot cooked rice or noodles.

# February 22

Somewhere around this date back in 1620, the Pilgrims landed at Plymouth Rock in Massachusetts. The first Thanksgiving Dinner wouldn't be served until 1631, twenty-one years later. The first public observance of Thanksgiving Day took place on this date in 1631 in the Massachusetts Bay Colony. Over time, this holiday has been moved to November. But I thought you'd find it interesting to know that the very first Thanksgiving meal was served on February 22.

## ALL AMERICAN POT ROAST

Prep. Time: 20-30 minutes / Cook Time: 3 hours

¼ cup vegetable oil
1 cup flour
1 (3-5 lb.) chuck roast, trimmed of fat
1 cup chopped onion
3 stalks celery, cut into 2-inch pieces
3 cups beef bouillon
⅓ cup ketchup
1 teaspoon salt
1 teaspoon dried thyme
¼ teaspoon pepper
6-8 medium potatoes, peeled and quartered
4 carrots, peeled, cut in 2-inch pieces
¼ cup cornstarch
1 teaspoon unseasoned meat tenderizer

Combine flour with salt and pepper. Rinse meat with water and coat with the seasoned flour. In a large skillet, brown roast in hot oil. Transfer meat to a large roasting pan. Sprinkle meat with meat tenderizer. Add onion, celery, bouillon, ketchup and thyme. Bake at 325 degrees for 2 hours. Turn up heat to 350 degrees and add carrots and potatoes. Cover and return to oven to cook for another 30 minutes or until vegetables are tender. Remove meat and vegetables from pan. Combine cornstarch and water, mixing until cornstarch is dissolved. Pour remaining pan drippings into the skillet used to brown the meat. Add dissolved cornstarch and bring mixture to a boil, stirring constantly to thicken. Boil for one whole minute. Pour gravy over roast and vegetables. Serve hot.

## MIRACLE WHIP™ CHOCOLATE CAKE

Prep. Time: 20 minutes / Cook Time: 30-40 minutes

1 cup Miracle Whip™ salad dressing
   (Miracle Whip Free™ and low fat does not
   work in this recipe)
1 cup sugar
1 teaspoon vanilla
2¼ cup sifted cake flour
½ cup cocoa
1 teaspoon baking powder
1 teaspoon soda
dash of salt

Combine salad dressing and sugar in bowl, blending until smooth. Add vanilla, mixing well. In a separate bowl, combine dry ingredients. Add dry ingredients alternately with ¾ cup cold water, mixing well after each addition. Pour batter into two greased and floured 8-inch round cake pans. Bake at 350 degrees for 25 to 30 minutes or until cake is done. Cool for 10 minutes before removing from pan. Frost with Cream Cheese Frosting or add a layer of vanilla ice cream in between cake layers and then frost.

## CREAM CHEESE FROSTING

Prep. Time: 15 minutes

1 (8 oz.) pkg. cream cheese, softened
1 tablespoon milk
1 teaspoon vanilla
dash of salt
4 cups confectioners' sugar

Combine all ingredients in a mixing bowl, beating with an electric mixer on low until of spreading consistency. Frost cooled cake.

# February 23

*If you find yourself short on time, try making your time serve double-duty. Listen to a book on audio cassette while chopping vegetables or preparing the evening meal. Check with your local library or nearest bookstore for a nice range of books on cassette. This way, you can keep up with the bestseller list or enjoy the classics.*

## TUNA-STUFFED BAKED POTATOES

*Prep. Time: 1 hour / Cook Time: 15 minutes*

8 potatoes, baked (wrap individually in aluminum foil and bake at 350 degrees for 50 - 60 min.)

2 tablespoons butter

2 (7 oz.) cans water-packed tuna

1 tablespoon grated fresh onion or minced dried onion

1 tablespoon dried parsley

1 (10¾ oz.) can cheddar cheese soup

¼ teaspoon paprika

1 teaspoon salt

4 slices American cheese, cut into halves

Cut baked potatoes in half lengthwise. Scoop out cooked potato, leaving the skins in-tact. Combine the potato meat with butter, tuna, onion, parsley, soup, paprika and salt. Mix well. Spoon mixture back into the potato shells. Top each potato with a half-slice of American cheese. Return potatoes to the oven and bake for 15 minutes at 350 degrees.

## BAKED FROZEN PEAS

*Prep. Time: 5-10 minutes / Cook Time: 45 minutes to 1 hour*

20 oz. frozen peas

1 can cream of celery soup

½ cup crushed cracker crumbs

4 tablespoons melted butter

Butter a quart casserole dish, break up frozen peas and mix in soup. Top with buttered crumbs and bake uncovered for 45 minutes to 1 hour at 400 degrees.

# February 24

## SWEDISH MEAT BALLS

*Prep. Time: 30 minutes / Cook Time: 30 minutes or longer*

1½ lb. lean ground beef

1 egg

1 tablespoon dried parsley flakes

1 teaspoon salt

1 teaspoon pepper

1 tablespoon Worcestershire sauce

¾ cup dried bread crumbs or quick cooking oatmeal

*Sauce:*

1 (12 oz.) bottle chili sauce

½ cup honey barbeque sauce

½ cup grape jelly

Combine all ingredients and mix well. Form into small balls and brown in skillet. Remove meatballs from skillet and place in a soup pan or crock pot. Combine sauce mix and pour over meatballs. Cook on low heat in soup pan or on the high setting in a crock pot for at least 30 minutes. Test one meatball by cutting it in half to make sure meatballs are cooked through before serving. Serve over a bed of rice or cooked noodles.

# CARROT CAKE & CREAM CHEESE ICING

2 cups all-purpose flour

2 teaspoons baking powder

2 teaspoons ground cinnamon

¾ cup oil

4 eggs

2 teaspoons baking soda

1 teaspoon salt

2 cups sugar

3 cups fresh grated carrots

2 cups raisins

¾ cup unsweetened applesauce

Combine oil, applesauce and sugar and add eggs. Beat with an electric mixer on low speed until mixture is creamy. Add dry ingredients alternately with eggs, adding eggs one at a time. Mix well. Fold in carrots and raisins. Pour into a 13x9 greased and floured cake pan. Bake at 300 degrees for 45 minutes or until a knife inserted in the center comes out clean.

### CARROT CAKE FROSTING

1 (8 oz.) pkg. cream cheese

4 cups powdered confectioners' sugar

2 teaspoons vanilla

½ stick butter, softened

Combine all ingredients in a medium mixing bowl and beat together with an electric mixer set on low speed. Beat until all ingredients form a creamy icing. Frost cooled cake and refrigerate until ready to serve.

## KID BREAK!

Here's a way for your little ones to help you tackle a big job. All kids love playing with water (that's why squirt guns are so popular!). Give each child a spray bottle filled with warm water. Instruct your child to spray all the dirty spots on your kitchen floor. Lay down a clean kitchen hand-towel for each bare foot and let each child then skate the dirt and water away!

# February 25

*A great time-saver when preparing meals is to pre-cook ground beef, sausage and/or chicken for other meals. Refrigerate or freeze the meat (and stock) for use later in the week. A quick zap in the microwave will have it ready for use in no time.*

## POTATO SAUSAGE CASSEROLE

*Prep. Time: 20-30 minutes / Cook Time: 1 hour or longer*

1 lb. mild sausage

1 (32 oz.) pkg. frozen hash browned potatoes, thawed

1 can cream of chicken soup

1 cup processed American cheese spread such as Cheese Whiz™

1 cup plain yogurt

½ to 1 cup chopped onion, depending upon your family's preferences

salt and pepper to taste

Brown sausage in skillet, stirring until crumbly. Drain. Add remaining ingredients, mix well. Spoon onto 9x13 inch baking dish. Bake at 350 degrees for 1 hour. Serve with scrambled eggs and toast.

## DIETER'S FRUIT DELIGHT

*Prep. Time: 5 minutes*

1 can cherry pie filling

1 can mandarin oranges, drained

1 can pineapple chunks, drained

3 bananas, sliced

2 cups miniature marshmallows

2 cups Fat Free Cool Whip™

Combine all ingredients and spoon into dessert dishes. Top with a cherry and serve.

# February 26

*Today kicks off National Pancake Week. We enjoy having breakfast meals at supper time for a change of pace. Make a double-batch of pancakes in order to have ready-made breakfasts in the freezer. To keep pancakes from freezing together, freeze individually on a baking sheet before stacking together. Seal in a gallon sized freezer bag and store in the freezer.*

## PANCAKES

*Prep. Time: 15 minutes / Cook Time: 3-6 minutes each*

2 cups all-purpose flour
1 teaspoon baking soda
½ teaspoon baking powder
½ teaspoon salt
2 tablespoons sugar
2⅓ cups buttermilk
2 eggs
3 tablespoons vegetable oil

Sift the dry ingredients together into a medium-size bowl. In a separate, smaller bowl, whisk together buttermilk, eggs and oil. (If you don't have any buttermilk on hand, measure out the milk and add a tablespoon of vinegar. Let milk set for five minutes to curdle, then use as buttermilk.) Pour the liquid into the dry ingredients, whisking just until they are incorporated. Don't over whisk the mixture, or the pancakes will be tough.

In a nonstick skillet over medium heat, pour ⅓ cup batter for each pancake. Cook until bubbles form on the top of the pancakes, about 3 minutes. Turn and cook until the bottom is golden and cooked, about 30 seconds to a minute longer. Serve immediately.

*Variations:*

• Add 1-2 cups fresh blueberries, raspberries or strawberries to batter.
• Puree 2 fresh bananas with 1 tablespoon milk and add to the batter mix.
• Add 2 teaspoons ground cinnamon and 1 extra tablespoon sugar to batter mix.
• Top plain pancakes with cherry pie filling or strawberry pie filling
  Serve pancakes with your choice of bacon strips, sausage links or eggs.

# February 27

*As soon as your children show an interest in cooking, I encourage you to cultivate that interest and to train both your daughters and sons how to cook. With a little supervision, today's menu is an easy one for kids to prepare.*

## EASY & DELICIOUS QUICHE

*Prep. Time: 15-20 minutes / Cook Time: 50-75 minutes*

1- 2 cup(s) shredded ham, crumbled bacon or cooked crumbled sausage
1 tablespoon dry onion flakes
2 cups grated cheddar cheese
8 eggs
1½ cups milk
¾ cup Bisquick™
1 teaspoon salt
½ teaspoon pepper

Cover bottom of greased casserole dish with meat and sprinkle on dry onion flakes. Top with grated cheese. In a blender, combine eggs, milk, Bisquick™, salt and pepper. Mix well and then pour egg mixture over the meat and cheese. Bake at 350 degrees for 50 minutes or until a knife inserted in the center comes out clean.

## GELATIN COCKTAIL

*Prep. Time: 15 minutes*

1 pkg. each lemon and lime gelatin
  (3 oz. boxes)
1 (8 oz.) pkg. cream cheese
1 large can fruit cocktail

Drain large can fruit cocktail and use juice plus enough hot water to make 1 quart liquid. Pour hot liquid over powdered gelatin and mix thoroughly.

Let cool, but not congeal. Pour over drained fruit and put into a 13x9 inch baking pan. Refrigerate until set. Serve in squares on a leaf of lettuce with a dollop of plain yogurt sprinkled with sugar in the center.

# February 28

*Sometimes family favorites are those dishes that have been passed down from one generation to the next. The sweet yeast bread recipe in today's menu is one that has been passed down through at least four generations. Special thanks goes to my sister-in-law, Melissa Stone, for sharing this bread recipe that has been prepared on her mother's side of the family for years. It has become one of my family's favorites.*

## SWEET YEAST BREAD

*Prep. Time: 8 hours plus / Cook Time: 30-40 minutes*

4 cups lukewarm water
2 pkgs. Active dry yeast
2 cups sugar
2 teaspoons salt
²/₃ cup shortening or stick butter
1 (5 lb.) bag of bread flour

In a very large bowl, dissolve yeast in lukewarm water. Let set for five minutes. (I use my hands instead of spoons when making this bread.) Mix together and add sugar, salt and shortening. Cream sugar in liquid mixture with your hands. Begin adding bread flour, mixing it with the liquid mixture using your hands. Continue adding bread flour until the dough is soft and pliable. (The dough will easily peel off of your hands at this stage.) Knead dough for five minutes. Place dough in an oiled bowl, coating dough with oil.

Turn on the oven and preheat at 400 degrees for two minutes. Turn off heat. Cover dough with a damp towel or cloth and put in oven. Let dough rise until doubled. Remove dough bowl from oven and with your fist, punch the dough in the center as hard and as fast as you can. This will eliminate

air bubbles from forming in your bread loaves while baking. Knead for two to three minutes and then divide dough into four loaves. Place loaves in greased bread pans. Turn on oven and preheat to 400 degrees for two minutes. Turn off heat. Return bread loaf pans to oven and let rise until doubled. When bread is at the size you desire, turn the oven on to 350 degrees and bake for 30 minutes or until bread is done. Bread is done when it is lightly browned and sounds hollow when thumped with your fingers. With a stick of butter, coat top crusts of bread loaves before wrapping individual loaves in plastic wrap.

## CUBED STEAK PARMIGIANA

*Prep. Time: 20-30 minutes / Cook Time: 60-75 minutes*

6 beef cubed steaks
3 tablespoons flour
1 teaspoon salt
½ teaspoon pepper
10 crackers, finely crushed
½ teaspoon dried basil
½ teaspoon ground oregano
grated Parmesan cheese
1 egg, beaten
3 tablespoons oil
1 (15 oz.) can tomato sauce
1 tablespoon sugar
1 clove garlic, crushed
1 cup grated mozzarella cheese
leaf oregano for garnish

Coat meat in flour seasoned with salt and pepper. Pound meat with a meat mallet until about doubled in size. In a separate bowl, combine cracker crumbs, basil and ¹/₃ cup Parmesan cheese. Add egg with 2 tablespoons water in bowl. Dip each steak into egg mixture. Then dredge each coated steak in cracker crumbs, evenly coating both sides. In a 13x9-inch baking pan, heat oil for 5 to 10 minutes in a 375 degree oven. Place steaks in baking pan on top of hot oil. Bake uncovered for 25 to 30 minutes or until meat is golden brown.

Remove meat from pan and pour off pan drippings

into a separate bowl. Combine tomato sauce with sugar, garlic and ground oregano. Pour over meat. Return meat to the baking pan and sprinkle on the Parmesan cheese. Bake for 20 minutes longer. Top with mozzarella cheese and a sprinkle of leaf oregano. Bake for 3 to 5 minutes longer.

Serve with mashed potatoes and your choice of vegetable and/or salad.

## MORE KITCHEN TRICKS

• Certain cheeses have a tendency to mold while being stored in the refrigerator. Due to the cultures within the cheese, the mold can simply be trimmed off and discarded and the remaining cheese is still good to eat.

• To help prevent your muffins or cupcakes from sticking to the papers, spray each one with a vegetable cooking spray before adding the batter. The papers will easily peel away from the cake, leaving it intact.

• Get some extra mileage from those shortening sticks and butter/margarine stick wrappers. Save the wrappers from each stick in a baggie. When you need to grease a pan, simply remove one of the wrappers and rub over the pan's surface. You never need to get your hands greasy again!

# March 1
## CHEESY CHICKEN BAKE

*Prep. Time: 35 minutes / Cook Time: 45 minutes to 1 hour*

1 chicken fryer cut up plus 2 chicken breasts
½ cup oil
1 cup crushed cracker crumbs
1 cup grated sharp cheddar cheese
¼ cup Parmesan cheese
1 teaspoon Accent™
1 teaspoon salt
$^1/_8$ teaspoon pepper
1 teaspoon dried chives
1 teaspoon dried sweet basil
fresh parsley for garnish

In a bowl, mix together the crushed cracker crumbs, Parmesan cheese, Accent™, salt, pepper, chives and basil. Dip each piece of chicken in water, then dredge in the crumb mixture. Place chicken in a large shallow baking pan about 1 inch apart. Pour oil over the chicken pieces. Bake at 350 degrees for 45 minutes or until the chicken easily comes away from the bone when pricked with a fork. While the chicken is baking, occasionally baste the chicken pieces with the standing oil in the pan.

Spinkle cheddar cheese over chicken 10 minutes before removing chicken from the oven. Serve with mashed potatoes and cooked peas.

# March 2

*Nothing is as inviting as the smell of fresh homemade bread. Plan ahead and serve some to your family with tonight's dinner meal. Here are a few of my favorite bread recipes that are great served with tonight's casserole.*

## MEATBALL DINNER

*Prep. Time: 20-30 minutes / Cook Time: 1 hour 15 minutes*

2 lbs. lean ground beef or ground chuck
1 medium onion, minced or finely diced
½ green bell pepper, finely diced
1 cup crushed saltine cracker crumbs
2 teaspoons salt
2 teaspoons chili powder
2 eggs, beaten
8 carrots, halved
6 to 8 potatoes, peeled and quartered
1 cup skim milk
2 cans tomato soup

Combine the first 7 ingredients in a large bowl, mixing well. Using a tablespoon for measurement, scoop up one tablespoon of meat mixture for every meatball. Form meat into a round meatball. Place meatballs in a baking dish and bake at 400 degrees for 15 minutes.

Remove baking dish from oven and drain off any meat drippings. Transfer meatballs to a roasting pan. Layer carrots and potatoes around meatballs. Prepare soups with milk and pour the soup over the top of all. Cover roasting pan with foil (or a lid) and return to the oven. Bake at 350 degrees for 1 hour or until vegetables are tender. Add salt and pepper to taste when serving.

## BEGINNER'S WHITE BREAD

*Prep. Time: 2½ hours / Cook Time: 20-30 minutes*

1 pkg. Active dry yeast
1 cup lukewarm water
¼ cup sugar
3 cups all-purpose flour (plus maybe up to a cup more)
2 tablespoons butter
1 teaspoon salt

In a large mixing bowl, dissolve the yeast in the lukewarm water. Add sugar and stir until dissolved. Let set for about 2 minutes to activate the yeast. Add 1 cup of flour, softened butter, salt and mix well. Gradually add the remaining flour until the dough becomes firm enough to form into a ball. You may or may not need more than 3 cups of flour, depending upon the level of humidity in the atmosphere when you make the bread. Don't add more than 4 cups of flour total though or your bread will be too dry.

Turn the dough out onto a lightly floured surface and knead it for about 10 minutes. Place the dough in a clean bowl and cover with a moist towel. Let bread dough set in a warm spot (68 to 72 degrees) until the dough has doubled in bulk. This will take about 45 minutes to 1 hour.

Preheat the oven to 375 degrees. Lightly oil a 9x5x3-inch bread loaf pan. Punch the dough down with one fast slam in the center of the dough. This will help eliminate air bubbles from forming during the baking of the bread. After punching dough down, form the dough into a loaf and place in the loaf pan. Return the dough to a warm spot and let the dough rise until it is slightly higher than the sides of the pan. This will take 30 to 45 minutes. When the dough has risen, bake the bread for 20-30 minutes at 375 degrees. Tap bread with fingers to test for doneness. The bread will echo a hollow sound when done. Remove from oven and turn it out immediately onto a wire rack to cool. While bread is still warm, coat the top crust with butter. Slice when cool.

# EASY WHEAT BREAD

*Prep. Time: 3 hours / Cook Time: 30-35 minutes*

1 pkg. Active dry yeast
4 cups all-purpose flour
2 cups whole wheat flour
1 tablespoon salt
⅓ cup oil
⅓ cup honey

Dissolve yeast in ¼ cup lukewarm water. In a separate bowl, add 2½ cups hot water, 2 cups all-purpose flour, all the whole wheat flour and salt. Mix well until dough is smooth. Pour in the yeast water and add the remaining flour, oil and honey. Mix with your hands, adding enough flour (as needed) to make a soft dough. Shape into 2 loaves and place in greased bread-loaf pans. Set in a warm spot (68 to 72 degrees) and cover with a moist kitchen towel. Let rise until dough is 1 to 2 inches above the bread pans. Turn the oven on to 400 degrees and let preheat for 1 minute then reduce heat to 350 degrees. Bake the two loaves at 350 degrees for 30-35 minutes or until bread is done (sounds hollow when tapped). Remove bread from oven when done and remove from pans. Let cool on a wire rack. Baste the top crust of both loaves with butter. Slice when cool.

# March 3

*For a fun and entertaining family night, plan a theme evening. Ask each person to find out some fact or bit of interesting information to share about the theme. Following are some suggestions for an Italian Night at home.*

*Cover the dinner table with a plain white tablecloth. Ask the children to make placemats using red and white and green construction paper (let them color a flag or draw a picture). Use a variety of dry pasta, red and green bell peppers and a bottle of Olive Oil with fresh garlic bulbs as your centerpiece spread. Check with your local library to see if they might have a selection of Italian classics on CD or cassette that you can play in the background during dinner. Turn the lights down low or eat by candlelight.*

# TOO EASY TO BE THIS GOOD LASAGNA

*Prep. Time: 20 minutes / Cook Time: 30 minutes*

1 pkg. lasagna noodles
1 can or jar spaghetti sauce
1 can or jar of pizza sauce
1½ lb. lean ground beef
2 cups grated cheddar cheese
2 cups grated mozzarella cheese
¼ cup Parmesan cheese
1-2 tablespoons dried minced onions
garlic powder
1 cup cottage cheese
1 egg
1 teaspoon dried Italian seasoning
1 teaspoon dried sweet basil
1 teaspoon dried oregano

Cook lasagna noodles according to package directions. When pasta is tender but still firm, drain hot water and rinse in cold water. In a separate pan, boil ground beef until done. Drain off water and crumble meat. In a large bowl combine the spaghetti and pizza sauces and stir until well blended. In another small container, combine cottage cheese with egg, Italian seasoning, sweet basil and oregano. Mix thoroughly.

In a 9x13 pan, lay down a layer of lasagna noodles with sides touching. Cover with sauce. Sprinkle ½ of the Parmesan cheese over sauce. Sprinkle with garlic powder. Sprinkle on minced onions. Spread a layer of crumbled ground beef over sauce. Dot on the cottage cheese mixture, using all of the mixture. Spread on ¼ cup each cheddar cheese and mozzarella cheese. Add another layer of lasagna noodles. Cover with remaining sauce. Sprinkle on remaining Parmesan cheese. Sprinkle garlic powder over sauce again and add remaining minced onions. Spread a layer of crumbled ground beef and sprinkle on remaining cheddar and mozzarella cheeses. Bake at 400 degrees for 30 minutes.

Serve with toasted Garlic Bread and a tossed salad.

# March 4

## DOUBLE-WRAPPED CHICKEN

*Prep. Time: 15 minutes / Cook Time: 1 hour*

1 small jar dried beef
6 chicken breasts, skinned
6 slices of bacon
2 cans cream of mushroom soup
2 cups plain yogurt
2 stalks celery
1 onion

Cover each chicken breast with three slices of dried beef and then wrap around one slice of bacon to hold the beef in place. Secure with a toothpick. Place chicken breasts in a 9x13 baking dish. In a separate container, whip together the cream of mushroom soup and the yogurt (do not add any water or milk to the soup). Spoon the soup mixture over the chicken, covering it completely. Cut celery in chunks and arrange over the chicken. Slice the onion and arrange over the celery. Bake at 350 degrees for 1 hour. Remove the onion and celery and discard before serving. The celery and onion are used only as seasoning for the dish.

Set the chicken on a platter to serve. Prepare enough instant rice to make 6 servings (following the directions on the rice box). When rice is ready to serve, pour the soup mixture from the chicken into the pan of rice and mix together thoroughly. Transfer to a serving bowl and serve with your choice of vegetables.

# KID BREAK!

### Creative Quality Time

At the beginning of each month, schedule a date with your kids on a weekly or bi-weekly basis. Mark it on the calendar. Somehow we always find the time to make it to business meetings, doctor appointments and parent-teacher conferences. Use the same strategy for your family. Make time to spend with your kids by marking it on the calendar and setting aside the time to do something together. Here are some suggested activities you can do with your child:

- put together a puzzle.

- use finger paints and cut brown paper sacks to custom design some wrapping paper for the next birthday present you have to wrap. Let your child make hand prints on the plain side of the brown sack.

- sort through old photographs and construct a family album or scrapbook. Help your child make frames for the pictures out of colored construction paper. Together work on writing out cute captions to place under the pictures. These scrapbooks make great gifts for grandparents, too!

- bake cookies and take them to a local nursing home. Ask if there is someone in particular that could use a cheer-me-up visit and some home baked cookies.

- plant a garden or some herb seeds for growing indoors. Let your child take ownership of the new plants that grow.

# March 5

*I believe the kitchen is the hub center of a home. One time-saver I've discovered for staying organized and preserving family history (like recording the funny things kids say or do or remembering that new recipe you just threw together) is to keep a notepad and pen in a drawer close by the telephone or storing it at the end of a counter. It comes in handy for leaving notes, giving directions for chores and keeping track of messages for others, too.*

## SCALLOPED POTATOES WITH SALMON

*Prep. Time: 15 minutes / Cook Time: 45 minutes*

6-7 potatoes, peeled and cubed
1 can salmon, drained
1 medium onion, finely diced
1 stalk celery, finely diced
1 can evaporated skim milk
2 teaspoons salt
½ teaspoon pepper
1 cup shredded cheddar cheese
1 tablespoon butter

In a skillet, sauté onion and celery in melted butter. When both are tender and the onion is transparent, stir in evaporated milk, salt and pepper. Spread cubed potatoes out in a 13x9 baking dish. Flake salmon over the potatoes in a thin layer. Pour seasoned milk and vegetable mixture over potatoes and salmon. Bake at 400 degrees for 35 minutes. Top with cheddar cheese and bake for 10 more minutes.

## CITRUS SALAD

*Prep. Time: 30 minutes Chill Time: 4 hours or longer*

1 (8 ½ oz.) can crushed pineapple
1 (3 oz.) pkg. orange gelatin
1 (3 oz.) pkg. cream cheese, softened (try with fat free cream cheese!)
2 cups Fat Free Cool Whip ™
1 carrot, grated

Drain the pineapple, reserving the juice. Add enough water to the pineapple juice to measure 1 cup of liquid. Bring this liquid to a boil. In a separate bowl, combine the gelatin and cream cheese and then pour in boiling liquid. Beat on low speed with an electric mixer until mixture is smooth. Set in refrigerator and let cool, stirring every 10 minutes for 1 hour. Remove from refrigerator and fold in remaining ingredients. Pour into mold and return to refrigerator to chill until firm, about 3 hours. To remove salad from mold, dip the outside of the mold in warm water and then invert onto a serving plate. Slice and serve.

# March 6

*Frozen food was first marketed in the United States on this date back in 1930. Since then just about any meal you desire can be found in the frozen foods section of the grocery store. But watch out! Buying the convenience-frozen food entrees can really put a dent in your grocery budget. Instead of spending the money for convenience foods, you can make this work for you for less money by cooking ahead and freezing entrees and ingredients at home. (Check out Deborah Taylor-Hough's **Frozen Assets: how to cook for a day and eat for a month** for a complete cookbook of foods to make and freeze—published by Champion Press, Ltd. see end pages for ordering information.) Today's dinner can be easily doubled if you'd like to freeze a portion for a quick weekend brunch.*

## MADE-FROM-SCRATCH BBQ

*Prep. Time: 3 hours or more / Cook Time: 1 hour*

1 (3 to 4 lb.) pork roast
2 onions, minced
1 tablespoon butter
2 cups ketchup
¾ cup chili sauce
3 tablespoons vinegar
3 tablespoons brown sugar
½ teaspoon dry mustard
1 teaspoon chili powder
1 teaspoon Worcestershire sauce
2 tablespoons grape jelly

Cover roast with water and bring to a slow boil over medium-high heat. Reduce heat to low and let simmer for 3 hours or until meat is tender. When roast is tender and done, drain off all water and let cool. In a separate pan, sauté onions in butter or margarine until they are transparent. Add the remaining ingredients and simmer on low heat for 1 hour. While sauce is simmering, cut up roast into shreds of bite-sized pieces. Add meat to the sauce and stir together. Allow the meat to reheat and then serve on buns or bread.

Serve with fresh vegetables and dip.

## SPINACH DIP

*Prep. Time: 15-20 minutes Chill Time: 1-2 hours*

1 pkg. Knorr ™ Vegetable Soup Mix
1 pkg. frozen chopped spinach, thawed and
     drained
1 cup sour cream
1 cup real mayonnaise
1 can chopped water chestnuts, drained
¼ cup chopped fresh onion

Combine all ingredients in a bowl and mix well. Refrigerate for 1 to 2 hours to let the flavors blend before serving.

## CHEESY DIP

*Prep. Time: 15-20 minutes Chill Time: 1-2 hours*

2 cups grated cheddar cheese
¾ cup real mayonnaise or 1 cup Miracle Whip ™
⅓ cup bacon bits
2 tablespoons minced onion
½ cup slivered almonds

Combine all ingredients in a mixing bowl and mix well. Refrigerate 1 to 2 hours to allow flavors to blend before serving.

# March 7

*It was on this date in 1897 that Dr. John Kellogg used his brother's new invention of Corn Flakes to feed his patients. The patients loved the corn flakes and Dr. Kellogg started selling them through mail-order. Now Kellogg's Corn Flakes™ are a common household staple. Today's menu uses Corn Flakes in a way you've probably never thought of—give it a try and see what you think!*

## OVEN-FRIED CHICKEN

*Prep. Time: 30 minutes / Cook Time: 1 hour*

2½ to 3 lbs. chicken, cut up
     (removing skin is optional)
1 can evaporated skim milk
2 eggs
2 cups corn flake crumbs
1 cup flour
salt and pepper to taste
2-3 tablespoons oil

Mix milk and eggs together. In a quart or gallon sized plastic bag, combine corn flake crumbs, flour, salt and pepper. Dip chicken pieces into the milk and egg mixture then drop one piece at a time into the bag. Shake bag to cover the chicken with the corn flake mixture. Place chicken on a baking sheet that has been coated with the oil. Bake for 30-40 minutes and then turn over and continue baking for 20-30 minutes or until chicken pulls away easily from the bone.

## FRIED BEANS

*Prep. Time: 20 minutes / Cook Time: 20 minutes, give or take*

2 cups cooked beans, mashed (pinto, kidney,
     navy, northern—any of these varieties)
¼ cup minced onion
2 cups corn flakes, crumbled
½ teaspoon salt
pepper to taste

Combine all ingredients in a bowl and then form mixture into at least 6 patties that are about ½ inch thick. Brown on both sides until lightly browned. Serve immediately.

## HONEY-CINNAMON ICE CREAM BALLS

*Prep. Time: 15-20 minutes Chill Time: 30 minutes or longer*

Vanilla ice cream
3 cups crushed corn flakes
½ cup sugar
2 tablespoons ground cinnamon
honey
Cool Whip™ and Maraschino Cherries, optional

Let ice cream soften until you can easily scoop out a ball. Mix together the sugar, corn flakes and cinnamon in a deep bowl. Roll the ball of ice cream in the crumb mixture and place in a serving dish. Return to freezer and let refreeze. When you're ready to serve, drizzle honey over the coated ice cream balls and top with whipped topping and a cherry if desired.

# March 8

*Where's my coffee??? I had just set my cup down on the kitchen table when I caught my then two-year-old son drinking from my cup. My mother tells me I was about that age when I developed my taste for coffee, too. If that's a taste you and your family enjoys, then you'll love tonight's decadent dessert!*

## CHICKEN CORNELIA

*Prep. Time: 15 minutes / Cook Time: 1 hour or longer*

6 skinless and boneless chicken breasts
2 cups plain yogurt
2 cans cream of chicken soup
2 envelopes dry onion soup mix
1 can chow mein noodles
salt and pepper to taste

In a large casserole dish, place chicken in a single layer. In a separate bowl, combine the yogurt, cream of chicken soup and dry onion soup mixes. Pour mixture over the chicken, being careful to coat each breast. Add salt and pepper. Bake uncovered at 400 degrees for 50 minutes. Sprinkle noodles over chicken and return to the oven for 10 to 15 minutes longer. Serve immediately.

## SEASONED PEAS AND VEGETABLES

*Prep. Time: 10-15 minutes / Cook Time: 30-40 minutes*

1 can small peas, drained (reserve juice)
½ cup pea liquid from canned peas
1½ teaspoon seasoned chicken stock
¼ teaspoon ginger
1 (5-oz.) can water chestnuts, sliced
1 (3-oz.) can sliced mushrooms
2 teaspoons cornstarch
1 tablespoon soy sauce

In a medium saucepan, combine the first 6 ingredients. Cover pan and heat to boiling. In a small bowl, combine the cornstarch with the soy sauce and mix until smooth. Reduce heat to low and add cornstarch mixture to peas. Stir continually until liquid thickens. Serve immediately.

Serve with mashed potatoes.

## MOCHA CAKE

*Prep. Time: 45 minutes to 1 hour Baking Time: 1 hour or longer*

8 eggs, separated
1 teaspoon cream of tartar
¾ teaspoon salt
1¼ cups sugar
1 tablespoon instant coffee
1 cup flour
⅓ cup hot water
¼ cup semi sweet chocolate chips
FROSTING:
4 cups Cool Whip™
¼ cup semi sweet chocolate chips

⅓ cup powdered sugar

1½ teaspoons instant coffee

1 teaspoon vanilla

In a large bowl, combine egg whites with cream of tartar and salt; beat on high speed with an electric mixer until soft peaks form. Gradually add ¾ cup sugar, beating until very stiff peaks form. In a small bowl, beat egg yolks until very thick and lemon colored. Gradually add remaining sugar, beating until thick.

Put chocolate chips in a blender and chop or grate. Dissolve 1 tablespoon instant coffee in hot water. Blend together the coffee, flour, ¼ cup grated chocolate chips and 2 teaspoons vanilla with the egg yolks. Beat 1 minute at low speed or just until well blended. Fold egg yolk mixture into egg whites. Pour into an ungreased 10-inch tube pan. Bake at 325 degrees for 50-60 minutes or until cake springs back when touched lightly in the center. Invert cake on funnel or soft drink bottle to hang until completely cooled. Remove cooled cake from pan and frost.

FROSTING: In a large bowl, stir together Cool Whip ™ with remaining grated chocolate (reserve 1 tablespoon grated chocolate for topping). Mix in the powdered sugar, the instant coffee and vanilla and beat on medium speed with an electric mixer until stiff peaks form. (Be careful not to over-beat.) Slice cake into two layers. Spread frosting on the top of the bottom layer and then add top layer of cake. Spread frosting over the top and down sides, if desired. Sprinkle on reserved chocolate for decoration. Store in refrigerator.

# March 9

*Craig is the official noodle maker in our home. I love snitching a bite or two while the noodles are air-drying. It brings back memories of when I was a kid and my mom would cover the cabinet tops and kitchen table with home-made noodles. You can make the homemade version of tonight's Beef 'n' Noodles or you can purchase your noodles already made from the grocery store. If I'm in a pinch for time, I'll use Reames Noodles ™ in the frozen foods section in place of the homemade variety.*

## BEEF 'N' NOODLES

*Prep. Time: 20 minutes to 4 hours, depending upon available beef and your choice of noodles / Cook Time: 30 minutes*

½ to 1 lb. cooked* beef roast

(can use the beef cubes packaged for beef stew; or use the leftovers from a roast)

2 cans beef broth stock*

3 cups water*

1 tablespoon beef bouillon

1 onion*

2 stalks celery*

1 teaspoon dried sweet basil*

1 teaspoon unseasoned meat tenderizer*

2 teaspoons salt*

¼ teaspoon pepper*

HOMEMADE NOODLES

1 beaten egg

2 tablespoons milk

½ teaspoon salt

1 cup flour

*If you need to cook the meat, then put the beef in a baking pan and add 3 cups water, 1 onion, sliced; 2 stalks celery cut in chunks, sprinkle basil, 1 teaspoon salt, pepper and meat tenderizer over the meat. Bake at 300 degrees for 2 hours or until meat is very tender. Remove meat from oven and shred it with your fingers when it is cool enough to handle. Scoop out meat juices and vegetables from pan and puree in a blender. Pour stock into a glass jar or large bowl and set in the refrigerator for 45 minutes to 1 hour. The fat will separate from the stock and will congeal at the top. When making your dish, discard the fat at the top of the beef stock.

If your meat is from a previous meal and is leftover and you have no stock, then you may substitute 2-3 large cans of beef broth stock available from the grocery store. If you do opt to use the already prepared beef broth, then add the beef bouillon for extra flavoring.

While your meat is cooking, make the noodles.

In a mixing bowl, combine egg, milk and salt. Stir in just enough flour to make a stiff dough. Cover and let dough rest for 10 minutes. Then on a floured surface, roll dough into a large rectangle that is about ⅛ of an inch thick. Let dough stand for 20 minutes to dry. Carefully roll up dough loosely from one end and cut into ¼ of an inch slices. Unroll and cut the slices into the desired length. Spread noodles out and let dry as a single layer for at least 2 hours. Store in an airtight container until ready to use or freeze them if you're not going to use them immediately.

To cook Beef 'n' Noodles, bring stock and 3 cups of water to a boil. (If you use the ready-made beef broth stock from the grocery store, add the beef bouillon to it before adding the meat.) Add meat and 1 teaspoon salt. Slowly add noodles to the boiling broth with meat. Cook, uncovered, 10 to 12 minutes or until noodles are firm and done.

## CARROTS IN ORANGE SAUCE

*Prep. Time: 10 minutes / Cook Time: 15 minutes*

1 cup orange juice
½ cup sugar
2 teaspoons butter
2 tablespoons flour
2 cans sliced carrots, drained

Set the drained carrots aside. In a medium saucepan, combine the orange juice, sugar, butter and flour together and cook until thick, stirring often. Add the carrots to sauce and cook just long enough for the carrots to heat through. Serve immediately.

# March 10

*Call your friends and plan a progressive dinner for tonight! Decide what course each of you will prepare; then get together and go from one home to the next for your evening meal. This is a great way to socialize, have fun and enjoy the home-cooking of a complete meal without having to do all the work yourself! Here are some company-pleasing recipes for whatever portion you decide to provide. Another fun socialization plan is a family potluck. Hook up with several friends and take turns hosting a family potluck on Sunday evenings.*

## APPETIZER: CHEESY CHOWDER

*Prep. Time: 15 minutes / Cook Time: 45 minutes*

1 medium onion, finely chopped
3 carrots, peeled and sliced or diced
1 stalk celery, thinly sliced
8 potatoes, peeled and cubed
1 large can chicken broth
3 tablespoons cornstarch mixed in ½ cup cold water
1½ cups milk
2 cups grated cheddar cheese
1 cup Cheese Whiz ™
salt and pepper
¼ cup chopped fresh parsley

Cook vegetables in chicken broth and 3 cups water. Add about a teaspoon of salt to vegetables. When vegetables are tender, add milk and both cheeses to the soup and stir until cheese is melted. Heat to a low boil and add cornstarch liquid. Season with salt and pepper to taste. Stir continuously until thickened. Garnish each serving with some fresh parsley. This can be made the day ahead and reheated.

# VEGETABLES: MARINATED VEGETABLES

*Prep. Time: 20 minutes Chill Time: 6 hours minimum*

1 head cauliflower
3 stalks celery
3 carrots
1 bunch broccoli
1 pint cherry-sized tomatoes
1 large bottle Italian salad dressing (fat free varieties work well, too)

In a large bowl, combine cauliflower florets, diced celery, sliced carrots, broccoli florets and halved cherry tomatoes. Pour a large bottle of Italian dressing over vegetables. Cover and refrigerate for at least 6 hours, stirring every 2 hours. When ready to serve, spoon out vegetables and discard the salad dressing. These can be eaten with your fingers or you can jab each piece with a cocktail stick or toothpick.

# ENTREE: HAWAIIAN PORK CHOPS

*Prep. Time: 20 minutes / Cook Time: 45 minutes*

6 pork chops
½ cup butter
3 cups instant cooked rice
1 tablespoon paprika
1 small can beef broth
½ teaspoon dried minced onions
2 green peppers cut into strips
2 tablespoons cornstarch
¼ cup soy sauce
1 large can of cubed pineapple, save the juice

In a skillet, melt butter and brown pork chops on both sides, until done. Set aside. In a small saucepan, blend together beef broth, pineapple juice, soy sauce, water, onions and cornstarch. Cook on low heat until the mixture is clear. Add peppers and cook about 15-20 minutes. Place cooked rice on large platter. Arrange pork chops on rice. Place pineapple mixture over chops and serve.

# STAINED GLASS DESSERT

*Prep. Time: 6 hours Chill Time: 3 additional hours*

1 (3 oz) pkg. red gelatin
1 (3 oz) pkg. green gelatin
1 (3 oz) pkg. lemon gelatin
1 (3 oz) pkg. orange gelatin
1 large tub Cool Whip ™
1 teaspoon vanilla
1 teaspoon sugar
25 crushed graham crackers
¼ cup melted butter
½ cup brown sugar
1 cup pineapple juice
1 envelope unflavored gelatin

Using 1½ cups hot water in each, dissolve each gelatin in a separate bowl and pour into a flat pan or cookie sheet to gel. Let gel for 4 to 6 hours. (Less time if pans can be placed in refrigerator.) Cut each colored gelatin into small squares. In a separate bowl, combine the crushed graham crackers with melted butter and brown sugar. Press into bottom of a large cake pan or dessert dish. Dissolve unflavored gelatin in ¼ cup cold water. Add 1 cup hot fruit juice. When unflavored gelatin is almost ready to gel, add it to the Cool Whip™ and beat until soft peaks form. Add sugar and vanilla and continue beating until stiff peaks form. Fold gelatin squares into the whipped cream mixture and pour onto crust. Let set 3 hours before serving.

---

### FAMILY IDEA

**Do the unexpected today!**
**Write a special note of appreciation and slip it under each person's plate. Express how each family member contributes joy and blessings to your life.**

# March 11

*The lowly peanut has grown in popularity ever since peanut farmer from Georgia, Jimmy Carter, was elected as president of the United States back in the late 1970s. Here are some of my family's favorite peanutty recipes.*

## STEAKS WITH PEANUT SAUCE

*Prep. Time: 10-20 minutes / Cook Time: 30 minutes, give or take*

6 beef steaks (sirloin, T-bone, or porterhouse), trimmed of fat
2 tablespoons olive oil
1 medium onion, chopped finely
1 cup water
½ cup chunky peanut butter
salt and pepper to taste

Heat olive oil in a large skillet over medium heat. Add the onion and cook, stirring frequently—until the onion is nearly transparent. Add the water and then stir in the peanut butter. Mix well. Reduce heat to low and simmer until the sauce thickens. Keep warm.

Lightly oil the grilling rack or broiler pan with vegetable or olive oil. Grill or broil steaks until done according to your preference. Salt and pepper steaks according to your taste and then top them with the peanut sauce. Serve immediately.

## LOWFAT SOUR CREAM AND CHIVE POTATOES

*Prep. Time: 1 hour / Cook Time: 20-30 minutes*

10 boiled, diced potatoes, cooled
1 cup fat free sour cream OR plain yogurt
2 teaspoons salt
2 cups nonfat or 1% cottage cheese
¼ cup finely chopped fresh chives
½ teaspoon garlic salt
½ cup grated American or cheddar cheese
paprika

Combine potatoes with sour cream, salt, cottage cheese, chives and salt. Mix well with an electric mixer on the low setting and pour into a 13x9 baking dish. Top with grated cheese and sprinkle with paprika for garnish. Bake at 350 degrees for 20-30 minutes.

Serve with a tossed salad, topped with toasted Spanish peanuts.

## CHOCOLATE PEANUT BUTTER PIZZA

*Prep. Time: 15-20 minutes / Cook Time: 20 minutes*

½ cup sugar
½ cup butter, softened
½ cup peanut butter
1 egg
2 cups miniature marshmallows
½ cup firmly packed brown sugar
½ teaspoon vanilla
1 cup semisweet chocolate chips

In a large bowl, combine sugars, butter, peanut butter, vanilla and egg; blend well. Lightly spoon flour into measuring cup and level it off. Stir in flour. Press dough evenly over the bottom of a 12-to-14-inch pizza pan, forming a rim along edge. Bake at 350 degrees for 10 minutes. Remove from oven, then sprinkle marshmallows and chocolate chips over the dough. Return to oven and continue baking for another 5-to-8 minutes or until marshmallows are puffy and lightly browned. Cool. Cut into wedges. Store any leftovers in a tightly covered container.

# COOKIES OF THE MONTH

## SNICKER DOODLES

2 sticks butter, softened

1½ cups sugar

2 eggs

2¾ cups flour

1 teaspoon baking soda

2 teaspoons cream of tartar

2 tablespoons cinnamon combined with 1
    cup sugar

Cream together butter with sugar and add eggs; mix well. Add baking soda and cream of tartar to the flour and sift flour into creamed mixture; mix well to form a soft dough. Roll dough in small balls with your hands and roll in cinnamon and sugar. Bake on greased cookie sheet at 400° for 8 to 10 minutes.

## OATMEAL COOKIES

2½ sticks butter, softened

¾ cup brown sugar, firmly packed

½ cup sugar

1 egg

1 teaspoon vanilla

1½ cups flour

1 teaspoon baking soda

1 teaspoon salt

1 teaspoon cinnamon

¼ teaspoon nutmeg

3 cups quick cooking oatmeal

Combine butter and sugars until creamy. Beat in egg and vanilla. Add baking soda, salt and spices to flour and add floured mixture gradually; mixing well after each addition. Stir in oats. Drop by rounded teaspoon onto ungreased cookie sheet. Bake at 375° for 8 minutes for a chewy cookie; 10 minutes for a crisp cookie. Cool for 1 minute on cookie sheet before removing.

1 cup raisins, chocolate chips or butterscotch chips may be added if desired.

## KRISPY COOKIES

6 tablespoons butter

½ cup miniature marshmallows

1 cup semi sweet chocolate chips

½ teaspoon vanilla

3½ cups crisp rice cereal

Melt butter and marshmallows in double boiler. Stir in chocolate chips and let melt. Remove from heat and add vanilla. Rub a large mixing bowl with butter, coating it evenly. Add the cereal to the buttered bowl. Pour chocolate mixture over cereal and mix thoroughly. Pour into a shallow pan and spread out. Let cool then cut into bars.

# March 12

*Although Coca-Cola ™ has been around for awhile, today is a notable date because it was on this day back in 1894 that the beverage was first sold in bottles. With this in mind, I thought I'd share with you some recipes calling for Coca-Cola ™.*

## BBQ COUNTRY RIBS

*Prep. Time: 2 hours / Cook Time: 20 minutes*

Boil ribs in a deep pan of water with 1 tablespoon salt added, so that the water covers the ribs. Boil for 2 hours, adding water when necessary. Remove ribs and discard salt water. Keep ribs warm while you prepare the sauce.

1 onion, finely diced
½ cup oil
2 cups ketchup
1 cup Coca-Cola ™
¼ cup firmly packed brown sugar
1 teaspoon cumin powder
1 cup vinegar
1 tablespoon celery seed
½ teaspoon dry mustard
1 tablespoon Worcestershire sauce
salt to taste

In a medium saucepan, slowly sauté onion in oil over low heat until the mixture is caramel colored. Then add the remaining ingredients. Stir together and heat through. When heated through, either pour or brush on to ribs. Place ribs on the grill or under the broiler and cook on each side for 3-5 minutes, marinating with the sauce at least three times on each side.

## POTATO CASSEROLE

*Prep. Time: 15 minutes / Cook Time: 1 hour*

2 lbs. frozen hash browns, thawed
¼ teaspoon pepper
1 teaspoon salt
½ cup melted butter
½ cup chopped onion
1 can cream of chicken soup
2 cups fat-free sour cream or plain yogurt
2 cups grated cheddar cheese
1 cup crushed corn flakes

Combine all ingredients in a 3-qt. casserole dish. Sprinkle over top: 1 cup crushed corn flakes with ½ cup melted butter. Bake at 350 degrees for 1 hour. Serve immediately.

## COCA-COLA™ SALAD

*Prep. Time: 20 minutes*

1 pkg. raspberry gelatin
1 pkg. cherry gelatin
1 large can crushed pineapple
1 can seedless cherries (not cherry pie filling)
1 cup pecans
1 (8-oz.) pkg. cream cheese (frozen)
2 cans Coca-Cola™ (partially frozen)

Dissolve gelatin in the juices drained from the cherries and pineapple. Heat until dissolved, stirring constantly. Pour into large bowl. Add partially frozen cokes, cherries, pineapple and nuts. Grate frozen cream cheese over top (to give the appearance of snow). Place in refrigerator until ready to serve.

## BLACK COW

*Prep. Time: 5 minutes*

vanilla Ice Cream
Coca-Cola™

Dip 2-3 scoops vanilla ice cream in to a parfait glass. Pour Coca-Cola™ over the ice cream and serve.

# March 13

## SWISS STEAK SUPPER

*Prep. Time: 30 minutes / Cook Time: 3-4 hours*

1 ½ to 2 lbs. cubed round steak, fat trimmed
¼ cup flour
1 teaspoon salt
2 tablespoons vegetable oil
1 teaspoon beef bouillon
1 can cream of mushroom soup
1 quart stewed tomatoes or juice
¼ teaspoon pepper

Combine flour and salt and dredge cubed meat in mixture, coating both sides. Pour oil in the bottom of a baking dish. Lay coated meat on top of oil. In a separate container, combine beef bouillon (dry) with condensed cream of mushroom soup. Add tomatoes (or tomato juice—your choice) and mix well. Pour over meat. Sprinkle with salt and pepper. Bake at 300 degrees for 3 to 4 hours.

During the last hour of baking, add peeled potatoes and carrots around meat and let bake until done.

## KITCHEN TRICKS

- To keep red cabbage from turning purple or blue, add a tablespoon of vinegar to the pan when cooking.

- To neutralize the smell of vegetables like cabbage, broccoli, Brussels sprouts and cauliflower, add a bread end or slice of red pepper to the pot when cooking. Remove and discard before serving.

- To perk up wilted vegetables such as celery, carrots, radishes, green onions, etc., soak in ice-cold water for 15 minutes before serving.

# March 14

## BREADED TENDERLOINS

*Prep. Time: 1 hour 45 minutes / Cook Time: 20 minutes*

6 to 8 butterfly tenderloins
2 cups milk
2 eggs
1 teaspoon salt
1 teaspoon pepper
1 ½ cups flour
1 tablespoon baking powder
½ cup cracker meal
½ cup yellow corn meal

With a meat mallet, beat tenderloins until they are flattened and thinned. Mix milk and eggs, then soak the beaten tenderloins in mixture for at least 1 hour. Mix all dry ingredients well. When ready to bread, don't shake off liquid mixture from meat; instead, press in the dry mixture and coat both sides well. Set aside and allow to dry for at least 30 minutes before cooking. These can then be frozen for later use or deep fat fried for tenderloin sandwiches.

## ONION RINGS

*Prep. Time: 45 minutes to 1 hour   / Cook Time: 20 minutes*

2 large sweet onions
1 egg
1 cup milk
1 cup flour
1 ½ teaspoons salt
½ teaspoon cayenne pepper
1 teaspoon paprika
¼ teaspoon ground black pepper
¼ teaspoon dried oregano
⅛ teaspoon dried thyme
⅛ teaspoon cumin powder
vegetable oil for frying

Beat the egg and milk together in a medium bowl. In a separate dish, combine the flour with spices and mix well. Slice onions and separate the rings. Dip each ring into the milk mixture and then dredge in the floured-spice mixture. Set aside to dry. When finished dipping all the onion rings, go back and repeat the same process again, double coating each ring with the milk and flour mixtures. Let the double-dipped onion rings rest in the refrigerator for at least 15 minutes before deep fat frying in the vegetable oil.

# March 15

*I'm a real cheapskate when it comes to feeding my family. I never accept inferior products, but I don't (and won't) pay high retail prices either. Did you know that most big name brand food distributors will also package their products under a generic label? This is true for milk, ice cream, cottage cheese, yogurt, hot dogs, sausage, cereals, crackers, etc. Don't be afraid to try an off-brand-name or a store-brand-named product in place of it's nationally advertised counterpart. You may end up buying the exact same product, just in different packaging! The end result will leave more money in your pocket.*

## TACO CASSEROLE

*Prep. Time: 30 minutes / Cook Time: 25-30 minutes*

1 lb. lean ground beef, cooked, drained and crumbled
1 lb. ground pork sausage (regular or mild), cooked, drained and crumbled
1 can refried beans
2 cups shredded cheddar cheese
1 medium onion, chopped
1 large bag nacho style chips, crushed
lettuce, shredded
1-2 tomatoes, chopped
sour cream, optional

In a 13x9 baking dish, place ½ the crushed nacho chips. In a separate bowl, spoon out refried beans from the can. Add enough water to the beans to make a thick paste that is spreadable. Spoon the

beans over the crushed chips, using all the beans. Then add the crumbled meats. Layer chopped onions over meats. Top with cheese, covering completely.

Bake at 350 degrees for 25 to 30 minutes or until golden brown. Remove from oven and add the remaining crushed chips, lettuce and tomatoes. Top each serving with a teaspoon of sour cream if desired.

# March 16

## BACON AND CHEESE PASTA CASSEROLE

*Prep. Time: 30 minutes / Cook Time: 30-45 minutes*

1 pkg. (8 oz.) elbow macaroni
1 can (14 ½ oz.) evaporated milk
½ cup water
1 can cream of mushroom soup, undiluted
½ lb. processed American cheese, cubed in chunks
2 tablespoons Parmesan cheese
1 teaspoon prepared mustard
1 lb. bacon

Cook macaroni according to package directions, drain and rinse in cold water. Cook bacon until crisp. Drain bacon on sheets of paper towel. (Reserve 3-4 strips of crisp bacon to use as garnish on top of casserole.) Combine milk, water, soup, cheeses and mustard in a medium sized pan. Cook on low heat until well blended. Crumble bacon into cheese sauce. Turn into a buttered 2-qt. casserole dish. Top with crumbled bacon. Bake at 350 degrees for 25 to 30 minutes.

# SEASONED GREEN BEANS

*Prep. Time: 5 minutes / Cook Time: 15 minutes*

2 cans green beans (or use 1 quart of
    home-canned), keep liquid
1 teaspoon ham-flavored seasoning mix or
    seasoned dry soup mix
2 teaspoons dried minced onions
1 teaspoon salt (do not add salt if the ham
    seasoning mix or soup mix has salt in it)

Pour green beans and their liquid in a medium sized saucepan. Add seasoning mix to the liquid and stir to dissolve. Add the minced onions. If you use a bouillon instead of a seasoning mix, then add salt—otherwise, do not add any additional salt. Bring green beans to a boil, stirring frequently to heat through. Serve when hot and dried onions have rehydrated.

# BUTTERSCOTCH PIE

*Prep. Time: 30 minutes / Cook Time: 20 minutes*

1 prepared 9" pie crust, baked
1 cup dark brown sugar, packed firmly
5 tablespoons flour
1½ cups skim milk
2 egg yolks
2 tablespoons butter
1 sprinkle of salt

Mix sugar, flour and salt. Gradually add milk and mix well. Beat egg yolks and add to the milk mixture, stirring constantly until thickened. Add butter and stir until melted and blended. Pour into baked pie shell and top with meringue. Brown at 350 degrees for 20 minutes.

# MERINGUE TOPPING

*Prep. Time: 15 minutes*

5 egg whites
½ teaspoon cream of tartar
½ cup sugar

Beat egg whites on high speed with an electric mixer until soft peaks form. Gradually add cream of tartar and sugar while beaters are still mixing. Continue beating on high speed until meringue forms stiff peaks. Spread over pie and bake.

# March 17

*Today is recognized as Saint Patrick's Day! Don't forget to wear something green today!*

# CORNED BEEF BOILED DINNER

*Prep. Time: 15 minutes / Cook Time: 4 hours or longer*

3-lb. corned beef
1 teaspoon peppercorns or ¼ teaspoon black
    pepper
6 whole cloves
1 bay leaf
6-8 potatoes, peeled and quartered
6 carrots, lengthwise cut in half and chunked
1 medium head cabbage, cut into 6 wedges
    (core removed)

In large cooking pot, cover corned beef with water. Add peppercorns, cloves and bay leaf. (If corned beef is packaged with a spice packet, omit peppercorns, cloves and bay leaf and use the spice packet instead.) Cover; simmer 3 to 3 ½ hours or until meat is tender. Add potatoes and carrots. Cover again; simmer for 15 minutes. Add cabbage; cook an additional 15 minutes or until all vegetables are tender. Remove bay leaf, if used. Cut meat into pieces and serve with broth and vegetables.

# LIME FRUIT SALAD

*Prep. Time: 10 minutes*

1 small carton fat free or 1% cottage cheese (or
    2 cups)
1 small box green (lime) gelatin
1 can crushed pineapple

1 can mandarin oranges

1 tub of Fat Free Cool Whip ™

Drain pineapple and oranges. Sprinkle gelatin over cottage cheese. Mix well until cottage cheese turns green and is well covered with the gelatin. Add both fruits and mix well. Top with a dollop of whipped topping and serve.

# March 18

*Today is the Pillsbury Dough Boy's™ birthday! The Pillsbury Dough Boy ™ was introduced on this day back in 1961. Tonight we'll incorporate some of the Dough Boy's fares into our menu.*

## SLOPPY JOE TURNOVERS

*Prep. Time: 30-45 minutes / Cook Time: 20-25 minutes*

1 lb. lean ground beef

1 medium onion, finely diced

1 packet sloppy joe seasoning mix

1 small can tomato sauce

1 pkg. Pillsbury ™ 10-ct. Biscuits

In a large skillet, brown ground beef and onions until done. Drain off all grease. Add sloppy joe mix and tomato sauce. Mix well. Separate dough into the 10 biscuits. On ungreased cookie sheet, press each biscuit to a 4"x4" square. Place about ¼ cup meat mixture in the center of square. Fold over corner to form a triangle. Bake at 375 degrees for 15 to 20 minutes or until biscuits are lightly browned. Brush on melted butter, if desired, when removing turnovers from the oven. Serve with French fries and salad.

# March 19

*Sometime during March 19 to the 25th, whatever day begins the third full week of the month, Americans celebrate the American Chocolate Week. In observance, let your family splurge a bit and enjoy tonight's rich chocolate dessert.*

## DOUBLE MEAT CASSEROLE

*Prep. Time: 30 minutes / Cook Time: 1 hour*

1 pkg. noodles, cooked and drained

4 cups diced-cooked chicken

1 cup diced ham

1 can cream of mushroom soup

1 can cream of chicken soup

½ green pepper, diced

1 medium onion, grated or finely chopped

¼ teaspoon celery salt

¼ teaspoon black pepper

3 cups grated American or cheddar cheese

Combine all ingredients in a large casserole dish. Spread cheese evenly over the top. Bake at 350 degrees for 1 hour.

## BLACK-EYED PEAS

*Prep. Time: 5 minutes / Cook Time: 10-15 minutes*

1 can black-eyed peas

1 teaspoon ham seasoning mix or dry soup mix

1 teaspoon minced onion

Pour black-eyed peas with liquid in a small saucepan. Add ham seasoning and minced onion and stir to blend well. Cook on medium-low heat until liquid begins to boil. Serve while hot.

# CHOCOLATE LAYERED DESSERT

*Prep. Time: 30-45 minutes*

FIRST LAYER:

2 sticks butter, melted

2½ cup flour

1 cup crushed nuts (your choice of either pecans, walnuts or almonds)

Mix these ingredients together and press into a 9x13 cake pan. Bake at 350 degrees for 10 minutes.

SECOND LAYER:

16 oz. cream cheese

8 oz. Cool Whip ™ or other non-dairy whipped topping

2 cups powdered sugar

Mix these ingredients together and spread on the cooled crust.

THIRD LAYER:

2 small boxes instant chocolate pudding

3 cups milk

Mix together the chocolate pudding mixes with the milk. Beat with an electric mixer until pudding is thick. Spread pudding on top of the second layer.

FOURTH LAYER:

Spread Cool Whip ™ over the pudding and garnish with chopped nuts. Refrigerate for at least an hour before serving.

## FOOD FOR THOUGHT

- Use your head to save your feet. Hopefully neither will be overworked.
- It is better to make the world smile at what you say than laugh at what you do.
- A smile is a language that even a baby understands.
- Love is blind and marriage is an eye-opener.
- Don't judge a woman's cooking by the cake she sends to the church bazaar.
- There is nothing that broadens one like travel, except pastry.

# March 20

## POTATO SUPREME NESTS

*Prep. Time: 1 hour / Cook Time: 25 minutes*

6 cups mashed potatoes, well seasoned with salt and butter

Shape potatoes into 4" nests on greased baking sheets. Bake at 450 degrees until well browned. Remove from oven.

3 tablespoons cornstarch dissolved in ½ cup cold water

2 cups skim milk

½ teaspoon salt

2 cups shredded cheddar cheese

2 cups cubed cooked ham

1 can carrots, drained

1 can peas, drained (opt.)

salt and pepper to taste

Heat milk over low heat until hot, but not boiling. Pour in cornstarch liquid, stir well. Add salt and pepper and cook for 5 minutes. Add cheese, ham, carrots and peas. Cook until vegetables are heated through and cheese has melted. Dip by spoonfuls, filling each potato nest with ham and vegetable mixture. Return to 450 degree oven and heat through for 10 minutes. Serve hot.

# March 21

*One evening I had some leftover ham that was too salty to eat on sandwiches or as an entree by itself. I decided to experiment (again) and tonight's menu is what I came up with. For a lack of anything else to call it, I named it my Keeper Soup. When I served it, all three of the kids ate their serving and asked for seconds! My husband gave me a thumb's up and declared, "This is a Keeper! Make sure you write down how you made this so we can have it again!"*

# KEEPER SOUP

*Prep. Time: 30 minutes / Cook Time: 1 hour*

10 medium potatoes, peeled, quartered and
    cubed
2 small yellow onions, peeled and diced
2 cups frozen cut broccoli
2 stalks celery, sliced
2 cups milk
1 cup American processed cheese
    (such as Cheese Whiz™)
2 teaspoons salt
¼ teaspoon pepper
1 tablespoon cornstarch
water

In a large soup pan, cube potatoes, add celery, onions, broccoli and salt. Cover all vegetables with water until there's about an inch of water above the vegetables. Bring to a boil and cook until vegetables are tender. (If you have picky eaters, remove vegetables at this point and puree with a little broth. This is what I did. Return to soup pot.) Add cheese, milk and pepper. Continue cooking until cheese melts and potatoes are tender.

In a separate container, mix together ½ cup water with cornstarch. Stir to dissolve. Pour into soup and stir. Serve when the soup has thickened into a creamed soup. Egg dumplings may be added, if desired.

# EGG DUMPLINGS

*Prep. Time: 10 minutes / Cook Time: 10 minutes*

2 eggs
1 cup flour
1 teaspoon salt
¼ teaspoon pepper

With a fork, beat all ingredients into a stiff dough. Drop by teaspoon into boiling soup. Let cook in boiling soup for at least 5 to 10 minutes before serving.

# March 22

## BEEF STIR-FRY

*Prep. Time: 15 minutes / Cook Time: 5-10 minutes*

4 tablespoons oil
1 tablespoon cornstarch
1 tablespoon soy sauce
1½ to 2 lbs. round steak, thinly sliced
2 green onions, sliced
1 bunch fresh broccoli, chopped

Combine 1 tablespoon oil, cornstarch and soy sauce in bowl. Add steak slices, mixing well. Brown onions in 2 tablespoons oil in a large skillet. Add marinated steak, cooking until brown. Add remaining oil and broccoli. Stir-fry for 5-7 minutes until broccoli is tender crisp. Serve over a bed of white or brown rice.

## FRESH STRAWBERRY PIE

*Prep. Time: 20-30 minutes*

1 cup sugar
2 tablespoons cornstarch
2 tablespoons light corn syrup
pinch of salt
2 teaspoons strawberry gelatin
red food coloring
3 cups fresh strawberries, washed, drained
1 9-inch pie shell, baked
Cool Whip™

Combine sugar, cornstarch, corn syrup and salt with 1 cup of water in a small saucepan. Cook over low heat until thick and clear, stirring constantly. Cool slightly and add gelatin and food coloring, stirring to dissolve. Arrange fresh strawberries in a baked pie shell. Pour the glaze over the berries. Top with Cool Whip ™ and additional strawberries, if desired. Chill for at least 2 hours before serving.

# March 23

## BREADED PORK CUTLETS

*Prep. Time: 15-20 minutes / Cook Time: 25 minutes*

¾ cup flour
1 teaspoon salt
½ teaspoon paprika
¼ teaspoon pepper
2 eggs, slightly beaten
2 teaspoons Worcestershire sauce
6-8 pork cutlets (boneless lean pork that has
    been cubed)
¾ cup crushed saltine cracker crumbs
3-4 tablespoons oil

In small bowl, combine flour, salt, paprika and pepper. In another small bowl, combine egg and Worcestershire sauce. Rinse each piece of pork with warm water and then dredge in the seasoned flour. Then dip in egg mixture and coat with cracker crumbs. In large skillet, brown cutlets in hot oil until golden brown. Continue cooking over medium heat until meat has cooked through, 7 to 10 minutes.

## BAKED HASHBROWNS

*Prep. Time: 15 minutes / Cook Time: 1 hour*

2 lb. frozen hashed brown potatoes, thawed
½ cup melted butter
1 teaspoon salt
¼ teaspoon pepper
1 can cream of mushroom soup
2 cups grated cheddar cheese
½ cup chopped onion
2 cups fat free sour cream or plain yogurt

Combine all ingredients in large bowl, mixing well. Spread in a 9x13 baking pan. Bake at 350 degrees for 1 hour.

## WHOLE WHEAT ZUCCHINI BREAD

*Prep. Time: 30 minutes / Cook Time: 1 hour or longer*

3 eggs
½ cup oil
½ cup unsweetened applesauce
1 cup brown sugar, firmly packed
2 cups grated zucchini, peeled
1 teaspoon vanilla
2 cups whole wheat flour
1 cup flour
½ teaspoon baking soda
1 teaspoon salt
1 teaspoon baking powder
1 tablespoon cinnamon
1 cup chopped nuts (optional)

Beat eggs in bowl until frothy. Add oil, applesauce, brown sugar, zucchini and vanilla; mixing well. Sift together dry ingredients and add to the egg mixture; beating well. Stir in nuts if desired. Pour into 2 greased bread-loaf pans. Bake at 325 degrees for 40 minutes or until bread tests done when a clean knife is inserted in the middle and comes out clean. Remove from pans and cool before slicing and serving.

### KITCHEN TRIVIA
*Did you know that 63% of the population spends more time cleaning the kitchen than any other room in the house?*

# March 24

*Make a wish today! Set a votive candle before each place setting on tonight's dinner table. When everyone has gathered around the table, light each candle. Tell everyone to close their eyes and make a wish, then open their eyes and blow out their candle. Over dinner, get everyone talking about what they wished for and how you can all help to make others' wishes come true.*

## PARMESAN MEAT LOAF DINNER

*Prep. Time: 15 minutes / Cook Time: 1 hour 30 minutes*

1 large carrot, grated
1 large potato, grated
3 eggs, beaten
1 teaspoon minced onion
2 teaspoons salt
½ teaspoon black pepper
¾ cup Parmesan cheese
1 cup crushed saltine cracker crumbs
1 cup water
3 lbs. lean ground beef

Thoroughly mix first 9-ingredients, then add ground beef and mix well. Form into 2 loaves. Place in a baking pan. Add water and cover loosely with foil. Bake at 350 degrees for 1 hour and 15 minutes. Uncover, baste with ketchup, and bake 15 minutes longer.

## SWEET CORN

1 can corn
¼ cup sugar
2 tablespoons butter
1 teaspoon salt
⅛ teaspoon pepper

Combine all ingredients in small saucepan and heat through on medium heat. Remove from heat and serve when liquid starts to boil.

## BLUEBERRY PIE

*Prep. Time: 10 minutes / Cook Time: 45 minutes to 1 hour*

1 quart fresh blueberries (may use frozen if thawed and drained)
⅔ cup sugar
1 tablespoon lemon juice
2½ tablespoons tapioca
pinch of salt
1 (9") prepared pie crust
pie crust top
½ cup brown sugar
½ stick butter

Combine all ingredients and pour into a 9-inch prepared pie crust. Sprinkle with ½ cup brown sugar, dot with butter, and cover with a top crust. Flute edges to seal. Fork holes in the top to allow steam to escape. Bake at 400 degrees for 45 minutes to 1 hour.

# March 25

*In 1775 on this day, George Washington planted pecan trees given to him by Thomas Jefferson. As a result, today is observed as Pecan Day.*

## BAKED CHICKEN WITH PECANS

*Prep. Time: 15 minutes / Cook Time: 40 minutes*

6 skinless boneless chicken breasts
1 cup Miracle Whip Free ™
2 cups diced celery
½ cup chopped pecans
3 cups cooked rice
1 can cream of chicken soup
1 onion, diced
1 teaspoon salt

Combine Miracle Whip ™ with celery, pecans, cooked rice, soup, diced onion and salt. Lay chicken breasts in the bottom of a shallow casserole dish that has been sprayed with vegetable spray. Pour the rice mixture over chicken. Bake at 400 degrees for 40 minutes.

# COOL FRUIT SALAD

*Prep. Time: 25 minutes*

1 small box vanilla instant pudding
1 can fruit cocktail, undrained
1 small can mandarin oranges, drained
1 small can pineapple tidbits, drained
1 cup miniature marshmallows
1 small carton Cool Whip ™ or other non-dairy frozen whipped topping
½ cup chopped pecans

Sprinkle dry pudding mix over fruits. Add Cool Whip ™ and mix. Pour into a 13x9 dish and garnish with sprinkled chopped pecans. Refrigerate for at least 2 hours before serving.

# March 26

## BAKED CUBED PORK

*Prep. Time: 25 minutes / Cook Time: 1 hour*

6 pieces cubed pork
2 cans chow mein noodles, browned in butter
3 tablespoons butter
2 cans cream of mushroom soup
6 cups crushed saltine cracker crumbs
2 cups water
salt and pepper to taste

Melt butter in skillet. Toss chow mein noodles in hot butter, coating evenly. After browning chow mein noodles, brown pork in the same skillet using the remaining butter. Once both sides are browned, add 2 cups water and cook on medium heat for 20 minutes. Remove meat and place in a 13x9 baking pan or casserole dish in a single layer. Spread condensed soup over meat. Top with crushed cracker crumbs. Bake at 375 degrees for 40 minutes.

# ORIENTAL SALAD

*Prep. Time: 25 minutes*

1 head lettuce, torn in small pieces
1 small can mandarin orange slices, drained
5 oz. slivered almonds, browned in bacon grease
¼ lb. bacon, fried crisp
1 can French fried onions

Layer lettuce, oranges, almonds, crumbled bacon and French fried onion rings in a large salad bowl.

DRESSING:
2½ tablespoons tarragon vinegar
½ teaspoon dry mustard
½ teaspoon celery salt
¼ teaspoon paprika
1 teaspoon dried minced onion
3 tablespoons honey
½ tablespoon lemon juice
⅓ cup sugar

Combine all dressing ingredients in a small saucepan. Over medium heat, cook dressing until sugar is dissolved. Cool and then add ½ cup oil. Shake well and pour over salad just before serving.

# March 27

## GROUND BEEF CASSEROLE

*Prep. Time: 20 minutes / Cook Time: 40 minutes*

1 - 2 lbs. lean ground beef
1 teaspoon garlic salt
salt and pepper to taste
1 medium onion, finely chopped
1 can tomatoes, cut into pieces
2 cans tomato soup
2 cups frozen peas, thawed
2 cups instant rice

In skillet, combine ground beef with garlic salt, onion, salt and pepper. Stir and fry until done. Drain off grease. Stir in tomatoes and tomato soup. In the bottom of a 9x13 pan, put a layer of peas. Sprinkle the dry rice on top of the peas. Next, pour the meat and tomato mixture over the rice. Bake at 350 degrees for 40 minutes.

## APPLE CRISP PIE

*Prep. Time: 15 minutes / Cook Time: 30 minutes*

1 (9-inch) prepared pie crust
1 can apple pie filling
1 cup quick cooking oatmeal
½ cup sugar
½ cup brown sugar
1 tablespoon cinnamon
½ stick butter

Pour apple pie filling into the 9-inch pie crust. In a separate container, combine the oatmeal with the sugars and cinnamon. Mix well. Sprinkle an even layer on top of the pie filling. Place pats of butter around and through the center of the topping. Bake at 375 degrees for 30 minutes. Serve warm with a slice of American cheese melted on top.

# March 28

## DROPPED BISCUITS 'N' HAM CASSEROLE

*Prep. Time: 30 minutes / Cook Time: 30-45 minutes*

3 cups cubed ham
4 cups diced potatoes
2 cups diced or sliced carrots
1 cup peas
1 cup corn
2 cups flour
1 tablespoon baking powder
1 teaspoon salt
2 tablespoons shortening
1 cup milk

In a large skillet, brown the ham. Add potatoes, carrots and water. Add enough water to cover vegetables. Cover skillet with a lid and cook until vegetables are tender. In another container, combine 1 tablespoon flour with just enough water to make it pasty. Add the flour liquid to the boiling water. Continue cooking for 5 minutes. Transfer ham and vegetables to a 13x9 cake pan or casserole dish. In a separate bowl, combine the rest of the flour, baking powder, salt and milk. Drop by tablespoon into the pan of ham and vegetables. Bake at 350 degrees from 20 to 30 minutes until done.

## PISTACHIO SALAD

*Prep. Time: 15 minutes*

1 can crushed pineapple
1 pkg. instant pistachio pudding mix
1 cup miniature marshmallows
½ cup chopped nuts
1 large container Fat Free Cool Whip™
2 cups fat free or 1 % cottage cheese

Pour dry pudding mix over cottage cheese and stir well. Add pineapple (with juice) and blend well. Add Cool Whip ™ and chopped nuts. Beat on low speed with an electric mixer until well blended. Fold in marshmallows. Pour into a serving dish and refrigerate for 3 hours before serving.

# March 29

## GARDEN QUICHE

*Prep. Time: 25 minutes / Cook Time: 30-45 minutes*

2 cups chopped fresh broccoli
1 cup finely chopped onion
1 cup shredded cheddar cheese
1½ cups milk
1 cup Bisquick ™ baking mix
5 eggs
1 teaspoon salt
¼ teaspoon pepper

Lightly grease pie pan. In a sauce pan, heat 1-inch of salted water to boiling. Add broccoli, cover and heat to boiling. Cook until broccoli is tender, about 5 minutes; drain thoroughly. Combine cooked broccoli with onion and cheese in pie plate. Beat milk, Bisquick ™ mix, eggs, salt and pepper until smooth (15 seconds in the blender or 1 minute beating by hand). Pour egg mixture into pie plate, covering vegetables. Bake until golden brown and knife inserted halfway between center and edge comes out clean (35-40 minutes). Let stand 5 minutes before cutting. Refrigerate any remaining pie.

Serve with sausage links.

## CINNAMON ROLLS

*Prep. Time: 2½ hours / Cook Time: 10-20 minutes*

2 cups milk, scalded and cooled to room temperature
1 cup sugar
1 cup flour
2 pkgs. active dry yeast
¾ cup butter, melted
2 eggs, beaten
4 ½ cups flour
2 teaspoons salt
cinnamon and sugar, mixed together

Combine the first four ingredients in bowl, mixing well. Let rise for 1 hour. Add the next 5 ingredients, mixing well. Let rise, covered with a moist towel, in a warm place until doubled in bulk. Turn dough out on a lightly floured surface. Knead dough until smooth and elastic. Roll dough out on a floured surface. Spread soft butter or margarine over dough. Sprinkle cinnamon and sugar over butter. Roll dough as for a jelly roll and cut into ¼" to ½" slices. Place in a greased baking pan and let rise until doubled in bulk. Bake at 375 degrees for 10 minutes or until golden brown. Frost while warm and serve immediately.

### FROSTING CINNAMON ROLLS:

2-3 cups powdered sugar
1 tablespoon butter, softened
2 tablespoons milk
1 teaspoon vanilla

Start with 2 cups powdered sugar combined with butter, milk and vanilla. If icing is too runny, add more powdered sugar and continue stirring until smooth. Drizzle over cinnamon rolls while rolls are still warm.

# March 30

*Make tonight another themed family night. This time, assign your kids to look up information about Spain. Clay pottery is real popular in Spain, so use some to decorate your kitchen and table for tonight's meal. Throw a red tablecloth over the table and place a sombrero in the center. Find a picture of a bull in a coloring book and let your kids trace the shape on sheets of colored construction paper. Use the bull drawings as your placemats! Olè!*

## SPANISH STEAKS

*Prep. Time: 25 minutes / Cook Time: 1 hour*

2 lbs. lean ground beef
2 eggs
1½ cups crushed cracker crumbs
1 medium onion, finely chopped
½ cup evaporated skim milk
2 teaspoons salt
½ teaspoon pepper

Combine all ingredients and shape into 8 large patties. Flatten out steaks. Cook in a skillet just until steaks are browned on both sides.

In a separate bowl, combine 1 tablespoon Worcestershire sauce, 1 (8 oz.) can tomato sauce, ½ cup water, 1 tablespoon sugar, 1 tablespoon chili powder and ½ teaspoon salt. Stir well to blend and then pour sauce over steaks in the skillet. Reduce heat to low and simmer until sauce has thickened and meat is cooked through and tender.

## SPANISH RICE

*Prep. Time: 25 minutes   / Cook Time: 30 minutes*

3 cups cooked rice
1 can tomato sauce
1 medium onion, finely chopped
½ cup chopped green pepper
2 tablespoons A-1 Steak Sauce ™
1 teaspoon salt
½ teaspoon garlic powder
¼ teaspoon pepper

Combine all ingredients and pour into a casserole dish. Bake at 375 degrees for 30 minutes. Remove from oven and sprinkle ½ cup Parmesan cheese over rice. Serve immediately.

## PLUM CAKE

*Prep. Time: 35 minutes / Cook Time: 1 hour 15 minutes*

½ cup oil
½ cup unsweetened applesauce
2 cups sugar
1 oz. red food coloring
2 small jars baby food plum pudding with tapioca
2 cups sifted flour
1 teaspoon cinnamon
½ teaspoon baking soda
¼ teaspoon salt
3 eggs
1 cup chopped nuts

Combine all ingredients in a large mixing bowl and beat with an electric mixer on medium speed for three full minutes. Fold in nuts. Pour into a greased bundt or tube pan. Bake at 325 degrees for 1 hour and 15 minutes or until done.

Meanwhile, make frosting for plum cake:

1 (3 oz) pkg. cream cheese, softened
1 tablespoon milk
1 teaspoon vanilla
dash salt
2½ cups powdered sugar

Blend cream cheese with milk, vanilla and salt; gradually add sugar, beating until smooth and of spreading consistency. If icing is too thick, add more milk a teaspoon at a time.

# March 31

## CHINESE BEEF

*Prep. Time: 20 minutes / Cook Time: 10-20 minutes*

1 clove garlic
3 tablespoons oil
salt and pepper
1½ lbs round steak, cut in ⅛-inch strips
water
1½ cups beef broth or bouillon
½ lb. fresh mushrooms (may substitute with
    canned if necessary)
3 tablespoons cornstarch
1 tablespoon soy sauce

Place oil and garlic in heavy frying pan. Cook gently about 2 minutes and remove garlic. Meanwhile, salt and pepper the meat. After removing garlic, add the meat slices and onion, cooking over a moderate heat, stirring constantly, until meat is nicely browned. Add the beef broth and sliced mushrooms. Cover pan tightly and cook on medium heat for about 10 minutes. Add soy sauce to cornstarch with enough water to make a thin paste. Mix well into broth, cooking over a low heat and stirring constantly until broth thickens. Serve at once, piping hot with cooked rice.

## SPINACH SALAD

*Prep. Time: 30 minutes*

⅓ cup vinegar
¾ cup sugar
1 cup oil
1 medium onion, finely diced
1 teaspoon Worcestershire sauce
1 teaspoon salt

Blend above ingredients in a blender. Set aside.

1 lb. spinach leaves, cleaned and dried
1 can bean sprouts, drained and chilled

1 can water chestnuts, sliced
1 can chow mein noodles
½ lb. bacon, fried crisp and crumbled
2 hard-boiled eggs, chopped

Toss all salad ingredients except for the chow mein noodles. Pour dressing over salad and mix well. Sprinkle chow mein noodles on top of each serving.

This month celebrates:
• National Fresh Celery Month
• National Garden Month
• National Recycling Month

# April 1

*It's no foolin' that today is also recognized as "Sorry Charlie Day." This day is for people, who like Charlie the Tuna, get turned down but never give up.*

## EASY TUNA BAKE

*Prep. Time: 15 minutes / Cook Time: 15-20 minutes*

1 can cream of mushroom soup
¼ cup water
1 (3 oz.) can chow mein noodles
1 stalk celery, finely chopped
½ cup salted cashews, broken into pieces
1 small yellow onion, finely chopped
dash of pepper
1 (7 oz.) can tuna, drained

Combine soup and water; add 1 cup noodles. Drain tuna. Add tuna to soup and noodles, mix well. Add the remaining ingredients and toss lightly. Sprinkle remaining noodles on top. Bake in ungreased 9x13 baking dish at 375° for 15 to 20 minutes.

Serve with baked tater tots and seasoned peas.

# COCONUT CUSTARD PIE

*Prep. Time: 5 minutes / Cook Time: 40-50 minutes*

½ stick butter

½ cup Bisquick™

½ cup sugar

2 cups skim milk

3 eggs

1 teaspoon vanilla

pinch of salt

2 cups flaked coconut

Combine all ingredients in a blender, except for 1 cup of coconut; and blend for 2 minutes. Pour into a greased and floured pie plate. Sprinkle top with remaining 1 cup of the flaked coconut. Bake at 350° for 40 to 50 minutes.

# April 2

## SWEET & SOUR MEATBALLS

*Prep. Time: 20 minutes / Cook Time: 20-25 minutes*

1- 2 lbs. lean ground beef

5 tablespoons A-1™ Steak sauce

1 egg, beaten (use 2 eggs if you use 2 lbs. ground beef)

½ cup crushed saltine crackers (use 1 cup if you use 2 lbs. ground beef)

1 medium clove garlic, crushed

1 teaspoon salt

1 can (8 oz.) pineapple chunks, undrained

1 cup sliced carrots

1 cup sliced celery

¾ cup beef broth

2 tablespoons soy sauce

1 tablespoon cider vinegar

¼ teaspoon ground ginger

1 tablespoon cornstarch

1 large green pepper cut into strips

Combine beef, 2 tablespoons steak sauce, egg, cracker crumbs, garlic and salt. Mix well and form into meatballs. In large skillet brown meatballs.

When meatballs are browned, drain off all grease. Add remaining ingredients except cornstarch and peppers. Cover and simmer for 5 minutes. Dissolve cornstarch in 1 tablespoon water. Stir into the mix and add the green pepper slices. Simmer uncovered for 5 minutes longer. Serve over cooked rice.

# EVE'S APPLE PUDDING

*Prep. Time: 15 minutes / Cook Time: 30-40 minutes*

½ cup butter

1 cup sugar

1 cup flour

2 teaspoons baking powder

¼ teaspoon salt

1 teaspoon cinnamon

1 cup milk

5 apples, peeled and sliced

Melt butter in a 2-qt. casserole dish. Combine the next six ingredients and pour on top of the melted butter. Pile apples in center of batter. Bake at 350° for 30 to 40 minutes. Serve with Cool Whip™ if desired.

# April 3

## SMOKED SAUSAGE IN SCALLOPED POTATOES

*Prep. Time: 20-30 minutes / Cook Time: 1 hour 15 minutes*

1 lb. skinless smoked sausage, cut into ¼" slices

1 can cream of mushroom soup

²/₃ cup skim milk

1 cup shredded cheddar cheese

1 teaspoon salt

8 medium potatoes, peeled and sliced thin

Combine the mushroom soup and milk until well blended. Add ½ cup cheese and salt. Mix well. Add the raw, sliced potatoes and mix well. Stir in the slices of smoked sausage. Pour into a casserole dish. Bake for 1 hour. Test doneness of potatoes. If done, add remaining cheese as a topping and bake until cheese melts.

## CARROT SALAD

*Prep. Time: 25 minutes*

3 cups grated carrots
1 cup raisins
⅓ cup sugar
¼ cup oil
¼ cup orange juice

Mix together and chill for at least an hour before serving.

# April 4

## BATTER-FRIED PERCH

*Prep. Time: 10-15 minutes / Cook Time: 20 minutes*

1-2 lbs. frozen perch fillets, thawed
2 cups milk
5 eggs
¼ cup lemon juice
flour
cracker meal
salt and pepper, to taste

Combine milk, eggs and juice; beat well. Roll fish in plain flour then dip in milk mixture. Dredge in cracker meal. Let set for 5 minutes before deep frying until golden brown. Salt fillets after removing them from the pan.

Serve with oven baked seasoned Potato Wedges (see page 11) and a tossed salad.

# April 5

## PIZZA POTATOES

*Prep. Time: 15 minutes / Cook Time: 30-40 minutes*

2 packages of boxed scalloped potatoes
1 can prepared pizza sauce
1 pkg (4 oz.) sliced pepperoni
1 medium onion, finely chopped
1 cup shredded mozzarella cheese

Empty potato slices and packet of seasoned sauce mix into a casserole dish. In a saucepan, heat together the tomato sauce and onion with the amount of water called for on the scalloped potato mixes. Bring to a boil and then pour over the potatoes. Arrange pepperoni over the top and sprinkle with cheese. Bake at 400 degrees for 30-35 minutes or until potatoes are cooked.

Serve with bread sticks.

## STRAWBERRIES & PRETZELS DESSERT

*Prep. Time: 30 minutes*

2 cups pretzels, finely crushed
1 (8 oz.) pkg cream cheese
1 large carton Fat Free Cool Whip™
2½ cups boiling water
1 (10 oz.) pkg frozen strawberries
¾ cup butter, melted
2 cups powdered sugar
2 pkgs strawberry gelatin
2 cups miniature marshmallows

Mix the pretzel crumbs in the melted butter and press into a 9x13 pan. Blend the softened cream cheese, powdered sugar, marshmallows and Cool Whip™. Spread over the crust and chill. Meanwhile, prepare the gelatin, dissolved in the boiling water, and add the frozen strawberries. Make sure the strawberries are well blended into the gelatin.

Spoon this layer over the cream cheese mixture. Chill until gelatin is firm. Cut into squares. Serve with a dab of Cool Whip™ on top.

# April 6

*In 1930, James Dewar invented the original junk food treat: Hostess Twinkies™. Today is the national "Twinkie" day. Try your hand at making some homemade twinkies for tonight's dessert.*

## CREAM OF CARROT SOUP

*Prep. Time: 20 minutes / Cook Time: 30 minutes*

2 cups sliced carrots, cooked and drained
¼ cup finely chopped onion
¼ cup finely chopped celery
¼ cup butter
2 tablespoons flour
½ teaspoon salt
¼ teaspoon pepper
2 cups chicken broth
1½ cups skim milk

In medium saucepan, saute onion and celery in butter until vegetables are tender. Stir in flour, salt and pepper. Cook for 1 minute, stirring constantly, until smooth and bubbly. Gradually stir in chicken broth and milk; cook until slightly thickened, stirring constantly. Do not boil. Stir in carrots. Heat thoroughly.

KITCHEN TIP: Once a month, run 1 cup apple cider vinegar through your coffee and tea makers. This is to remove lime buildup from hard water. It will help to clean the insides of your beverage makers. Throw away the vinegar after it has "brewed." Fill the chambers with water and rinse the beverage makers twice, tossing out the brewed water and replacing with fresh water. After two rinses, your coffee and tea makers should not smell or taste like vinegar and you should be able to use them again for brewing your coffee and tea.

# SUBMARINE SANDWICHES

*Prep. Time: 20 minutes*

6-8 hoagie buns
your choice of condiments: mayo, mustard, ketchup, BBQ sauce, etc.
deli-styled sliced ham
deli-styled sliced chicken breast
American cheese slices
lettuce, torn into pieces
onion, thinly sliced
green pepper, thinly sliced and de-seeded
ripe tomato, sliced

Spread your choice of condiment on bread. Layer on meat, cheese and vegetables. Add top half of bread and cut in half to serve. Enjoy with a creamed soup!

## "TWINKIE" CAKE

*Prep. Time: 2 hours / Cook Time: 45 minutes*

1 yellow cake mix with pudding in the mix
eggs, oil and water as called for on the cake mix box
1 cup milk
5 tablespoons flour
1 cup sugar
½ teaspoon salt
½ cup butter
1 teaspoon vanilla

Bake cake mix according to package directions. Pour into 2 cake pans so you'll have two layers. When cake is cool, split each layer in half.

In a saucepan, mix together milk, flour and sugar. Bring to a boil, stirring until thick. Pour into a large mixing bowl and let set until room temperature. Then beat until fluffy. Add the remaining ingredients, beating after each addition, until well mixed. Spread between layers of cake. Then slice and serve!

# April 7

*Did you know that on the average, a mother will clean up after her child over 40,000 times during her lifetime? This doesn't include wiping up over 16,000 spills or multiplying these numbers for more than one child! So enjoy today! The Wellness Permission League in New York, NY has proclaimed today as "NO HOUSEWORK DAY!"*

## OVEN BBQED CHICKEN

*Prep. Time: 20 minutes / Cook Time: 1 hour 30 minutes*

1-2 whole chickens, cut up
¼ cup oil
½ cup ketchup
2 tablespoons lemon juice
1 tablespoon brown sugar
1 tablespoon Worcestershire sauce
1 tablespoon vinegar
1 tablespoon prepared mustard

(Chicken may be skinned, if desired.) In skillet, brown chicken slowly in oil. When browned, transfer to a large baking dish. Add all remaining ingredients to the skillet and ⅓ cup water. Season to taste. Simmer for 15 minutes; skim off excess fat. Pour sauce over chicken. Bake uncovered at 325° for 1 hour and 15 minutes, basting 3 or 4 times with the sauce.

## SCALLOPED HASH BROWNS

*Prep. Time: 5-10 minutes / Cook Time: 1 hour 30 minutes*

1 (30 oz.) pkg frozen hash browns, thawed
1 onion, finely chopped
1 can cream of potato soup
1 can cream of celery soup
1 large (12 oz.) container fat free sour cream or plain yogurt
1 cup shredded cheddar cheese
3 tablespoons butter
salt and pepper to taste

Layer hash browns in a lightly greased 9x13 baking pan. In a separate bowl, combine soups with sour cream and add onion. Pour over potatoes. Sprinkle cheese over top. Drizzle melted butter over all. Bake at 325° for 1 hour 30 minutes.
Serve with Cheesy Broccoli (see page 40)

# April 8

*Did you know that today is the "World Grits Day?" If you haven't ever tried this southern dish, today would be a good day to try it! Serve it along side a "breakfast supper."*

## EGGS BENEDICT

*Prep. Time: 20 minutes / Cook Time: 20 minutes*

8 slices ham or Canadian Bacon
English muffins
1 stick butter
8 eggs

Wrap meat in foil and heat in oven at 350° while preparing the rest. Split, toast and butter English muffins. Wrap English muffins in foil and set in oven to keep warm. In cupcake pans, place a pat of butter in each cup. Set pan in oven for a few minutes to melt the butter. When melted, remove from oven and break an egg into 8 of the cups. Sprinkle with salt and pepper. Place the cupcake pan back into the oven and leave until the whites are just done (watch very closely).

While eggs are cooking, prepare the sauce: (As this heats, it must be stirred constantly)

HOLLANDAISE SAUCE:
4 egg yolks, well beaten
1½ sticks butter
2 teaspoons unsweetened lemon juice
salt and pepper

In a double boiler, place ½ of the butter. After it is melted, add beaten egg yolks, all the time stirring continuously with a wooden spoon. Add remainder of butter. Sauce will begin to thicken as butter melts. Just as sauce begins to thicken, add lemon juice, salt and pepper. It is very important that sauce be ready just at serving time. On each warm toasted muffin half, place 1 slice of meat, poached egg and spoon on Hollandaise Sauce. Serve immediately while everything is hot.

Serve with a bowl of steaming grits. Make according to package directions. Season with butter, salt and pepper or with milk and sugar.

# April 9

## BEEF UPSIDE DOWN PIE

*Prep. Time: 20 minutes / Cook Time: 20-25 minutes*

1½ cups flour
1 teaspoon black pepper
1 teaspoon salt
5 tablespoons shortening
¾ cup skim milk
1 onion, diced
1 can sliced carrots, drained
1 can peas, drained
1 can cream of tomato soup
1 lb. lean ground beef

Mix flour, pepper, salt and 3 tablespoons shortening. Add milk. Melt the remaining shortening in a skillet. Brown ground beef and onion. Drain off all grease. Add soup, carrots and peas and bring to a boil. Pour into a 9x13 baking dish. Sprinkle the flour mixture on top, coating evenly and covering the entire pan. Bake at 400° for 20-25 minutes. Turn out upside down on a large platter or serve directly from the casserole dish, flipping each serving over when you put it on the plate.

KITCHEN TIP: A paint scraper works great for cleaning off baked-on sauces from your stove top. It's also the perfect tool for cleaning sticky and dried on messes on countertops.

# BUTTERFINGER™ DESSERT

*Prep. Time: 15-25 minutes*

2 cups crushed graham crackers
1 cup crushed saltine crackers
½ cup sugar
½ cup melted butter
4 bars of Butterfinger™ candy, crushed
1 quart vanilla ice cream
2 pkgs vanilla instant pudding
2 cups skim milk
Cool Whip™

Mix together graham crackers, saltine crackers, sugar, melted butter and Butterfinger™ candy. Press in a 9x13 pan and set aside. In a mixing bowl, combine instant pudding mixes with milk and beat on high with an electric mixer until thickened. Add 1 quart softened vanilla ice cream. Spread on cooled crumbs and freeze. When ready to serve, spread Cool Whip™ on top and sprinkle with candy bar crumbs.

# April 10

## CHICKEN TETRAZZINI

*Prep. Time: 45 minutes / Cook Time: 30 minutes*

1 chicken, cooked and cut into bite sized pieces
1 lb. spaghetti, cooked according to package directions
1 can cream of mushroom soup
1 can cream of chicken soup
1 can cream of celery soup
1 cup celery, chopped
1 can sliced water chestnuts
1 small onion, finely diced
1 can chicken broth (you may use 2 cups of broth left from cooking chicken, if desired)
2 cups grated American cheese

Mix cooked spaghetti and chicken and all other ingredients except for ½ cup cheese in a large bowl. Pour into a greased 9x13 pan and sprinkle remaining cheese over the top. Bake at 350° for 20-30 minutes (until hot and bubbly and starting to brown).

# RED VELVET CAKE

*Prep. Time: 20 minutes / Cook Time: 30-40 minutes*

2 oz. red food coloring
3 tablespoons Nestle's Quik™ chocolate (other brands are too strong tasting)
½ cup butter
1½ cup sugar
2 eggs
1 cup buttermilk
2¼ cups sifted cake flour
1 teaspoon salt
1 teaspoon baking soda
1 teaspoon vanilla

Blend together food coloring and chocolate with a fork. Cream butter and sugar until fluffy. Add eggs, one at a time, and blend well. Stir in coloring mixture. Beat in buttermilk and flour and salt, a little at a time. Add alternately the vanilla and baking soda, beat well. Pour into greased and floured 8-inch round cake pans and bake at 350° for 30-40 minutes.

# FROST WITH 7-MINUTE FROSTING

*Prep. Time: 20-30 minutes*

1½ cups sugar
⅓ cup cold water
2 egg whites
2 teaspoons light corn syrup OR ¼ teaspoon cream of tartar
1 teaspoon vanilla

In the top of a double boiler (set on the cabinet—while combining these ingredients, get water to boiling in the bottom part of the double boiler) combine sugar, cold water, egg whites, corn syrup and a dash of salt. Beat 30 seconds on low speed with an electric mixer. Set top part of the double boiler over the bottom part containing the boiling water. Be careful that the water does not touch the top part of the pan. Cook for about 7 minutes while beating constantly on high speed with the electric mixer or until frosting forms stiff peaks. Remove from heat and add vanilla. Beat 2 to 3 minutes longer or until it is of spreading consistency. Spread on a cooled cake.

# April 11

## FRANKS AND BEANS

*Prep. Time: 10 minutes / Cook Time: 30 minutes*

1 (1 lb.) can pork and beans
1 pkg hot dogs
2 tablespoons ketchup
1 teaspoon prepared mustard
1 tablespoon brown sugar
3 slices of bacon, fried crisp

Cut hot dogs into small, round pieces. Open beans and scoop out into a casserole dish. Mix hot dog bites together with beans. In a small bowl, combine ketchup, mustard and brown sugar, mix well. Add sauce to the beans and mix well. Crumble up bacon and sprinkle on top of the casserole. Bake at 350° for 30 minutes.

# CHERRY CAKE

*Prep. Time: 15 minutes / Cook Time: 45 minutes*

¼ cup butter

½ cup unsweetened applesauce

1 cup sugar

¾ cup flour

¾ cup milk

1 teaspoon vanilla

2 teaspoons baking powder

1 can cherry pie filling

Melt butter in 8x8 baking dish. In a medium bowl, combine applesauce, sugar, flour, milk, vanilla and baking powder and mix well. Pour over melted butter. Top with the pie filling. Bake at 350° for 45 minutes. Serve with a scoop of vanilla ice cream.

# April 12

## CHICKEN FRIED STEAK AND GRAVY

*Prep. Time: 30-45 minutes / Cook Time: 2 hours or longer*

1 round steak,
   cut into serving portions ½ inch thick

2 eggs

2 tablespoons water

½ cup flour

⅓ cup cornmeal

1 teaspoon salt

½ teaspoon pepper

½ teaspoon poultry seasoning

1 cup flour

4-6 tablespoons oil

Beat eggs and water together. Mix the ½ cup flour, cornmeal, poultry seasoning, salt and pepper on a sheet of waxed paper. Put the 1 cup flour on another sheet of waxed paper. Dip meat in flour, then in egg mixture, then in cornmeal mixture.

Brown meat, 2 pieces at a time, in hot oil on both sides in a large skillet. Return all meat to skillet; lower heat and cook for 10-15 minutes.

Remove steaks to platter. Pour off all but 3 tablespoons of the pan fat.

GRAVY:

3 tablespoons pan fat

2 tablespoons flour

½ teaspoon salt

⅛ teaspoon pepper

1½ cups milk

Blend flour, salt and pepper into fat and stir into a paste; stir in milk. Continue cooking and stirring until gravy thickens and bubbles for 1 minute. If gravy is too thick, add a bit more milk.

Place meat in a baking dish and pour gravy over the meat. Bake at 300° for 2 hours or until the meat is very tender. Serve with Green Beans and Cornbread.

# April 13

## SAUSAGE AND MACARONI BAKE

*Prep. Time: 25 minutes / Cook Time: 30 minutes*

1 lb. bulk mild sausage

2 tablespoons flour

½ teaspoon salt

1 medium onion, finely chopped

½ green pepper, finely chopped

1½ cups skim milk

2 cups shredded cheddar cheese

1 (8 oz.) pkg macaroni, cooked and drained

Crumble sausage in a skillet and add onion and green pepper; cook on medium heat until cooked through. Drain excess fat. Add flour and salt to meat, blending well. Gradually add milk and cook over low heat stirring constantly until thickened. Stir in cooked macaroni and 1 cup cheese. Cook until cheese melts and macaroni is tender. Pour mixture into a lightly greased casserole dish and sprinkle remaining cheese on top. Bake at 400° for 30 minutes.

# BANANA SALAD

*Prep. Time: 25 minutes*

²/₃ cup sugar

2½ tablespoons cornstarch

½ teaspoon salt

1 tablespoon flour

3 cups skim milk

3 egg yolks

1 tablespoon butter

½ teaspoon vanilla

1 cup crushed graham crackers

¾ cup crushed peanuts

3 bananas

In a saucepan, mix together the sugar, cornstarch, salt and flour. Gradually stir in milk over a medium heat and bring to a boil. Let boil for 1 minute. In a small bowl, beat egg yolks. Blend 1 cup of the hot mixture in with the eggs. Then blend egg mixture into saucepan, bring to a boil and let boil 1 more minute, stirring constantly. Remove from heat. Blend in 1 tablespoon butter and ½ teaspoon vanilla. Let cool. Arrange in dish alternating layers with crushed graham crackers, crushed peanuts, banana slices and the saucepan dressing. Serve warm or cold.

# April 14

## CHICKEN ROLL-UPS

*Prep. Time: 30-45 minutes / Cook Time: 1 hour 15 minutes*

6 boneless and skinless chicken breasts

1 family-sized pkg. Stovetop Stuffing Mix™, prepared according to pkg. directions

3 tablespoons butter

1 can cream of chicken soup

1 can cream of mushroom soup

1 can water

salt and pepper

Cut each chicken breast in half, leaving 12 thin chicken breasts. Cut each chicken breast into 1-2 inch strips. Prepare Stovetop Stuffing Mix™ according to package directions. Put as much prepared stuffing on a strip of chicken as will stay on. Carefully, roll the chicken strip up and secure with a toothpick. Fry each roll in butter until it is golden brown all around. Transfer chicken rolls to a baking dish and lay them in a single layer.

In hot frying pan, add the soups and water. Heat, stirring until smooth and hot. Pour gravy over chicken and bake for at 350° 1 hour. Carefully remove toothpicks. Serve immediately.

# BAKED HERB POTATOES

*Prep. Time: 20 minutes / Cook Time: 30-45 minutes*

8-10 medium sized potatoes, peeled and sliced

1 onion, minced

1 cup minced celery

½ cup melted butter

2 tablespoons dried parsley flakes

2 teaspoon salt

¼ teaspoon pepper

1 teaspoon poultry seasoning

Slice potatoes into a large saucepan and cover with water. Bring to a boil and let cook for 10 minutes. Remove from heat and drain off water. Add all other ingredients and mix well. Pour into a casserole dish and bake at 350° for 30-45 minutes, or until potatoes are tender.

# April 15

*This date is observed as the anniversary day for the opening of fast-food chain, McDonald's. Des Plaines, Illinois was the hometown for the first McDonald's restaurant back in 1955. Ronald McDonald didn't appear on the scene until 1963 and it was in Washington, D.C. It's reported that under the red wig and in the 14½ inch shoes was NBC's "Today" show weatherman, Willard Scott!*

## HOMECOOKED BIG MACS

*Prep. Time: 25 minutes / Cook Time: 5-10 minutes*

*For each serving, you'll need:*
2 hamburger buns
2 cooked ground beef patties
salt
1 tablespoon Thousand Island dressing
1 teaspoon minced onion
¼ cup chopped lettuce
1 slice American cheese
2 to 3 dill pickle slices

For the bun in the middle of the sandwich, take a serrated knife and cut the top off the extra bun half, leaving about ½ to ¾ inch thick slice. Save remaining parts of bun for dried bread crumbs and use in another recipe.

Spray a griddle with vegetable spray and heat griddle. Place the three bun halves face down on the hot griddle until lightly browned. Remove and set aside. Cook the patties on the hot griddle over medium heat until done. Salt lightly on each side when patties are done cooking. Start with the bottom bun. Place half of the Thousand Island dressing, half of the onion, half of the lettuce, slice of cheese and the beef patty. Place middle bun on top of beef patty and add the remainder dressing, onion and lettuce. Top lettuce with pickle slices and second beef patty. Top with the bun top. Enjoy!

Serve with French fries prepared according to package directions.

# April 16

## EASY CHICKEN CASSEROLE

*Prep. Time: 40 minutes / Cook Time: 45 minutes*

4 skinless, boneless chicken breasts
2 cups crushed cracker crumbs
2 tablespoons chopped parsley flakes
1 teaspoon salt
¼ teaspoon pepper
2 eggs, beaten
1½ cup chicken stock (use the water you cooked the chicken in)
1½ cup skim milk
1 can French-fried onions (the same kind used for Green Bean Casseroles)

Cook chicken breasts in a pan of water until done. Remove from water and dice. Place a layer of crumbs in a greased casserole dish. Add a layer of diced chicken. Top with parsley, salt and pepper. Add another layer of crumbs followed by a layer of chicken. In a separate bowl, beat eggs and add milk and broth. Pour over the crumbs and chicken layers. Sprinkle top with salt and pepper (according to taste). Bake at 350° for 30 minutes. Add a can of crumbled French-fried onions and bake another 15 minutes.

## PEACHY SWEET POTATOES

*Prep. Time: 15 minutes / Cook Time: 35-40 minutes*

½ cup brown sugar, firmly packed
3 tablespoons flour
¼ teaspoon nutmeg
2 tablespoons butter
⅓ cup chopped pecans (optional)
2 (16 oz.) cans sweet potatoes, drained
1 (16 oz) can sliced peaches in light syrup, drained
3 cups miniature marshmallows

Combine sugar, flour and nutmeg in a small mixing bowl. Cut in butter until mixture resembles coarse crumbs. Add nuts, if desired. In a casserole dish, layer half of the sweet potatoes, peaches and sugar mixture, plus 1 cup marshmallows. Repeat layers of potatoes, peaches and sugar mixture. Bake at 350° for 30 minutes. Top with remaining marshmallows and return to the oven to bake for 5-10 minutes longer, until marshmallows start to melt and turn lightly brown.

# April 17

## BEEFY RICE BALLS

*Prep. Time: 20-30 minutes / Cook Time: 45 minutes to 1 hour*

1½ lb. lean ground beef
1 cup uncooked instant rice
½ cup onion, finely chopped
¼ teaspoon pepper
1½ teaspoons salt
1 cup water
2 (8 oz.) cans tomato sauce

Mix ground beef, rice, onion and seasonings together, making 1-inch balls. Fry, turning often until browned. Transfer meatballs to a casserole dish and cover with tomato sauce and water. Cover and bake at 400° for 45 minutes to 1 hour, until meatballs are done in the center.

## BROCCOLI-CAULIFLOWER SALAD

*Prep. Time: 30 minutes Chill Time: 2 hours*

1 cauliflower head, buds chopped
1 large bunch broccoli, chopped
½ cup onion, chopped
1 cup Miracle Whip Free™
1 tablespoon sugar
1 tablespoon vinegar
salt and pepper to taste

Combine vegetables in a large salad bowl. In a smaller bowl, combine Miracle Whip™, sugar and vinegar. Mix well and pour over vegetables. Toss to coat all vegetables. Let set in refrigerator for at least 2 hours before serving. Add salt and pepper to taste when served.

## CINNAMON WHAT-IS-IT?

*Prep. Time: 5-10 minutes / Cook Time: 20 minutes*

1 cup flour
1 teaspoon baking powder
½ cup sugar
½ cup milk
1 teaspoon vanilla
¾ cup brown sugar, firmly packed
¾ cup sugar
3 tablespoons cinnamon
½ stick butter

In a mixing bowl, combine flour, baking powder, ½ cup sugar, milk and vanilla. Mix well and spread in bottom of a pie pan or other pan. In the same mixing bowl, combine sugars and cinnamon. Sprinkle sugar/cinnamon mixture on top of pastry dough. Dot with slices of butter. Bake at 350 degrees for 20 minutes.

### QUICK TIP:

Purchase a new powder puff and store it in your flour canister. When a recipe calls for a pan to be greased and floured, the powder puff will distribute the flour dust effortlessly and with a whole lot less mess.

# April 18

## ONE-SKILLET SAUSAGE AND ZUCCHINI DINNER

*Prep. Time: 15 minutes / Cook Time: 20 minutes*

1 onion, finely diced

1 can stewed tomatoes

1 medium (fresh) zucchini, sliced

½ cup Parmesan cheese

1 cup shredded mozzarella cheese

1 lb. smoked sausage or Kielbasa in large
    chunks

8 medium potatoes, peeled and boiled

½ teaspoon garlic powder

1 teaspoon dried chives

salt and pepper to taste

In a large skillet, brown sausage in ½ cup water. Add onion, tomatoes, zucchini and seasonings and sliced potatoes. Cover and let simmer for 20 minutes. Remove lid and sprinkle with both cheeses. Allow cheese to start to melt before serving.

## STRAWBERRIES & ANGELFOOD CAKE DESSERT

*Prep. Time: 15 minutes*

1 Angelfood cake, already prepared

1 quart fresh (or frozen and thawed) strawber-
    ries, hulled

2 cups sugar

1 (8 oz) pkg cream cheese

1 large container Fat Free Cool Whip™

Reserve 8-10 strawberries for garnishing. Tear up Angelfood cake in pieces and place in casserole dish. Slice strawberries and add 1½ cups sugar. Mix well and set aside. In a small bowl, beat cream cheese with ½ cup sugar at low speed using an electric mixer. Add all but 1 cup Cool Whip™ to the cream cheese and mix on low speed until well blended. Spoon cream cheese mixture into strawberry slices and stir well. Add to the cake and stir well. Top with remaining cup of Cool Whip™ and decorate with whole or sliced strawberries. Refrigerate until ready to serve.

# April 19

## CORN CHOWDER

*Prep. Time: 20-25 minutes / Cook Time: 30 minutes*

½ lb. bacon

1 small green pepper, chopped

1 medium onion, finely chopped

2 cups skim milk

2 cans cream style corn

6 medium potatoes, peeled and diced

salt and pepper to taste

Cook bacon until crisp. Remove bacon and saute pepper and onion in bacon grease. Add potatoes and toss to absorb the remaining bacon grease. Transfer all from skillet and put in soup pan. Add corn, milk, salt and pepper. Cook over very low heat, stirring often to prevent sticking. Chowder will be done when the potatoes are tender. Add crumbled crisp bacon to soup bowls right before ready to eat.

## QUICK TIP:

Here's an easy way to clean your microwave. First, dissolve 2 tablespoons baking soda in 1 cup of water and set cup in the center of microwave. Cook on high for one minute. As soon as the microwave shuts off, wipe down the inside of the microwave. Stubborn stains should lift right off.

## FRUITY PUDDING

*Prep. Time: 10 minutes / Cook Time: 35 minutes*

1½ cup flour
1 cup sugar
1 teaspoon baking soda
½ teaspoon salt
1 egg, slightly beaten
1 can fruit cocktail
1 cup brown sugar

Sift flour, sugar, baking soda and salt together. Add egg and fruit cocktail. Mix together and pour into a greased 9x9 pan. Sprinkle brown sugar evenly over entire top. Bake at 350° for 35 minutes.

# April 20

## EASY BEEF MANHATTENS

*Prep. Time: 10 minutes / Cook Time: 20 minutes*

1 - 2 lbs. sliced roast beef from the deli
leftover or instant mashed potatoes to serve 6
6 slices white bread
2 packets brown gravy mix

Prepare brown gravy mixes in a medium saucepan. After whisking to dissolve mixes, add meat and cook until heated through. Heat mashed potatoes in the microwave or make 6 servings of instant mashed potatoes according to package directions. For each serving, lay down 1 slice of bread. Spoon 1 to 2 slices of meat with gravy on top of bread. With an ice-cream scoop (or large spoon) dip out a ball of mashed potatoes and put in the center of the meat. Drizzle a bit more gravy over the top of the mashed potatoes and serve.

Serve with peas and carrots.

## MANDARIN ORANGE CAKE

*Prep. Time: 10 minutes / Cook Time: 45 minutes to 1 hour*

2 cups flour
2 cups sugar
2 teaspoons baking soda
2 teaspoons vanilla
1 teaspoon salt
2 eggs
2 small cans mandarin oranges, drained

Mix all ingredients together in a mixing bowl. Pour into a lightly greased 9x13 cake pan. Bake at 350° for 1hour.

## FROSTING FOR MANDARIN ORANGE CAKE

*Prep. Time: 5 minutes / Cook Time: 10 minutes*

1 cup brown sugar
4 tablespoons butter
4 tablespoons skim milk

Mix brown sugar, butter and milk in a saucepan and bring to a boil. Let boil for 2 minutes then pour over the cake. Serve warm.

# April 21

## HOMEMADE CHICKEN PILAF

*Prep. Time: 30 minutes / Cook Time: 10 minutes*

1 cup finely diced celery
1 medium onion, finely diced
2 tablespoons butter
½ small red or green bell pepper, finely chopped
4 cups cooked rice
4 boneless, skinless chicken breasts, cooked
    and cut into bite-sized pieces
salt and pepper to taste

Using a large skillet, saute celery and onion in butter. Add red sweet pepper, cooked rice and chicken. Salt and pepper to taste. Simmer for 10 minutes, stirring constantly. Serve hot.

# CARROTS IN HONEY BUTTERSAUCE

*Prep. Time: 15 minutes / Cook Time: 30 minutes*

5 large carrots, sliced
¼ cup butter
2 tablespoons pecan pieces
3 tablespoons honey
2 tablespoons golden raisins
salt and pepper to taste

In medium covered saucepan, cook carrots in enough boiling water to just cover carrots. Cook for 15 to 20 minutes or until tender. Drain off water. Stir in remaining ingredients and bring to a brisk boil. Let boil until liquid is absorbed and carrots are glazed. Stir often. Serve hot.

# April 22

# TACO VEGIE CASSEROLE

*Prep. Time: 15 minutes / Cook Time: 25 minutes*

1 lb. lean ground beef or ground turkey
¼ cup chopped onion
1 cup whole kernel corn
1 can stewed tomatoes
2 tablespoons chili powder
1 teaspoon sugar
1 teaspoon oregano
¼ teaspoon salt
⅛ teaspoon pepper
2 cups shredded cheddar cheese
1 (9½ oz.) pkg corn chips
1 large head iceberg lettuce

Brown ground beef and onion together in a large skillet. Stir until meat is crumbly. When meat is done and onion is transparent, drain off grease. Stir in corn, tomatoes and seasonings. Bring mixture to a boil, stirring often. Let boil for about a minute then reduce heat;simmer over low heat for 10 minutes. Stir in 1 cup cheese and corn chips. Cook until the cheese is partially melted. Tear up

lettuce into bite size pieces and layer it on a large platter. When taco mixture is done, spoon it onto the lettuce. Sprinkle the remaining cheese over the top and serve immediately.

# POKE 'N' POUR CAKE

*Prep. Time: 10 minutes / Cook Time: 30-35 minutes*

1 pkg white or yellow cake mix
eggs, oil and water as called for on the cake mix box
1 small box gelatin, any flavor
1 large box vanilla instant pudding
2 cups Fat Free Cool Whip™

Prepare mix according to package directions and bake until done. When cake is done, poke holes in cake using the handle of a wooden spoon. Prepare gelatin according to package directions and pour over the cake, filling the holes with liquid gelatin. Refrigerate cake until gelatin is firm. Prepare instant pudding according to package directions and add Cool Whip™. Frost cake with pudding/Cool Whip™. Refrigerate until ready to serve.

# April 23

# CHIPPED BEEF CASSEROLE

*Did you know an average pair of adult lungs can hold 2 gallons of air; but most people settle for only 2 pints. Deep breathing helps a body to concentrate, solve problems and release stress. That's why we're told to take a deep breath and relax.*

*Prep. Time: 20 minutes / Cook Time: 30 minutes*

6-7 medium potatoes, peeled and thinly sliced
4 tablespoons bacon grease
1 medium onion, finely chopped
2 (3-to-4-ozs) pkgs chipped beef
2 cans cream of mushroom soup
⅔ cup water
saltine cracker crumbs

In a large skillet, heat bacon grease and heat until melted. Add potatoes, onion, and dried beef torn into little pieces. Fry until potatoes begin to brown. Add 1 cup water and cover skillet with a lid and steam until potatoes are tender. Turn potatoes frequently to avoid sticking. When water has evaporated, remove skillet from heat. In a large casserole dish, combine soups with water. Stir well. Add potato mixture. Top with cracker crumbs. Cover casserole dish and bake at 350° for 30 minutes.

Serve with raw vegetables and dip.

## APPLE CAKE

*Prep. Time: 30 minutes / Cook Time: 45 minutes*

2 eggs
½ cup oil
2 cups sugar
1 teaspoon vanilla
2 cups flour
½ teaspoon salt
1 teaspoon baking soda
¼ teaspoon nutmeg
2 teaspoons cinnamon
4 cups diced apples

Beat eggs until light and fluffy. Gradually add sugar, oil and vanilla. Sift together flour, salt, baking soda, cinnamon and nutmeg, adding gradually to the egg mixture. Stir in apples. Pour into greased 9x13 cake pan. Bake at 350° for 45 minutes. Let cake cool while preparing Cream Cheese Frosting. (see page 47)

# April 24

## SOUPY BAKED CHICKEN BREASTS

*Prep. Time: 5-10 minutes / Cook Time: 1 hour*

4-6 chicken breasts
1 can cream of chicken soup
1 can cream of celery soup
1 soup-can full of water
1 teaspoon salt
pepper to taste
8-10 medium potatoes, peeled
1 onion, sliced

Remove skin from chicken breasts and discard. Place breasts in a single layer in a large roasting pan. Add potatoes, whole. In a separate container, combine soups with water. Pour over meat and potatoes. Sprinkle salt evenly and pepper as desired. Place sliced onions on top of both the meat and potatoes. Cover with roasting pan lid and bake at 350° for 1 hour. To serve, scoop potatoes out and place in one serving bowl and the chicken on a serving platter. Discard the soups and onion, or puree and freeze as a chicken-stock base for a creamed soup later on.

### KITCHEN TIP:

Before you put those electric mixer beaters in that cake mix, give them a quick spray with nonstick vegetable spray or dip them in hot water and dry quickly. The batter will mix more evenly and not stick to the beaters.

# CRUNCHY RANCH SALAD

*Prep. Time: 20 minutes*

*Special thanks goes to my mother, Joyce James, for sharing with me some of her "custom" recipes. This Crunchy Ranch Salad is one of them I'm sure you'll enjoy.*

1 bunch fresh broccoli
1 head cauliflower
1 bunch (12) green onions
2 medium green bell peppers
3 ripe red tomatoes (optional)
½ cup sugar
¾ teaspoon salt
⅛ teaspoon pepper
Ranch salad dressing

Wash and cut off florets of broccoli and cauliflower. Clean and dice all of the onions. Wash and dice bell peppers and tomatoes. Place vegetables in a deep bowl. In a separate container, combine sugar, salt, pepper and Ranch dressing. Mix well and pour over all the vegetables. Stir in order to coat well. Seal container and let set for 3 to 4 hours before serving.

# April 25

# BROWN GRAVY MEATLOAF

*Prep. Time: 10-15 minutes / Cook Time: 90 minutes*

2 lb. lean ground beef or turkey
2 eggs
2 cups crushed crackers
3 pkgs brown gravy mixes
1 tablespoon minced onion
½ cup diced green bell pepper
1 tablespoon Worcestershire Sauce
2 teaspoons salt
½ teaspoon pepper

In a large bowl combine all ingredients except gravy mixes and blend well. Form mixture into a loaf shape and place in the center of a roasting

pan. Cover pan and bake at 350º for 40 minutes. Remove pan from oven and drain off all meat drippings. Prepare 3 packets of gravy mix according to package directions and pour over the meatloaf. (Gravy will thicken as it cooks.) Add slices of fresh onion for seasoning and garnish. Bake at 350º for another 25 minutes.

# SOUR CREAM MASHED POTATOES

*Prep. Time: 15 minutes / Cook Time: 1 hour*

10-14 medium potatoes, peeled and sliced
water
1 teaspoon salt
1 teaspoon butter
¾ cup skim milk
¼ cup fat free sour cream or plain yogurt
¼ cup butter
1 teaspoon salt
⅛ teaspoon pepper
1 teaspoon dried chopped chives

Peel and slice potatoes into a large pan. Cover potatoes with water. Add 1 teaspoon salt and 1 teaspoon butter. Cook over medium-to-high heat for 40 minutes, or until potatoes are tender. Drain off all water. Add milk, sour cream, butter, salt and pepper. With a potato masher, beat potatoes until mashed.

Serve with Honey-Bear Carrots (see pg 17)

# April 27

# SCALLOPED POTATOES WITH HAM

*Prep. Time: 20 minutes / Cook Time: 1 hour*

1 medium onion, finely chopped
2 tablespoons butter
2 tablespoons flour
1¼ cups skim milk
4 to 6 cups sliced potatoes

1 lb. diced ham
2 cups shredded Cheddar cheese
1 cup Cheese Whiz™
1 teaspoon salt
½ teaspoon pepper

In a large skillet, cook onion in butter until transparent. Stir in flour, salt and pepper. Add milk, all at once, and continue stirring until mixture thickens into a gravy of sorts. Add processed cheese and stir until dissolved. Remove from heat. In a casserole dish, alternate layers of sliced potatoes with ham and the shredded cheddar cheese. Reserve ½ cup of shredded cheese. Pour gravy mixture over potatoes and bake covered at 350° for 45 minutes. Uncover, add remaining cheese, and bake 15 to 20 minutes longer or until potatoes are tender and cheese is lightly browned.

# PEA SALAD

*Prep. Time: 15-20 minutes*

1 (10 oz.) pkg frozen baby peas
1 cup diced celery
1 cup chopped cauliflower
6 green onions, finely chopped
1 cup chopped salted cashews
½ cup fat free sour cream or plain yogurt
1 cup fat free Ranch salad dressing
4 slices bacon, fried crisp

Combine all ingredients. Sprinkle crumbled bacon over top. Chill for an hour before serving.

# ALOHA CAKE

*Prep. Time: 10 minutes Bake Time: 30 to 40 minutes*

1 box yellow cake mix
1 (11 oz.) can mandarin orange sections, undrained
2 small pkgs instant vanilla pudding mix
2 cups crushed pineapple in its own juice, undrained
4 eggs
1 (8 oz.) pkg cream cheese
1 large carton Fat Free Cool Whip™

1 cup powdered sugar
1 teaspoon vanilla
Maraschino cherries

In mixing bowl, combine dry cake mix, 1 package dry pudding mix, 1 cup pineapple with juice, entire can of mandarin orange sections with juice and 4 eggs. With an electric mixer, blend on high for four minutes. Pour batter into a greased 9x13 cake pan. Bake at 350° for 30 to 40 minutes or until sides of cake pull away from the sides of the pan. Remove from oven and refrigerate to cool.

Combine remaining cup of pineapple with juice, 1 package dry pudding mix, cream cheese, vanilla and powdered sugar and beat with electric mixer on high until well blended. Spread on cooled cake. Garnish with maraschino cherries and maraschino cherry juice. Keep refrigerated.

# April 27

## TUNA PATTIE MELT

*Prep. Time: 15 minutes / Cook Time: 3 to 6 minutes*

2 (6 ½ oz) cans tuna, drained
1 cup crushed saltine crackers
1 carrot, grated
2 eggs, beaten
½ cup Miracle Whip Free™
¼ cup sliced green onions
½ teaspoon salt
pepper to taste
vegetable spray
6-8 slices American cheese

Combine all ingredients except cheese in a large bowl. Mix well and form into patties. Brown in a skillet or on a griddle over medium heat using vegetable spray to prevent patties from sticking. Heat about 3 minutes and turn, continue cooking until lightly browned (about 3 more minutes). Just before removing from heat, top each pattie with a slice of American cheese, letting it melt. Serve immediately.

## Recycling

With this being "National Recycling Month," here are some great ideas for how to pull double-duty from what you'd otherwise throw away as trash.

• Save small boxes, canisters and containers instead of throwing them away. Purchase different colors of paints (water-based) from a craft store and put your kids to work painting the containers and making them into buildings. The next time you have a rainy day, let your kids design their own city with the painted buildings and drive matchbox cars around the streets.

• Concentrated cardboard juice cans make great pencil/pen holders, wooden spoon holders, etc. Decorate with paper or material or paint. The limit is your imagination!

• Plastic 2-liter soda bottles make great banks for the kids to make and use! Cut a coin slot about an inch below the neck of a plastic soda bottle. Decorate the bank with construction paper and make it into an animal, cartoon character, plant or a piece of modern art!

• Wooden popsicle sticks make great plant markers. If you want to use them outdoors, write the name of the plant on the stick with a permanent marker and seal with a coat of clear fingernail polish. You can do the same thing with plastic spoons!

# SPAGHETTI SALAD

*Prep. Time: 20-25 minutes*

1 (1 lb.) box spaghetti
2 medium green bell peppers
2 bunches (20-24) green onions
2 large, ripe tomatoes
1 cup pitted ripe (black) olives, drained
½ cup Parmesan cheese
salt and pepper to taste
1 cup sugar
1 large jar creamy Italian salad dressing
1 small jar French salad dressing

Cook and drain spaghetti, rinsing it in cold water when it is "al dente" (firm, yet still tender). Chop green peppers, green onions and tomatoes and put in a deep salad bowl. Add cooked and cooled spaghetti noodles. Add olives and Parmesan cheese. Mix all ingredients in bowl together. Combine salad dressings and pour over salad bowl mixture. Mix well. Add salt and pepper to taste and stir again. Cover with a lid and let set for 12 hours or overnight before serving.

# April 28

*If your previous theme nights were a success, go with another one tonight! This time make it an Oriental night. Let your kids make small paper kites of different shapes and sizes. Use them to decorate the room. If you're real energetic, check out a book from the library on how to make origami sculptures. Use chop sticks instead of the usual silverware. Instead of setting at the kitchen table, put big pillows (or rolled up sleeping bags/blankets) around the living room coffee table and use that as your dinner table. Burn votive candles to add to the oriental setting.*

# BAKED CHOP SUEY

*Prep. Time: 25 minutes / Cook Time: 1 hour 15 minutes*

1 lb. ground pork
2 medium onions, chopped
1 can cream of chicken soup
1½ cups warm water

1 cup rice (uncooked)
3 cups fresh broccoli florets
1 cup fresh sliced mushrooms
1 cup bean sprouts, drained
1 can cream of mushroom soup
½ cup soy sauce
⅛ teaspoon pepper
chow mein noodles

Brown ground pork as you would hamburger and drain off all grease. Add cans of soup and water and let simmer until heated through. In casserole dish, combine chopped onions with uncooked rice, broccoli, mushrooms and bean sprouts. Mix well. In soup mixture, stir in soy sauce and pepper. Pour over the vegetables. Cover with a lid and bake at 350° for 1 hour. Remove from oven, cover with chow mein noodles and return to oven to bake for 15 minutes longer. Serve immediately.

# FRIED RICE

*Prep. Time 10 minutes / Cook Time: 8-10 minutes*

6 slices bacon, cut up
1 stalk celery, chopped
4 green onions, chopped
1 egg
2 cups cooked rice
2 to 3 tablespoons soy sauce

Cook bacon until crisp. Add celery and onion and saute in bacon grease until tender. Push vegetables and bacon to the side and add egg. Scramble egg and add cooked rice and soy sauce. Combine all ingredients and mix well. Sprinkle with chopped green onions and serve when lightly browned.

Serve with Fortune Cookies (available at most grocery stores)

# April 29

## SOUTHERN CHICKEN 'N' DUMPLINGS

*Prep. Time: 25 minutes / Cook Time: 1-2 hours*

1 whole chicken, cut in pieces
water
2 teaspoons salt
½ teaspoon black pepper
1 medium onion, finely chopped
1 green pepper, finely chopped
2 stalks celery, diced

Removed skin from chicken and discard. Put chicken in a large pot and cover with water. Add remaining ingredients and cook over medium heat until chicken is done and comes away from the bone easily. Remove chicken and let cool. Meanwhile, mix up the dumplings.

## DUMPLINGS:

*Prep. Time: 10 minutes / Cook Time: 15 minutes*

1½ cup flour
⅓ cup shortening
1 teaspoon salt
2 eggs
½ cup milk

Combine flour, shortening and salt in a bowl. Work shortening into the flour. Add eggs and milk to flour mixture. Knead together. Put 1 cup flour on counter top. On a floured surface, work the dough and roll it out like pie crust. Cut in squares. More flour may be added, if needed. Drop dumplings into the pot of hot broth. Cook uncovered for at least 15 minutes.

As soon as the dumplings are in the pot cooking, go back to the chicken. Pick meat off bones and return meat to the pot. Discard bones. Simmer together for about 5 minutes to reheat chicken and then serve.

# CORN-BROCCOLI BAKE

*Prep. Time: 15 minutes / Cook Time: about 1 hour*

10 oz. pkg broccoli cuts, thawed
2 cans creamed style corn
1 tablespoon minced onion
2 tablespoons butter, melted
1 egg
salt and pepper to taste
½ cup butter, melted
1 cup croutons

Put thawed broccoli in a casserole baking dish. Combine corn, onion, 2 tablespoons melted butter, egg, salt and pepper and pour over broccoli. Melt the ½ cup butter and toss croutons until well coated. Put croutons on top of casserole and bake at 350° for 1 hour.

# OREO™ COOKIES DESSERT

*Prep. Time: 10 minutes*

1 pkg Oreo™ cookies, crushed
1 (8 oz.) pkg cream cheese, softened
3½ cups skim milk
2 (3 oz.) pkgs instant vanilla pudding
1 large container Fat Free Cool Whip™

Crush cookies and press into a 9x13 pan, reserving ⅓ of the cookies for the topping. In mixing bowl, combine cream cheese, milk and pudding until smooth and thick. Fold in the Cool Whip™. Pour over Oreo™ crust. Sprinkle with remaining crushed cookies. Chill until ready to serve.

# April 30

# HOT DOG CASSEROLE

*Prep. Time: 15 minutes / Cook Time: 25 minutes*

1 pkg hot dogs
1½ cups boiling water
1 teaspoon Worcestershire sauce
1 tablespoon onion, minced
½ teaspoon salt
1 cup peas (cooked or canned)
1 cup grated cheddar cheese
5 cups macaroni, cooked
⅛ teaspoon pepper
1 can cream of potato soup

Add hot dogs to boiling water and simmer for 5 minutes. Remove from water and let cool. In a large casserole baking dish, combine cooked macaroni with the peas and onion. In a separate container, stir together Worcestershire sauce, salt, pepper and cream of potato soup. Add 1 cup water. Pour over macaroni mixture. Cut hot dogs into 1-inch round bites. Mix in with macaroni mixture. Bake at 400° for 20 minutes. Top with grated cheddar cheese and bake for 5 minutes longer. Serve immediately.

# APPLE OATMEAL SQUARES

*Prep. Time: 25 minutes / Cook Time: 45 minutes or longer*

2 cups quick cooking oatmeal
2 cups sifted flour
1½ cups brown sugar, firmly packed
½ cup butter, melted
1 teaspoon vanilla
½ teaspoon salt
¼ cup sugar
4 teaspoons cinnamon
8 cups sliced, pared tart apples

Combine flour, brown sugar, butter, vanilla and salt. Mix until crumbly. Press half of mixture in a greased 13x9 pan. Top with sliced apples. Combine sugar and cinnamon; sprinkle over apples. Top with remaining crumb mixture. Bake at 350° for 45 minutes or until apples are tender. Serve with ice cream.

# COOKIES OF THE MONTH

## JIFFY PEANUT BUTTER COOKIES

1 pkg. yellow cake mix
1 cup crunchy peanut butter
½ cup oil
2 tablespoons water
2 eggs

Combine all ingredients and mix well. Drop by teaspoon on to ungreased cookie sheet. Flatten each cookie with the tines of a fork. Bake at 350° degrees for 10-12 minutes.

## CANDY HASH

¼ cup sliced roasted almonds
1 cup dry roasted peanuts
1 cup Captain Crunch™ cereal
1 cup Rice Krispies™ cereal
1 cup minature marshmallows
1 lb. white chocolate coating mix

Combine almonds, peanuts, cereals and marshmallows in a large bowl. Melt white chocolate coating mix in a double boiler. Pour white chocolate over mixed ingredients in bowl. Stir well. Drop by teaspoon onto waxed paper.

## TEA COOKIES

1 cup butter
1 teaspoon vanilla
¼ teaspoon salt
½ cup powdered sugar
2¼ sup flour
¾ cup chopped pecans, optional

Cream butter with sugar, add vanilla and mix well. Combine flour and salt and add nuts; gradually add flour mixture to the sugar mixture; beating well after each addition. Chill dough for 2 hours. Pinch off and roll dough into 1-inch balls. Place on ungreased baking sheet. Bake at 400° for 8-10 minutes.

Nationally, May is observed as the:
- National Barbecue Month
- National Egg Month
- National Hamburger Month
- National Salad Month
- National Stawberry Month

One thing is certain—there's a *lot* to enjoy during the month of May!

# May 1

## SPAGHETTI AND MEATBALLS

*Prep. Time: 20 minutes / Cook Time: 20-30 minutes*

1 lb. lean ground beef
1 egg
1 cup crushed saltine crackers
½ teaspoon salt
⅛ teaspoon pepper
½ cup finely diced onion
1 lb. spaghetti pasta
1 jar or can of traditional spaghetti sauce
1 packet of spaghetti sauce seasoning mix
1 can tomato sauce

Mix together ground beef with the egg, cracker crumbs, salt, pepper and onion. Roll into 1½-to- 2 inch balls and brown in a skillet, turning often. Cook until all sides are browned and the meatballs are cooked through. Drain them on a paper towel.

In a large pan, cook spaghetti pasta according to package directions. When pasta is tender, but still firm, drain off water and rinse in cold water to stop the cooking. Return pasta to the pan. Add the jar or can of spaghetti Sauce, ½ of the seasoning packet of spaghetti Sauce mix, and the can of tomato sauce. Mix thoroughly with spaghetti. Add meatballs and reheat until hot. Serve immediately.

Serve with baked Garlic Bread, available in your grocer's freezer section.

# May 2

## PORK AND RICE

*Prep. Time: 15 minutes / Cook Time: 90 minutes*

4-6 lean pork chops or steaks
1 can evaporated skim milk
2 packets pork gravy mix
2 cups water
2 cups uncooked instant rice
1 can French-fried onions, crumbled
1 teaspoon salt
¼ teaspoon pepper

In a deep baking dish, combine skim milk with both packets of gravy mix and water. Whisk together until well blended. Add pork, trying to coat each piece with the gravy sauce. Cover with a tight-fitting lid and bake for 1 hour and 15 minutes at 350º. Remove dish from oven and take out the pork. Set aside to let cool. Add rice and stir into the gravy sauce. Cover with lid and return to oven to bake for 5 minutes longer. While rice is cooking, pick meat off the bone and tear into bite-sized pieces. When rice is done, add meat back to the casserole dish. Add salt and pepper and mix well. Crumble French-fried onions over top, reserving ¼ of the can. Mix the crumbled onions into the rice and meat. Sprinkle the remaining ¼ of the onions on top. Return to the oven, uncovered, for 10 minutes longer. Serve immediately.

## MISSISSIPPI MUD CAKE

*Prep. Time: 10 minutes / Cook Time: 35 minutes*

2 cups sugar
1 cup shortening
4 eggs
1½ cups flour
¼ cup cocoa
1 teaspoon vanilla
1 cup chopped pecans (optional)

dash salt

1 (7 oz.) jar marshmallow creme

Preheat oven to 350°. Cream sugar and shortening together; add eggs and beat by hand. Sift flour, cocoa and salt and add to creamed sugar mixture. Add vanilla and nuts, mix well. Pour into ungreased 13x9 cake pan and bake for 30-35 minutes or until a knife inserted in the center comes out clean. Spread marshmallow creme on hot cake and let it melt. When cake is cool, frost with the following icing recipe.

## MISSISSIPPI MUD CAKE ICING

*Prep. Time: 10 minutes / Cook Time: 3 minutes*

1/3 cup butter

4 tablespoons cocoa

1/3 cup milk

1 teaspoon vanilla

2½ cups powdered sugar

Melt butter in a saucepan. Add cocoa and stir well, cook for 1 minute. Remove from heat and add milk, vanilla and powdered sugar. Stir until smooth and then pour over the cooled cake, spreading evenly to coat the entire cake.

**TAKE A BREAK:**
With Mother's Day around the corner take a break from cooking! Turn this recipe book over to your kids. For young children, check the contents page for a list of oven-free recipes.

# May 3
## KITCHEN SINK CASSEROLE

*Prep. Time: 25 minutes / Cook Time: 1 hour*

1 lb. lean ground beef or turkey

1 cup chopped onions

6 cups cubed potatoes

4 medium carrots, sliced

1 cup celery, diced

1 can green beans, drained

1 cup tomato sauce

1 cup kidney beans, rinsed and drained

1 cup uncooked rice

2 teaspoons salt

1½ tablespoons Worcestershire sauce

2 teaspoon chili powder

1 teaspoon pepper

2 cups water

Brown meat and onion together, drain grease. Combine all ingredients in a large casserole dish and cover with a tight fitting lid. Bake at 350° for 1 hour or until all vegetables are cooked through and tender.

## CLOUD BISCUITS

*Prep. Time: 20-30 minutes / Cook Time: 15 minutes*

2 cups flour

1 tablespoon sugar

4 teaspoons baking powder

½ teaspoon salt

½ cup shortening

1 egg

2/3 cup milk

Sift together the dry ingredients; cut in shortening until mixture resembles coarse crumbs. Combine egg and milk; add to flour mixture. Stir until dough follows fork around bowl. Turn out on lightly floured surface. Knead gently with heel of hand about 20 times. Roll out and cut with a biscuit cutter or the rim of a drinking glass. Place on ungreased cookie sheet. Bake at 450° for 15 minutes.

# May 4

## BAKED CUBED STEAK WITH BROWN GRAVY

*Prep. Time: 15 minutes / Cook Time: 1 hour*

6 pieces cubed steak
½ cup flour
1 teaspoon salt
½ teaspoon pepper
1 teaspoon unseasoned meat tenderizer
2-3 tablespoons oil
2 packets brown gravy mix
3 cups water
1 onion, sliced
2 teaspoons cornstarch

With a meat mallet, pound each cubed steak until about doubled in size. In a plastic bag or a deep bowl, combine flour, salt, pepper, meat tenderizer and mix well. Dredge each piece of meat in flour mixture, coating well on both sides. Brown meat on both sides in hot oil then place in a casserole dish. Prepare gravy mixes according to package directions, adding ½ cup additional water with each packet. Pour gravy over meat. Slice onion and place rings over meat. Cover and bake at 350° for about 1 hour. Just before serving, dissolve cornstarch in a little cold water. Remove meat and place on a platter. Pour cornstarch liquid into gravy and stir well. This will help to thicken the gravy a bit more.

## PARSLEY POTATOES

*Prep. Time: 15 minutes / Cook Time: 35-40 minutes*

8-10 medium potatoes, peeled and cubed
water
2 teaspoons salt
¼ teaspoon pepper
2 tablespoons butter
1 tablespoon parsley flakes
¼ to ½ cup butter (optional)

Cover cubed potatoes with water and add remaining ingredients. Bring potatoes to a boil over medium heat and cook until potatoes are tender. Drain off half of the water and, if desired, add ¼ to ½ cup more melted butter. Stir well to coat potatoes.

## GREEN BEAN CASSEROLE

*Prep. Time: 15 minutes / Cook Time: 35 minutes*

2 cans French-styled green beans, undrained
1 can cream of mushroom soup
1 small to medium onion, finely diced
1 can French-fried onions

Combine green beans with mushroom soup and onion. Stir well. Bake at 350° for 25 minutes. Remove from oven and sprinkle French-fried onions on top of casserole. Return to oven and bake for 10 minutes longer. Serve immediately.

## HOMEMADE ICE CREAM CAKE

*Prep. Time: 20 minutes / Cook Time: 30 minutes*

2 chocolate flavored cake mixes
1 large box instant chocolate pudding
6 eggs
½ cup oil
2 cups water
vanilla ice cream
1 large tub Cool Whip™

Prepare both cake mixes in large mixing bowl, according to package directions. (This will use the eggs, oil and water.) Be sure to mix cake batter on high speed for a full two-minutes. Add pudding mix and mix for one-minute longer. Pour batter into two 8 or 9-inch round cake pans. Bake cakes according to package directions. When cakes are done, remove from oven. Invert one layer immediately onto a round platter. Invert the other layer on to a wire rack to cool. While cakes are cooling, get the ice cream out of the freezer to soften. Spread a 2-to-3 inch layer of ice cream on top of the bottom cake layer. Add top cake layer and immediately place in freezer. When cake and ice cream are frozen, remove from freezer and frost with Cool Whip™. Return cake to freezer until ready to serve.

# May 5

*Cinco de Mayo is the Mexican Independence Day. Make tonight's dinner a Mexican theme evening. In addition to making Mexican dishes, purchase a ready-to-fill piñata and let your kids fill it with individually wrapped pieces of candy and gum. Following dinner, invite the neighborhood kids over for a game of break the piñata! Everyone wins!!!*

## CHICKEN ENCHILADAS

*Prep. Time: 15 minutes / Cook Time: 25 minutes*

2 cups fat free sour cream or plain yogurt

1 can cream of chicken soup

1 medium onion, minced

½ teaspoon salt

¼ teaspoon pepper

12 flour tortillas

1 (4 oz.) can diced green chilies

2 cups boned, cooked chicken

1 teaspoon chili powder

½ teaspoon garlic powder

2 cups shredded cheddar cheese

Blend sour cream and soup together. Spread 1 cup of mixture into a 9x13 pan; set aside. In a 2-quart pan, combine chicken, ½ cup sour cream

mixture, chilies, onion, 1 cup cheese, salt, pepper, chili powder and garlic. Cook over low heat, stirring occasionally until heated through.

Preheat oven to 450°. Heat tortillas a few at a time in skillet or microwave. Spread ¼ cup chicken mixture along center of the tortilla. Fold sides over and place seam side down in baking dish. Spread the remaining sour cream mixture over top of the tortillas. Sprinkle with remaining cheese. Bake 10 minutes or until cheese is melted. Serve hot.

## TACO SALAD

*Prep. Time: 15 minutes*

1 large can refried beans

1 large jar taco sauce

16 oz. container fat free sour cream or plain yogurt

3 medium tomatoes, diced

½ head lettuce

6 green onions

1 package taco seasoning mix

2 cups shredded cheese

1 can sliced ripe olives (optional)

Mash refried beans in bottom of a large cake pan. Layer the remaining ingredients in order listed. Can be refrigerated a few hours prior to serving.

# COOKIES OF THE MONTH

## CRISP LEMON COOKIES

1 pkg. lemon cake mix
1 cup crisp rice cereal
1 stick butter
1 egg, slightly beaten

In large bowl, combine all ingredients and mix well. Shape into 1-inch balls, pressing firmly on ungreased cookie sheet. Place cookies about two inches apart. Bake at 350° for 9 to 12 minutes or until light golden brown around edges. Cool for two minutes before removing from cookie sheet.

## GERMAN CHOCOLATE CHEWS

1 pkg. German chocolate cake mix
⅓ cup coconut
½ cup butter, softened
1 egg
2 cups semi-sweet chocolate chips
2 cups miniature marshmallows
1 can ready-to-spread coconut pecan or
    coconut almond frosting
2 cups crisp rice cereal
½ cup chopped pecans or walnuts, if desired

In large bowl, combine cake mix, coconut, butter and egg; blend well. Press in bottom of

ungreased 15x10-inch jelly roll pan or 13x9 cake pan. Bake at 350° for 15 to 25 minutes or until light golden brown. Remove from oven and let cool.

In large saucepan, heat chocolate chips, marshmallows and frosting over low heat, stirring constantly until marshmallows are melted. Stir in cereal; spread over cooled cookie base.

Sprinkle with nuts and lightly press them in. Refrigerate for 1 hour and then cut into bars.

# May 6

## HOAGIE SANDWICHES

*Prep. Time: 15 minutes*

hoagie buns, enough for each person
Miracle Whip Free™
mustard and ketchup, if desired
1-2 tomatoes, sliced
1-2 onions, sliced
1 lb. shaved ham
1 lb. shaved turkey breast
1 lb. shaved roast beef
dill pickle slices
1 green pepper, sliced thin

Spread your choice on condiments on inside of buns. Layer meats and vegetables as desired. Serve with chips.

## STRAWBERRY SHORTCAKE

*Prep. Time: 20 minutes / Cook Time: 30-40 minutes*

1 pkg. white or yellow cake mix
eggs, oil and water as called for on cake mix
    directions
1 quart fresh strawberries
2 cups sugar
Cool Whip™

Prepare cake mix as directed. Pour into a 13x9 inch cake pan and bake. Wash and hull strawberries. Slice into a bowl and stir in sugar. Use a potato masher and partially mash berries. Pour strawberries and juice over the top of cooled cake. Top each serving with a dollop of Cool Whip™.

# May 7

## BEEFY ZUCCHINI CASSEROLE

*Prep. Time: 20 minutes / Cook Time: 1 hour*

1 sliced zucchini
1 large onion, diced
1 large tomato, diced
2 cups cooked rice
2 lbs. lean ground beef, cooked and crumbled
1 teaspoon salt
1 can cream of mushroom soup

Place a layer of zucchini in the bottom of pan or large skillet. Place half of onion, half of tomato, 1 cup cooked rice and half of ground beef over zucchini. Pour half of the soup over the top. Make layers again, starting with zucchini. Cook on top of stove on low to medium heat for 1 hour, stirring occasionally to prevent sticking.

## RAISIN CAKE

*Prep. Time: 20 minutes / Cook Time: 50 minutes to 1 hour*

2 cups water
½ cup butter
½ cup unsweetened applesauce
1 (15 oz.) pkg. raisins
3 cups sugar
2 teaspoons baking soda
¼ cup warm water
2 eggs, beaten
4 ½ cups flour
1 teaspoon ground cloves
1 teaspoon ground allspice
1 teaspoon ground cinnamon
½ teaspoon baking powder

Bring 2 cups water to a boil in large saucepan. Stir in butter and raisins, boil uncovered about 5 minutes. Remove from heat and cool until lukewarm. Stir in sugar and applesauce. Dissolve baking soda in ¼ cup cold water, add to raisins.

Stir in eggs. Combine flour, spices and baking powder; gradually add to raisin mixture, stirring after each addition. Spoon batter into a 10" Bundt pan coated with Vegetable Spray. Bake at 375 degrees for 50 minutes to 1 hour or until knife inserted in center comes out clean. Cool in pan for 10 minutes then remove cake from pan.

# May 8

*Coca-Cola was first introduced to the public on this date in 1886. It was concocted by John Pemberton, an Atlanta, Georgia pharmacist.*

## BAKED COCA-COLA™ PORK CHOPS

*Prep. Time: 5 minutes / Cook Time: 45 minutes*

6-8 pork chops, trimmed of fat
1 (12 oz.) can of Coca-Cola™
1 cup ketchup
4 tablespoons Worcestershire sauce
½ teaspoon salt
pepper

In a mixing bowl, combine Coca-Cola™, ketchup, Worcestershire sauce, salt and pepper. Dip each pork chop in mixture, coating both sides. Lay in a single layer on a baking pan. Pour Coca mixture over each chop. Cover pan with foil and bake at 350° for 45 minutes.

## JEWEL RICE

*Prep. Time: 10 minutes / Cook Time: 20 minutes*

¾ cup chopped onion
4 tablespoons butter
2 cups instant rice, uncooked
2 chicken bouillon cubes
1 teaspoon salt
½ teaspoon pepper
½ teaspoon dried thyme
½ teaspoon dried parsley flakes

½ teaspoon dried chives
½ teaspoon dried sweet basil
1 10-oz. pkg. frozen peas, thawed, drained
1½ cups orange sections

Sauté onion in skillet until tender. Add the rice, cooking until golden. Stir in the next four ingredients and 2 cups water. Simmer, covered, for about 15 minutes. Add peas. Cook 5 minutes longer or until rice is tender and water is absorbed. Add orange sections and heat through. Serve immediately.

# May 9

## CHEDDAR CHICKEN AND PASTA BAKE

*Prep. Time: 15 minutes / Cook Time: 30 minutes*

Italian-breaded chicken fingers, enough for each person
1 lb. spaghetti
2 jars traditional spaghetti sauce
2 cups shredded cheddar cheese
1 teaspoon salt
1 teaspoon butter
Parmesan cheese (optional)

Place chicken pieces in a shallow baking dish and bake at 400° for 10 minutes. While chicken is cooking, put a large pan of water on to boil. Add salt to water. When water boils, add spaghetti pasta and butter. Remove chicken from oven and remove from baking dish. When pasta is tender, drain off all water and rinse in cold water to stop cooking. Return pasta to pan. Pour in the jars of prepared spaghetti sauces and stir well. Transfer pasta to baking dish. Top pasta with 1 cup shredded cheddar cheese. Lay chicken on top of cheese. Top chicken layer with remaining cheese. Bake at 400° for 15 minutes. Use Parmesan cheese as desired.

Serve with tossed salad and garlic bread.

# OREO™ COOKIE PIE

*Prep. Time: 10 minutes*

1 can crushed Oreo™ cookies (or 2½ cups crushed cookies if you want to do them yourself)
1 (8 oz.) pkg. cream cheese
1 large tub Fat Free Cool Whip™
¼ cup sugar
1 teaspoon vanilla

Spread cookie crumbs in the bottom of a casserole dish, reserving ½ cup. In separate bowl, combine cream cheese with sugar and vanilla. Beat on low with an electric mixer until well mixed. Add Cool Whip™ and continue beating with mixer until smooth. Spread creme layer on top of cookie crumbs. Top with remaining ½ cup cookie crumbs. Refrigerate for at least 30 minutes before serving.

# May 10

# BAKED CORNISH GAME HENS

*Prep. Time: 15 minutes Bake Time: 1 hour*

6 Cornish Game Hens, thawed
3 cups uncooked instant rice
1 large or 2 small yellow onions, finely chopped
2 stalks celery, finely chopped
½ cup butter, melted
1 cup chicken stock
1 tablespoon seasoned salt
2 teaspoons pepper
½ cup orange juice
½ cup currant jelly
1 cup raisins
water

Heat oven to 350°. Prepare instant rice according to package directions. In separate skillet, sauté celery, onions and raisins in melted butter. Add half the salt, half the pepper, and chicken stock. Stir well to blend seasonings. Scoop out 3 cups cooked rice and add to raisin mixture, stir well.

Using a spoon, stuff the insides of each Cornish hen with rice and raisins mixture. Rub the outer sides of the hens with softened butter and place in a single layer on a foil wrapped baking pan. Sprinkle remaining salt and pepper on hens. Bake, covered, for 45 minutes. Combine orange juice and currant jelly in saucepan and stir until melted. Brush hens with glaze. Combine remaining rice with remaining raisin mixture and spread over and around the hens. Return pan to oven and bake for an additional 15 minutes uncovered. Serve immediately.

# COMPLIMENTARY CARROTS

*Prep. Time: 20 minutes / Cook Time: 45 minutes*

6-8 carrots, peeled and sliced thin
1 cup golden raisins
½ cup honey
½ cup light brown sugar
½ cup butter, melted
¼ teaspoon ground ginger
¼ teaspoon cinnamon

In a medium saucepan, cover carrots with water. Bring to a boil and cook for about 10 minutes. Drain off water. In a separate bowl, combine raisins, honey, brown sugar, spices and melted butter. Mix well. Pour mixture over carrots and mix well. Turn carrots out into a lightly greased casserole dish. Bake at 400° for 30 minutes or until carrots are cooked.

# May 11

## POPCORN SHRIMP

*Prep. Time: 5 minutes / Cook Time: 10 minutes*

1-2 lbs. breaded popcorn shrimp
1 jar prepared cocktail sauce
3 tablespoons olive oil

Normally, shrimp is deep-fat fried. If you'd like to skip the added fat-calories, try oven-frying the shrimp instead. Simply coat a baking sheet with the olive oil. Preheat oven to 450°. Layer shrimp in a single layer and bake for 5 minutes. Using a spatula, flip over shrimp and bake for 5 minutes longer. Serve with cocktail Sauce.

## SEASONED BAKED POTATOES

*Prep. Time: 15 minutes / Cook Time: 1 hour*

6-8 medium baking potatoes, scrubbed clean
½ cup olive oil
1 teaspoon dill weed
1 teaspoon dried chives
1 teaspoon salt
¼ teaspoon pepper
½ teaspoon garlic powder

After scrubbing potatoes, pat dry. In a small bowl, combine olive oil with spices and mix well. Using a sharp knife, make X cuts (3 to 4, more if room allows) along the sides of the potatoes, cutting all the way through potato. Lay potatoes on counter and do the same again, this time cutting from the top into the bottom with two crossing slits. Make at least 3 X slits on the top to the bottom. Roll each potato in olive oil mixture. Drizzle seasoned oil into the potato slits. Wrap each potato in aluminum foil, making sure to completely wrap the potato. Bake at 400° for about 1 hour or until potatoes are soft when squeezed.

Serve with fresh vegetables and your choice of dip(s).

# May 12

## BEEF BBQ CUBES

*Prep. Time: 20 minutes / Cook Time: 2 hours*

1-2 lbs. round steak, trimmed of fat and cut into cubes
3 tablespoons brown sugar
2 teaspoons salt
3 tablespoons Worcestershire sauce
1 tablespoon vinegar
¼ teaspoon dill weed
¼ teaspoon dried chives
¼ teaspoon dried parsley flakes
¼ teaspoon dried sweet basil
¼ teaspoon dry mustard
1 cup ketchup
1 cup water
1 tablespoon grape jelly
2 tablespoons cornstarch dissolved in ½ cup cold water

The secret to this recipe is cooking the meat slowly for a long time. Preheat oven to 400°. In mixing bowl, combine all ingredients except for the meat. Stir well. Add meat cubes. Pour meat and sauce into a baking dish. Cover with foil, reduce heat to 325° and bake for 2 hours.

## STUFFED MUSHROOMS

*Prep. Time: 30 minutes / Cook Time: 5 minutes*

24 (or more) large mushrooms
1½ cup crushed Ritz™ crackers
1 stalk celery, chopped finely
1 medium yellow onion, chopped finely
1 tablespoon butter
1 teaspoon dry mustard
¼ teaspoon soy sauce
¼ teaspoon salt
½ teaspoon oregano

2 tablespoons skim milk

olive oil flavored non-stick vegetable spray

Wash mushrooms and remove stems from caps. Set caps aside to dry. Toss mushroom stems in blender and add the chopped onion. Blend on GRATE setting for 10 seconds on, 10 seconds off, until both are finely minced. In skillet, melt butter. Add celery and minced onion and mushrooms. Cook over medium heat until onion is transparent. Stir frequently. When vegetables are tender, add dry mustard, soy sauce, salt, oregano and milk. Stir until well mixed. Add cracker crumbs and mix well.

Place mushroom caps (cavity side down) on a baking sheet that has been sprayed with olive oil non-stick vegetable spray. Spray the tops of mushroom caps with olive oil vegetable spray. Set under broiler for 2 minutes. Remove and invert caps. Spray inside caps with olive oil vegetable spray. Stuff each cap with the mixture in the skillet, heaping a spoonful in each mushroom. Set pan back under broiler and broil for 3 minutes. Serve immediately.

---

### BREAK TIME

The kitchen isn't only for cooking! With Mother's Day in the air, why not pamper yourself with items from the kitchen. Try this fantastic facial for quick and easy relaxation. Pour four cups of boiling water into a large bowl, add a quarter cup of dried herbs or rose petals. Drape a towel over your head and the bowl and steam your face for 5 to 10 minutes. Next, combine one cup cornmeal and ¼ cup honey in a small bowl and stir into paste. Gently smooth onto face, avoiding eye area and leave on for 3 to 5 minutes. Rinse and pat dry. Follow with a moisturizer.

---

# May 13

## TOASTED HAM & CHEESE SANDWICHES

*Prep. Time: 10 minutes / Cook Time: about 15 minutes*

12 slices bread (enough for two slices per sandwich, 1 sandwich per person)

light butter spread

vegetable Spray

12 slices either fat free or low fat American cheese slices

36 slices deli-shaved ham

12 slices either fat free or low fat Mozzarella cheese slices (may substitute for Swiss, if desired)

Spread a thin coating of butter on every slice of bread. Spray griddle with the non-stick vegetable spray. Lay bread on griddle, buttered side down. On each slice of bread, lay the slice of American cheese, 3 slices of deli-shaved ham and a slice of Mozzarella (or Swiss) cheese. Top with another slice of bread, buttered side out. Cook over medium heat for about 5 minutes. Using a spatula, flip sandwiches over and cook for about 5-6 minutes longer. Sandwiches are done when cheese is melted and the outer sides of the bread are lightly toasted.

Serve with Tomato Soup and celery sticks.

## LEMON SURPRISE CAKE

*Prep. Time: 10 minutes / Cook Time: 45 to 50 minutes*

1 ¼ cups flour

1 ½ cups sugar

3 teaspoons baking powder

1 teaspoon salt

½ cup butter-flavored shortening, softened

1 cup skim milk

1 teaspoon vanilla

2 tablespoons concentrated lemon juice

3 eggs

## KID BREAK!

If a Mom can take a break for a facial in the kitchen, why not let kids take a break and do a science experiment? In the book *Getting to Know Kids in Your Life* by Jeanne McSweeney and Charles Leocha they suggest making a volcano with baking soda and vinegar. They write, When vinegar and baking soda are mixed, foam is created. Try pouring some vinegar on baking soda in a coffee mug to test the reaction. Use your imagination to create a volcano.

Sift together flour, sugar, baking powder and salt. Add shortening, milk and vanilla and beat with an electric mixer until well blended. Add eggs and lemon juice, beat for three full minutes on high speed. Grease and flour a 9x13 cake pan. Pour batter in pan and bake at 350° for 45 to 50 minutes or until a knife inserted in the middle comes out clean.

## LEMON SURPRISE FROSTING

*Prep. Time: 20 minutes*

1 ½ cups sugar
⅓ cup cornstarch
1 ½ cups cold water
1 egg
2 cups Fat Free Cool Whip™
¼ cup concentrated lemon juice
1 tablespoon grated lemon rind (zest)
4 drops yellow food coloring

In a small saucepan, mix together water and cornstarch. When cornstarch is dissolved, add sugar, lemon juice and slightly beaten egg. Cook over medium heat, stirring constantly until mixture thickens and comes to a boil. Add food coloring and stir well. Remove from heat and let cool. When lemon mixture is cool, fold in the Cool Whip™. Spread over cooled cake and sprinkle with lemon zest.

# May 14

*Mother's Day falls on different dates, but always on the second Sunday in the month of May. At the very first Mother's Day observance, held in 1907, Anna Jarvis of Philadelphia, Pennsylvania asked her church to hold a special service on the anniversary of her mother's death. Mother's Day has been observed every year since. See what a difference just one person can make in history! Here's a nice dinner for Mother's Day—made even better when someone else cooks it for you!*

## GRILLED MARINATED RANCH CHICKEN

*Prep. Time: 2 hours / Cook Time: 8-15 minutes*

6 boneless, skinless chicken breasts
1 bottle fat-free Ranch salad dressing
salt and pepper

Pour Ranch dressing over thawed chicken breasts and let marinate for at least 2 hours in the refrigerator. Heat grill until hot. Place chicken breasts on grill and lightly salt and pepper. Let cook for 3-4 minutes, then turn. Brush on more Ranch dressing and lightly salt and pepper each piece of chicken. Let chicken cook for another 3-4 minutes. Turn again, and test for doneness. If more cooking time is needed, then continue cooking until done. It is not necessary to baste chicken on each side more than once in the cooking process.

## STUFFED TOMATO SALADS

*Prep. Time: 15 minutes*

6 large meaty tomatoes
3 cups cottage cheese
6 lettuce leaves
6 green onions
18 spinach leaves

Cut the core out of the tomatoes and discard. Remove the inside flesh of the tomatoes, leaving it as a bowl. Diagonally cut wedges around the top of the tomatoes. Chop up the tomato flesh and seeds and combine with the cottage cheese. Fill each tomato cavity with a half cup of the cottage cheese and tomato mixture. Set tomatoes on lettuce leaves and garnish with three leaves of spinach set around the base. Chop up the green onions, including the green tops, and sprinkle on the cottage cheese fillings. Refrigerate until ready to serve.

# CARAMEL & NOUGAT CAKE

*Prep. Time: 25 minutes / Cook Time: 30 to 40 minutes*

2 sticks butter

2 cups sugar

4 eggs

2½ cups flour

½ teaspoon baking soda

1 cup buttermilk

½ cup chopped nuts

3 Milky Way™ candy bars

Break up the candy bars and put the pieces in a saucepan with 1 stick butter. Melt over low heat, stirring often. In a separate bowl, cream together other stick of butter and sugar. Add eggs and mix well. Stir in flour, baking soda and buttermilk. When candy and butter are melted, pour the candy in to the cake batter. Add nuts and mix well. Pour into a greased and floured 9x13 cake pan. Bake at 350° for 30 to 40 minutes or until a knife inserted in the center comes out clean. Frost cake with prepared chocolate icing if desired.

# May 15

## EGGS FOR DINNER CASSEROLE

*Prep. Time: 15 minutes / Cook Time: 40 minutes*

8 eggs, beaten

1 cup skim milk

1 teaspoon salt

½ teaspoon pepper

1½ cups diced Canadian bacon

2 tablespoons chives

1 tablespoon minced onion

2 cups grated Cheddar cheese

1 tablespoon butter

3 cups grated potatoes or thawed (uncooked) hashbrowns

Melt butter in skillet and sauté minced onion and chives. Stir in Canadian bacon and cook for about 5 minutes. In a bowl, combine eggs with milk, salt, pepper, potatoes and 1 cup cheese. Add the Canadian bacon mixture and stir well. Pour into a 13x9 baking dish and bake for 30 minutes. Sprinkle the remaining cup of cheese over the top and bake for 10 minutes longer or until casserole has cooked through and is firm. Cut into squares and serve with toasted English muffins.

# TURTLE CAKE

*Prep. Time: 25 minutes / Cook Time: 25 minutes*

1 pkg. German chocolate cake mix

3 eggs

¼ cup oil

½ cup water

14 oz. bag caramels

½ cup butter

½ cup chopped pecans

1 can (7 oz.) Eagle™ Brand Sweetened Condensed Milk

1 cup semi-sweet chocolate chips

In a large mixing bowl, combine cake mix with eggs, oil and water. Beat on low speed with an electric mixer until well mixed, then beat on high speed for a full two minutes. Pour half of batter into a greased and floured 13x9 cake pan. Bake at 350° for 15 minutes. While cake is baking, combine remaining ingredients (but not the reserved batter) in the top of a double-boiler and melt. Cool mixture slightly and pour over the baked portion of cake, reserving 1 cup. Pour the remaining batter over caramel layer. Drizzle with remaining caramel mixture. Bake for 25 minutes at 350° or until cake tests done.

# May 16

## HAMBURGER, MACARONI AND TOMATOES

*Prep. Time: 25 minutes / Cook Time: 15 minutes*

1 lb. lean ground beef
2 quarts stewed tomatoes
4 cups elbow macaroni
2 teaspoons salt
½ teaspoon pepper
water

Crumble the ground beef into a pot of water. Bring the meat to a boil and cook until done. In a separate pan of water, prepare the elbow macaroni according to package directions. Drain both the meat and pasta. Rinse pasta in cold water. In either pan, add the other. Blend the tomatoes in a blender on the puree setting for about 10-15 seconds and then pour the tomatoes in the pan with the meat and pasta. Add salt and pepper. Stir well and heat through.

We enjoy this quick and easy meal with slices of bread and butter.

## CITRUS CAKE

*Prep. Time: 15 minutes / Cook Time: 30-40 minutes*

½ cup butter, softened
1 cup sugar
2 eggs
⅔ cup buttermilk
2 cups flour
2 teaspoons baking powder
½ teaspoon baking soda
½ cup orange juice
zest from one orange (grate rind very fine)
½ cup sugar

Cream together butter and sugar, then add eggs and buttermilk. Sift together flour, baking powder and baking soda. Add floured mixture to the creamed mixture and blend well. Fold in orange zest. Spread batter into a greased and floured 9x13 cake pan and bake at 350° for 30 to 40 minutes. Combine orange juice with the half cup of sugar and stir until sugar is dissolved. As soon as the cake comes out of the oven, pour the orange juice over the top of the cake and let it soak in. Serve with ice cream or Cool Whip™.

# May 17

## MARINATED ITALIAN CHICKEN BREASTS

*Prep. Time: less than 5 minutes / Cook Time: 35 minutes, more or less*

6 skinless, boneless chicken breast filets
1 bottle fat free Italian salad dressing

Shake dressing well and pour over chicken breasts. Let chicken marinate for at least an hour before cooking. (Refrigerate while marinating.) When you're ready to cook them, place chicken breasts in a shallow baking dish. Bake at 400°. Baste chicken breasts every 5 minutes for 20 minutes and then turn them over. Baste again and bake for 15 minutes longer or until chicken is cooked through.

# SEASONED RICE

*Prep. Time: 5 minutes / Cook Time: 15 minutes*

3 cups instant rice
1 can cream of chicken soup
1 can cream of celery soup
1 soup can full of water
1 teaspoon salt
¼ teaspoon pepper

In a medium saucepan (with a tight fitting lid) mix soups with water. When soups are hot, stir in salt and pepper. Heat until almost boiling and then add the rice. Stir well to coat all of the rice with the soup mixture. Cover pan with a tight-fitting lid and remove from heat. Let set for 5-7 minutes; stir and serve.

# STEAMED SUMMER SQUASH (YELLOW SQUASH)

*Prep. Time: 5 minutes / Cook Time: 15 minutes*

1-2 summer squashes, washed and sliced thin
1 tablespoon butter
½ teaspoon salt
¼ teaspoon pepper
1 cup water

In small saucepan, melt butter. Add water, salt and pepper. Stir well then add sliced yellow squash. Cover with lid and cook over medium heat until squash is tender.

## FOOD FOR THOUGHT:

- You can always get someone to love you, even if you have to do it yourself.
- Never judge the appearance of a dumb blond by her hair color. She may actually be a very smart brunette!
- When ignorance leads to woe, let bluffing be thy choice!
- When a job is once begun, never leave it till it's done
- Be the labor great or small, do it well or not at all.
- Success is the journey—not the destination.

# May 18

## GRILLED SHISKABOBS

*Prep. Time: 20 minutes / Cook Time: 15 minutes*

3-4 cans small white potatoes, left whole
1½ - 2 lbs. beef round steak, cut into cubes
fresh mushrooms, left whole
fresh green peppers, cut into wedges
fresh yellow or red onions, cut into wedges
fresh red or yellow tomatoes, cut into wedges
fat-free Italian salad dressing

On each skewer, place a piece of meat and then a wedge of onion, a potato, a wedge of green pepper, a mushroom and a wedge of tomato. Repeat sequence for as long as the skewer space allows. Place skewers on a hot grill, baste with Italian salad dressing and let cook for 3-5 minutes. Turn skewers and baste with Italian salad dressing. Cook for 3-5 minutes longer. Turn skewers for a third time and baste. Cook for 3-5 minutes or until fresh vegetables are cooked to the tender crisp stage.

# May 19

## HOMEMADE CORN DOGS

*Prep. Time: 10-12 minutes / Cook Time: 3-5 minutes*

1 cup flour
1½ cups skim milk
2 tablespoons oil
1 cup corn meal
2 eggs
1 teaspoon salt
3 pkgs. hot dogs
4 cups oil

In a large bowl, combine all ingredients except oil and hot dogs to make the batter. Dip hot dogs, one at a time, into the batter and then drop into a frying pan of hot oil. Cook for 3 to 5 minutes or until batter turns firm and is dark brown. Use a brown paper sack to drain corn dogs on before serving. Using paper towels will make the corn dogs mushy. Let set about 5 minutes before serving.

## GERMAN POTATO SALAD

*Prep. Time: 45 minutes*

8 medium potatoes
½ lb. bacon
1 medium onion, chopped finely
4 hard boiled eggs, diced
2 tablespoons celery seed
2 tablespoons flour
¾ cup water
4 tablespoons sugar
½ cup vinegar
½ teaspoon salt
pepper to taste

Boil potatoes until tender. Peel off skins and cube into bite-sized pieces. Fry bacon until crisp. Pour off all but ¹/₃ cup bacon grease. Cook onion in bacon grease until it is transparent. Stir in flour and water. Add celery seed, sugar, vinegar, salt and pepper. Cook until slightly thickened, then pour over the potatoes and eggs. Crumble bacon over potatoes and mix well, serving warm.

## BAKED BEANS

*Prep. Time: 10 minutes / Cook Time: 20 minutes*

2 large cans Pork 'n' Beans
1 onion, finely chopped
½ cup ketchup
¾ cup brown sugar
1 tablespoon prepared mustard
1 tablespoon Worcestershire Sauce

Combine all ingredients in a casserole dish and bake until heated through, about 20 minutes. Serve warm or cold.

# May 20

## FRIED CATFISH NUGGETS

*Prep. Time: 10 minutes / Cook Time: 15 minutes*

2 lbs. fresh catfish nuggets (ask for this at your grocer's meat dept.)
2 cups skim milk
5 eggs
¼ cup lemon juice
2 cups flour
2 cups cracker meal
½ cup yellow corn meal
4 cups oil

In one bowl, mix together milk, eggs and lemon juice. Make sure eggs are well beaten. In another bowl, combine the flour, cracker meal and corn meal, mixing thoroughly. Dip catfish nuggets in milk mixture and then roll in flour/meal mixture. Drop into hot oil and deep fry until done, about 3 to 5 minutes.

# HUSHPUPPIES

*Prep. Time: 10 minutes / Cook Time: About 2 minutes each*

1 cup buttermilk
2 eggs, beaten
1 medium onion, finely chopped
¼ cup water
1 ¾ cups yellow cornmeal
1 cup flour
1 tablespoon sugar
2 teaspoons baking powder
1 teaspoon salt
½ teaspoon baking soda

In bowl, beat eggs then add buttermilk. Add chopped onions and water. Set aside. In another bowl, combine all the remaining ingredients, mixing well. Add egg/milk mixture to the flour mixture, stirring until just moistened. Drop by tablespoon into hot oil and fry until done, about 2 minutes. (You may need to turn Hushpuppies over to cook uniformly.) Drain on brown paper or paper towels. Serve hot plain or with butter, if desired.

# May 21

## STUFFED GREEN PEPPERS

*Prep. Time: 25 minutes / Cook Time: 30 minutes*

6 large bell peppers
1 lb. lean ground beef
4 cups cooked rice
1 quart stewed tomatoes
2 teaspoons salt
½ teaspoon pepper
6 slices American cheese

Core peppers and discard seeds. Rinse out and place in a large pan of hot water. Bring water to a boil and then remove from heat. Prepare rice according to package directions. Blend tomatoes in the blender on the puree setting for about 10 seconds. Pour tomatoes in with the rice. In a skillet, sprinkle 1 teaspoon salt over crumbled ground beef and brown

until cooked through. Drain meat on paper towel and then add to the rice. Add remaining teaspoon salt and the pepper to the rice mixture. Stir well. Remove peppers from water and drain. Place peppers, cavity side up, in a deep casserole dish or baking pan. Spoon rice mixture into pepper cavities. If you have remaining rice and meat, just layer it around the bell peppers. Bake at 350° for 20 minutes. Top each pepper with a slice of American cheese and let bake until cheese melts. Serve immediately.

# BLUEBERRY CHEESECAKE

*Prep. Time: 10 minutes*

1 prepared graham cracker pie crust
1 (8 oz.) pkg. cream cheese, softened
1 tub Fat-Free Cool Whip™
½ cup sugar
1 can blueberry pie filling

In a large bowl, combine cream cheese with Cool Whip™ and sugar. Beat on high with an electric mixer until smooth. Spoon filling into the graham cracker crust. Top with the blueberry pie filling. Refrigerate until ready to serve.

# May 22

## GRILLED RIBEYES

*Prep. Time: 10 minutes / Cook Time: 20 minutes*

6 Ribeye Steaks
Worcestershire Sauce
salt and pepper

On a hot grill, lay ribeyes in a single layer. Shake enough Worcestershire Sauce on each steak to coat it well. Salt and pepper according to your tastes. Cook for about 5 minutes and then turn. Repeat the process again, cooking for another 5 minutes. Turn again, and repeat the process. Check for doneness. Continue cooking until steaks are done the way you like them.

Serve with baked potatoes and a tossed salad.

# RICE CUSTARD

*Prep. Time: 20 minutes / Cook Time: 45 to 50 minutes*

5 eggs, beaten
1 cup sugar
4 cups skim milk
2 teaspoons vanilla
3 cups cooked rice
½ teaspoon ground cinnamon

Scald milk and then remove from heat. In a mixing bowl, combine eggs and sugar. Stir in scalded milk, vanilla and cinnamon. Add rice and stir well. Pour into a 2-qt. baking dish. Set casserole dish in a pan of hot water that is 1 inch deep. Bake at 350° for 45 to 50 minutes.

# May 23

## VERMICELLI DELIGHT

*Prep. Time: 20 minutes / Cook Time: 30 minutes*

1½ lbs. lean ground beef
2 onions, finely chopped
1 clove garlic, minced
1 stick butter
2 cups fresh mushrooms, sliced
1 can creamed-styled corn
2 cans tomato soup
3 soup cans water
1 (8 oz.) pkg. vermicelli (uncooked)
1 cup grated cheese of your choice
salt and pepper

In a large skillet, melt butter and sauté onion and garlic. Add crumbled ground beef and cook until beef is done. Add mushroom slices, corn and soup with water. Heat until almost boiling, then add vermicelli. Stir well. When pasta is tender, pour all ingredients into a large casserole baking dish. Bake at 350° for 30 minutes. Remove from oven and stir. Return to oven and continue baking for another 30 minutes. Right before serving, top with grated cheese.

# TOFFEE DELICIOUS

*Prep. Time: 10 minutes*

1 Sara Lee™ pound cake, slightly thawed
1 box instant butterscotch pudding mix
2 cups skim milk
3 Heath™ bars, crushed
1 (8 oz.) tub Fat-Free Cool Whip™

Slice pound cake into 1-inch thick slices and arrange in an 8x8 inch baking pan. Prepare pudding according to the package directions, using the 2 cups milk. Spread pudding over cake slices. Sprinkle Heath Bar candy on top of pudding. Top with Cool Whip and refrigerate until ready to serve.

# May 24

## PARMESAN-ROMANO CHICKEN

*I love this saying! Do good with what you have, or it will do you no good. How true!*

*Prep. Time: 15 minutes / Cook Time: 50 minutes*

6 skinless, boneless chicken breasts
1 yellow onion, finely chopped
1 can tomato soup
1 soup can water
⅛ teaspoon garlic powder
½ teaspoon dried oregano
½ teaspoon dried sweet basil
¼ cup Parmesan-Romano Cheese
1 cup mozzarella cheese

In a blender, combine tomato soup, water, onion and spices. Whiz for ten seconds on the blend setting. Arrange chicken in a single layer in a baking dish. Pour soup mixture over chicken. Sprinkle Parmesan-Romano cheese over chicken and bake at 350° for 45 minutes. Top with grated mozzarella or sliced mozzarella cheese and bake 5 minutes longer.

## BUTTERED CHEESE NOODLES

*Prep. Time: 1-2 minutes / Cook Time: 20 minutes*

1 pkg. medium-wide egg noodles
   (such as No Yolks™)
water
1 teaspoon salt
½ teaspoon pepper
½ teaspoon salt
½ cup butter, melted
¼ cup Parmesan-Romano Cheese
1 teaspoon dried chopped chives

In a large saucepan, cover noodles with water and add 1 teaspoon salt. Add a pat of butter and bring noodles to a boil. Let cook until noodles are tender. Drain off water. Add remaining butter and stir to coat evenly. In a small container or baggy, combine Parmesan-Romano Cheese, chives, ½ teaspoon salt and ½ teaspoon pepper. Mix well and sprinkle on noodles, stirring often to mix well.

## PINEAPPLE UPSIDE DOWN CAKE

*Prep. Time: 15 minutes / Cook Time: 30 minutes*

½ cup butter
2 cups brown sugar, firmly packed
1 can sliced pineapple
maraschino cherries
6 eggs, separated
1½ cups flour
1½ cups sugar
½ teaspoon salt
2 teaspoons baking powder
8 tablespoons pineapple juice, or more
2 teaspoons vanilla

In the bottom of a 9x13 cake pan, melt butter and stir in brown sugar. Arrange pineapple and cherries on top of brown sugar/butter. In small mixing bowl, whip egg whites on high speed with an electric mixer and gradually add 3 tablespoons sugar. Continue whipping on high speed until stiff peaks form. (To test for stiff peaks, stop mixer and lift out beaters. If peaks remain from the removal of beaters, then you have stiff peaks.) In separate bowl, mix dry ingredients and egg yolks. Stir in pineapple juice. This batter will be very thick, but if is too thick, add more pineapple juice one tablespoon at a time. Mix until batter is spreadable consistency. Fold in beaten egg whites and spread batter over the pineapple in the baking dish. Bake at 375° for 30 minutes or until a knife inserted in the center comes out clean. Invert cake on a platter before serving.

# May 25

## SLOPPY JOES

*Prep. Time: 15 minutes / Cook Time: 20 minutes*

1 lb. lean ground beef
1 (8 oz.) can tomato sauce
1 tablespoon Worcestershire sauce
1 green pepper, chopped finely
1 yellow onion, chopped finely
1 teaspoon salt
¼ teaspoon pepper
1 teaspoon Italian seasoning
1 teaspoon dried oregano
1 teaspoon dried sweet basil
½ teaspoon garlic powder

Brown ground beef in a skillet with onion and green pepper. Drain off all grease. Stir in tomato sauce, Worcestershire sauce and all other seasonings. Simmer over low heat for 10 minutes. Serve on either bread or buns.

Serve with potato wedges (see page 11) and fresh vegetables and dip.

# FRESH STRAWBERRY SHORTCAKE

*Prep. Time: 20 minutes*

**Complete Buttermilk Pancake Mix**
**1 quart fresh strawberries**
**2 cups sugar**
**Fat Free Cool Whip™**

Prepare 6 skillet-sized pancakes according to package directions. Hull strawberries, wash and slice into a mixing bowl. Add 2 cups sugar and stir. Use a potato masher and partially mash strawberries. Layer pancakes with crushed strawberries. Pour any remaining strawberries and juice over the top. Serve warm or cold with a big dollop of Cool Whip™.

# May 26

## UPSIDE DOWN PIZZA PIE

*Prep. Time: 20 minutes / Cook Time: 25 minutes*

**1 lb. mild bulk sausage**
**24 pepperoni slices**
**1 jar (32 oz.) traditional spaghetti sauce**
**2 cups shredded mozzarella cheese**
**2 cups shredded cheddar cheese**
**1 small onion, finely chopped (optional)**
**1 small green pepper, finely chopped (optional)**
**sliced mushrooms, (optional)**
**²/₃ cup flour**
**½ teaspoon salt**
**⅛ teaspoon garlic powder**
**½ cup skim milk**
**2 eggs**

Brown sausage and drain off all grease. Combine crumbled cooked sausage with spaghetti sauce. Pour meat sauce in the bottom of a 9x13 pan. Layer pepperoni with onion, green pepper and mushrooms. Top with 1 cup mozzarella and 1 cup cheddar cheese. In a separate bowl, mix together the flour, salt, garlic powder, milk and eggs. Beat

well. Carefully spread dough out and lay on top of the cheeses. Add on top of the dough the remaining cheeses. Bake at 350° for 25 minutes.

# May 27

## STIR-FRIED CHICKEN

*Prep. Time: 20 minutes / Cook Time: 10-15 minutes*

**5 skinless, boneless chicken breasts**
**2 stalks celery, chopped**
**1 cup fresh broccoli, chopped**
**1 small onion, finely chopped**
**1 cup sliced fresh mushrooms**
**2 tablespoons oil**
**1 cup bean sprouts, drained**
**½ cup water chestnuts, chopped**
**4-5 cups cooked rice**
**1 tablespoon soy sauce**

Cut chicken into bite-sized pieces. Heat oil in large skillet or wok. Stir fry chicken for about 5 minutes or until meat is done. Add soy sauce and all the vegetables. Stir fry for 5-10 minutes longer until vegetables are "tender-crisp". Serve over a bed of cooked rice.

## KEY LIME PIE

*Prep. Time: 25 minutes*

**1 9-inch graham cracker pie shell**
**⅓ cup sugar**
**1 envelope unflavored gelatin**
**¼ cup lime juice**
**3 egg yolks, slightly beaten**
**2 teaspoons grated lime peel (zest)**
**2 cups Cool Whip™**
**green food coloring**

In top of double boiler, combine sugar and gelatin. Add lime juice and egg yolks and cook over simmering water until thick, stirring constantly. Remove from heat, stir in lime peel and cool. In a separate bowl, add food coloring to Cool Whip™

and mix well. Fold green Cool Whip™ into gelatin lime mixture. Pour into crust and chill until firm.

# May 28

## ZUCCHINI 'N' BEEF

*Prep. Time: 25 minutes / Cook Time: 35 to 40 minutes*

1½ lbs. zucchini, cut in ¼ inch thick slices
1 lb. lean ground beef
1 medium yellow onion, finely chopped
2 cups cooked rice
2 cups small curd fat free (or 1 %) cottage cheese
2 cups grated sharp cheddar cheese
1 teaspoon oregano
½ teaspoon basil
1 can cream of mushroom soup
1 teaspoon salt
¼ teaspoon pepper

Cook zucchini in boiling water until almost done—about 5 minutes. Drain well. In skillet, brown ground beef and onion together. Drain off all grease. Add rice, salt, pepper, oregano and basil; stir well to distribute spices. In the bottom of a 9x13 pan, put a layer of zucchini slices on the bottom. Add beef mixture. Spoon cottage cheese over beef mixture. Cover with remaining zucchini slices. Spread soup over all. Sprinkle with grated cheese. Bake uncovered at 350° for 35 to 40 minutes.

## 7-UP™ BREAD

*Prep. Time: 5 minutes / Cook Time: 20-25 minutes*

3 cups self-rising flour
3 tablespoons sugar
1 (7 oz.) can 7-Up™ at room temperature

Mix ingredients together and form into a loaf. Place loaf in greased bread pan. Bake at 350° for 25 minutes.

# May 29

## PORK BURGERS

*Prep. Time: 15 minutes / Cook Time: 20-25 minutes*

1 lb. ground pork
½ lb. ground bulk sausage
1 can cream of mushroom soup
1 tablespoon Worcestershire sauce
1 teaspoon salt
¼ teaspoon pepper
2 cups crushed saltine cracker crumbs
2 teaspoons prepared mustard
2 eggs

Combine all ingredients in a large bowl. Form into patties and brown on both sides until cooked through. Serve on buns with dill pickle spears on the side.

## BAKED PEAS 'N' CELERY

*Prep. Time: 5 minutes / Cook Time: 45 minutes*

1 pkg. (20 oz.) frozen peas
1 stalk celery, diced
1 can cream of celery soup
½ cup crushed Ritz™ crackers
¼ cup butter, melted

Lightly butter casserole dish. Break up frozen peas and mix in soup and celery. Top with crushed crackers and pats of butter. Bake uncovered at 400° for 45 minutes.

## BAKED PEACH PUDDING

*Prep. Time: 20 minutes / Cook Time: 50-60 minutes*

2 cups sliced raw peaches
2 cups sugar
½ cup milk
¼ cup butter
1 teaspoon baking powder
1 cup flour
1 tablespoon cornstarch

¼ teaspoon salt

1 cup boiling water

Layer sliced peaches in a greased 9x13 cake pan. Combine ¾ cup sugar and butter and cream together. Add baking powder, milk and flour. Spread batter over peaches. Mix 1 cup sugar, cornstarch and salt together and sprinkle this mixture over the batter. Pour boiling water over all and bake at 325° for 50 to 60 minutes. Serve warm with a dip of vanilla ice cream.

# May 30

*With Memorial Day here, it's a perfect time to bring out the grill and start enjoying outdoor cooking. Tonight's dinner is perfect for the grill.*

## GRILLED BURGERS AND DOGS

*Prep. Time: 5 minutes / Cook Time: about 20 minutes*

1 lb. lean ground beef

1 teaspoon salt

½ teaspoon pepper

1 tablespoon Worcestershire sauce

2 tablespoons smoked BBQ sauce

1 pkg. hot dogs

Mix salt, pepper, Worcestershire and BBQ sauces in with ground beef and form into patties. Place on a hot grill and cook for 5 minutes. Turn over and cook for another 5 minutes. Continuing cooking and turning burgers until meat is cooked through. As soon as the burgers come off the grill, put the hot dogs on the grill. Let hot dogs cook for about 2 minutes and then roll them. Cook for 2 minutes longer. When the skins of the hot dogs start to bust, hot dogs are done. Remove them from the grill and serve hot.

## GRILLED POTATOES

4 potatoes, scrubbed clean and cubed

3 tablespoons butter

¾ cup mushrooms, diced

½ cup onion, diced

salt and pepper

Spread out aluminum foil and place cubed potatoes on foil. Add other ingredients and wrap into a log shape. Place on grill for 20-30 minutes or until potatoes are tender. If cooking for kids, divide potatoes into two sections and make one without mushrooms and onions.

## PEA SALAD

*Prep. Time: 15 minutes*

1 pkg. frozen peas, thawed

2 tablespoons minced onion

¼ cup minced celery

1 cup shredded cheddar cheese

½ cup Miracle Whip Free™

2 hard boiled eggs

¼ teaspoon salt

$\frac{1}{8}$ teaspoon pepper

Cook peas for about 10-15 minutes, then drain. Combine all ingredients and mix well. Refrigerate overnight to blend flavors. Serve chilled.

Serve with fresh apples, pears, bananas and oranges for dessert.

# May 31

## QUICK FIX BEEF & TATORS

*Prep. Time: 20 minutes / Cook Time: about 30 minutes*

1 lb. lean ground beef or turkey
1 pkg. tator tots
1 can peas, drained
1 can corn, drained
1 small onion, finely chopped
1 can cream of mushroom soup
1 can cream of celery soup
1 teaspoon salt
½ teaspoon pepper

Boil meat in a soup pan until done. Drain off all water. Combine both soups with meat and onion. Add salt and pepper and mix well. Pour into a 13x9 casserole dish. Stir in corn and peas and mix well. Lay tator tots over the top of the casserole. Bake at 350° for about 30 minutes. This may be topped with grated cheese if you desire.

## FRUIT COCKTAIL CAKE

*Prep. Time: 15 minutes / Cook Time: 40 minutes*

1½ cups flour
1 cup sugar
1 teaspoon salt
1 teaspoon baking soda
½ teaspoon ground cinnamon
2 eggs, beaten
1 No. 2 can fruit cocktail with juice
1 teaspoon vanilla
1 cup brown sugar
½ cup chopped pecans (or walnuts)

Sift together flour, salt, baking soda, and cinnamon. Stir in sugar. Add beaten eggs and fruit cocktail (with juice) and vanilla. Mix well and pour into a greased and floured 9x13 cake pan. Sprinkle the top with brown sugar and chopped nuts. Bake at 350° for 40 minutes. Let cake cool for at least 10 minutes before cutting.

# June 1

## TURKEY CHILI

*Prep. Time: 15 minutes Cook Time: 30 minutes*

1 lb. ground turkey (or beef, chicken or pork)
½ cup finely chopped green onions
2 cans (15 oz.) chili styled tomatoes
1 can red kidney beans, drained
1 cup water

Brown meat and onions together over medium heat, adding salt and pepper to taste. Drain. Put meat into a soup pan and add tomatoes, beans and water. Simmer for about 20 minutes on low to let the flavors blend.

## FROZEN CHOCOLATE YOGURT OVER M & M BARS

*Prep. Time: 10 minutes Cooking Time: Approximately 10 minutes*

1 cup brown sugar
½ cup sugar
1 cup butter-flavored shortening
2¼ cups flour
2 eggs
1 teaspoon baking soda
1 teaspoon salt
2 teaspoons vanilla
2 teaspoons water
1½ cups M&M's™

Cream together shortening with sugars. Add eggs and mix well. Stir in water and vanilla. Sift dry ingredients together in another bowl and gradually add the dried mixture to the first, beating well after each addition. Stir batter until smooth. Pour batter into a 9x13 greased pan. Spread M&M's™ over the top and lightly push them down into the batter. Bake at 375° for 10 minutes or until the entire pan of batter is lightly browned. Remove from oven and let cool for 10 minutes before cutting. Cut into bars and serve with a scoop of chocolate frozen yogurt.

# June 2

## C SALAD WITH TOMATOES AND HERBS

*Prep. Time: 20 minutes Cook Time: about 20 minutes*

4 grilled ears of corn with kernels cut off cob
(about 2¾ cups)
6 grilled chicken breasts halves, cut in 1-inch-
long by ¼-inch-wide strips
3 to 4 large red tomatoes, chopped
2 cucumbers, peeled and sliced in ½-inch
pieces
½ cup loosely packed fresh basil, coarsely
chopped
1 tablespoon chopped chives
¼ teaspoon garlic powder
¼ cup olive oil
¼ cup lime juice
2 teaspoons salt

After grilling corn and chicken, combine all
ingredients in a large bowl and mix well to evenly
coat meat and vegetables. Serve as the main
entree with some fresh papaya for dessert.

# June 3

## EASY CHEESE BROCCOLI QUICHE

*Prep. Time: 15 minutes Cooking Time: about 40-45 minutes*

1 cup finely chopped broccoli (fresh or frozen,
doesn't matter)
1 lb. ground sausage
1 cup grated cheddar cheese
12 eggs
½ cup skim milk
1 teaspoon salt
¼ teaspoon coarse pepper

Put broccoli in the blender and chop until very fine.
Brown sausage and cook until done; drain. In casserole dish, mix eggs with milk, salt and pepper. Stir in
crumbled meat, grated cheese and broccoli. Bake at
350° for 40 to 45 minutes. The eggs will be firm and
the top will be a light golden brown. Slice and serve
with warm bagels and creamed cheese.

## RUM APPLES

*Prep. Time: 15 minutes Cooking Time: 20 minutes*

2 cups water
1 cup sugar
¼ teaspoon ground nutmeg
2 tablespoons dark rum or ½ teaspoon each of
rum and vanilla extract
1 teaspoon cinnamon
6 to 8 apples, peeled, quartered and cored
1 cup raisins (optional)

Bring water and spices to a boil in a large deep
skillet. Boil for about 5 minutes, stirring occasionally
until some of it has evaporated. Add rum and apples.
Cover and simmer over low heat 10 to 15 minutes,
gently stirring 2 or 3 times, until apples are tender.
Remove from heat and stir in raisins. Serve warm or
cold. This goes great with a scoop of vanilla frozen
yogurt.

# June 4

## DRIED BEEF GRAVY OVER TOAST

*Prep Time 15-20 minutes. Cook Time: 15-20 minutes.*

2-3 oz. dried beef
3 tablespoons oil
1½ tablespoon flour
½ teaspoon salt, more to taste
¼ teaspoon pepper, more to taste
3 cups milk
toasted bread

Heat oil in large skillet. Add flour and stir to form a paste. Immediately stir in milk. Tear beef into small pieces and add to skillet. Add salt and pepper. Stir frequently until thickened. Serve over toasted bread. This is good with Fresh Broccoli and Tomato Salad (see page 24).

# June 5

## CHEESEBURGER BISCUITS

*Prep. Time: 15-20 minutes . Cook Time: 20-25 minutes*

2 lbs. lean ground beef
1 medium onion, finely chopped
1 pkg. chili seasoning mix
1 (8 oz.) can tomato sauce
6 slices American cheese
2 canisters refrigerated prepared biscuits (10 to a can)

Brown meat and onion in a skillet, stirring often to crumble. When meat is brown and onion is transparent, drain off all grease. Add seasoning mix and tomato sauce. Mix well and let simmer for about five minutes. Meanwhile, open one canister of biscuits and press them flat into a 9x13 pan or baking dish. Spoon the meat mixture over the biscuit crust and top with American cheese slices. Open other canister of biscuits and flatten those, laying biscuits over the top of the cheese and meat. Bake at 400° for 20-25 minutes or until the biscuits are golden brown.

## DOMINO BROWNIES

*Prep. Time: 20 minutes Cook Time: 45 minutes*

2½ cups flour
2¾ cups sugar
1 stick butter
½ cup babyfood plums
½ cup cocoa
1 teaspoon vanilla
5 eggs
white chocolate chips

Cream the butter and cocoa together. Beat in eggs, plums and vanilla and gradually add sugar until batter is the consistency of a sponge cake. Mix in alternately the flour and the butter and cocoa. Pour into a greased pan and bake for 40-45 minutes at 300°. Remove brownies from oven and let cool for about 15 minutes. Carefully, using a hot knife, cut the brownies into rectangles. Lightly score each rectangle down the middle. Invert the white chocolate chips and push them down in the brownies making each brownie look like a domino. Serve when completely cooled.

## Kitchen Tips

• A great time-saver when preparing meals is to pre-cook ground beef, sausage and/or chicken for other meals. Refrigerate or freeze the meat (and stock) for use later in the week. A quick zap in the microwave will have it ready for use in no time.

• If you find yourself short on time for yourself, try making your time serve double-duty. Listen to a book on audio cassette while chopping vegetables or preparing the evening meal. Check with your local library or nearest bookstore for a nice range of books on cassette. This way, you can keep up with the bestseller list or enjoy the classics.

• One of the best ways to stay organized in the kitchen is to keep a running list of spices and ingredients that you use up. That way, you always know what items you need to purchase when you make your next trip to the grocery store. For maximum freshness, store opened cans in the refrigerator and gravy mixes and spice packets in the freezer. Dried spices in jars will keep best if stored in the refrigerator. They are fine stored at room temperature in a kitchen cabinet, but their shelf-life reduces to about three months of potency.

• When you make out your daily To Do list, check it over twice. Be realistic. Did you know that on an average people tend to write down at least 30% more than what they can actually accomplish?

# June 6

## ISLAND PORK DELIGHT

*Prep. Time: 15-20 minutes Cook Time: about 1 hour or longer*

1½ - 2 lbs. lean pork, cut into 1-inch cubes
1 egg, slightly beaten
2 tablespoons flour
½ teaspoon salt
⅛ teaspoon pepper
2 green peppers, cut into ½-inch strips
10 mushrooms, sliced
2 tablespoons cornstarch
¼ cup apple cider vinegar
3 tablespoons soy sauce
2 cups chow mein noodles
¼ cup sugar
1 cup pineapple chunks, reserve juice
pineapple juice and water to equal ½ cup water
oil

Combine egg, flour, salt and pepper in a medium bowl. Dip meat cubes into batter and coat well. Drop cubes in hot oil to cook. Reduce heat to low, cover skillet and let pork cubes cook for about 30 minutes. Remove cubes from oil and drain on brown paper. Pour off all liquid. Place the green peppers and mushrooms in skillet and lightly sauté, then add water to cover vegetables and boil for 10 minutes. Drain off water and add pineapple chunks. Combine all in deep skillet: cooked pork cubes, green peppers, mushrooms and pineapple. In a separate container, mix together soy sauce, cornstarch, sugar, vinegar and ½ cup pineapple juice. Pour mixture over meat and vegetable mixture, stirring well. Cook over medium low heat until the broth becomes thick and clear. Serve over the chow mein noodles.

# COOKIES OF THE MONTH

## PECAN PIE BARS

1 box yellow cake mix
4 eggs
½ cup butter, melted
1 cup brown sugar, firmly packed
1½ cup dark corn syrup
1 teaspoon vanilla
1 cup chopped pecans

Combine ⅓ of the cake mix with 1 egg and butter in bowl; mix well. Press into a greased 9x13 cake pan. Bake at 350° for 15 minutes. Combine remaining cake mix, 3 eggs, brown sugar, corn syrup and vanilla in bowl. Beat for two minutes with electric mixer at medium speed. Pour over crust. Sprinkle with pecans. Bake for 30-35 minutes longer or until light brown. Cool and then cut into bars.

## PINEAPPLE COOKIES

1 cup shortening
1 cup brown sugar, firmly packed
1 cup sugar
4 cups flour
2 teaspoons baking powder
½ teaspoon baking soda
½ teaspoon salt
2 eggs
1 cup crushed pineapple
1 teaspoon vanilla
1 cup chopped nuts, if desired

Cream shortening and sugars together in bowl. Sift dry ingredients together, set aside. Add 1 egg, half the pineapple and half the dry ingredients; beating well after each addition. Repeat and add all remaining ingredients. Drop by teaspoons onto greased cookie sheet. Bake at 400° for 10 minutes or until lightly browned.

## SHAPED SCOTCH SHORTBREAD

1 cup sugar
2 cups butter
4 cups flour

Cream sugar into butter. Knead in flour gradually until smooth. Roll out to ½ inch thick. Cut into desired shapes. Sprinkle lightly with granulated sugar. Bake at 325° for 15 to 20 minutes.

# June 7

## SUMMER SEA SALAD

*Prep. Time: 20 minutes*

1 (7 oz.) pkg. macaroni—cook, drain and rinse
   in cold water
½ cup Miracle Whip Free™
½ cup plain yogurt
½ teaspoon celery seed
½ teaspoon onion salt
1 (6½ oz.) can tuna, drained
1 can peas, drained
1 cup shredded cheddar cheese
2 tablespoons minced green pepper
2 boiled eggs, diced

Mix everything together in a large bowl and chill to blend flavors. Serve over a bed of lettuce.

## FLUFFY PINEAPPLE WHIP

*Prep. Time: 5 minutes*

1 can pineapple chunks, drain and reserve juice
1 (13 ½ oz.) pkg. Fat Free Cool Whip™
1 small box instant vanilla pudding
½ cup pineapple juice

Combine pudding mix with pineapple juice and mix well. Add pineapple chunks and fold in Cool Whip™. Refrigerate until ready to serve.

# June 8

## SWEET 'N' SAUCY CHICKEN

*Prep. Time: 15 minutes Cook Time: 1 hour*

1 whole chicken cut up and skinned
1 bottle Kraft Fat Free Russian™ salad dressing
1 small jar apricot preserves
1 tablespoon olive oil

Spread oil over the surface of a baking pan. Arrange chicken in a single layer in pan. Pour entire bottle of salad dressing over chicken, equally coating each piece. Spread one teaspoon apricot preserves over each piece. Bake at 350º for an hour or until chicken is done and comes away from the bone easily. Baste with the Russian dressing every 15 minutes. Reapply the apricot preserves during the final 15 minutes of baking time.

## STUFFED SUMMER SQUASH

*Prep. Time: 15 minutes Cook Time: 25-30 minutes*

6 small summer squashes
6 tablespoons butter
⅔ cup honey
⅛ teaspoon salt
¼ teaspoon cinnamon

With a sharp knife, cut each squash down the middle into halves. Carefully scoop out the squash pulp. Put all ingredients in a blender and whiz blender on the BLEND setting. Fill each squash shell with pulp mixture. Place in shallow baking pan on a rack over ¼-inch of water. Bake in 350º for 25 to 30 minutes.

# June 9

## SOUTH OF THE BORDER BAKE

*Prep. Time: 15-20 minutes Cook Time: 20-25 minutes*

1 ½ lbs. lean ground beef or turkey
2 tablespoons chili powder
1 large onion, finely diced
1 packet (mild) enchilada sauce mix
1 packet (mild) taco sauce mix
1 can (8 oz.) tomato sauce
1 can cheddar cheese soup
1 can cream of mushroom soup
1 pkg. flour tortillas
1 cup shredded cheddar cheese

Brown meat, onion and chili powder in a large skillet. Drain. Add the sauce mixes and tomato sauce; stir well. Add cheese and mushroom soups. Stir often and cook over low heat until mixture starts to boil. In a large baking dish, put a layer of tortillas in the bottom of the pan. Pour mixture over the tortillas until they're covered. Put down another layer of tortilla shells. Pour remaining meat mixture over the shells. Top with 1 cup grated cheddar cheese. Bake at 400° for 20-25 minutes. Serve with fat free sour cream.

# June 10

## HONEY BBQ SANDWICHES

*Prep. Time: 10 minutes Cook Time: 45 minutes*

2 lbs lean ground beef (or turkey)
1 green pepper, chopped
1 cup diced celery
1 can (8 oz.) tomato sauce
1 small onion, diced
1 tablespoon salt
¼ cup honey
2 tablespoons apple cider vinegar
2 teaspoons chili powder

Add green pepper, celery and onion to ground beef and brown until done. Drain. Add all remaining ingredients and let simmer over low heat for about 45 minutes in order to blend flavors. Serve hot on buns.

## OVEN BAKED FRENCH FRIES

*Prep. Time: 2 minutes Bake Time: 15-20 minutes*

frozen french fries
2-3 tablespoons oil

In a jellyroll pan, spread oil over the pan's surface. Layer french fries out in a single layer. Bake at 400 degrees for about 10 minutes. Flip fries over and lightly salt. Let bake another 5 to 10 minutes or until a light brown.

# June 11

## OLD-FASHIONED MACARONI & CHEESE

*Prep. Time: 20 minutes Cook Time: 30 minutes*

3 cups elbow macaroni
8 American cheese slices
2 cups shredded cheddar cheese
1 can cream of chicken soup
½ cup skim milk
1 cup colby cheese cubes
1 teaspoon salt
⅛ teaspoon pepper

Cook macaroni until tender. Drain and rinse in cold water. Put drained macaroni in a deep casserole dish. In a medium saucepan, combine cream of chicken soup, milk, salt and pepper, 1 cup shredded cheddar cheese, 4 American cheese slices and the colby cheese cubes. Pour melted cheese mixture over macaroni and stir well. Tear up remaining slices of American cheese and stir into the macaroni. Top with remaining cup of shredded cheddar cheese. Bake at 350° for about 30 minutes or until cheese is bubbly and lightly browned on top.

Serve with fresh vegetables and dip.

## BLUEBERRY CAKE

*Prep. Time: 5 minutes Cook Time: 35 minutes*

1 box yellow cake mix
1 can blueberry pie filling
1 teaspoon vanilla
2 eggs, beaten

Combine all ingredients until well blended. Pour into a 9x13 cake pan that has been greased and floured. Bake at 350° for 30-35 minutes. Frost with your favorite prepared white icing.

# June 12

## MEAT BALLS & NOODLES

*Prep. Time: 20 minutes Cook Time: 30-40 minutes*

2 lbs. lean ground beef or turkey

2 cups crushed saltine cracker crumbs

2 eggs

½ cup skim milk

2 tablespoons minced onion

2 tablespoons Worcestershire sauce

2 teaspoons salt

¼ teaspoon pepper

1 large green pepper, chopped

3 tablespoons butter

3 tablespoons flour

4 cups canned tomatoes

2 cups fat free sour cream or plain yogurt

Combine meat, crumbs, egg, milk, onion, Worcestershire sauce, salt and pepper. Shape into balls and brown over medium-low heat in a skillet. When meatballs are completely browned, let them drain on a sheet of brown paper. Empty skillet of all meat drippings and wipe clean with a paper towel. Melt butter and green pepper and cook until

green pepper is tender-crisp. Stir in flour and continue cooking for about a minute. Add canned tomatoes, stirring until thick and smooth. Add sour cream and mix well. Put meatballs in a deep casserole dish. Pour tomato mixture over the meatballs. Bake at 300º for about 30 minutes. Serve over cooked, buttered noodles.

## ZUCCHINI NUT BREAD

*Prep. Time: 15-20 minutes Cook Time: 50-60 minutes*

2 cups sugar

½ cup oil

½ cup unsweetened applesauce

3 eggs

2 cups grated raw zucchini

1 teaspoon vanilla

3 cups flour

½ teaspoon baking powder

1 teaspoon baking soda

½ teaspoon salt

1 teaspoon ground cinnamon

1 teaspoon ground ginger

1 teaspoon ground cloves

1 cup chopped pecan (or walnut) pieces

Cream together sugar, oil, applesauce, eggs, zucchini and vanilla. In a separate bowl, sift together the flour, baking powder, baking soda, salt, cinnamon, ginger and cloves. Add dry ingredients to the creamed mixture gradually, mixing well. Stir in chopped nuts. Pour into greased and floured loaf pans. This will make 2 large or 3 small loaves. Bake at 325º for about 50-60 minutes.

# June 13

## FRESH GREEN BEANS 'N' HAM

*Today is called the Kitchen Klutzes of America Day to celebrate the not-so-accomplished cook. For those of you who consider yourself a genuine Kitchen Klutz you'll love tonights easy dinner.*

*Prep. Time: 30 minutes Cook Time: 1 hour*

2 lbs. fresh green beans, washed and snapped

1 lb. ham cubes (available prepackaged at most grocery stores)

6-8 new red potatoes, scrubbed clean

2 teaspoons salt

water

1 medium onion, diced

In a very large pot, combine green beans, ham and potatoes. Cover with water until there is about an inch of water above the vegetables. Add salt. Cook over medium-high heat for about an hour. Add water when needed and stir occasionally.

## LIME-PINEAPPLE-ORANGE DESSERT

*Prep. Time: 5 minutes*

1 small carton fat free cottage cheese (or 1%)

1 (8 oz.) small tub Fat Free Cool Whip™

2 cups miniature marshmallows

1 small pkg. lime gelatin

1 small can pineapple tidbits, drained

1 small can mandarin oranges, drained

Mix all ingredients together and refrigerate for at least an hour before serving. Desserts don't come any easier than this!

# June 14

## STUFFED ROUND STEAK

*Prep. Time: 10 minutes Cook Time: about 2 hours*

*(Note: The long cooking time is required for tenderizing the meat. This is a dish you can put in the oven to bake while you go do something else.)*

1½ - 2 lbs. round steak, pounded thin with a meat mallet

1 onion, finely diced

6 slices of bacon

¼ teaspoon sage

2 cups bread crumbs

salt and pepper

1 cup tomato paste

1 can cream of mushroom soup

½ cup water

Fry bacon until crisp. At the same time, cook onions in the bacon grease. When onions are tender, add bread crumbs and sage; crumble up bacon. Cook until moistened. Spread this mixture on the round steak and then roll it up, securing with toothpicks. Combine tomato paste and cream of mushroom soup with ½ cup water. Put meat roll in a baking pan and pour tomato mixture over meat. Cover and bake at 325° for 2 hours. Salt and pepper to taste.

## GARDEN SALAD

*Prep. Time: 15 minutes*

1 can French-styled green beans, drained

1 can peas, drained

1 green pepper, sliced thin

1 large red onion, sliced (separate rings)

4 stalks celery, chopped into bite-size pieces

1 can ripe (black) pitted olives, drained

1 cup sugar

½ cup vinegar

¼ cup salad oil

1 teaspoon salt

1 teaspoon water

In a small saucepan, combine sugar, vinegar, oil, salt and water. Heat until sugar dissolves. Combine all vegetables in a large salad bowl. Pour dressing over vegetables and toss to coat all vegetables with the dressing. Cover container and refrigerate for at least 2 hours before serving to allow flavors to blend.

# June 15

## SAUCY DOGS OVER RICE

*Prep. Time: 10 minutes Cook Time: 15 minutes*

3 tablespoons apple cider vinegar

1 small onion, diced

1 can tomato soup

¼ cup brown sugar

½ cup chopped green pepper

1 pkg. hot dogs

2 tablespoons butter

¼ cup water

1 tablespoon Worcestershire sauce

4 cups cooked rice

Cut hot dogs into bite-sized pieces and brown in skillet. Add all ingredients except green peppers. Cover and simmer over low heat for about 5 minutes. Add green peppers and simmer for about 10 minutes. Serve over cooked rice.

## CUCUMBER SALAD

*Prep. Time: 10 minutes*

3-4 large cucumbers, peeled and diced

1 medium red onion, diced

½ large green pepper, diced

1 cup fat free sour cream

1 teaspoon dill

1 teaspoon chives

Mix dill and chives into sour cream. Combine vegetables in bowl and add seasoned sour cream. Toss well and chill until ready to serve.

# June 16

## GRILLED HERBED CHICKEN

*We've all heard how expensive it is to raise a child these days. But have you heard that the cost for raising a medium sized dog to the old age of 11 is over $6,400?! And that doesn't include the cost of all those doggie treats!*

*Prep. Time: 3 hours Cook Time: 15 minutes*

½ cup olive oil

juice of 1 lemon

2 tablespoons minced onion

1 clove garlic, minced

¼ teaspoon rosemary

¼ teaspoon tarragon

¼ teaspoon thyme

1 teaspoon salt

¼ teaspoon pepper

½ teaspoon Accent™

¼ cup white wine

Combine all ingredients in a jar and shake well. Pour over boneless, skinless chicken breasts or chicken tenderloins to marinade for at least 3 hours before grilling.

## BROCCOLI SURPRISE

*Prep. Time: 20 minutes Cook Time: 30-35 minutes*

1 pkg. frozen chopped broccoli

2 cups instant rice

4 tablespoons butter

1 small jar Cheese Whiz™

½ cup water chestnuts, sliced thin

slivered almonds

Cook broccoli in a saucepan or microwave until done. Drain off any liquid. Prepare rice according to package directions. Add butter, Cheese Whiz™, broccoli and water chestnuts to the rice and mix well. Pour into a casserole dish and top with slivered almonds. Bake at 350° for 30-35 minutes.

# Easy Elephant Ears

*Prep. Time: 2 minutes Cook Time: 20 minutes*

2 canisters of prepared refrigerator biscuits
1 cup sugar
2 teaspoons cinnamon
2 cups oil

Mix cinnamon and sugar together in a dish. Heat oil over medium heat. Flick a drop of water into oil and when it sizzles, the oil is ready. Open biscuits. You can poke a hole in the middle to make a donut or flatten biscuit to make an elephant ear. (I also make donut holes by dividing one biscuit into two and rolling them into balls.) Drop biscuits in hot oil and watch carefully. Turn biscuits over when the bottom starts to turn light brown. When both top and bottom are about the same color, remove from oil and roll in cinnamon/sugar mixture. Test one by eating it. If it is still doughy inside then turn the heat down under the oil and let oil cool a bit before continuing. These taste great hot or cold!

# June 17

## Tamale Casserole

*Prep. Time: 15 minutes Cook Time: 1 hour*

1 medium onion, finely chopped
1 green pepper, finely chopped
1 lb. lean ground beef or turkey
3 cups chopped fresh tomatoes
1½ cups corn meal
½ teaspoon chili powder
½ teaspoon cumin
½ teaspoon garlic salt
1 teaspoon salt
¼ teaspoon pepper
1 cup shredded cheddar cheese

Crumble meat into a large skillet and cook over a medium heat. Add chopped onion and green pepper. Cook until meat is done and vegetables are slightly tender. Drain off all grease and wipe skillet clean with a paper towel. Return meat mixture to the skillet and add remaining ingredients (except cheese), stirring well. Heat through and then pour contents into a casserole dish. Bake at 350° for 40 minutes. Top with shredded cheese. Bake another 10-20 minutes. Serve with fat free sour cream over salad greens.

# Banana Creme Cake

*Prep. Time: 20 minutes Cook Time: 20-25 minutes*

1 yellow cake mix
½ cup butter
2 eggs
1 cup chopped pecans
4 cups miniature marshmallows
1 box vanilla instant pudding
3 mashed ripe bananas

Combine yellow cake mix with ½ cup butter, 2 eggs and the nuts. Spread one-half of this mixture in the bottom of a greased 13x9 cake pan. In a saucepan, melt marshmallows. Add mashed bananas and the dry pudding mix to the melted marshmallows. Stir well. Pour the marshmallow/banana mixture over the bottom layer in the cake pan. Sprinkle the remaining cake mixture over the filling. Bake at 350° for 20-25 minutes.

# June 18

## SUPER EASY STUFFED PORK CHOPS

*Today was the first observed Father's Day held in Spokane, Washington in 1910. It was made a national holiday in 1966. Now it is always observed on the third Sunday of June.*

*Prep. Time: 10 minutes Cook Time: 40-50 minutes*

6-8 pork chops, trimmed of fat
1 box pork stuffing mix
2 envelopes brown gravy mix
½ lb. bacon
1 medium onion, sliced

Lay pork chops in the bottom of a 13x9 pan. Prepare stuffing mix and gravy mixes according to package directions. Lay strips of bacon over pork chops. Cover with prepared stuffing and then pour the brown gravy over all of it. Garnish (and season!) with slices of onion. Bake at 375º for 40-50 minutes.

Serve with Steam-fried Potatoes, (see page 10)

## CANDY APPLE SALAD

*Prep. Time: 25 minutes Cook Time: 15-20 minutes*

10 red apples (Gala works best!)
1 large can crushed pineapple
1 cup sugar
2 eggs
3 tablespoons flour
1 teaspoon vinegar
2 cups unsalted peanuts
1 tub Fat Free Cool Whip™

Drain pineapple and save juice. In a saucepan combine pineapple, sugar, flour, eggs and vinegar; stir well. Cook over medium low heat until mixture turns thick. Stir occasionally to avoid sticking. When mixture is thick, remove from heat and let cool. Meanwhile, core apples and cut into bite-sized chunks. Add peanuts and sauce and mix well. Fold in Cool Whip™. Refrigerate until ready to serve.

# June 19

## LASAGNA

*Prep. Time 20-30 minutes. Cook time 30-50 minutes*

1 lb. lasagna noodles
2 lbs lean ground beef or turkey
1 jar (32-40 oz.) spaghetti sauce
1 jar or can pizza sauce
4 cups ricotta cheese
4 cups shredded mozzarella cheese
2 cups shredded cheddar cheese
¼ cup grated Parmesan cheese
2 eggs
1 tablespoon chopped parsley
1 teaspoon sweet basil
2 teaspoons oregano
1 teaspoon salt
¼ teaspoon pepper

Brown the meat and drain off fat. Add the spaghetti and pizza sauces, salt and pepper. Set aside. Cook lasagna noodles according to package directions. Set aside. Mix together ricotta cheese, 2 cups mozzarella cheese, Parmesan cheese, eggs, and herbs. In the bottom of a 13x9 pan, lay down a layer of cooked lasagna noodles. Cover with ⅓ of the meat sauce and ½ of the cheese mixture. Cover with another layer of lasagna noodles. Cover with ⅓ of the meat sauce and the rest of the cheese mixture. Cover with another layer of lasagna noodles. Cover with remaining meat mixture. Top with remaining shredded cheeses. Bake at 350º for 30-50 minutes.

Serve with a tossed salad and garlic bread sticks.

# CUSTARD PIE

*Prep. Time: 10 minutes Cook Time: 35-45 minutes*

3 eggs
6 tablespoons sugar
1/8 teaspoon salt
2 cups skim milk
1 teaspoon vanilla
sprinkle with nutmeg
1 (9-inch) unbaked pie shell

Beat eggs slightly then add sugar, salt, vanilla and milk. Pour into unbaked 9-inch pie crust. Sprinkle with nutmeg. Preheat oven to 400°. Place a pan of water in the bottom of the oven. Put the pie in the center of the oven on the rack. Bake for 10 minutes then reduce heat to 350°. Continue baking for 25-30 minutes or until custard is firm.

# June 20

## CHEF SALAD

*Prep. Time: 15 minutes*

1 head iceberg lettuce
1 pkg. fresh spinach leaves
1 head Romaine lettuce
1 red onion, sliced
2 ripe tomatoes, diced
1 fresh cucumber, diced
6 boiled eggs, chopped
1/2 cup bacon bits
2 cups shredded cheddar cheese
2 cans chicken, tuna or other cooked meat, drained
choice of salad dressing

Wash and dry all vegetables. Tear lettuces up into bite-sized pieces. Add all remaining ingredients. Toss and serve. Top with your choice of salad dressing.

## FAT-BUSTERS

*Here are some ideas for trimming fat from your diet:*

• Use 1% or 1/2% milk instead of 2% or whole milk.

• In recipes using chocolate (such as brownies or cakes) substitute 1/2 of the oil or fat called for in the recipe with an equal amount of baby food plums. The plums will enhance the chocolate flavor as well as reduce the total fat grams. PLEASE NOTE: Recipes in THIS book have already been converted to lower fat recipes.

• In bread or muffin recipes, substitute one-half of the fat (oil) called for with unsweetened applesauce. PLEASE NOTE: Recipes in THIS book have already been converted to lower fat recipes.

• Use non-fat vegetable spray in place of grease or oil when sautéing or pan frying.

• Use butter-flavored nonfat vegetable spray in place of actual butter when seasoning potatoes, rice or vegetables.

• To season baked potatoes, use hot bouillon instead of butter and sour cream.

• In recipes calling for sour cream, use nonfat plain yogurt instead.

• When browning ground beef, turkey or bulk sausage, you can boil it to cook it and drain more grease off of the meat this way than after pan frying.

# BUTTERSCOTCH BROWNIES

*Prep. Time: 15-20 minutes Cook Time: 25-30 minutes*

½ cup butter, melted
2 eggs
2 cups light brown sugar, firmly packed
1 teaspoon vanilla
1½ cups flour
2 teaspoons baking powder
½ teaspoon salt
1 cup chopped pecans

In a large mixing bowl, beat eggs until light and foamy (about 3-6 minutes) with an electric mixer. Beat in sugar, vanilla and butter. In a separate bowl, combine flour with baking powder and salt. Add to egg mixture and mix at low speed until well blended. Stir in nuts and spread batter in a greased 13x9 pan. Bake at 350° for 25 to 30 minutes or until top is light brown. Cool for 10-15 minutes. Cut into bars.

# June 21

## TOASTED SWISS HAM SANDWICHES

*Prep. Time: 15 minutes Cook time: 10-15 minutes*

1-2 lbs shaved ham
slices of Swiss cheese, enough for 1 slice per sandwich
bread
butter

Butter bread on one side. Put bread buttered-sides-down on a hot grill. Add 2-3 ounces of shaved ham and a slice of Swiss cheese. Top with another slice of buttered bread, buttered side out. Cook over medium heat and flip sandwiches over when cheese starts to melt. Cook until bread is lightly toasted on both sides. Serve immediately.

# CREAM OF BROCCOLI SOUP

*Prep. Time: 20 minutes Cook time: 15 minutes*

1 bunch of fresh broccoli
3 tablespoons flour
3 tablespoons butter
2 cups skim milk
1 teaspoon seasoned salt
1 bay leaf
2 cups cheddar cheese, shredded or cubed

Put broccoli in a large saucepan and cover with salted water. Cook until tender and then set aside. In a medium saucepan melt butter over medium heat. Stir in flour until pasty. Add milk and seasoned salt. Stir constantly over medium heat until sauce begins to thicken. Add bay leaf. Mix half of the broccoli and half of the sauce in a blender and puree. Chop the rest of the broccoli into bite-sized pieces. Mix the broccoli/sauce mixture with the remaining sauce and chopped broccoli in a large soup pan. Add cheese and heat over medium-low heat until cheese melts. Serve hot.

# June 22

## CRUNCHY CHICKEN CASSEROLE

*Prep. Time: 20 minutes Cook Time: 30 minutes*

4 cups cooked chicken, cut up
2 cups diced celery
1 cup slivered almonds
2 teaspoons lemon juice
1 cup Miracle Whip Free™
2 cans cream of chicken soup
2 cups shredded Co-Jack cheese
2 cups crushed potato chips (or nacho chips)

In a large casserole dish, combine the chicken, celery, almonds, lemon juice, Miracle Whip™ and chicken soup. Mix well. Cover casserole with shredded cheese. Top with crushed chips. Bake at 350° for about 30 minutes.

# Baked Apple Donuts

*Prep. Time: 30 minutes Cook Time: 20-25 minutes*

3 cups flour
1 cup sugar
3½ teaspoons baking powder
1 teaspoon salt
¼ teaspoon nutmeg
¾ cup butter
1 cup grated apple (no peel)
1 cup vanilla flavored yogurt
2 beaten eggs
½ cup butter, melted
1 cup sugar combined
  with 2 teaspoons cinnamon

Combine flour, sugar, baking powder, salt and nutmeg; cut in butter with a pastry blender. Combine apple, yogurt and eggs; stir into flour mixture. Divide and spoon into greased muffin tin. Bake at 350° for 20-25 minutes. Remove from tins and roll in melted butter, then into cinnamon/sugar mixture.

# June 23

## Smothered Chicken Breasts

*Prep. Time: 15 minutes Cook Time: 20 minutes*

6 skinless, boneless chicken breasts
¼ cup butter, melted
1 cup sliced mushrooms
6 green onions, chopped
½ cup Parmesan cheese
1 cup shredded cheddar cheese
seasoned salt
pepper

Brush chicken breasts with butter and salt and pepper on both sides. Place them on a hot grill to cook. Turn breasts every 3-4 minutes, each time basting with the butter. When chicken is done, remove from grill and arrange on a serving plate.

Top each piece of meat with mushroom slices, green onions and sprinkle on Parmesan cheese. Cover each with some shredded cheddar cheese and pop the platter in the microwave on high just long enough to melt cheese. Serve immediately.

# Rice Pilaf

*Prep. Time: 15 minutes Cook Time: 50-60 minutes*

2 cups uncooked long grain rice
1 cup celery, chopped very fine
1 medium onion, chopped very fine
¼ cup butter
4 cups water
4 cubes chicken bouillon
1 teaspoon Worcestershire Sauce
1 teaspoon soy sauce
1 teaspoon dried oregano
1 teaspoon dried thyme
1 teaspoon dried sweet basil

Dissolve chicken bouillon cubes in 4 cups hot water. In skillet, sauté rice, celery and onion in butter until the rice is lightly browned and vegetables are tender. Pour into a casserole dish. Combine all ingredients and pour over the rice. Cover with a lid or tightly with aluminum foil. Bake at 325° for 50-60 minutes.

# June 24

## Stuffed Manicotti

*Prep. Time: 20 minutes Cook Time: 25 minutes*

1 (8 oz.) box manicotti shells
1 (16 oz.) Ricotta cheese
dash of nutmeg
1 (10 oz.) pkg. frozen spinach, cooked and
  drained
1 jar spaghetti sauce
1 medium onion, finely chopped
1 can water chestnuts, finely chopped

Cook and drain manicotti shells, rinse in cold water. Mix Ricotta, nutmeg, spinach, onions and water chestnuts in a bowl. Stuff each shell with spinach mixture. Arrange shells in a baking dish that has been sprayed with a non-fat vegetable spray. Pour sauce over all shells and bake uncovered for 25 minutes.

Serve with a toss salad.

## DIRT CAKE

*Prep. Time: 20 minutes*

1 large pkg. Oreo™ cookies, crushed
1 (8 oz.) pkg. cream cheese, softened
1 stick butter, softened
1 cup powdered sugar
2 pkgs. instant French vanilla pudding mixes
3 ½ cups skim milk
1 container Fat Free Cool Whip™
Gummy™ worms (optional)

Blend cream cheese, butter and powered sugar together. Set aside. In separate bowl, combine vanilla pudding mixes with milk and beat with an electric mixer until pudding thickens. Add Cool Whip™ and cream cheese mixture, beat well. Fill dessert cups half full of crushed Oreo™ cookies. Add ½ cup pudding and cream cheese mixture. Cover pudding with additional crushed cookies. Top with Gummy™ worms. Serve with a play shovel or fork.

### FOOD FOR THOUGHT

- You are only limited in accomplishments by how small you think.

- Doing nothing for others is the undoing of ourselves.

- Blessed are they who go around in circles for they shall be called Big Wheels!

- People don't plan to fail, they just fail to plan!

- I am not stubborn. I just want things done my way.

# June 25

## STOVE-TOP TUNA CASSEROLE

*Prep. Time: 15 minutes Cook Time: 20 minutes*

2 boxes (or 1 family-sized box) Macaroni & Cheese™
1 can cream of mushroom soup
1 can cheddar cheese soup
2 cans tuna in spring water, drained
1 pkg. frozen peas and carrots, cooked and drained
2 tablespoons butter
½ cup milk

Prepare macaroni according to package directions. Stir in butter, milk and powdered cheese (from the mixes). Add soups, tuna and vegetables. Stir over low heat until it is heated all the way through. Serve with slices of bread and butter.

## EASY MONKEY BREAD

*Prep. Time: 15 minutes Cook Time: 50 minutes*

4 cans (10-count) refrigerated biscuits
1 cup white sugar, divided
1 cup brown sugar, divided
1 tablespoon ground cinnamon
1 cup butter
1 cup chopped nuts, optional
non-fat vegetable spray

Spray a 10-inch bundt pan with the vegetable spray. Set aside. Cut each biscuit into 4 pieces. In a paper or plastic bag, combine ½ cup white sugar, ½ cup brown sugar and the cinnamon. Mix well. Place half of the biscuit pieces, a few at a time, in the bag and shake well to cover. Place biscuit pieces in Bundt pan. In a saucepan, mix together remaining white and brown sugars with butter and nuts. Heat until butter melts and sugars dissolve, but do not boil. Pour half of syrup mixture over biscuits in the bundt pan. Shake remaining biscuit pieces in bag of sugar mixture. Place in pan and add remainder of butter mixture on the top. Bake at 350° for 40-50 minutes, but do not over bake or syrup will crystallize. Cool just long enough to flip pan over onto a serving plate. Remove pan and serve.

# June 26

## MEXICAN ROLL-UPS

*Prep. Time: 20 minutes Cook Time: 20-25 minutes*

- 1 lb. lean ground beef, turkey or cooked chopped chicken
- 2 tablespoons salsa
- 1 (16 oz.) can fat free refried beans
- 1 to 2 jalapeno peppers, seeded and finely chopped
- 1 clove garlic, minced
- 1 small onion, finely diced
- ½ teaspoon ground cumin
- 2 cups shredded cheddar cheese
- 10 to 12 (6-inch) flour tortillas
- fat-free sour cream
- salsa

If you're using ground beef or turkey, pan fry the meat until done. Drain off all fat. Combine meat with 2 tablespoons salsa, refried beans, chopped jalapeno peppers, minced garlic, onion and cumin. Spread mixture over each tortilla, covering the entire piece. Roll each one up and place seam side down in a greased 13x9 baking pan. Cover pan with aluminum foil and bake for 20 minutes or until tortillas are heated through. Remove foil and cover tortillas with shredded cheese. Let stand until cheese melts—or you may return pan to oven for an additional 5 minutes or so. Serve with sour cream and salsa if desired.

## FRUIT PIZZA

*Prep. Time: 20 minutes Cook Time: 10 minutes*

- 1 tube Pillsbury™ sugar cookie dough
- pineapple tidbits, drained
- mandarin orange sections, drained
- green seedless grapes, cut in halves
- strawberries, cut in halves
- 3 kiwis, peeled and sliced
- 2 bananas, peeled and sliced
- 1 cup powdered sugar
- 1 (8 oz.) pkg. cream cheese, softened
- Fat Free Cool Whip™

Press sugar cookie dough onto bottom of cookie sheet; bake at 350° for 8 to 10 minutes. Remove from oven and set aside to cool. Meanwhile combine powdered sugar and cream cheese in a small mixing bowl. Blend on low speed with an electric mixer until smooth. Add 1 cup Cool Whip™ to cream cheese mixture and whip until smooth. Spread this mixture on to the cooled cookie crust. Randomly arrange fruit so each bite will be a delightful surprise! Cut and serve, topping each piece with a dollop of Cool Whip™.

# June 27

## SALISBURY STEAK

*Prep. Time: 15 minutes Cook Time: 45 minutes*

- 1 can golden mushroom soup
- ½ cup bread crumbs
- 1 small onion, finely diced
- ½ teaspoon prepared mustard
- ½ teaspoon dried parsley flakes
- ½ teaspoon pepper
- 1½ lbs. lean ground beef or turkey
- 1 egg
- ½ teaspoon Worcestershire sauce
- ⅓ cup water

Combine ¼ cup golden mushroom soup with bread crumbs, onion, mustard, parsley, pepper, meat, egg and Worcestershire sauce. Shape into 6 oblong patties and place in shallow pan. Bake at 350° for about 30 minutes. Drain off all pan drippings. Combine remaining soup and water and pour over patties. Bake another 10 minutes.

Serve with mashed potatoes.

## HARVARD BEETS

*Prep. Time: 10 minutes Cook Time: 15 minutes*

2 cans sliced beets
½ cup sugar
2 tablespoons oil
¼ cup vinegar
2 teaspoons cornstarch
   dissolved in ¼ cup cold water

Combine sugar and flour. Add oil, vinegar and cornstarch water. Boil 5 minutes. Add beets. Cook over low heat for 5-10 minutes.

# June 28

## B-L-T RANCH SALAD

*Prep. Time: 25 minutes*

1 lb. bacon or turkey bacon
1 head iceberg lettuce
4 large tomatoes
½ cup low-fat mayonnaise
½ cup Ranch salad dressing
salt and pepper

In a large salad bowl, tear up lettuce into bite-sized pieces. Dice tomatoes. Fry bacon until crisp, then drain on paper towel. Crumble bacon over tomatoes. Combine mayonnaise and Ranch dressing and pour over salad. Toss to coat and distribute dressing.

# June 29

## TOSS-TOGETHER CASSEROLE

*Prep. Time: 20 minutes Cook Time: 25 to 30 minutes*

1 lb. lean ground beef or turkey
3 cups elbow macaroni
1 medium onion, finely chopped
½ green pepper, finely chopped
1 stalk celery, finely chopped
2 (8 oz.) cans tomato sauce
¼ lb. Velveeta™ cheese, cubed
¼ teaspoon pepper
1 teaspoon salt

Brown meat in skillet with onions and green pepper and celery. Drain. Add tomato sauce, cheese, salt and pepper. Cook macaroni according to the package directions; drain and rinse. Mix with beef mixture and pour all into a casserole dish. Bake at 350° for 25 to 30 minutes.

## CINNAMON APPLE SALAD

*Prep. Time: 20 minutes*

9 cinnamon balls (candy)
½ cup boiling water
1 pkg. cherry gelatin
1 cup hot water
1 cup diced celery
1 cup died apples
½ cup chopped nuts

Dissolve the cinnamon balls in the ½ cup boiling water. When the cinnamon balls are dissolved, finish filling the ½ cup of water with enough water to equal 1 cup. Prepare the gelatin, using the cinnamon water in place of the 1 cup cold water. Refrigerate until just barely starting to gel. Fold in apples, celery and nuts. Refrigerate until ready to serve.

# June 30

## BBQ SPANISH RIBS

*Prep. Time: 15 minutes Cook Time: about 30 minutes*

4 lbs spare-ribs, cut into 2-to-3 rib pieces
1 tablespoon salt
¼ teaspoon pepper
¼ teaspoon cayenne or red pepper
1 teaspoon paprika
1 teaspoon chili powder
1 cup ketchup
1 cup water
2 tablespoons vinegar
2 onions, sliced

In a very large pan, boil spare-ribs in salted water until done. Drain. Combine all remaining ingredients except for the onions and pour over the ribs. Arrange slices of onion over the ribs and sauce. Cover pan and simmer on low heat for about 10-15 minutes.

## POPPY SEED CAKE

*Prep. Time: 10 minutes Cook Time: 45 minutes*

1 pkg. white cake mix
1 pkg. instant vanilla pudding
½ cup orange juice
½ cup water
½ cup oil
5 eggs
2 tablespoons poppy seeds
1 tablespoon almond extract

Mix all ingredients in a large bowl and beat at high speed with an electric mixer. Pour into a greased and floured bundt cake pan. Bake at 350° for about 45 minutes or until cake tests done when a knife is inserted in the middle. The cake is done when the knife comes out clean. Remove from oven and invert pan.

## LEMON GLAZE

*Prep. Time: 3-5 minutes*

2 cups powdered sugar
3 tablespoons milk
1 tablespoon butter, softened
2 tablespoons lemon juice

Combine all ingredients in a small bowl and beat on high with an electric mixer until smooth. Drizzle glaze over cake.

---

*July is recognized as:*
National Baked Beans Month, National Hot Dog Month, National Ice Cream Month, National Peach Month, National Picnic Month and of course, July belongs to *Blueberries Month!*

---

# July 1

## BULGARIAN SPAGHETTI SAUCE

*Craig's aunt married a man from Bulgaria. As she's learned to cook for him, she's introduced the rest of the family to some of the delicious Bulgarian dishes. Tonight's homemade spaghetti recipe is one of my family's favorite. In fact, I make several batches of this sauce and we can them to use throughout the year. Special thanks goes to Joetta Aglikin of Marion, Indiana, for sharing her recipes with me.*

*Prep. Time: 20 minutes Cook Time: 1 hour*

1 quart tomatoes or enough to equal 4 cups
1 (12 oz.) can tomato paste
1 large onion diced to equal ¾ cup
dash of garlic powder
1 cup water
1½ teaspoon salt
½ teaspoon pepper
1½ teaspoon oregano
1-2 Bay leaves

Combine all ingredients in a large soup pan and let cook over low heat for about an hour. Serve hot over cooked spaghetti pasta. Meatballs may be added, if desired.

# July 2

## TENDER PORK LOINS

*Prep. Time: 5 minutes Cook Time: 1 hour 15 minutes*

6-8 pork loins, trimmed of fat
2 cans cream of mushroom soup
1 small onion, sliced
1 small green pepper, sliced
1 teaspoon seasoned salt
¼ teaspoon pepper
1 tablespoon Worcestershire sauce
1 cup water

Combine all ingredients and submerge meat in the soup mix in a large oven proof pan with a lid. Put in a preheated 400° oven and bake for 1 hour and 15 minutes. Remove meat and arrange on a serving platter.

## STEAMED PEA PODS & CARROTS

*Prep. Time: 10 minutes Cook Time: 15 minutes*

1 lb. fresh snap sweet pea pods
1 lb.  baby carrots
2 tablespoons butter
2 cups water
1 teaspoon salt

Wash pea pods and carrots. Put vegetables in boiling salt water and add butter. Cover and cook for 10 minutes. Remove lid and stir, continue cooking for about 5 more minutes or until vegetables are cooked to a "tender-crisp" stage.

# July 3

## TACO PIE

*Prep. Time: 20 minutes Cook Time: 20-25 minutes*

1 ¼ lbs. lean ground beef or turkey
1 pkg. taco seasoning mix
½ cup water
1 can refrigerator crescent dinner rolls
2 cups crushed corn chips
1 cup fat free sour cream
1 cup shredded cheddar cheese
1 cup sliced ripe olives
shredded lettuce
avocado slices, optional

Brown meat in a large skillet and drain off all pan drippings when done. Stir in seasoning mix, water and olives. Simmer 5 minutes over a low heat. Separate crescent dough into 8 triangles. Place triangles in ungreased 9"-10" pie pan, pressing to form a crust. Sprinkle 1 cup crushed corn chips over top of crust. Spoon meat mixture over crust and top with remaining corn chips. Spread sour cream over meat mixture; cover with cheese. Bake at 375° for 20 to 25 minutes. Serve on top of shredded lettuce and garnish with avocado slices.

## PEACH CRISP

*Prep. Time: 10 minutes Cook Time: 40 minutes*

6 cups peeled peach slices
¾ cup packed brown sugar
½ cup flour
¼ teaspoon nutmeg
¼ teaspoon cinnamon
¼ teaspoon salt
⅓ cup butter
½ cup quick cooking oatmeal

Place peaches in a 9-inch square pan. Combine sugar, flour, spices and salt; cut in butter until mixture resembles coarse crumbs. Stir in oats.

Sprinkle mixture evenly over peaches. Bake at 350° for about 40 minutes. Serve warm.

# July 4

## CHEESEBURGERS

*Prep. Time: 5 minutes Cook Time: 15-20 minutes*

2 lbs. lean ground beef or turkey
1 small onion
1 tablespoon Worcestershire sauce
1 teaspoon salt
½ teaspoon pepper
American cheese slices
buns
your choice of condiments
dill pickle slices
red onion slices
lettuce
tomato slices

Chop onion finely and add to ground beef. Add Worcestershire sauce, salt and pepper. Mix well and form into patties. Cook meat on a hot grill, hot griddle on top of the stove, or broil it in the oven. Be sure to turn burgers in order to evenly cook through. As soon as burgers come off the heat, add a slice of American cheese and let it melt. Serve on a bun with your choice of condiments, lettuce, tomato, pickles and onion.

Serve with French fries.

## ALL-AMERICAN APPLE PIE

*Prep. Time: 10 minutes Cook Time: 35-40 minutes*

1 unbaked 9-inch pie shell
4 cups tart apples, peeled and sliced
1½ cups sugar
2 tablespoons flour
2 tablespoons butter
1 teaspoon cinnamon
1 cup milk
1 cup quick cooking oatmeal
½ cup sugar
1 teaspoon sugar
½ cup brown sugar, firmly packed

Sprinkle one tablespoon flour in bottom of the pie shell. In a large bowl, combine sliced apples, 1½ cups sugar, 1 teaspoon cinnamon, remaining flour and milk. Mix well to evenly coat apples. Pour into pie shell. Dot with pats of butter. In a separate container, combine oatmeal with ½ cup sugar, 1 teaspoon cinnamon and brown sugar. Mix well and sprinkle on top of pie. Bake at 400° for 35 to 40 minutes. Serve with a big scoop of vanilla ice cream.

# July 5

## HAM & CHEESE SOUFFLÉ

*Prep. Time: 15 minutes Cook Time: 45 minutes*

8 eggs, beaten
2 cups skim milk
6 slices bread, soft and cubed
2 cups ham, in small cubes
½ cup chopped mushrooms
2 cups sharp cheddar cheese, shredded
1 teaspoon dry mustard
½ teaspoon salt
pepper to taste

Combine all ingredients and mix well. Pour in a casserole dish. Refrigerate for at least 6 hours or longer. Bake at 350° for 45 minutes. May sprinkle top with more cheese if desired during the final 5 minutes of baking.

> **KITCHEN TIP:**
> If you've over salted the soup, add a peeled potato and cook it for 15 to 20 minutes. Remove potato and discard before serving. The potato will absorb most of the unwanted salt.

# EASY BLUEBERRY PANCAKES

*Prep. Time: 10 minutes Cook Time: 3-5 minutes each*

2 pkgs. Jiffy™ blueberry muffin mixes

4 cups flour

½ cup sugar

2 teaspoons salt

2 tablespoons baking powder

4 eggs

2 cups milk, maybe a little more

Combine all ingredients in a large bowl. Mix well. Pour by ¼ cup onto a hot greased griddle. Cook 3 to 4 pancakes at a time, turning when the edges start to turn brown. Serve hot with syrup or fresh blueberries.

# July 6

## PORK CHOP SUEY

*Prep. Time: 15 minutes Cook Time: 15 minutes*

3 cups Minute Rice™, uncooked

3 pork steaks, cut in strips

2 medium onions, chopped

1 stalk celery, chopped

2 tablespoons butter

1 can chop suey vegetables, drained

1 can mushrooms, drained

1 can water chestnuts, drained and chopped

1 tablespoon La Choy™ brown gravy sauce

1 tablespoon cornstarch

¼ cup water

Prepare rice according to package directions. Melt butter in a skillet and sauté meat strips with onion and celery. Add vegetables and brown gravy sauce. Mix well. Dissolve cornstarch in cold water and add to vegetable mixture. Heat until boiling and sauce begins to thicken. Serve over cooked rice.

# PUDDING ICE CREAM

*Prep. Time: 20 minutes Freeze time: 1-2 hours*

2 pkgs. instant pudding (any flavor you desire for the ice cream)

1 cup sugar

1 teaspoon vanilla

2 cups milk

7 eggs

¼ teaspoon salt

2 large cans Milnot™

**Extra milk may be needed**

Prepare both packages of pudding according to package directions. Beat eggs well with sugar, salt and vanilla. Add to pudding mixture, stir or beat until smooth. Add Milnot™. Put in freezer tub of an ice-cream maker. Add enough milk to fill the tub to within 2-inches of the top. Stir well with a long-handled spoon. Pack ice and salt around tub and work ice cream freezer until too stiff to turn.

# July 7

## EASY STEAK & POTATOES

*Prep. Time: 10 minutes Cook Time: 1 hour*

2 lb. round steak, cut ¾ inch thick

1 tablespoon oil

2 cans cream of mushroom soup

1 cup water

1 large onion, chopped

3 tablespoons steak sauce

1 tablespoon Worcestershire sauce

1 clove garlic, minced

8-10 medium potatoes, peeled and cut in half

Pound steak thin and cut into serving size pieces. Brown meat in oil. Drain. In a large baking dish or pan, combine soups with water, onion, sauces and garlic. Add meat and immerse. Place potatoes around the outer edge. Bake at 350° for 1 hour. (Note: If you desire your meat to be more tender, reduce heat to 325° and add another hour of baking time.)

# BAKED BROCCOLI & CHEESE

*Prep. Time: 20 minutes Cook Time: 45 minutes*

2 pkgs. frozen chopped broccoli, thawed
1 cup mayonnaise
1 cup shredded Cheddar cheese
3 eggs
1 can cream of mushroom soup
1 small onion, finely chopped

Cook broccoli in boiling salt water. Drain and pour into a large casserole dish. Combine remaining ingredients in a large mixing bowl and beat with an electric mixer for about 2 minutes. Pour over broccoli and bake at 350° for about 45 minutes.

# HOMEMADE VANILLA ICE CREAM

*Prep. Time: 15 minutes Freeze Time: 1-2 hours*

4 eggs
2 cups sugar
2 quarts milk
1 pkg. instant vanilla pudding mix
1 can evaporated milk
2 tablespoons vanilla

Beat eggs until light and gradually add sugar. Beat in milk, evaporated milk, pudding mix and vanilla. Pour into tub of an ice cream freezer. Pack ice and salt around tub and work ice cream freezer until the tub is too stiff to turn.

KITCHEN TIP:
Fried potatoes will be golden brown if sprinkled lightly with flour before frying.

# July 8

# MEXICAN LASAGNA

*Prep. Time: 25 minutes Cook Time: 50-60 minutes*

2 lbs. lean ground beef or turkey
1 (16 oz.) can fat free refried beans
12 lasagna noodles (I always do a few extra in case one breaks)
2 cups water
2 teaspoon dried oregano
1 teaspoon ground cumin
½ teaspoon garlic powder
2½ cups salsa
2 cups (or 1-16 oz. carton) fat-free sour cream
1 bunch green onions, chopped
½ cup sliced ripe (black) olives
1 cup shredded Monterey Jack cheese
1 cup shredded cheddar cheese

Brown meat in a large skillet and drain off fat. Combine beans, oregano, cumin and garlic powder with meat. Mix well. Boil noodles for about 2 minutes to cook firm—not soft. Rinse with cold water. Place 4 firm noodles in the bottom of a 13x9 baking pan. Add a little water to bottom of noodles. Spread half the mixture over the noodles. Sprinkle a handful of cheddar cheese over meat. Add another layer of 4 noodles. Spread on remaining meat mixture. Cover with remaining cheddar cheese. Add final layer of noodles. Combine remaining water with salsa and pour over top of noodles. Cover pan tightly with aluminum foil and bake at 350° degrees for about 40 minutes. Check noodles for tenderness. When noodles are tender, spread sour cream over noodles. Add green onions and olive slices and top with Monterey Jack cheese. Return pan to oven to bake uncovered for another 5-10 minutes. Serve with nacho chips.

# SUNDAE PIE

*Prep. Time: 20 minutes*

1 prepared 9-inch chocolate graham cracker
    crust
½ gallon vanilla ice cream
choice of toppings: blueberry, strawberry,
    fudge, etc.
Fat Free Cool Whip™
maraschino cherries

Either let ice cream set at room temperature to soften or stick it directly in the microwave from the freezer. Microwave on high for 45 seconds. Spread ice cream in the crust of the pie pan. Invert lid from the pie shell over the ice cream. Return to freezer and let refreeze. When ready to serve, remove pie from freezer and cut into 8 equal pieces. Top each slice with your choice of ice cream toppings, a dollop of Cool Whip™ and a cherry.

# July 9

# BAKED GLAZED HAM

*Prep. Time: 10 minutes Cook Time: 30-40 minutes*

6-8 half-inch slices of ham off the bone
1 cup brown sugar
1 cup dark corn syrup
2 tablespoons prepared mustard
1 tablespoon maple flavoring

Heat oven to 325°. Place ham on a rack in a shallow roasting pan. Put ham in oven and bake for 15-20 minutes. Combine remaining ingredients and mix well. Increase oven temperature to 400° and pour glaze over ham. Bake for 15 to 20 minutes longer, basting with glaze about every 5 minutes.

# TOMATOES AND ZUCCHINI

*Prep. Time: 15 minutes Cook Time: 15 minutes*

5-6 medium zucchini
2 tablespoons butter
¼ cup honey
2 cups stewed tomatoes

Slice zucchini lengthwise and slice into 2-to-3 inch pieces. Sauté lightly in butter. Add honey and tomatoes and bring to a boil. Cook 5 to 10 minutes longer.

# DONUTS

*Prep. Time: 2 hours 25 minutes Cook Time: 3-5 minutes*

½ cup sugar
½ cup oil
1 teaspoon salt
1 teaspoon vanilla
1½ cups milk
2 cakes yeast dissolved in ½ cup warm water
2 beaten eggs
4 cups flour, or more
GLAZE:
1 box powdered sugar (about 2 cups)
1 teaspoon vanilla
milk (add until you get to the right consistency
    for a glaze)

Scald milk. Pour over mixture of sugar, oil, salt and vanilla. Dissolve yeast in warm water and add beaten eggs. Mix well. Add flour and knead until well mixed. (Dough will sometimes require up to ¾ cup more flour.) When dough is firm and elastic, put into a greased bowl. Let rise (about 1 hour). Punch down and let rise again (about 1 hour). Roll out to 3/8-inch thick and cut out donuts. Let rise again (about 20-30 minutes). Deep fat fry until brown on both sides. While hot, dip in glaze mixture and set on a rack to cool.

# COOKIES OF THE MONTH

## ENGLISH TOFFEE COOKIES

1 cup brown sugar
¼ cup butter
¼ cup shortening
yolk of 1 egg
1 teaspoon almond flavoring
2 cups flour
1 egg white, beaten
ground pecans

Cream together butter, shortening and sugar. Add egg yolk, almond flavoring and mix. Add flour and mix. Spread in 10x13 cookie pan. Beat egg white stiff and spread on mix. Sprinkle with ground pecans. Bake at 350° for 12 minutes. Cut immediately. Do not let brown.

## FRENCH BUTTER COOKIES

1 stick real butter, room temperature
½ cup sugar plus 2 tablespoons
1 egg yolk (reserve egg white)
1 cup flour
½ teaspoon vanilla

Combine butter with sugar and mix until smooth. Add egg yolk, flour and vanilla; mix well. Press dough evenly in 15x10 pan. Beat egg white until frothy and spread on top of cookie dough. Sprinkle with chopped pecans. Bake at 350° for 15 minutes. Remove from oven and cut into squares. Serve when cooled.

## APRICOT BALLS

1 lb. powdered sugar
⅓ cup melted butter
2 tablespoons orange juice
1 (12 oz.) pkg. dried apricots, ground
¾ cup finely chopped nuts

Combine sugar, butter and orange juice. Add apricots and knead in bowl until ingredients are well mixed. Form into 1-inch balls and roll in chopped nuts. Store in refrigerator or freeze in covered container. Flavor improves with storage.

# July 10

## IN A PINCH SPAGHETTI

*Prep. Time: 20 minutes Cook Time: 1-1½ hours*

1 lb. lean ground beef or turkey
2 (16 oz.) cans tomato sauce
water
1 medium onion, finely chopped
1½ teaspoons brown sugar
1 teaspoon oregano
1 teaspoon sweet basil
½ teaspoon garlic salt
1 teaspoon Italian seasoning
1 pkg. spaghetti pasta
Parmesan cheese, optional

Crumble meat in a soup pan. Add onion and cover with water. Boil until meat is done. Drain off all water. Return meat and onion to pan. Add tomato sauce, brown sugar and spices. Cook over low heat for about an hour. In another pan, cook spaghetti according to package directions. When pasta is tender, drain off water and rinse in cold water to stop the cooking action. Drain and add to the meat sauce. Stir well and reheat pasta, letting it continue cooking for 15-20 more minutes. Serve hot with garlic bread sticks.

## KID BREAK!

Summer is the perfect time for blowing bubbles! Make your own colored bubble mix with the following: 3 parts dish detergent; 3 parts water; 2 parts glycerin and food coloring (optional).

# July 11

## SKILLET "BAKED" BEANS

*Prep. Time: 20 minutes Cook Time: 45 minutes*

1 medium onion, finely chopped
1 green pepper, finely chopped
½ cup BBQ sauce
2 tablespoons brown sugar
¼ cup honey
⅛ teaspoon garlic powder
2 lg. cans pork and beans
½ lb. bacon

Fry bacon until crisp. Set aside. Measure out 3 tablespoons bacon grease and empty out the rest. Add 3 tablespoons bacon grease back to skillet. Sauté onion and green pepper in grease. Add all ingredients except for bacon. Mix well. Cook over medium heat until beans are no longer soupy— about 45 minutes. Right before serving, crumble up bacon and sprinkle over the top.

Serve with Homemade Macaroni and Cheese (see page 125).

## BLUEBERRY ANGEL WHIP

*Prep. Time: 15 minutes Cook Time: 20 minutes*

1 pint fresh blueberries, washed and stemmed
1 cup sugar
2 tablespoons cornstarch dissolved in ¼ cup cold water
3 egg whites
¾ cup sugar
1 prepared Angel Food Cake™

First, put mixing bowl and electric beaters in freezer. Next, put washed berries in a medium saucepan with 1 cup sugar. Cook over medium heat, mashing and stirring occasionally. When hot, add dissolved cornstarch. Cook until liquid turns transparent and thickens. Remove from heat and let cool. Remove mixing bowl and beaters from freezer. Combine egg whites and ¾ cup sugar and beat on high with an electric mixer. When soft peaks form, add blueberries. Mix on low speed until well blended. For each serving, cut a piece of Angel Food Cake™ and pour blueberry whip over each slice.

# July 12

## T-BONE STEAKS ON THE GRILL

*Prep. Time: 5 min. (Marinating time: 1 hour) Cook Time: 8-12 min.*

## STEAK MARINADE

*Prep. Time: 5 minutes Cook Time: 10 minutes*

3 tablespoons Worcestershire sauce
2 tablespoons steak sauce
1 teaspoon garlic powder
1 teaspoon salt
⅛ teaspoon pepper
1 teaspoon dried minced onion
¼ cup water

Combine all ingredients in a small sauce pan and bring to a boil. Remove from heat and brush on each steak. Let each steak set for about an hour before grilling. Add more marinade right before grilling and use it as a baste while grilling. Cook on a hot grill, turning to cook evenly on both sides. Be sure to baste meat often. Serve with a baked potato with your choice of toppings.

## CARAMEL DUMPLINGS

*Prep. Time: 20 minutes Cook Time: 40-50 minutes*

1 cup brown sugar
1½ cups sugar
2 tablespoons butter
3 cups boiling water
2 teaspoons vanilla
1 cup sugar
2 tablespoons butter
1 tablespoon baking powder
1 cup milk
4 cups flour

Boil the 1 cup brown sugar, 1½ cups white sugar, butter, boiling water and vanilla. Keep hot. Then take remaining sugar, 1 tablespoon butter, baking powder, milk and flour and mix together adding flour and milk alternately, until thoroughly mixed. Drop this batter from a spoon into the hot syrup. Let dumplings cook in syrup for about 5 minutes. Then pour entire dish into a casserole dish and bake at 350° for about 30 minutes. Serve with a scoop of vanilla ice cream.

# July 13

## SMOKIN' SHISKABOBS

*Prep. Time: 15 minutes Cook Time: 20 minutes*

1 lb. smoked sausage
2 green peppers, quartered
2-3 cans whole baby potatoes
1 can chunk pineapple, reserve juice
2 cans carrot fingers or baby carrots
½ cup brown sugar
2 tablespoons butter
reserved pineapple juice

Cut sausage into chunks. Quarter green peppers. Drain liquid off of potatoes and carrots. In a small saucepan, combine brown sugar, butter and ¼ cup pineapple juice. Heat until sugar dissolves and mixtures becomes like a glaze. Remove from heat. Alternately place sausage chunks, green pepper quarters, whole potatoes and baby carrots on to a skewer. Place on hot grill. Brush each skewer with glaze several times as cooking. Cook over a hot grill for 12-18 minutes or until thoroughly heated.

# HONEY NUT ICE CREAM

*Prep. Time: 20 minutes*

2 pints heavy whipping cream, shake well
    before opening
¾ cup honey
1 teaspoon vanilla
2 cups crushed nuts (pecans recommended)

Grind nuts in a blender, set aside. In a cold mixing bowl, using beaters that have been chilled in the freezer, beat the whipping cream on high with an electric mixer until it becomes like whipped cream. Add vanilla and honey and continue beating on high for an additional minute. Fold in pulverized nuts. Pour into a freezer container and freeze until ready to serve.

# July 14

## FRUITY CHICKEN BAKE

*Prep. Time: 5 minutes Cook Time: 90 minutes*

6 boneless, skinless chicken breasts
1 bottle Seven Seas Fat Free Raspberry
    Vinaigrette™ dressing
1 can pineapple chunks
salt and pepper to taste

Lay chicken in a single layer in a baking pan. Pour entire bottle of dressing over chicken. Top with chunks of pineapple and the juice. Cover tightly and bake at 350° for 90 minutes. (If you use chicken tenderloins or cut the breasts in half, you can cut the baking time in half.) To serve, remove from pan. Salt and pepper each piece according to your taste.

# CHICKEN RICE AND PEAS

*Prep. Time: 5 minutes Cook Time: 15 minutes*

1 pkg. frozen baby peas, thawed
3 cups instant rice
2 tablespoons butter
2 teaspoons salt
1 can cream of chicken soup

Follow directions on box to prepare rice. Before adding rice to boiling water, cook peas for about 5 minutes, then stir in cream of chicken soup. Add rice to boiling mixture and remove from heat. Stir in butter and salt, mix well. Serve with chicken.

# July 15

## INDIVIDUAL PIZZA PIES

*Prep. Time: 20 minutes Cook Time: 15 minutes*

2 pkgs. English muffins
1 can prepared pizza sauce
2 cups shredded mozzarella cheese
1 cup shredded cheddar cheese
pepperoni slices

Combine cheeses and mix well. Separate muffins and place on a cookie sheet. Spread a tablespoon of pizza sauce on each half. Put a handful of mixed cheese on each slice and top with pepperoni slices. Bake at 350° for 10-15 minutes.

    Enjoy your choice of fresh fruit for dessert.

## KID BREAK!

A fun summertime activity for your family to do is to compile a time capsule in some kind of nondegradable container or box. Did you know there are an estimated 10,000 time capsules buried worldwide?

# July 16

## SPICY BEEF STIR FRY

*Prep. Time: 25 minutes Cook Time: 5-8 minutes*

1½ lbs. beef round tip steaks, cut ⅛-inch to ¼-inch thick
1 clove garlic, crushed
2 tablespoons olive oil
3 small zucchini, thinly sliced
1 pint cherry tomatoes, cut in halves
1 cup sliced mushrooms
1 medium onion, chopped
½ cup fat free bottled Italian salad dressing
6 cups hot cooked pasta
2 tablespoons Parmesan cheese
salt and pepper

Cut the beef steaks crosswise into 1-inch wide strips. Cut each strip crosswise in half. Stir the garlic in oil in a large non-stick skillet or wok. Cook over medium heat for one to two minutes. Remove the garlic. Add the beef strips, a few at a time, and stir-fry for 1 to 2 minutes or until cooked through. Season with salt and pepper. Remove from oil, but keep warm. Repeat steps for cooking meat until all meat is cooked. Next add the zucchini, mushrooms and onions and stir- fry for 2 to 3 minutes or until tender crisp. Return beef to skillet (or wok) and add tomato halves. Add salad dressing and heat through. Sprinkle Parmesan cheese over all. Serve over hot pasta.

## PEACH DELIGHT

*Prep. Time: 30 minutes Cook Time: 30-40 minutes*

1 pkg. yellow cake mix
eggs and oil as called for on the cake mix package
1 teaspoon cornstarch
¼ cup water
2 tablespoons apricot jam or preserves
½ teaspoon lemon juice
3 teaspoons sugar
1 cup sliced canned peaches

Prepare cake mix as directed on package. (I like to fix the recipe that makes the cake into a pound cake—but the choice is yours.) While cake is baking, combine water and cornstarch in a medium saucepan. Add jam, lemon juice and sugar. Bring to a boil. Reduce heat to low and cook for 2 more minutes. Add peaches and heat through. Serve over cake.

# July 17

## TACO SALAD

*Prep. Time: 25 minutes*

1 head iceberg lettuce
1 medium onion, chopped
1 lb. lean ground beef
1 jar taco sauce
2 cups shredded cheddar cheese
2 large tomatoes, diced
Dorito™ Nacho Chips or Tortilla Chips
1 small can tomato sauce
1 pkg. taco seasoning mix
fat free sour cream (optional)

Brown meat and onion in a skillet. Drain grease. Add tomato sauce and taco seasoning packet. Let simmer for 5 minutes over low heat. Tear up lettuce into bite-sized pieces. Put a bed of lettuce on each plate. Add a spoonful of meat. Top with tomatoes and cheese. Crumble chips over all and pour taco sauce over salad as the dressing. Top with sour cream if desired.

**KITCHEN TIP:** Make your own croutons by buttering bread on both sides. Sprinkle on your favorite seasoning and toast it on a cookie sheet in the oven set on 200 or 250 degrees. Once the bread has been buttered, you can cut it up in strips or cubes.

# July 18

## PITA SANDWICHES

*Prep. Time: 15 minutes Cook Time: about 5 minutes*

1 lb. shaved deli ham
1 lb. shaved deli turkey breast
shredded lettuce
chopped tomato
Miracle Whip Free™
pita bread, enough for each person

Cut pitas in half. In each half, spread some Miracle Whip™. Stuff each half with either or both meats, lettuce and tomato. Serve with cottage cheese mixed with pineapple chunks.

# July 19

## CHILI CHOPS

*Prep. Time: 20 minutes Cook Time: 25-30 minutes*

6 pork chops
salt and pepper to taste
1 medium onion, diced
1 can (8 oz.) tomato sauce
1 can (15½ oz.) chili style kidney beans
1 teaspoon chili powder
¼ teaspoon ground cumin
1 small green pepper, chopped
cooked rice, enough for each person

Trim chops of any excess fat and discard. Brown chops in a large skillet. Drain off any excess fat. Add salt and pepper according to your tastes. Add all remaining ingredients except for rice. Cover and let simmer over medium low heat for 25 to 30 minutes. Serve over a bed of rice.

## VEGETABLE SCRAMBLE

*Prep. Time: 25 minutes Cook Time: about 10 minutes*

2 tablespoons butter
4 cups shredded or grated cabbage
1 cup celery, sliced thin
1 small green pepper, finely chopped
2 cups diced, peeled tomatoes
1 medium onion, sliced thin
1 teaspoon salt
⅛ teaspoon pepper

In large skillet, melt butter. Add all vegetables and salt and pepper. Cover with a tight fitting lid and cook for 5-8 minutes. Remove lid, stir and continue cooking for a few minutes until vegetables are tender crisp.

## PECAN PIE DESSERT

*Prep. Time: 20 minutes Cook Time: 50-60 minutes*

1 pkg. butter or yellow cake mix
1 egg
½ cup butter
1 cup chopped pecans
FILLING:
⅔ cup reserved cake mix
½ cup brown sugar, firmly packed
1½ cups dark corn syrup
1 teaspoon vanilla
3 eggs

Generously grease sides and bottom of a 13x9 cake pan. Reserve ⅔ cup dry cake mix for filling. In a large bowl, combine remaining dry cake mix, butter and 1 egg. Mix until crumbly. Press in prepared pan. Bake at 350° for 15 to 20 minutes until golden brown. Meanwhile prepare filling. In large bowl, combine all ingredients; beat at medium speed 1 to 2 minutes. Pour filling over partially baked crust; sprinkle with pecans. Return to oven and bake for 30 to 35 minutes until filling is set. Cool. Cut into bars and serve.

# July 20

## LINGUINI WITH ITALIAN CHEESES

*Prep. Time: 20 minutes Cook Time: 15 minutes*

1 pkg. linguini
2 tablespoons olive oil
1 clove garlic, crushed
2 medium tomatoes, chopped
2 medium zucchini, sliced
1 cup sliced fresh mushrooms
1 small green pepper, diced
6 green onions, chopped
1 tablespoon fresh chopped parsley
1 teaspoon dried basil
½ teaspoon salt
⅛ teaspoon pepper
1 cup shredded Provolone cheese
¼ cup Parmesan cheese

Cook linguini according to package directions. In a large skillet, sauté garlic in olive oil for about 2 minutes. Remove garlic and discard. Stir in all remaining ingredients except for cheeses. Sauté until tender, about 8-10 minutes. Drain linguini and arrange on a large platter. Add cheeses to vegetable mixture and mix well. Spoon vegetables and cheese on to pasta and toss gently before serving.

## COFFEE CAN ICE CREAM

*Prep. Time: 5 minutes Freeze Time: 25-30 minutes*

1 (3 lb.) empty coffee can with lid,
   washed and dried
1 (1 lb.) empty coffee can with lid, washed & dried
1 can Milnot™
1 cup milk
⅓ cup sugar
1 egg, beaten
1 teaspoon vanilla

your choice of flavorings

Mix all ingredients well and pour into the 1 lb. coffee can. Seal can with lid. Place the smaller can inside the larger can. Pack the larger can with ice cubes and ½ cup canning salt. Rotate salt and ice cubes to distribute salt. Put lid on the larger can and roll on the floor with your feet or hands—going back and forth for 5 minutes. Add more ice and salt. Replace lid and repeat for another 5 minutes. Do this for a total of 20 minutes, then check the inner can's mixture. If ice cream is still too soft, continue rolling for another 10-15 minutes.

# July 21

## PRESSURE-COOKED CHICKEN & VEGIES

1 or 2 whole chickens
6-8 potatoes, peeled
6 carrots
2 cups water
2 yellow onions, peeled and quartered
2 stalks celery, cut in thirds
1 teaspoon salt
pepper to taste

Clean chicken(s) and remove cavity items. Stuff chicken with celery and onion. Arrange chicken(s) and vegetables in large pressure-cooker pan. Add water, salt and pepper. Cover with lid. Bring up to 10 lbs. of pressure over high heat, then reduce heat to medium and let cook for 45 minutes.

## CHERRY CITRUS SALAD

*Prep. Time: 5 minutes*

1 can cherry pie filling
1 can pineapple tidbits, drained
1 can mandarin orange sections, drained
2 cups miniature marshmallows
1 cup chopped pecans

Mix all ingredients together. Chill until ready to serve.

# July 22

## BLT SANDWICHES

*Prep. Time: 0 Cook Time: 15 minutes*

bread or buns
1 - 2 lbs. bacon (may use Turkey Bacon)
lettuce
2 large sandwich tomatoes
Fat Free Miracle Whip™

Fry bacon until crisp and drain on a paper towel or brown paper. Spread Miracle Whip™ on each slice of bread/bun. Put a leaf of lettuce on the bottom. Add tomato slices and 3 to 4 slices of crisp bacon. Add top piece of bread/bun.

## FRESH FRUIT SALAD

*Prep. Time: 20 minutes Cook Time: 15 minutes*

1 cup water
¾ cup sugar
2 eggs
¼ teaspoon salt
1 tablespoon cornstarch
1 lemon (juice and grated rind)
2 oranges (navels work best)
2 bananas
2 unpeeled apples
1 pint strawberries
1 cup seedless green grapes, cut in halves

In a medium saucepan, combine water, sugar, eggs, salt, cornstarch and lemon. Whisk until well blended. Cook over medium heat until mixture starts to boil and thickens. Remove from heat and refrigerate to cool. While sauce is cooling, peel oranges and break them apart into sections. Peel and slice bananas. Core and chop apples. Wash and de-stem strawberries, cutting them into quarters or slices. Wash grapes and cut each in half. When sauce is cool, pour over fruit and toss gently to evenly coat each piece. Refrigerate for an hour to let flavors blend. Serve well chilled.

# July 23

## HOMEMADE HAMBURGER HELPER

*Guess how many black spots Disney animators drew for the animated movie of 101 Dalmatians. Give up? The answer is 6,469,952. Now my question for you is who took the time to count all of them?*

*Prep. Time: 15 minutes Cook Time: 25 minutes*

1½ lbs. ground beef
3 cups instant rice
1 medium onion, chopped finely
1 tablespoon chili powder
1 (8 oz.) can tomato sauce
½ cup water
1 bay leaf
1 cup shredded cheddar cheese
1 teaspoon salt
⅛ teaspoon pepper
¼ teaspoon oregano

Brown ground beef and onion together in a large skillet. Drain off all grease when meat is done. Add chili powder, salt, pepper, tomato sauce and bay leaf. Simmer for about 5 minutes over medium heat. When sauce starts to boil, stir in uncooked rice. Cover with a tight-fitting lid and remove from heat. Let set for about 15 minutes. Uncover and stir, removing bay leaf. Sprinkle cheese over the top and return lid for another 3-5 minutes just long enough to let cheese melt. Serve directly from the stove-top.

## CLOWN HEADS

*Prep. Time: 15 minutes*

Ice Cream (your choice of flavors)
1 sugar cone for each serving
M&M's ™

Dip out one large scoop of ice cream and place on each dessert dish or in a disposable bowl. Put a sugar ice cream cone upside down on the top of the ice cream—make it look like a pointed hat. Use

M&M's™ to make a face on the ice cream. Return to freezer until ready to serve.

# July 24

## TENDER HERB GRILLED CHOPS

*Prep. Time: 10 minutes Cook Time: 20 minutes*

6 pork chops
2 teaspoons seasoned salt
⅛ teaspoon coarse black pepper
¼ teaspoon turmeric
¼ teaspoon sage
¼ teaspoon rosemary
3 tablespoons butter

Trim chops of excess fat and discard. In a small saucepan, combine butter and seasonings. Heat over low heat until well blended. Light grill and let it heat up before putting meat on to cook (about 10 minutes). Use a small paintbrush or a pastry brush and coat each pork chop with butter and herbs. Place on a searing hot grill and cook for 2-3 minutes. Turn and baste, cook for 2-3 minutes. Turn again and baste. Repeat until chops are cooked through.

## STUFFED POTATO PEPPERS

*Prep. Time: 20 minutes Cook Time: 15 minutes*

6 cups mashed potatoes
   (may use leftovers or instant)
6 medium green peppers
1 cup grated carrots
1 tablespoon parsley, chopped
6 green onions, chopped finely
   (including green tops)
½ cup Parmesan cheese
1 teaspoon garlic powder
1 teaspoon salt
¼ teaspoon pepper
1 cup skim milk
1½ cups shredded Cheddar cheese

Heat potatoes in a microwave on high until heated through—3-4 minutes or longer. Add milk and stir until smooth. Add parsley, chopped green onions, Parmesan cheese, garlic powder, salt and pepper and stir well. Stir in 1 cup shredded cheese. (Take a taste test—add more seasonings to taste.) Put cup of grated carrots in microwave and cook on high for 3 minutes. Stir grated carrots into potatoes. Core and remove seeds from each green pepper. Wash and pat dry. Fill each green pepper cavity with the mashed potatoes. Set upright in a microwaveable casserole dish. Microwave on high for about 5 minutes. Sprinkle each pepper with remaining cheddar cheese. Microwave on high for another 2-3 minutes.

# July 25

## CHILI DOGS OFF THE GRILL

*Prep. Time: 15 minutes Cook Time: 10-15 minutes*

1 pkg. bun-length hot dogs
1 pkg. hot dog buns
2 cans hot dog chili sauce
1 large onion, diced
1 cup shredded Cheddar cheese

Put hot dogs on a hot grill. In a small saucepan, empty Chili sauce and heat through on grill. Serve each hot dog on a bun topped with Chili sauce, diced onions and cheddar cheese.

### KID BREAK!

Use a dry-erase marker to write messages or love notes on the bathroom mirror to surprise your children or spouse. A quick spray of window-cleaner and a paper towel will clean the mirror's surface when you're ready to change the message.

# BAKED BEANS

*Prep. Time: 20 minutes Cook Time: 30-40 minutes*

1 lb. lean ground beef
1 large onion, finely chopped
3 (16 oz.) cans pork 'n' beans
1 cup brown sugar, firmly packed
1 tablespoon vinegar
1 teaspoon salt
1 cup ketchup
1 tablespoon prepared mustard
¼ cup honey BBQ sauce

Brown the ground beef and onions together until done. Drain. Pour into a deep casserole dish. Add all remaining ingredients and mix well. Bake at 400° for 30 to 40 minutes. Serve hot or cold.

# POTATO SALAD

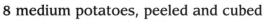
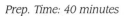

*Prep. Time: 40 minutes*

8 medium potatoes, peeled and cubed
3 eggs
1 small onion or 6 green onions, chopped
2 stalks celery, chopped
¼ cup sweet pickle relish
¾ cup mayonnaise or Miracle Whip™
1 tablespoon prepared mustard
1 teaspoon salt
pepper to taste

Cover potatoes with water in a large saucepan. Cook until tender. Drain. At the same time the potatoes are cooking, put eggs in a small saucepan and bring them to a boil. Boil for at least 5 minutes for hard boiled eggs. Remove from heat, cool in cold water. Peel eggs and chop. In a large bowl, combine cooked and cooled potatoes, chopped eggs and all remaining ingredients. Mix well. Refrigerate until ready to serve.

# HOMEMADE CHOCOLATE ICE CREAM

*Prep. Time: 5 minutes Freeze Time: 1-2 hours*

4 eggs, beaten well
3 cups sugar
3 quarts milk
1 can Milnot™
1½ teaspoons vanilla
¾ cup chocolate syrup
¼ teaspoon salt

Combine all ingredients and pour into an ice cream freezer. Add coarse salt and ice around the ice cream tub and work freezer until too stiff to turn.

---

**KITCHEN TIP:**
Here are some substitutes you can use if you find you're out of one of these:
*If you're out of....Use instead...*

1 TEASPOON ALLSPICE—
¼ teaspoon ground cinnamon and
½ teaspoon  ground cloves

1 TEASPOON BAKING POWDER—
½ teaspoon cream of tartar plus
¼ teaspoon  baking soda

1 CUP BROWN SUGAR—
1 cup white sugar plus
1½ tablespoons molasses

1 CUP CAKE FLOUR—
1 cup sifted all-purpose flour minus
2 tablespoons

# July 26

## LEMON ORANGE ROUGHY WITH DILL

*Prep. Time: 5 minutes Cook Time: 5-10 minutes*

2 lbs Orange Roughy fish fillets
2 lemons
1/3 cup butter
3 teaspoons dill weed
1 teaspoon marjoram leaves
1/2 teaspoon salt

Squeeze fresh lemon juice over fish fillets. Combine dill weed, marjoram leaves and salt and sprinkle over each filet, coating evenly. Dot each filet with butter. Broil for 5 to 10 minutes or until fish flakes easily. Serve with tartar sauce.

## MACARONI SALAD

*Prep. Time: 30 minutes*

3 cups cooked elbow macaroni
1/2 cup mayonnaise or Miracle Whip
1 stalk celery, finely diced
1 green pepper, finely diced
1 teaspoon prepared mustard
1 teaspoon salt
1/3 cup sweet pickle relish

Combine drained macaroni with all ingredients. Mix well. Refrigerate until ready to serve in order to blend flavors.

## CHOCOLATE ZUCCHINI CAKE

*Prep. Time: 25-30 minutes Cook Time: 60 to 90 minutes, depending upon size of pan*

3 cups finely grated peeled zucchini
4 eggs, slightly beaten
1 cup oil
1/2 cup baby food plums
3 1/4 cups sugar
2 squares (2 oz.) baking chocolate, melted
3 1/4 cups flour
1 1/2 teaspoons cinnamon
1 teaspoon salt
2 teaspoons baking powder
1 cup chopped pecans, optional
2 teaspoons baking soda

Grate and drain zucchini, add beaten eggs. Stir in oil, plums, sugar and melted chocolate and beat on low speed with an electric mixer. In a separate bowl, sift together flour, cinnamon, salt, baking soda and baking powder. Measure out 1/2 cup of flour mixture and stir in with chopped nuts. Gradually add flour mixture to zucchini, beating by hand to mix well. Stir in the flour-coated nuts and stir until well blended. Pour batter into a greased and floured bundt pan or two 9x5-inch pans. Bake at 350° for 60 to 90 minutes if using the bundt pan; 50 to 60 minutes if using the two smaller pans. Test for doneness by inserting a knife in the center. Remove from pan and let cool. This tastes like a rich chocolate pound cake. Serve with non-fat non-dairy whipped topping or chocolate fudge sauce.

# July 27

## WAGON WHEEL DINNER

*Prep. Time: 5-8 minutes Cook Time: 20-35 minutes*

1 pkg. hot dogs, halved lengthwise
1/2 cup butter
6 cups frozen hash brown potatoes, thawed
1 large onion, finely chopped
1 small green pepper, finely chopped
6 eggs, slightly beaten
2 cups American processed cheese, cubed
1 teaspoon salt
1/4 teaspoon pepper

In a large skillet, melt butter. Add hashbrowns, onions and green pepper. Sprinkle on salt and pepper; stir to combine. Add cheese cubes and stir occasionally until cheese begins to soften and melt. Cover with a lid and reduce heat to low. Cook for 10-15 minutes, stirring occasionally to distribute cheese. When cheese is melted, pour eggs evenly over the top. Arrange the hot dogs as "spokes of a wagon wheel" on top. Cover and cook over low heat for another 10 minutes to allow hot dogs and eggs to heat through.

## KITCHEN TIPS

### What to do with Herbs and Seeds

To dry fresh herbs such as Sage, Chives, Rosemary and Thyme, pick and wash with clear lukewarm water. Pat dry with power towels. Arrange herbs on 3 layers of paper towels and set in microwave. Dry herbs by running microwave for 3-4 minutes on the highest possible setting. Remove and store in an air-tight bag or dry spice bottle. Use as you would the store-bought variety.

For Parsley, Basil, Oregano, Peppermint, Spearmint, Chives, Sage and Rosemary, you can also gather several stems of the plant and tie them together with a rubber band. Use a push-pin and "thumb-tac" the herb bundles so they hang suspended under your kitchen cabinets. Allow herbs to air dry for 6-12 weeks. As herbs dry and shrink, the rubber band will tighten around the bunch, holding them secure. To use, roll dried herb (one at a time) in-between your hands, crumbling the dried leaves over a large bowl. Pour dried herb into an air-tight bag or dry spice bottle. Discard stems. Use as you would the store-bought variety.

### Fresh Peppermint or Spearmint "Candy"

Wash fresh peppermint or spearmint and remove leaves from stems. Pat dry with paper towels. Set aside. In a small bowl, beat 1 egg white on high speed with an electric mixer until frothy. Dip each leaf in egg white mixture and then coat both sides in granulated sugar. Set each leaf on waxed paper and let air dry over night. Store in an air-tight bag. Use on cakes, desserts or to each like candy.

### Sunflower Seeds

Wash and drain fresh sunflower seeds. Pat dry with paper towels. Sauté 3 cups of seeds with 2 tablespoons butter or 1½ tablespoons corn oil and 1 teaspoon salt in a large skillet for about 3-4 minutes. Drain seeds and arrange them on a baking sheet in a single layer. Sprinkle salt over seeds. Bake seeds at 250° for 30-45 min.

# July 28

## BARBECUED CHICKEN

*Prep. Time: 25 minutes Cook Time: 1 hour 30 minutes*

1 - 2 whole chickens, cut up and skinned
2 lemons
1 large onion
1½ cups ketchup
⅔ cup Worcestershire sauce
2 teaspoons chili powder
2 teaspoons salt
½ teaspoon pepper
2½ cups water

Place meat in shallow roasting pan. Place a slice of unpeeled lemon and a thin slice of onion on each piece (as the juices from the lemon and onion penetrate the meat as it cooks, it becomes a natural tenderizer). Preheat oven to 450°. Insert uncovered roasting pan and let chicken bake for about 20-25 minutes. Meanwhile, combine the remaining ingredients in a medium saucepan. Stir well and bring mixture to a boil. When sauce begins to boil, remove from heat. Remove roasting pan from oven and remove lemon and onion slices. Baste each piece of meat with the BBQ sauce. Reduce oven temperature to 350°. Return pan to oven and continue baking until chicken is done, about 1 hour. Every 15 minutes or so, turn chicken and baste with sauce. If sauce becomes too thick, add a little water to thin.

## CREAMY PEAS & POTATOES

*Prep. Time: 15 minutes Cook Time: about 40 minutes*

15-20 tiny to small new (red) potatoes
2 cups fresh peas (or frozen peas, thawed)
6 green onions, finely chopped
3 tablespoons butter
3 tablespoons flour
2 cups milk

2 teaspoons salt

Scrub potatoes and put them in a large soup pan. Cover with water. Add 1 teaspoon salt. Boil potatoes for about 15 minutes. Add peas and chopped onions to potatoes and continue boiling for another 10 to 15 minutes. Drain. Make a white sauce in a small saucepan by combining melted butter with flour, a dash of salt and milk. Stir until thick and gravy like. Pour sauce over vegetables. Sprinkle with remaining teaspoon of salt and stir well. Cook for an additional 3 to 5 minutes.

# July 29

## STOVE-TOP KIELBASA DINNER

*Prep. Time: 20 minutes Cook Time: about 35 minutes*

2 lbs. Kielbasa, cut into half-inch slices
1 cup sour cream
3 tablespoons prepared mustard
1 teaspoon salt
1 large Spanish (or sweet) onion, sliced
1 medium red onion, sliced
6 cups shredded cabbage
½ teaspoon coarse black pepper
8 small new red potatoes, scrubbed and cut in quarters
2½ cups water

In large skillet, combine kielbasa, onion slices, cabbage and potatoes. Add water and cover skillet with a tight fitting lid. Cook over medium heat for about 20 minutes or until cabbage and onions are soft and somewhat translucent. Stir in sour cream, mustard, salt and pepper; mix well. Return lid to skillet and cook for another 10 to 15 minutes.

Serve with chilled wedges of watermelon.

# July 30

## MEATBALLS IN CREAM SAUCE

*Prep. Time: 25 minutes Cook Time: 20 minutes*

1½ - 2 lbs. lean ground beef
1 medium onion, finely chopped
½ cup crushed saltine crackers
2 eggs
2 tablespoons parsley flakes
1 tablespoon sweet basil
2 tablespoons Worcestershire sauce
1 can cream of celery soup
1 can cream of mushroom soup
1 cup water
3 tablespoons dill pickle, minced (like relish)
6 cups cooked rice

In a large bowl, combine ground beef with onion, crushed crackers, eggs, parsley, basil and Worcestershire sauce. Mix well and form into 1-2 inch balls. Brown meatballs in a skillet, turning often. When meatballs are cooked through, remove from skillet and drain off all pan drippings. Pour in soups with water and minced pickle. Heat until almost boiling. Add meatballs and cover with a lid, reduce heat to low and let simmer for about 20 minutes. Serve over cooked rice.

# July 31

## SKILLET-ROASTED CHICKEN

*Prep. Time: 20 minutes Cook Time: 35-40 minutes*

6-8 pieces chicken, skinless
2 tablespoons flour
¼ teaspoon ground sage
¼ teaspoon dried thyme
¼ teaspoon salt
⅛ teaspoon coarse black pepper

½ teaspoon parsley flakes
½ cup buttermilk
2 tablespoons butter
1 can cream of chicken soup
½ cup water
cooked buttered egg noodles

In a large plastic bag, combine flour with sage, thyme, salt, pepper and parsley. Dip chicken in buttermilk and then drop in bag. Shake bag to evenly coat each piece of chicken with the flour and spices. In a large skillet over medium heat, melt butter. Add each coated piece of chicken and let cook for about 10 minutes, turning once or twice. Remove chicken. Add soup and water to skillet, stirring to loosen any browned bits. Reduce heat to low. Add chicken to soup, cover with a tight fitting lid and cook for another 20 to 30 minutes or until chicken is tender and juices run clear. Serve over buttered egg noodles.

## PEACH FLUFF

*Prep. Time: 2-3 minutes*

1 can crushed pineapple, in its own juice
1 can peach pie filling
1 can evaporated milk
1 tub Fat Free Cool Whip™

Combine all ingredients in a mixing bowl and blend well. Spoon into individual serving dishes and chill until ready to serve.

# August 1

## POPCORN SHRIMP & SPAGHETTI

*Prep. Time: 20 minutes Cook Time: 25 minutes*

2 lbs. breaded popcorn shrimp
1½ cups oil
1 lb. thin spaghetti pasta
1 quart prepared spaghetti sauce
¼ cup Parmesan cheese
¼ cup Romano cheese

Heat oil in a small saucepan and deep-fat fry popcorn shrimp until cooked. Remove from oil and drain on absorbent paper towel. Cook pasta according to package directions. When pasta is cooked, drain and rinse. Add spaghetti sauce to pasta and toss. Add fried shrimp to pasta and serve. Sprinkle Parmesan and Romano cheeses to each plate just prior to serving.

## APPLE & CELERY SALAD

*Prep. Time: 20 minutes*

6-8 apples
1 cup raisins
2 stalks celery, finely chopped
¾ cup Miracle Whip Free™
2 tablespoons sugar
¼ cup skim milk
2 teaspoons lemon juice
1 cup shredded cheddar or colby cheese

Core apples and cut into bite-sized chunks. Combine lemon juice in ¼ cup water and pour over apples. Let set. Pour boiling water over raisins and let set for 5 minutes. Drain off water. In a mixing bowl, combine Miracle Whip™, sugar and milk; mix well. Drain off lemon water from apples and add apples and raisins. Chop celery and add to apples. Mix well to evenly coat apples, raisins and celery with "dressing." Stir in cheese if desired. Let chill for at least an hour before serving in order to blend flavors.

# August 2

## GRILLED LEMON-THYME CHICKEN

*Prep. Time: 15 minutes (Marinating time: about 2 hours) Cook Time: 8-10 minutes each*

6 boneless chicken breast halves, skinned and slightly flattened
1 large or 2 medium garlic cloves, crushed with the side of a knife
½ cup lemon juice (about 1½ lemons)
2 tablespoons olive oil
½ teaspoon dried thyme
salt and black pepper to taste

Put the breasts in a glass baking dish that will hold them in one layer. Beat the remaining ingredients in a small bowl with a fork and pour over the chicken. Cover with plastic wrap and refrigerate for 2 hours. Turn the breasts once during that time.

Preheat the broiler. Remove the breasts from the marinade and broil 4 minutes on each side or until cooked through.

## TOMATO BOWLS

*Prep. Time: 15 minutes*

6 large firm tomatoes
½ cup lowfat (or fat free) cottage cheese per person (3 cups for 6 servings)
6 large leaves lettuce (your choice)
salt and pepper to taste
2 tablespoons Miracle Whip Free™

Core tomatoes and cut out the flesh from inside, making each tomato into a "bowl." Dice tomato flesh and set aside. In a medium bowl, combine cottage cheese and Miracle Whip™. Stir to mix

well. Add diced tomatoes and mix well. Fill each tomato cavity with cottage cheese mixture. Set each tomato on a leaf of lettuce and salt and pepper to taste.

# August 3

## HAM & POTATO PIE

*Prep. Time: 20 minutes Cook Time: 30 minutes*

non-stick vegetable spray
1½ cups lean ham, finely chopped
1 medium onion, finely chopped
1 small green pepper, finely chopped
½ cup fat-free chicken broth
1 can creamed-styled corn
2 cups mashed potatoes (use either leftover or instant)
1 tablespoon Worcestershire Sauce
salt and pepper to taste

Preheat oven to 425°. Spray a large skillet with non-fat vegetable spray and sauté the onion over medium heat until softened, about 2 minutes. Add the green pepper, chicken broth, salt, pepper and Worcestershire sauce and simmer uncovered for 10 minutes.

In a bowl, combine the ham, corn and onion mixture; then spoon this into an ungreased baking dish. Cover with the mashed potatoes, roughen the surface with a fork, and bake uncovered for 30 minutes, or until the top is flecked with brown. If necessary, run the dish under the broiler to brown.

## HARVEST SALAD

*Prep. Time: 15-20 minutes Cook Time: 15-20 minutes*

3 slices bacon
1 medium onion, diced
1 small green pepper, diced
1 large zucchini, sliced and quartered
2-4 ears fresh corn, cut from the cob
5 fresh tomatoes, cored and cut in wedges

1 cup green beans, snapped

1 tablespoon Accent™

1 tablespoon sugar

1 teaspoon salt

⅛ teaspoon pepper

¾ teaspoon cumin

½ cup V-8 Juice™

Fry bacon until crisp and remove to drain. In remaining bacon grease cook onion and green pepper until tender. Add zucchini and continue cooking for another 3 to 4 minutes. Add corn, tomatoes, juice, beans and seasonings. Simmer for 8-10 minutes. Serve when vegetables are tender. Crumble bacon over vegetables and serve. Other vegetables may be substituted according to your taste and what is available in season.

# August 4
## PARTY TIME MEATBALLS

*Prep. Time: 20-25 minutes Cook Time: 25 minutes*

vegetable oil spray

1 egg

½ cup low-fat or non-fat cottage cheese

½ cup skim milk

3¼ teaspoons allspice

¾ teaspoon nutmeg

⅛ teaspoon ground cloves

1 teaspoon salt

½ teaspoon pepper

1 cup finely chopped onion

1 lb. lean ground pork (not sausage)

1 lb. lean ground turkey

1 recipe Fresh Herb Sauce (see below)

Preheat oven to 375°. Lightly spray a large broiler pan with vegetable spray. In a blender combine egg, cottage cheese, milk and spices. Process until smooth. Pour mixture into large bowl. Add onion and meats. Thoroughly blend with hands. Form meat mixture into balls. Place on prepared pan and bake uncovered 25 minutes.

Heat Fresh Herb Sauce in a small saucepan over medium heat. Transfer meatballs to a serving bowl. Pour Fresh Herb Sauce over meatballs and serve immediately.

## FRESH HERB SAUCE

*Prep. Time: 15 minutes*

½ cup low-fat or non-fat cottage cheese

2 tablespoons butter

1½ cups skim milk

3 tablespoons flour

1 tablespoon finely chopped fresh dill

1 tablespoon finely chopped fresh basil

1 tablespoon snipped fresh chives

1 tablespoon finely chopped fresh parsley

dash pepper

Combine cottage cheese and milk in a blender. Process until smooth and set aside. Melt butter in a saucepan over medium heat. Stir in flour and cook 1 minute. Add milk and cottage cheese mixture. Bring to a boil, stirring constantly. Cook until thickened. Remove from heat; add herbs and pepper. Stir well.

## BUTTERED PARSLEY EGG NOODLES

*Prep. Time: 5 minutes Cook Time: about 15 minutes*

1 bag dried egg noodles, medium width

water

1 teaspoon salt

¼ cup butter

2 teaspoons dried parsley

1 teaspoon salt

¼ teaspoon pepper

Cook noodles in boiling salt water. (Add the 1 teaspoon salt to water.) Drain off water when noodles are tender. While noodles are still hot, add butter, parsley, salt and pepper. Mix well then serve.

Serve with fresh vegetables and your choice of dips.

## KITCHEN WISDOM

Did you know that those spices and ingredients in your kitchen cabinets can be used for home-medical remedies as well?

• After having teeth pulled, bite down on warm wet tea bags. The tea acts as a poultice, drawing out any infection. This will help to reduce swelling and prevent dry socket from forming.

• To stop a bad case of hiccups, swallow a teaspoon of granulated sugar without drinking anything with it.

• Dissolve baking soda in water, making it into a thick paste. Spread on bee stings or insect bites to take the burning sting away.

• For a sore throat, dissolve a teaspoon of salt in ½ cup warm water and use as a gargle.

• Ammonia will eliminate the burning sting associated with bee stings. If you don't have any plain ammonia on hand, a quick spray of window cleaner with ammonia will work, too.

# August 5

## SMOKED SAUSAGE SANDWICHES

*Prep. Time: less than 5 minutes Cook Time: 15 minutes*

Your choice: skinless smoked sausage cut into bun-length pieces; individual smoked sausage "dogs"; or 2 smokie links per serving
hot dog buns
mustard or your choice of condiments
water

Cook sausage in boiling water for about 10-15 minutes. Remove from water and drain. Place sausage on buns and top with your favorite condiment.

## HOT SLAW

*Prep. Time: 15 minutes Cook Time: 25 minutes*

2 tablespoons butter
¼ teaspoon dry mustard
dash cayenne pepper
2 tablespoons flour
1 egg, beaten
2 tablespoons sugar
¾ cup evaporated milk
½ teaspoon salt
⅓ cup weak vinegar (fill measuring cup half full of vinegar and add water to fill to ⅓ cup)
3 cups finely grated cabbage
1 cup finely grated carrot

In a small saucepan, melt butter. Add dry mustard, cayenne and flour. When smooth, stir in beaten egg, sugar, milk, salt and vinegar. Put in a double boiler. Cook, stirring until thick. Add cabbage and carrots and steam for about 15 minutes. Serve warm.

# MELON SALAD

*Prep. Time: 15 minutes*

1 cantaloupe
1 honey dew melon
¼ to ½ red watermelon

Peel rind from each melon and remove seeds. Cut melons into wedges and then slice into bite-sized pieces. Or use a melon baller to make a melon ball salad. Gently toss together to make a colorful melon salad. Serve chilled.

# August 6

## BEEF AND TOMATOES

*Prep. Time: 5 minutes Cook Time: 15-20 minutes*

1 lb. lean ground beef
1 quart stewed tomatoes
1 medium onion, chopped
2 teaspoons salt
½ teaspoon pepper
cooked rice

In a large skillet, brown meat and onion until cooked. Drain off all grease. Whiz stewed tomatoes in a blender for a minute and then pour over meat. Add salt and pepper; mix well. Heat over medium heat until tomatoes begin to boil. Serve over a bed of cooked rice.

## STUFFED CELERY & GREEN PEPPERS

*Prep. Time: about 20 minutes*

1 bunch celery
4 large green peppers
soft cream cheese
spreadable cheddar cheese (cheese from a can works well)
peanut butter
raisins

3-trays ice cubes
water

Wash stalks of celery and cut into 3-4-inch pieces. Wash green peppers, remove cores and seeds. Cut peppers into wedges. Fill sink with cold water and add 3 trays of ice cubes. Let celery and peppers soak in ice-cold water until you're ready to fill them. The cold water will make them crisp to eat. Fill celery sticks and pepper wedges with your choice of: cream cheese, cheddar cheese or peanut butter. For the ones filled with peanut butter, add 3-4 raisins on top. (I especially like green pepper wedges filled with cream cheese.)

# August 7

## PAPRIKASH CHICKEN

*Prep. Time: 15 minutes Cook Time: about 40 minutes*

2-3½ pound broiler-fryer chicken, cut up, remove skin
2 large onions, chopped
1 teaspoon salt
1 garlic clove, minced
1 small ripe tomato, peeled, seeded
3 tablespoons olive oil
½ green pepper, cut into small shreds (use a food grater)
1¼ cups fat-free chicken broth
2 tablespoons paprika (Hungarian paprika works best)
1 cup lowfat or non-fat sour cream

In a large soup pan, sauté the onions and garlic in the olive oil until softened. Add the green pepper and the paprika and mix well. Sprinkle the chicken pieces with salt, add to the pot, then add the tomato and 1 cup of chicken broth. Stir, bring to a boil, then cover, lower heat and simmer slowly, until the chicken is tender, about 25 minutes. Turn the chicken pieces from time to time so they cook evenly. Taste and adjust seasonings. Transfer the chicken pieces to a warm platter. Add the remain-

# COOKIES OF THE MONTH

## GINGER SNAP COOKIES

¾ cup shortening, creamed
1 cup brown sugar, firmly packed
¼ cup molasses
1 egg
2¼ cups sifted flour
1½ teaspoons baking soda
1 teaspoon cinnamon
1 teaspoon ground ginger
¼ teaspoon ground cloves
¼ teaspoon salt

Combine shortening, sugar, molasses and egg and beat thoroughly. Add baking soda, cinnamon, ginger, cloves and salt to flour and sift together, adding gradually to shortening mixture. Cover and chill. Roll into 1-inch balls and then roll in granulated sugar. Bake on greased cookie sheet at 325° for 8 minutes.

## BANANA-OATMEAL DROPS

¾ cup shortening
1 cup sugar
1 egg
1 medium banana, mashed
½ teaspoon lemon juice
1½ cups flour
½ teaspoon baking soda
1 teaspoon salt
¾ teaspoon cinnamon
¼ teaspoon nutmeg
1½ cups oatmeal
½ cup chopped nuts

Cream shortening and sugar together and add egg, banana and lemon juice; mix well. In a separate bowl, sift together the flour, baking soda, salt, cinnamon and nutmeg. Mix dry ingredients in with creamed mixture, mixing well. Stir in 1½ cups oatmeal and ½ cup chopped nuts. Mix well and drop by teaspoon on greased cookie sheet. Bake at 350 degrees for 7-10 minutes.

## CONFETTI COOKIES

1 cup sugar
½ cup brown sugar, firmly packed
1 cup shortening
2 eggs
1 teaspoon vanilla
1 teaspoon salt
1 teaspoon baking soda
2½ cups flour
1 cup cut up gumdrops, different colors
½ cup chopped nuts

Cream together sugars and shortening; add eggs and vanilla; add dry ingredients and cream mixture. Add gumdrops and nuts and mix well. Drop on greased cookie sheet. Bake at 350° for 15 minutes.

ing ¼ cup broth to the pot and bring to a boil, scraping up bits from the bottom and sides. Add the sour cream, more paprika if desired, and stir until smooth. Pour the sauce over the chicken and serve at once with noodles or rice.

## ZUCCHINI BREAD

*Prep. Time: 10 minutes Cook Time: 1 hour or more*

non-fat vegetable spray
3 cups flour
3 large eggs
½ teaspoon baking soda
1 teaspoon baking powder
1 cup oil
1 teaspoon salt
1 cup brown sugar, firmly packed
1 cup sugar
3 teaspoons ground cinnamon
2 cups grated zucchini, tightly packed
1 teaspoon vanilla

Combine the eggs, oil and sugar in a large bowl. Stir in the zucchini and the vanilla.

In another bowl, sift together the flour, baking soda, baking powder, salt and cinnamon. Add to the zucchini mixture and stir lightly to blend. Spray two bread loaf pans with the vegetable spray, making sure to coat the sides well. Divide between the prepared pans and bake at 325° for 1 hour or until bread tests done. Cool for 20 minutes on a wire rack before removing from pan. Keep refrigerated, wrapped in foil, or freeze.

# August 8

## BEEF BURGUNDY

*You won't believe this, but this date is known as Sneak Zucchini onto your neighbor's porch night. Really it is! If you're one of those lucky neighbors to discover zucchini on your porch, go ahead and grate the zucchini. Measure into 2 cups and put in freezer bags. Store bags in the freezer. This way, you can enjoy the fresh zucchini recipes all year long.*

*Prep. Time: 10-15 minutes Cook Time: 25 minutes\**

2-4 lbs. beef round steak
1 cup Burgundy wine
1 medium onion, finely chopped
1 large clove garlic, crushed
1 can cream of mushroom soup
1 pkg. dry-onion soup mix
1 bay leaf
1 tablespoon finely snipped fresh parsley
1 cup water
1 can whole mushrooms, drained

Trim meat of fat and discard. Cut meat into bite-sized pieces. In a pressure cooker, combine soup with water, dried soup mix, Burgundy wine, onions, garlic and mushrooms. Mix well and stir in beef. Add bay leaf and parsley. Cover with lid and bring cooker up to 10 lbs. pressure. Cook for 25 minutes and then serve over cooked noodles. *\*You can bake this instead of using a pressure cooker. To bake, combine ingredients in large casserole dish with a tight fitting lid. Cover and bake at 325° for 2½ hours.*

## BAKED ZUCCHINI

*Prep. Time: 20 minutes Cook Time: 45 minutes*

2 large or 5 small zucchini, washed, peeled & grated
4 eggs, lightly beaten
½ cup flour
1 cup grated muenster cheese
1 cup shredded cheddar cheese
¼ cup minced fresh parsley
¼ cup plus 1 tablespoon butter
1 tablespoon oregano

Sprinkle salt on zucchini and let it set for about 15 minutes. After 15 minutes, squeeze zucchini to remove all water. Return dry zucchini to bowl and add remaining ingredients. Mix well. Pour into a buttered casserole dish and dot the top with pats of butter. Bake at 375º for about 45 minutes or when zucchini is puffed-up and lightly browned.

# August 9

## SAUSAGE PILAF

*Prep. Time: 10 minutes Cook Time: about an hour*

1 lb. pork sausage

1 cup chopped celery

1 medium onion, chopped

1 small green pepper, chopped

1¼ cups skim milk

¾ cup uncooked rice

½ teaspoon poultry seasoning

¼ teaspoon salt

1 can cream of mushroom soup

2 tablespoons butter

1 cup crushed Ritz™ crackers

Brown sausage and drain off all grease. Add celery, onion and green pepper to skillet. Cook until tender, but not brown. Add soup, milk, rice, salt and seasoning. Pour into a large casserole dish and bake at 350º for about 45 minutes. Combine cracker crumbs with 2 tablespoons butter and sprinkle mixture over the top of the casserole. Bake, uncovered, for 10-15 minutes longer.

## FUDGE CREAM PIE

*Prep. Time: 25 minutes Cook Time: about 20 minutes*

1 baked 9-inch pie shell

1⅓ cups sugar

¼ cup flour

¼ cup cocoa

1⅔ cups (a tall can) evaporated milk

3 egg yolks, slightly beaten (save egg whites for meringue topping)

2 tablespoons butter

1½ teaspoons vanilla

meringue topping

Sift together sugar, flour and cocoa; gradually stir in evaporated milk. Pour this into a medium saucepan and heat over medium heat until mixture comes to a boil and thickens. Reduce heat; cook and stir for about 4 minutes. Add small amount of hot mixture to egg yolks, stirring well after each addition. Once all of the cocoa mixture is combined with egg yolks, return all to pan. Cook over medium-low heat for 1 to 3 minutes—mixture will become very thick. Remove from heat and stir in butter and vanilla. Cool for about 5 minutes and then pour into the pie shell. Cover with meringue, sealing well around the edges. Bake at 350º for 12 to 15 minutes.

### MERINGUE:

¼ teaspoon cream of tartar

½ teaspoon vanilla

3 egg whites

½ cup sugar

In a mixing bowl, combine egg whites with cream of tartar and vanilla. Beat at high speed with an electric mixer until soft peaks form. Gradually add sugar and continue beating at high speed until stiff peaks form and sugar is dissolved. Cover pie with meringue and bake to lightly brown.

# August 10

## QUICK 'N' EASY PIZZA CASSEROLE

*Prep. Time: 15 minutes Cook Time: 20 minutes*

1 pkg. dry egg noodles

1 jar or can of prepared pizza sauce

1 lb. sausage links (like Smokie Links™), sliced

2 cups shredded mozzarella cheese

1 cup shredded cheddar cheese

1 pkg. sliced pepperoni

Cook noodles until tender; drain off water and rinse in cold water. Combine drained noodles with meats and pizza sauce. Spread out in a 9x13 pan and top with both cheeses. Bake at 350° for about 20 minutes or until cheese is melted. Serve with garlic bread sticks.

## FROZEN CREAMED CHERRIES

*Prep Time: 5 minutes*

1⅓ cups (15 oz. can) Eagle Brand™ sweetened condensed milk
¼ cup lemon juice
1 can (1 lb. 5 oz.) prepared cherry pie filling
1 cup crushed pineapple, well drained
¼ teaspoon almond extract
1 teaspoon vanilla
2 cups (1 pt.) heavy cream

In small mixing bowl, beat heavy cream on high speed with an electric mixer until it is the consistency of whipped cream. Set aside. In large bowl combine all other ingredients and mix well. Fold in the whipped cream. Freeze until solid and then cut into servings.

## KID BREAK!

On a rainy summer afternoon, try making flubber! You will need two containers. In the first container mix 1½ cups warm water, 2 cups of of Elmer's™ white glue and a few drops of food coloring. In your second container mix 1¹/₃ cups of warm water and 3 level teaspoons of Borax™. Mix both containers thoroughly. Next, mix the Borax™ mixture into the glue mixture, until combined. (There will probably be some liquid left at the bottom of the container.) Remove flubber from leftover liquid and place on a tray. Let stand for a few minutes. When not using, store flubber in an airtight container. It will keep for 10-14 days.

# August 11

## APPLE-CABBAGE KIELBASA

*Prep. Time: 20 minutes Cook Time: 16 minutes*

3 tart apples
6 cups shredded cabbage
½ cup thinly sliced red onion
2 tablespoons butter
2 tablespoons water
1 tablespoon apple cider vinegar
¼ teaspoon salt
¼ teaspoon pepper
1 lb. Kielbasa

Core and slice 2 apples. Combine with cabbage and onion. Sauté apple mixture in butter for about 5 minutes. Stir often to avoid sticking. Add water, vinegar, salt and pepper. Pierce sausage and cut into bite-sized pieces. Place over apple and cabbage mixture. Cook, covered, for about 10 minutes or until cabbage is barely cooked and sausage has heated through. Core and wedge remaining apple. Add to skillet and cook, covered, for a minute longer. Serve immediately.

## APPLE DIPLICIOUS

*Prep. Time: 10 minutes*

apples, sliced and covered with orange juice
1 (8 oz.) pkg. cream cheese
¾ cup brown sugar, firmly packed
2 teaspoons vanilla
¼ cup sugar

In a small mixing bowl, combine cream cheese with both sugars and vanilla. Use the low setting on an electric mixer to blend well. Chopped nuts may be added, if desired. To serve, remove apple slices from orange juice and dip into the creamed cheese mixture.

# August 12

## BEEF WELLINGTON

*Prep. Time: 30 minutes (Marinade time: at least 2 hours) Cook Time: 90 minutes*

MARINADE:

1 tablespoon dry mustard

1 cup water

1 cup soy sauce

3 cloves garlic

4 tablespoons beef bouillon

6 tablespoons brown sugar

CRUST:

2 cups flour

1 teaspoon salt

$2/_3$ cup shortening

5 to 7 tablespoons water

2 lbs round steak

2 cups sliced mushrooms

1 medium red onion, cut into wedges

1 egg

¼ cup milk

flour

Trim meat of any fat and discard. Cut round steak into bite-size pieces. Slice mushrooms and cut onion into wedges. Combine marinade ingredients and add to meat, mushrooms and onions. Cover and refrigerate to marinade for at least 2 hours. (Best if left for longer.) In a shallow baking dish, bake meat and vegetables covered at 325° for 90 minutes.

While meat and vegetables are baking, prepare crust. In mixing bowl, combine flour and salt. Cut in shortening, using a pastry blender. Sprinkle water over the mixture, a tablespoon at a time. Add water until dough is moist. Form it into equal balls. Flatten each to about a half inch thickness and cut into 6x6 squares. In a shallow baking dish, place a pastry square on the bottom. Top with marinated meat and vegetables. Cover with another pastry top. Coat each "Beef Wellington" with beaten egg and milk so pastry will brown evenly while baking. Bake at 350 degrees for 12 to 15 minutes until pastry is golden brown.

# August 13

## VANISHING EGG SALAD FOR SANDWICHES

*Prep. Time: 25 minutes*

1 dozen eggs

1 lb. bacon

2 cups shredded cheddar cheese

½ cup Miracle Whip Free™ (may need more, add a tablespoon at a time)

½ teaspoon celery seed

¼ teaspoon seasoned salt

⅛ teaspoon salt

⅛ teaspoon coarse black pepper

Boil eggs until hard-boiled. Fry bacon until crisp. Peel eggs and quarter them. In a food processor or blender, process 3 to 4 eggs at a time until they are of a spreadable consistency. When finished with eggs, tear bacon up in small pieces and process bacon. Add the two together. Add cheese and Miracle Whip™ and seasonings; mix well. Let salad chill for at least an hour before serving. Although this is real good when it's first made, the blending of flavors improves as it "ages" making it down-right delicious when served! (NOTE: This is an egg salad to serve to those who say they don't like egg salad!)

# "White" Chocolate Cake

*Prep. Time: 20 minutes Cook Time: 45 minutes*

¼ lb. white chocolate (melted)
1 cup butter
2 cups sugar
5 eggs
2¾ cups cake flour
½ teaspoon salt
1 teaspoon baking powder
1 cup buttermilk
1 teaspoon vanilla
1 cup flaked coconut, optional
1 cup chopped pecans

Cream together butter and sugar. Add melted chocolate and eggs, beating well after each addition. Sift dry ingredients together and add alternately with buttermilk. Stir in vanilla, coconut and nuts. Pour into greased and floured 10x15 or three 8-inch round cake pans. Bake at 350° for 45 minutes or until a knife inserted in the center comes out clean. Frost with "White Fudge Icing."

# "White" Fudge Icing

*Prep. Time: 15 - 20 minutes*

1 cup white chocolate, melted
3 tablespoons flour
1 cup milk
1 cup butter
1¼ cups sugar
2 teaspoons vanilla

In a medium saucepan over low heat, combine melted white chocolate and flour. Stir this into a paste and then add milk, stirring constantly. Cook until mixture is very thick. Remove from heat and let cool completely. In a large mixing bowl, cream together butter, sugar and vanilla. Beat this mixture with an electric mixer set on high for 3 full minutes. Gradually add cooled chocolate mixture and continue beating at high speed until icing is the consistency of whipped cream. If you're frosting three cake layers, spread icing only on top of each layer. Toasted flaked coconut may be sprinkled on top as a garnish if desired.

# August 14

## Adobo Pork

*Make tonight another theme evening. Try celebrating the heritage passed down for generations in the Phillipines. Stop by your local library to find out how to decorate for the evening.*

*Prep. Time: 10-12 minutes Cook Time: 45-55 minutes*

3 lbs. pork, trimmed of fat, cut in 1-inch cubes
1 cup water
1 cup rice vinegar
¼ cup soy sauce
⅛ teaspoon salt
1 tablespoon butter (or shortening)
cooked rice

In a medium saucepan over low heat, combine vinegar, water, soy sauce and salt. Add pork cubes and cook uncovered for about 30 minutes, stirring often. When sauce has cooked down to about 1 cup, transfer meat and sauce to a large skillet. Continue cooking over low heat until sauce evaporates and meat is almost dry. Add butter and increase heat to medium, cook for about 10 minutes longer. Serve over rice.

Serve with fresh fruits such as pineapple wedges, papaya, kiwis, oranges.

# August 15

## Sweet & Sour Meatballs

*Prep. Time: 20 minutes Cook Time: 20 minutes*

1½ lbs. ground pork sausage
1½ lbs. ground turkey sausage
1½ cups ketchup
½ cup dark brown sugar, firmly packed
½ cup water
2 tablespoons soy sauce
1 tablespoon lemon juice

1 can pineapple chunks in its own juice, drained

Combine meat and form into 1-inch balls. In a large skillet over medium heat, brown meat balls, turning often. When meat balls are lightly browned, remove from skillet and drain on a paper towel or piece of brown paper. Empty skillet of all meat drippings and wipe clean with a paper towel. Return balls to skillet and add all remaining ingredients except for pineapple. Simmer over medium heat for about 10 minutes and then add pineapple chunks. Cover and simmer for about another 5 minutes.

## SMART SHOPPING:

*Try these tips to save money at the grocery store!*

- Go grocery shopping with cash only.
- Don't buy non-food items at the grocery store. These items (housewares, greeting cards, over-the-counter medicines, toiletries) can be purchased elsewhere for less money.
- Look high-and-low on grocery store shelves—usually the most expensive products are kept at eye level.
- Stick to the outer aisle of your grocery store for most of your shopping. Expensive convenience foods are kept in middle aisles. Instead of going up and down each aisle, just go in for what you need.
- Bakery, dairy and produce departments often mark down items for quick sales. Ask the department managers what time of day they usually do this.

—courtesy of Deborah Taylor-Hough author of *Frozen Assets: how to cook for a day and eat for a month*

# CARROT NUT SALAD

*Prep. Time: 15 minutes*

3 cups grated carrots
1 cup chopped roasted peanuts (chop in blender)
1 tablespoon grated onion
½ teaspoon salt
½ cup Miracle Whip Free™ (or mayonnaise)
2 cups raisins
leaf lettuce
1 tomato, cut into thin wedges (optional)

Combine carrots, peanuts and raisins in salad bowl. In a small bowl, combine onion, salt and Miracle Whip ™; mix well and add to carrots. Toss well to evenly coat. Serve on crisp lettuce and garnish with tomato wedges.

# August 16

## EGGPLANT PARMIGIANA

*Prep. Time: 20 minutes Cook Time: 15-20 minutes*

4 small eggplants (or zucchini)
1 cup olive oil
4 large ripe tomatoes
1 clove garlic
1 teaspoon garlic powder
1 teaspoon dried basil
1 teaspoon dried oregano
¼ to ½ cup Parmesan cheese
2 cups shredded mozzarella cheese

Slice eggplant into thin slices. In a large skillet, combine olive oil and 1 whole clove of garlic; stir often. Cook eggplant in hot olive oil until lightly browned on both sides. Remove from oil and drain. Dip a paper towel in olive oil and grease a 9x13 pan or casserole dish. Spread a layer of fried eggplant on bottom. Add single layer of sliced tomatoes. Sprinkle garlic powder, basil and oregano over tomatoes. Sprinkle Parmesan cheese over tomatoes and top with another layer of eggplant. Repeat until eggplants and tomatoes are used. Cover top of casserole dish with shredded mozzarella. Bake in a hot oven at 425° for 15 to 20 minutes. Cheese will be melted and bubbly and tomatoes and eggplant will be tender.

# APPLESAUCE 'N' SPICE CAKE

*Prep. Time: 5 minutes Bake Time: 25-30 minutes*

1 pkg. white cake mix
¾ cup applesauce
1 egg
1 teaspoon cinnamon
¼ teaspoon ground cloves
¼ teaspoon nutmeg
¼ teaspoon ginger
Cool Whip™

Combine all ingredients in a mixing bowl and beat on medium speed with an electric mixer until smooth. Pour into a greased 8-inch cake pan. Bake at 350° for 25 to 30 minutes or until a knife inserted in the middle comes out clean. Serve warm with a dollop of Cool Whip™ on top.

# August 17

## CHILI 'N' CHEESE FOOT LONG HOT DOGS

*Prep. Time: 10 minutes Cook Time: 15 minutes*

1 pkg. foot long hot dogs
1 pkg. foot long hot dog buns
2 cups shredded cheddar cheese
1 large onion, diced
2 cans hot dog chili sauce

In a small saucepan, heat the chili sauce until warm. Either heat hot dogs on stove-top, in the microwave or on an outdoor grill. When both dogs and sauce are warmed through, put each dog in a bun and serve with a generous portion of chili

sauce, shredded cheese and onions if desired.
Serve with oven baked tator tots or french fries.

# GELATIN WIGGLES

*Prep. Time: 10 minutes*

2 pkgs. gelatin (your choice of flavor—use same flavor for both packages)
3 envelopes Knox™ Unflavored Gelatin
1 cup boiling water
2 cups club soda, cold

Dissolve gelatin in the hot water. Add cold club soda and stir until well mixed. Pour into a flat pan and place in the refrigerator. When gelatin is firm, either cut into blocks or use cookie cutters to cut out shapes.

# August 18

## CHEESE 'N' ONION ENCHILADAS

*Prep. Time: 15 minutes Cook Time: 15 minutes*

4 cups shredded "Four Cheese" mix (cheddar, mozzarella, monterey Jack and American or colby)
8 to 12 large flour tortillas
8-12 green onions, chopped (including green tops)
1 jar prepared enchilada sauce

Spray a baking dish with vegetable spray. In the center of each tortilla, spread out a handful of the mixed cheese. Add some chopped onion. Begin at one side and roll up tortillas, placing each one seam side down in the baking dish. Cover with enchilada sauce and remaining cheese and onions. Bake at 350° for about 15 minutes or when cheese is melted and bubbly.

# SAUCY REFRIED BEANS

*Prep. Time: 5 minutes Cook Time: 15 minutes*

2 cans fat free refried beans
1 cup prepared taco sauce or enchilada sauce
1 cup shredded cheese (your choice)
3-4 green onions, chopped

Combine sauce with both cans refried beans. Pour into a small casserole dish. Sprinkle cheese and onions over the top and bake at 350° until heated through and cheese is bubbly, about 15 minutes.

# August 19

## MARINATED PORK LOINS

*Prep. Time: 10 minutes (Marinade time: 6-8 hours or longer) Cook Time: 25 to 45 minutes NOTE: Prepare these in the morning and let them stand in the refrigerator until you're ready to cook them.*

6 lean ½ inch slices pork loin
Marinade:
1 tablespoon water
2 teaspoons dried thyme
2 teaspoons dried sweet basil
2 teaspoons sugar
1 teaspoon apple cider vinegar
¼ teaspoon salt
⅛ teaspoon ground black pepper
1 clove garlic, minced
1 teaspoon dried parsley

Combine marinade mixture in a small mixing bowl. Dip each piece of meat into the spiced mixture and lay flat in a pie pan or baking dish. Pour any remaining spice mixture over the top of the meat. Cover with plastic wrap and refrigerate at least 6 hours. When you're ready to cook these, they can be put on a hot grill and cooked 10-15 minutes; placed in an oven set at 350° and baked for 45 minutes or until tender; or fried in 2 tablespoons olive oil on top of the stove top.

Serve with Steamed Fried Potatoes (see page 10) and fresh corn on the cob.

# MIXED BERRIES

*Prep. Time: 20 minutes*

1 pint strawberries
1 pint blueberries
1 pint red or black raspberries
1 cup sugar

Wash and hull strawberries. Slice strawberries in half. Wash and remove stems from blueberries and raspberries. Combine all berries in a large bowl. Cover with sugar and stir until sugar coats all the berries. Serve in dessert dishes or over hot pancakes for dessert.

# August 20

*Today is "Sit Back and Relax" day. Sounds good to me! Tonight's dinner is one you can ask the kids to make while you take it easy!*

## THREE MEAT SALAD

*Prep. Time: 20 minutes*

½ lb. shaved smoked ham
½ lb. shaved smoked chicken breast
½ lb. shaved smoked turkey
1 head iceberg lettuce
2 cups fresh spinach leaves, washed and dried
2 cups shredded cheddar cheese
1 pint cherry tomatoes
¼ cup bacon bits
1 cup chow mein noodles
**Ranch salad dressing**

Tear up meats into bite-size pieces. Tear up lettuce and spinach into bite-sized pieces. Combine meats with lettuce and spinach. Add bacon bits, shredded cheddar cheese, and chow mein noodles. Toss to evenly distribute. Divide up into individual serving bowls. Add salad dressing and a few cherry tomatoes on top of each salad.

Serve with bread sticks.

# August 21

## PIZZA BEEF BURGERS

*Prep. Time: 15 minutes Cook Time: 20 minutes*

2 lbs. lean ground beef (or turkey or half and half)
1 can prepared pizza sauce
individually wrapped slices mozzarella cheese
2 cups sliced mushrooms
1 cup diced onion
2 small green peppers, thinly sliced
1 teaspoon salt
¼ teaspoon pepper
1 egg
1 tablespoon Worcestershire sauce

Combine ground meat with egg, salt, pepper and Worcestershire sauce. Form into patties and either grill or broil until cooked through. While still hot, top each burger with a tablespoon pizza sauce, mushroom slices, diced onions, sliced green peppers and a slice of mozzarella cheese. (You may need to return these to the oven for a few minutes or microwave on high for about a minute.) Serve when cheese starts to melt over the top of the burgers.

## KID BREAK!

### Bath Crayons

These crayons are fun to make and make washing much more fun!

Mix 4½ cups of baby-safe soap flakes with ¼ cup of water in a mixing bowl. Mix until this forms a thick, smooth paste. Separate the mix into four smaller bowls. Add 10-12 drops of food coloring to each bowl. Place colored paste into an ice cube tray. Set the tray in a dry place for a couple of days or until hardened through.

**SPECIAL DAY:**
August 22 is "Be An Angel Day." What three things can you do to help those around you?

# August 22

## CHICKEN STIR-FRY

*Prep. Time: 20 minutes Cook Time: 15-20 minutes*

2 tablespoons olive oil
6 skinless, boneless chicken breasts, cut into strips
1 can cream of mushroom soup
1 can cream of celery soup
2 tablespoons soy sauce
1 teaspoon garlic powder
1 bag frozen stir-fry vegetables, thawed
chow mein noodles

In a large skillet or wok, cook chicken in olive oil. When chicken is done, add stir-fry vegetables and cook until tender. Stir in soups, soy sauce, and garlic powder and mix well, cooking until soups are boiling. Spoon out on individual serving plates and top each with a generous portion of chow mein noodles.

## DUMP CAKE

*Prep. Time: 5 minutes Cook Time: 1 hour*

1 pkg. white or yellow cake mix
1 pint fresh blueberries, strawberries, raspberries or peaches
1 can crushed pineapple
½ cup chopped pecans
1½ sticks butter, melted
1 cup sugar

Clean fruit and place in a medium mixing bowl. Cover with sugar and stir to mix well. Place in a greased baking dish. Cover with crushed pineapple (undrained). Sprinkle on the dry cake mix and scatter nuts over the top. Drizzle butter over all. Bake at 350° for about 1 hour. Serve with ice cream or Cool Whip™.

# August 23

## GARDEN MINESTRONE

*Prep. Time: 20 minutes Cook Time: 1 hour 30 minutes*

STOCK:

3 cups beef broth

2 cups water

1 can (15 oz.) tomato sauce

2 cups tomato juice (or pureed stewed tomatoes)

2 tablespoons dried parsley flakes

1 clove garlic, minced

2 teaspoons dried basil

1 teaspoon dried oregano

1 teaspoon salt

¼ teaspoon coarse black pepper

1 teaspoon sugar

VEGETABLES:

2 large (yellow or white) onions, chopped

2 stalks celery, chopped

1 can (15 oz.) kidney beans, not drained

3 large carrots, sliced

2 small or 1 medium zucchini, diced

1 cup corn (fresh off the cob is great!)

2 cups green beans

Optional Vegetables:

chopped summer squash

shredded cabbage

diced turnips

garbanzo beans

PASTA:

2 cups dry alphabet pasta (may use elbow macaroni, spaghetti noodles or your choice of pasta)

In a large soup pan, combine all ingredients for the stock and bring to a boil. Cook for about 5 minutes at the boiling stage, then reduce heat to medium and add the vegetables. Simmer for about an hour, stirring occasionally to prevent sticking. Add pasta and cook for 20 minutes more.

# August 24

## HOT TURKEY SANDWICHES

*Prep. Time: 10 minutes Cook Time: 10 minutes*

6 submarine rolls, separated in half

1 lb. deli shaved turkey breast

2 pkgs. dry turkey gravy mixes

2 cups water

In a medium saucepan, add water to gravy mixes and cook according to package directions. Add turkey meat and heat through. For each serving, spoon meat and gravy over each bun half. Top with your choice of toppings: lettuce, tomato, onion, pickle, etc. Add top bun half and serve.

## MUSHROOM RICE

*Prep. Time: 10 minutes Cook Time: 15 minutes*

2 cans cream of mushroom soup

2 soup cans water

½ cup fresh sliced mushrooms

3 green onions, finely chopped

3 cups instant rice

In a medium saucepan, combine soup, water, mushrooms and onion. Heat until boiling. Stir in rice. Cover pan and remove from heat. Let pan set for 10 minutes before serving.

Serve with cooked peas and carrots.

For dessert, top a toasted waffle with fresh fruit and powdered sugar.

# August 25

## STOVE TOP TUNA MAC CASSEROLE

*Prep. Time: 5 minutes Cook Time: 15 minutes*

1 family-sized pkg. Velveeta Shells and Cheese™
2 small cans water-packed tuna
2 cups frozen peas

Cook pasta according to package directions. At the same time, in the same water, cook the peas. Drain off water and add the cheese. Drain tuna and add it to the pasta. Stir well to thoroughly distribute peas and tuna. Serve immediately.

## ZUCCHINI CAKE

*Prep. Time: 10 minutes Cook Time: 1 hour*

3 eggs
2 cups sugar
½ cup unsweetened applesauce
½ cup butter, melted
2 cups flour
1 teaspoon baking powder
1 teaspoon salt
½ teaspoon baking soda
1 tablespoon cinnamon
2 cups grated raw zucchini
2 teaspoons vanilla

In a large mixing bowl, beat eggs and add sugar; mix well. Add applesauce and butter; mix well. Sift together flour, baking powder, salt and baking soda; add to egg mixture and beat well. Add cinnamon and mix well. Add vanilla and zucchini and mix well. Pour into a greased and floured 9x13 cake pan and bake at 325° for about an hour or until a knife inserted in the middle comes out clean. Glaze cake with Brown Sugar Icing Glaze.

## BROWN SUGAR ICING GLAZE

*Prep. Time: 5 minutes Cook Time: 10-15 minutes*

2 tablespoons cornstarch
¾ cup water
1 cup brown sugar
1 teaspoon cinnamon
2 tablespoons butter

Combine all ingredients in a small saucepan and cook over medium heat until slightly thickened, about 8 to 10 minutes. Pour over Zucchini Cake.

# August 26

## BEEF STIR-FRY

*Did you know that when a person is engaged in deep thought, his or her brain can generate as much as 14 watts of power?*

*Prep. Time: 20 minutes Cook Time: 25-30 minutes*

1½ lbs. beef round steak, ½-inch thick, cut into strips
2 tablespoons olive oil
1 can tomato soup
¼ cup water
2 tablespoons soy sauce
2 teaspoons vinegar
1 teaspoon garlic powder
¼ teaspoon red pepper
1 large onion, sliced in wedges and separated
2 cups fresh broccoli florets
2 cups cherry tomatoes, cut in halves
2 cups sliced mushrooms
cooked rice

In a large skillet, cook meat in oil over medium-high heat until cooked through. Stir often. Add condensed soup, water, soy sauce, vinegar, garlic powder and pepper to meat and heat to boiling. Add vegetables and cook until tender, stirring often. Serve over rice.

# PEANUT BUTTER PIE

*Prep. Time: 10 minutes Cook Time: 45 minutes or until done*

1 cup smooth peanut butter

2 teaspoons vanilla

½ teaspoon salt

1½ cups sugar

¼ cup light brown sugar

3 eggs

1½ cups milk

1 unbaked 9-inch pie shell

Combine all ingredients in a mixing bowl and pour into an unbaked 9-inch pie shell. Bake at 350° for 45 minutes or until the center of the pie is firm and the shell is done. Let cool before serving.

# August 27

## CHICKEN CAESAR SALAD

*Prep. Time: 25 minutes*

5 skinless, boneless chicken breasts

2 teaspoons seasoned salt

¼ teaspoon black pepper

water

1-2 pkgs. ready-to-use romaine salad greens mix

1 red onion, sliced

Caesar salad dressing

seasoned croutons

Parmesan cheese

In a medium saucepan, cover chicken breasts with water and add seasoned salt and pepper. Cook over medium heat until chicken breasts are cooked through. Remove from heat and drain. Cut into thin strips. In a large salad bowl, toss salad greens with sliced onions and chicken strips. Divide into individual serving bowls and top each with seasoned croutons, Parmesan cheese and Caesar salad dressing.

Serve with chilled watermelon wedges.

# August 28

## PORK FAJITAS

*Prep. Time: 15 minutes Cook Time: 20 minutes*

1½ lbs. boneless pork loin

2 tablespoons orange juice

2 tablespoons apple cider vinegar

1 clove garlic

1 teaspoon oregano

1 teaspoon basil

½ teaspoon thyme

½ teaspoon cumin

1 teaspoon seasoned salt

¼ cup oil

1 medium onion, diced

1 green pepper, diced

2 stalks celery, diced

Tortillas

Trim meat of any visible fat and rub garlic clove over both sides of the meat. Cut into thin strips. In a large skillet, combine orange juice, vinegar and seasonings. Add meat and toss until well mixed. Add onion, celery and green pepper. Add ¼ cup oil and cook until meat is cooked and vegetables are tender, stirring and tossing often. Serve with warm tortillas.

## COOKED GREENS

*Prep. Time: 10 minutes Cook Time: 20-30 minutes*

2 cans mixed greens, drained

¼ lb. bacon, cut into tiny pieces

1 medium onion, finely chopped

apple cider vinegar

Drain greens and with kitchen scissors or a sharp knife, cut greens into shreds. Combine cut greens with bacon pieces and onion in a medium skillet. Cook over medium heat until bacon begins to fry crisp. Stir often to prevent sticking. Cook until onion is transparent and bacon is cooked. Serve hot with a teaspoon of apple cider vinegar drizzled over each serving, if desired.

# August 29

## GROUND STEAK PATTIES

*Prep. Time: 15 minutes Cook Time: 35 minutes*

2 lbs lean ground beef
2 tablespoons minced onion
1 tablespoon Papa Dash™
2 tablespoons Worcestershire sauce
2 tablespoons A-1™ Steak Sauce
¾ cup chopped green pepper
2 eggs
1 cup crushed saltine cracker crumbs
2 pkgs. brown gravy mix
2 cups water

In a large bowl, combine ground meat with onion, Papa Dash™, Worcestershire and steak sauces, green pepper, eggs and cracker crumbs. Mix well and form into ¼ lb. patties. Cook under a hot broiler for 3 to 5 minutes on each side. Remove and place in a 9x13 baking dish. In a small saucepan, prepare two packages brown gravy mix according to package directions. Cook until gravy begins to thicken. Pour over the cooked beef patties. Bake at 350° for about 15 minutes.

Serve with mashed potatoes and a tossed salad.

# August 30

## CHICKEN BOBS

*Prep. Time: 20 minutes Cook Time: 12-15 minutes*

4-5 skinless, boneless chicken breasts
3 large onions, cut into wedges
3 stalks celery, cut into chunks
frozen broccoli florets, thawed
frozen cauliflower florets, thawed

cherry tomatoes
Italian salad dressing
salt and pepper

Coat chicken breasts with Italian salad dressing and cook over a hot grill for 3 to 5 minutes on each side. When juices run clear, remove chicken from grill. Cut into chunks. Load skewers with chunks of meat and vegetables. Coat with Italian salad dressing. Sprinkle with salt and pepper and place over a hot grill for about 5-6 minutes, turning every two minutes or so. Remove when vegetables are cooked tender-crisp and are heated through.

## STRAWBERRY FIZZ CAKE

*Prep. Time: 15 minutes Cook Time: 25 to 30 minutes*

2¼ cups sugar
1 cup butter-flavored shortening
3 ¼ cups cake flour
2 teaspoons baking powder
½ teaspoon salt
1 cup strawberry soda, at room temperature
6 egg whites
2 teaspoons vanilla

Cream together sugar and shortening; set aside. Sift together flour, baking powder and salt. Add the creamed sugar mixture alternately with the strawberry soda and the flour mixture. In a separate small mixing bowl, beat egg whites on high speed with an electric mixer until soft peaks form. Fold in vanilla. Add whipped egg whites to cake mixture, stirring to fold in egg whites. Pour into a greased cake pan and bake at 350° for 25 to 30 minutes. Cake will test done when a knife inserted in the center comes out clean. Let cake cool before icing with prepared strawberry icing.

# August 31

## BEEF QUESADILLAS

*Prep. Time: 15 minutes Cook Time: 5-10 minutes*

1 lb. lean ground beef
1 medium onion, finely chopped
1 can cheddar cheese soup
thick and chunky salsa
2 cups shredded "Four Cheese" Mexican blend
8-inch flour tortillas
sour cream (fat free)

Brown ground beef and chopped onion in a large skillet over medium heat. Drain. Add cheddar cheese soup and 1½ cups salsa and heat to boiling. Stir to mix well. Place tortillas on greased cookie sheets. Top each tortilla with about ⅓ cup meat and cheese mixture. Spread to within ½-inch of edge. Sprinkle shredded "Four Cheese" Mexican blend over each tortilla. Moisten edges of each tortilla with water and add a top tortilla. Press the edges of tortillas together to seal. Bake 5 to 10 minutes in a 350° oven. Using a pizza cutter, cut each layered tortilla in fourths. Top each "Quesadilla" with a spoon full of salsa and sour cream.

## HOMEMADE M&M™ FREEZE

*Prep. Time: 10 minutes*

½ gallon vanilla or chocolate frozen yogurt
2-3 cups M&Ms™
2 cups skim milk

In a blender, combine 1 cup milk with 1 cup M&Ms™ and ¼ of the frozen yogurt. Blend until M&Ms™ are chopped and yogurt and milk make a thick shake. Spoon into serving dishes and repeat, using the remaining ingredients. Top each serving with a few M&M's™. Serve with a spoon.

## FOOD FOR THOUGHT

✦ A woman's age doesn't really matter; what matters most is how long she has been that age.

✦ One of the troubles with growing old is that you stop feeling your oats and start feeling your corns instead.

✦ The best way to improve your appetite is to go on a diet.

✦ Falling in love in awfully simple, but falling out is simply awful.

✦ He who laughs last didn't get the joke at first.

September is celebrated as: The All American Breakfast Month, National Chicken Month, National Honey Month, National Rice Month and National Potato Bread Month!

# September 1

*Start the month out with this easy breakfast supper! It's one of our favorites!*

## CHICKEN-FRIED STEAK & EGGS

*Prep. Time: 10 minutes Cook Time: 20 minutes*

6 pieces of cubed steak
1 pkg. original fried chicken coating mix
1 egg
¼ cup milk
3 tablespoons oil
2 tablespoons flour
3 cups milk

With a meat mallet, pound each cube steak until thin. In a small bowl, combine egg and ¼ cup milk and beat well. Dip each piece of meat in egg mixture and then coat with the chicken coating mix. Fry in hot oil in a large skillet, turning every 3 to 5 minutes until meat is done. Remove meat and keep warm. When all the meat is cooked, add the flour to the pan drippings and stir until pasty. Add milk and continue stirring constantly until well blended. Turn the heat up to medium-high and continue stirring until gravy starts to thicken. When the gravy is thick, pour it over the meat and keep warm until ready to serve.

Serve with poached eggs and hashbrowns.

# September 2

## CHICKEN AND RICE

*Prep. Time: 20 minutes Cook Time: 30 minutes*

6 boneless, skinless chicken breasts
2 stalks celery
1 medium onion
1 teaspoon salt
water
1 can cream of mushroom soup
1 can cream of chicken soup
2 cups water
3 cups uncooked instant rice
¼ teaspoon coarse black pepper

In a medium saucepan, cover chicken, onion and celery with water. Add a teaspoon of salt and bring water to a boil. Cook chicken for about 20 minutes. Remove celery and onion with about a cup of liquid and puree vegetables in a blender. Add enough water to blender to equal two cups. Discard remaining water from meat. Combine pureed vegetables/liquid with both cans of soup and stir well. Cut chicken breasts up into strips and return to pan. Add pepper and stir well. Heat to boiling, then stir in rice. Cover with a lid and remove pan from heat. Let set for 5-8 minutes, then fluff rice with a fork. Serve immediately.

Serve with cooked baby peas and carrots.

## KID BREAK!

While preparing dinner one night, set your kids up with supplies to make Macaroni Necklaces. You'll need medium size macaroni, food coloring, rubbing alcohol, string and plastic zipper bags. First, open up a zipper bag and put in 1 tablespoon of food coloring and 2 tablespoons of rubbing alcohol. Then add a few handfuls of macaroni. Zip closed and shake. When macaroni is colored, empty it onto a plate or tray to let dry. Continue process to make additional colors, then string and enjoy.

# September 3

## SWEET HONEY BBQ SANDWICHES

*Prep. Time: 5 minutes Cook Time: 20 minutes*

2 lbs. ground turkey
2 tablespoons oil
1 green pepper, chopped
2 teaspoons celery seed
1 cup stewed tomatoes, pureed
1 medium onion, finely chopped
½ teaspoon chili powder
1 tablespoon salt
¼ cup honey
¼ cup light brown sugar
2 tablespoons apple cider vinegar
2 teaspoons prepared mustard, optional
buns

In a large skillet, heat oil and add green pepper, onion and ground turkey. Cook until meat is cooked through and vegetables are tender. Add pureed tomatoes, celery seed, chili powder, salt, honey, brown sugar and vinegar. Mix well. Cook for about 5 minutes over medium heat. Taste sauce. If it tastes too sweet, add 2 teaspoons prepared mustard and stir well. Continue simmering over low heat for about 10-15 minutes. Spoon meat mixture onto buns and serve each with a slice of cheese and some dill pickles.

## BAKED CINNAMON APPLES WITH HONEY SAUCE

*Prep. Time: 15 minutes Cook Time: 45 minutes*

8-10 tart apples, peeled and sliced (use Gala, Jonathan, Macintosh, Granny Smith, etc.)
½ cup light brown sugar
2 teaspoons cinnamon
2 tablespoons butter
1 cup honey
¼ cup apple juice
2 tablespoons lemon juice

Sprinkle lemon juice over peeled and sliced apples. Toss to coat evenly. In a casserole dish, melt butter and stir in brown sugar and honey. Add cinnamon and stir well. Add apple slices and stir to coat each apple slice with the honey mixture. Bake at 350° for 35 to 45 minutes, stirring often to distribute honey sauce over apples. Serve with a scoop of vanilla frozen yogurt or ice cream.

# September 4

*Labor day gives us all one final fling before admitting that our summer days are really over. To a lot of folks, this is the unofficial end to summer. Make the most of today and enjoy the quick and easy menu for tonight's dinner!*

## GRILLED SIRLOIN TIPS AND MUSHROOMS

*Prep. Time: 10 minutes (Marinating Time: 4 hours) Cook Time: 20 minutes*

2 lb. beef sirloin, cut into small chunks
3 tablespoons oil
2 onions, sliced
4 cups whole mushrooms, washed and dried
1 cup red wine
2 tablespoons A-1™ Sauce
1 tablespoon Worcestershire Sauce
1 teaspoon salt
¼ teaspoon pepper

Combine red wine with A-1™ Sauce, Worcestershire Sauce, salt and pepper. Add chopped sirloin to boil and mix well. Cover and refrigerate for at least 4 hours. Over a hot grill, add oil to a large skillet. Add sirloin tips, separated slices of onion, whole mushrooms and about a quarter cup of the marinade. Cook meat and vegetables as if preparing a stir-fry meal, about 20 minutes or when meat and vegetables are cooked through.

Serve with hot baked potatoes and a tossed salad.

# September 5

## ZITI CASSEROLE

*Prep. Time: 20 minutes Cook Time: 25-30 minutes*

1 pkg. Ziti pasta

2 cups ricotta cheese

1 egg

½ teaspoon black pepper

1 teaspoon salt

2 teaspoons dried oregano

2 teaspoons dried basil

2 teaspoons dried parsley flakes

¼ cup Parmesan cheese

1 lb. ground beef (or turkey)

1 medium onion, chopped

1 green pepper, chopped

2 jars (15 oz.) spaghetti sauce

2-3 cups sliced mushrooms, optional

2 cups shredded mozzarella

Prepare pasta according to package directions. Drain off water when pasta is tender. Rinse in cold water. Set aside. In a large skillet, brown meat, onion and green pepper. Drain off all grease when meat is cooked and vegetables are tender. Add sliced mushrooms and spaghetti sauce. Heat to boiling over medium heat, then lower heat and let simmer while you prepare the cheese sauce. In a medium mixing bowl, combine ricotta cheese with the egg, pepper, salt, oregano, basil, parsley and Parmesan. Mix well and add cooked Ziti pasta. Stir to evenly coat pasta. Pour into a greased 9x13 baking pan. Pour spaghetti sauce/meat over pasta and stir to evenly coat pasta. Top with mozzarella cheese and bake at 350° for about 15-20 minutes, just long enough to heat through. Serve with garlic bread sticks and a tossed salad.

# September 6

## COLA STEW

*Prep. Time: 15 minutes Cook Time: 1 hour*

2 cups Coca-Cola™

1 lb. cubed ham

2 cans French-style green beans, drained

1 can cream of mushroom soup

1 can cream of celery soup

2 cups water

6 potatoes, peeled and cubed

3 carrots, sliced

1 large onion, chopped

2 teaspoons salt

½ teaspoon pepper

Combine all ingredients in a large soup pan and cook over medium heat until vegetables are tender— about an hour.

## POTATO BREAD ROLLS

*Prep. Time: 20 minutes Cook Time: 20-25 minutes*

2 cups mashed potatoes (may use either leftover mashed potatoes or those reconstituted from instant mix)

4 ½ cups flour (may need up to ½ cup more)

1 pkg. active dry yeast

1 cup milk

½ cup butter flavored shortening

½ cup sugar

1 teaspoon salt

2 eggs

In a large mixing bowl, combine the dry yeast with two cups flour. In a saucepan, heat the milk and shortening until shortening melts. Add the mashed potatoes and stir well. Pour milk and potato mixture into the bowl with yeast and flour. Add eggs and beat at low speed with an electric mixer for about 30 seconds. Turn mixer on high and beat for a full three minutes. Remove beaters and add remaining flour, stirring by hand. Dough should be soft and elastic. Place dough in a greased bowl, turning once to grease surface. Cover with a damp cloth. Refrigerate the dough for several hours before making into rolls. When ready to bake, pinch dough off and form into 2-inch balls. Place on a greased baking sheet and let set at room temperature to rise until doubled, about 45 minutes. Bake at 375° for 20 to 25 minutes. NOTE: This dough may be made ahead and stored in the refrigerator for up to a week before making rolls.

# September 7

## BAKED STROMBOLI

*Prep. Time: 20 minutes Cook Time: 20-25 minutes*

2 loaves frozen garlic bread
1 lb. sausage, browned
1 lb. shaved ham
2 onions, sliced
pizza sauce
1 green pepper, sliced
1 cup sliced mushrooms
Mozzarella cheese slices

Open garlic bread's wrapper and bake in a hot oven, at 400° for 5 minutes. Remove from oven and separate the tops from the bottom halves. Spread pizza sauce on the bottom half and top with meats, vegetables and cheese slices. Put top half on each loaf and return to oven. Bake at 400° for 15 to 20 minutes. Cut each loaf into thirds or fourths and serve with chips.

# September 8

## TUNA POT PIE

*Prep. Time: 15 minutes Cook Time: 30 minutes*

2 cans (7 oz.) water-packed tuna, drained
2 cans cream of chicken soup
1 medium onion, chopped
½ teaspoon poultry seasoning
2 cups frozen peas, cooked and drained
3 cups cooked rice
½ cup heavy cream
2 teaspoons dried parsley flakes
2 cans refrigerator biscuits (10 count)

Combine all ingredients except for biscuits in a 9x13 baking pan. Bake at 450° for 20 minutes. Lay biscuits over the top, with sides touching, and bake for 10 minutes longer or until biscuits are lightly browned.

## COBBLER DESSERT

*Prep. Time: 5 minutes Cook Time: 40 minutes*

1 can pie filling, your choice of any flavor
2 cups flour
1¾ cups sugar
⅔ cup oil
2 eggs
2 teaspoons vanilla
3 teaspoons cinnamon
2 teaspoons baking soda
1 cup chopped nuts
1½ tablespoons butter, melted

Combine 1 cup sugar with oil, eggs and vanilla; beat well. Add pie filling and stir in flour, 2 teaspoons cinnamon, baking soda and nuts. Pour into a greased 9x13 cake pan. In another container, combine remaining sugar and cinnamon. Sprinkle mixture over the top of the dessert. Melt butter and drizzle over the top. Bake at 350° for 40 minutes.

# September 9

## BAKED PORK CUTLETS

*Prep. Time: 15-20 minutes / Cook Time: 25 minutes*

¾ cup flour
1 teaspoon salt
½ teaspoon paprika
¼ teaspoon pepper
2 eggs, slightly beaten
2 teaspoons Worcestershire sauce
6-8 pork cutlets (boneless lean pork that has
    been cubed)
¾ cup crushed saltine cracker crumbs
3-4 tablespoons oil

In small bowl, combine flour, salt, paprika and pepper. In another small bowl, combine egg and Worcestershire sauce. Rinse each piece of pork with warm water and then dredge in the seasoned flour. Then dip in egg mixture and coat with cracker crumbs. In large skillet, brown cutlets in hot oil until golden brown. Continue cooking over medium heat until meat has cooked through, 7 to 10 minutes.

## CHEESY VEGETABLE MEDLEY

*Prep. Time: 5 minutes Cook Time: 35-40 minutes*

1 bag (16 oz.) frozen mixed vegetables (such as
    cauliflower, carrots and broccoli)
1 can cream of mushroom soup
1 cup shredded cheddar cheese
⅓ cup sour cream
¼ teaspoon coarse black pepper
½ teaspoon salt
1 can French fried onions
6 slices American cheese

Combine vegetables with soup, sour cream, cheddar cheese, salt and pepper. Pour into a casserole dish. Crumble French fried onions over the top and lay slices of American cheese on top of onions. Bake at 350° for 30 to 40 minutes.

# September 10

*Special tribute goes to grandparents today. It's National Grandparents day. If yours or your children's grandparents live nearby—extend an invitation to join you for dinner tonight!*

## BEEF AND SNOW PEAS

*Prep. Time: 15-20 minutes Cook Time: 20 minutes*

1 lb. sirloin tip, thinly sliced
1 lb. fresh snow peas
3 cups boiling water
1 small onion, sliced
2 tablespoons oil
cooked noodles
MARINADE:
2 tablespoons soy sauce
1 teaspoon sugar
1 tablespoon cornstarch
¼ cup beef bouillon

Mix up marinade mixture and soak meat strips while preparing the rest of the meal. Pour boiling hot water over snow peas and cook for 5 minutes. Remove pan from heat. In a large skillet, heat oil. Sauté onion slices and meat, stirring often, until meat is cooked through. Add drained snow peas and 1 cup of liquid from the snow peas. Continue cooking until tender, stirring often. Serve over a bed of cooked noodles.

## GELATIN & ICE CREAM SALAD

*Prep. Time: 15 minutes*

1 pkg. gelatin (any flavor)
1 cup boiling water
1 pint vanilla ice cream
1 can crushed pineapple, drained
½ cup chopped nuts
1 cup miniature marshmallows

Dissolve gelatin in boiling water. Add ice cream

and stir until melted. Add drained crushed pineapple, nuts and marshmallows. Chill for at least 2 hours before serving.

# September 11

*Make tonight's dinner a theme evening featuring Japan. Give your children plain sheets of 8 ½ x 11 sheets of paper and a box of crayons. Let them color the paper as desired. Then fold the paper in half lengthwise and make 2 to 3-inch cuts in the paper spaced about a half-inch apart. Unfold and roll the cut paper into a tube. Tape, staple or glue the ends together and add a string hanger. Decorate with these homemade Japanese lanterns. For a truly authentic experience, try eating with chopsticks tonight!*

## SUKIYAKI

*Prep. Time: 15 minutes Cook Time: 15-20 minutes*

2 lbs. sirloin steak or filet mignon, cut thin and in strips
¼ cup oil
¾ cup soy sauce
½ cup beef bouillon
¼ cup sugar
2 bunches green onions, diced
1 cup sliced bamboo shoots
2 cups sliced mushrooms
2 stalks celery, sliced thin
1 cup shredded fresh spinach

Brown meat in oil. In a separate bowl, combine soy sauce, bouillon and sugar. Pour half of soy mixture in pan with meat. Push meat to one side and add onions and celery. Simmer for about 5 minutes. Add remaining soy mixture, bamboo shoots, mushrooms and spinach. Simmer for 3-5 minutes longer, stirring often. Mix all ingredients together and lower heat. Let cook on low heat while you prepare the rice.

Serve with cooked rice.

# September 12

## HAM & POTATOES AU GRATIN

*Prep. Time: 15 minutes Cook Time: 40-45 minutes*

2 pkgs. dried potatoes au gratin mix
1 lb. ham cubes
2 tablespoons dried minced onions
1 can mushrooms stems and pieces, drained
1 can peas, drained

Prepare potato mixes according to package directions. Add cubed ham, minced onions, drained mushrooms and peas. Stir together and bake at 400° for 40-45 minutes.

## PISTACHIO CAKE

*Prep. Time: 10 minutes Cook Time: about 30 minutes*

1 box white cake mix
¾ cup oil
1 cup water
4 eggs
3 pkgs. instant pistachio pudding
1 carton Cool Whip™

In a large mixing bowl, combine cake mix with 2 pkgs. pistachio pudding mix, oil, water and eggs. Pour into a greased and floured 9x13 cake pan. Bake at 350° for 20 to 30 minutes. When a knife is inserted in the center of cake and the blade comes out clean, cake is done. While cake cools, prepare remaining pkg. of pistachio pudding according to directions for pudding. Fold pistachio pudding in with Cool Whip™ and frost cooled cake. Refrigerate until ready to serve.

# September 13

## PANCAKES

*Prep. Time: 5 minutes Cook Time: 3-5 minutes each*

2 cups plain yogurt
4 eggs, separated
1½ cups flour
2 tablespoons sugar
2 teaspoons baking powder
2 teaspoons salt
1 cup butter, melted
1 teaspoon cinnamon

In large mixing bowl, sift together flour, baking soda, salt and cinnamon. In a smaller bowl, combine yogurt, sugar and egg yolks. Stir in melted butter. Add to flour mixture, beating to mix well. In a small bowl, beat egg whites until foamy. Gradually fold egg whites into floured mixture. Dip pancakes onto a greased hot griddle using a ¼ cup measuring cup. When batter begins to bubble, flip pancakes over and cook until lightly browned on both sides. Serve with warm syrup or fresh fruit.

NOTE: Fresh blueberries, strawberries, cherries or other fruit may be added for variation if desired. May need to increase cooking time when adding fresh fruit.

Serve with sausage patties or ham steaks.

# September 14

## CRUNCHY CHICKEN CASSEROLE

*Did you know that the average consumption of potato chips by the American population has risen to over 71 percent since 1980? Potato chips make great casserole toppings and they even make a pretty good cookie too! (see page 91 for cookie recipe.)*

*Prep. Time: 20 minutes Cook Time: 20-25 minutes*

2-2½ cups cooked chicken, diced
1 can cream of mushroom soup
1 can cream of celery soup
1 cup water
4 cups cooked noodles
2 cups mixed peas and carrots
3 cups crushed potato chips
8 slices American cheese

In a 9x13 pan, combine soups with water. Add chicken, noodles and vegetables; mix well. Place cheese slices over entire top and then add a layer of crushed potato chips. Bake at 400° for 20 to 25 minutes.

### KITCHEN TIP
Pour oil in a small squeeze bottle and keep it handy. It's easier to squeeze just the right amount of oil into the pan than it is to pour from a large bottle. This will save on oil and clean-up.

# September 15

## BEEF SURPRISE

*Prep. Time: 15 minutes Cook Time: 20-30 minutes*

1½ lbs. round steak
3 tablespoons oil
1 small onion, chopped
2 stalks celery, diced
1 green pepper, diced
2 cups fresh sliced mushrooms
1 can water chestnuts, drained and chopped
1 can green beans, drained
2 tablespoons cornstarch
3 tablespoons soy sauce
2 tablespoons water
1 clove garlic
cooked noodles or rice

Peel garlic clove and rub fresh garlic over both sides of meat. Add oil and garlic clove to a large skillet and heat until boiling. Cut meat into bite-sized pieces and add meat to hot oil. Remove garlic. Stir often and cook until meat is done. Add onion, celery, green pepper, mushrooms, water chestnuts and green beans. Continue cooking and stirring until vegetables are heated through and the fresh vegetables are tender-crisp. In another container, dissolve cornstarch with soy sauce and water. Pour over the meat and vegetables, continuing to stir until gravy thickens. Serve over cooked noodles or rice.

# September 16

## TENDER POT ROAST

*Prep. Time: 5 minutes Cook Time: 90 minutes*

1 beef roast (round, rump or sirloin tip)
1 envelope Lipton's™ dry onion soup mix
½ cup water
1 tablespoon flour
1 cooking bag

Put flour in cooking bag and shake it to coat the insides of the bag. Place roast in bag. Mix soup mix and water together and pour over the meat. Seal bag with the twist tie. Poke 3 to 4 holes in the top of bag to allow steam to escape. Bake, uncovered, in a roasting pan at 350° for 90 minutes or until meat is tender and cooked through.

## SKINNY MASHED POTATOES

*Prep. Time: 12-15 minutes Cook Time: 25 minutes*

12 potatoes
2 teaspoons salt
¼ teaspoon pepper
¾ cup fat free clear chicken broth
½ cup plain fat free yogurt
1 teaspoon chopped chives
water

Peel potatoes and slice them into a large pan. Cover potatoes with water and add 1 teaspoon of salt. Add a pat of butter and cook over medium high heat until water begins to boil. Continue cooking until potatoes are tender and cooked through—about 20 minutes. Drain off water and add chicken broth, yogurt, remaining salt, chopped chives and pepper. Mash potatoes with a potato-masher, mixing together the added ingredients. For lumpy mashed potatoes, serve directly from the pan. For smooth mashed potatoes, whip on low speed using an electric mixer.

# SAUCY CORN & BROCCOLI MIX

*Prep. Time: 15 minutes Cook Time: 15 minutes*

1½ lb. bunch of fresh broccoli, cut up into bite-sized pieces
1 can corn, drained
1 can cream of celery soup
1 cup water
¼ cup milk
1 cup shredded cheddar cheese
⅛ teaspoon pepper

In a medium saucepan, combine cut-up broccoli and water. Over high heat, bring the water to a boil. Reduce heat to low and cover pan with a lid. Continue cooking broccoli for about 10 minutes. When broccoli is tender, drain off water. Then add soup, milk, corn, cheese, salt and pepper. Mix well and return pan to burner, heating contents over medium-low heat. Stir often. Serve hot when cheese melts.

# September 17

## BAKED FISH WITH STUFFING

*Prep. Time: 15 minutes Cook Time: 40-45 minutes*

4 - 5 lbs. white fish or lake trout
1 teaspoon salt
¼ teaspoon pepper
1 teaspoon seasoned salt
½ teaspoon thyme
STUFFING:
¼ cup butter, melted
¼ cup green onions, chopped
1 cup fresh spinach, torn in little pieces
2½ cups soft bread crumbs
3 tablespoons heavy whipping cream
¼ teaspoon lemon juice
½ teaspoon salt
½ cup butter, melted

Wash fish and cut off heads. Combine 1 teaspoon salt, ¼ teaspoon pepper, 1 teaspoon seasoned salt and the thyme and sprinkle on fish, on both sides outside and in the inside cavity. Set aside while preparing stuffing. In a small skillet, melt ¼ cup butter and sauté green onions for about 2 minutes. Add spinach and stir-fry for a couple minutes longer. Transfer to mixing bowl and add bread crumbs, cream, lemon juice, salt and pepper. Stuff each fish cavity with the spinach mixture. Melt ½ cup butter in a shallow baking dish. Place each stuffed fish in buttered dish. Use a pastry brush and brush the top of each fish with the melted butter. Bake at 375° for 40-45 minutes, basting fish with melted butter every 5-6 minutes.

# BAKED BUTTERNUT SQUASH

*Prep. Time: 5 minutes Cook Time: 40-45 minutes*

3-4 butternut squash
½ cup sugar
1 tablespoon cinnamon
2 tablespoons brown sugar
½ cup butter, melted

Wash squash. In a large baking dish, set squash in hot oven and bake at 375° for about 20 minutes. Remove from oven and cut each squash in half. Scoop out seeds and discard. Remove stems if there are any. Combine sugar, brown sugar and cinnamon. Brush each open half of squash with melted butter and then sprinkle on the sugar mixture. Return to oven and bake for another 20-25 minutes or until the inside flesh of the squash is tender. To serve, give each person a half and let each scoop out the inside flesh of the squash. Additional butter and sugar mixture may be added, if desired.

# September 18

## ITALIAN BEEF PIE

*Prep. Time: 15 minutes Cook Time: 30 minutes*

½ cup flour
½ teaspoon salt
1 teaspoon baking powder
¼ cup shortening
½ cup sour cream or plain non-fat yogurt
1 egg
1 lb. lean ground beef
1 teaspoon salt
2 teaspoons oregano
½ teaspoon garlic powder
1 medium onion, chopped
1 small can (6 oz.) tomato paste
1 cup sliced mushrooms
1 cup shredded cheddar cheese
1 cup shredded mozzarella cheese

In a medium bowl, combine the flour with ½ teaspoon salt, baking powder and shortening. Stir and knead until well blended. Press dough in a greased pie pan or casserole dish. Set aside. Brown meat and onion in a medium skillet. Drain off all grease. In a separate container, combine sour cream, egg, salt, oregano and garlic powder. Add drained beef and onions; mix well. Stir in tomato paste and mix well. Pour meat mixture into the crust. Top with both shredded cheeses. Bake at 400° for about 30 minutes. Crust should be lightly browned and cheese should be melted and bubbly.

Serve with a tossed salad.

# September 19

## EASY BAKED PORK CHOPS

*Prep. Time: 5 minutes Cook Time: 45 minutes*

6-8 pork chops or pork steaks, trimmed of fat
1 cup ketchup
1 cup Coca-Cola™
1 teaspoon unflavored tenderizer
salt and pepper to taste

Sprinkle tenderizer over both sides of pork chops and lay them in a shallow baking dish. Combine the ketchup and cola and pour over the chops. Sprinkle on salt and pepper. Bake at 375° for about 45 minutes.

## SEASONED RICE

*Prep. Time: 1-3 minutes Cook Time: 8-10 minutes*

1 can cream of mushroom soup
1 can cream of chicken soup
1 tablespoon dried minced onion
½ teaspoon salt
⅛ teaspoon pepper
1 cup water
3 cups uncooked rice

In a medium saucepan, combine both soups, minced onion, salt, pepper and water. Heat over medium heat until boiling, stirring often. Add rice to liquid and stir when it starts to boil. Cover with a lid and remove from heat. Let pan set for 5-10 minutes and then fluff with a fork.

Serve with your choice of vegetables.

# September 20

## CHICKEN CORDON BLUE

*Prep. Time: 10 minutes Cook Time: 25-30 minutes*

3 whole chicken breasts, split in half, skinned
    and deboned
3 slices Swiss cheese, cut in half
3 slices boiled ham, cut in half
2 tablespoons butter
1 can cream of chicken soup
¼ cup milk
½ cup chopped celery
½ cup chopped onion
salt and pepper to taste

In a large skillet, melt butter and cook chicken over medium heat for about 10 minutes. Turn chicken over. Top each breast with a half slice of ham and a half slice of cheese over the ham. Secure with toothpicks. Stir in soup, milk, celery and onion. Cover and cook on medium-low heat for another 20 minutes or until chicken tests done (juices run clear).

## BOILED CINNAMON SWEET POTATOES

*Prep. Time: 10 minutes Cook Time: 25 minutes*

3-4 lbs. fresh sweet potatoes
¾ cup white corn syrup
3 tablespoons ground cinnamon
3 tablespoons butter
½ cup light brown sugar plus 2 tablespoons
water

In a large saucepan, cover sweet potatoes with water and add 1 tablespoon cinnamon and 2 tablespoons brown sugar. Bring water to a boil and let potatoes cook until skin begins to break. Drain off water and peel potatoes. Dice potatoes and return them to the pan. Add the corn syrup,

remaining cinnamon, butter and brown sugar. Using a potato masher, mash potatoes until smooth. Serve immediately.

**WORLD GRATITUDE DAY—SEPTEMBER 21**
Before your evening meal tonight, ask each person to name the top three things for which they are most thankful. It's good for all of us to stop and count our blessings from time to time. And what a more appropriate day than on this World Gratitude Day.

# September 21

## GROUND CHUCK CASSEROLE

*Prep. Time: 15 minutes Cook Time: 40 minutes*

1 lb. lean ground beef
1 can cream of mushroom soup
1 pkg. frozen tator tots
2 cups frozen chopped broccoli, thawed
1 cup shredded cheddar cheese
1 medium onion, chopped

Brown meat and onion in a skillet. Drain off all grease. Pour into a casserole dish. Stir in soup and broccoli. Cover with shredded cheese and top with tator tots. Bake at 400° for about 40 minutes.

## WILTED LETTUCE SALAD

*Prep. Time: 15 minutes Cook Time: 20 minutes*

1½ lbs. leaf lettuce
1 lb. fresh spinach
2 heads iceberg lettuce
½ lb. bacon
1 medium onion, chopped
2 teaspoons salt
½ teaspoon pepper
1 cup apple cider vinegar
1 cup water

1 cup sugar

Wash salad greens and break them into bite-sized pieces. Set salad greens in refrigerator while preparing the rest. In a large skillet, fry bacon until crisp. Remove bacon and drain on paper towel or brown paper. Measure ½ cup bacon grease and discard the remaining grease. Add the ½ cup grease back to the skillet. Chop onion and sauté in bacon grease until it turns transparent. Add water, vinegar, salt, sugar and pepper. Stir and bring this mixture to a fast boil. Remove salad greens from the refrigerator and crumble up bacon over the salad greens. When mixture in skillet is at a hard boil, pour over the salad greens and toss immediately. Serve warm.

# September 22

## OVEN-FRIED CHICKEN

*Prep. Time: 15 minutes Cook Time: 1 hour*

1 frying chicken, cut up, skin removed
½ cup corn meal (yellow or white)
1 cup flour
½ cup Parmesan cheese
½ cup Romano cheese
2 teaspoons salt
¼ teaspoon pepper
1 teaspoon garlic salt
1 cup butter, melted
2 eggs
¾ cup milk

Combine corn meal, flour, Parmesan and Romano cheese, salt, pepper and garlic salt. In a small bowl, combine eggs and milk; beat well. Dip each piece of chicken into milk and egg and then roll in the dry mixture to evenly coat the entire piece of meat. Lay each piece of meat in a shallow baking dish. Melt butter and drizzle over each piece of chicken. Bake at 350° for an hour or until meat is cooked through.

Serve with mashed potatoes and your choice of cooked vegetables.

# September 23

## BACON & TOMATO ELBOWS

*Prep. Time: 20 minutes Cook Time: 15 minutes*

½ lb. bacon
1 medium onion, finely chopped
4 cups stewed tomatoes
2 teaspoons sugar
1 teaspoon salt
½ teaspoon pepper
1 pkg. (16 oz.) elbow macaroni
1 tablespoon chopped parsley
2 teaspoons dried oregano
1 teaspoon dried basil

Fry bacon until crisp, remove and drain each piece on paper towel or brown paper. Measure out 2 tablespoons bacon grease and discard the rest. Add the 2 tablespoons bacon grease back to the skillet. Add the chopped onion and cook over medium heat until onion is transparent. Whiz tomatoes in a blender for about 30 seconds and then pour into skillet. Add sugar, salt, pepper, parsley, oregano and basil. Increase the heat to high and bring mixture to a boil. Meanwhile, prepare elbow macaroni according to package directions. Drain water from macaroni when it is tender and add macaroni to skillet. Mix well and serve. Crumble up bacon over each portion and serve immediately.

# APRICOT CAKE

*Prep. Time: 15 minutes Cook Time: 50-60 minutes*

1 box butter-flavored yellow cake mix
½ cup sugar
4 eggs
¼ cup oil
½ cup unsweetened applesauce
1 cup apricot nectar
2 cups powdered sugar
½ cup apricot nectar

Combine cake mix with sugar, eggs, oil, applesauce and 1 cup apricot nectar and beat on high speed for four full minutes. Pour into a greased and floured 9x13 cake pan and bake at 350° for 45 to 50 minutes or until a knife inserted in the center comes out clean. When cake is done, remove from oven and prepare icing. In a small mixing bowl, combine the ½ cup apricot nectar with 2 cups powdered sugar. Beat on high speed using an electric mixer until smooth. Drizzle over warm cake and serve.

# September 24

## HAMWICHES

*Prep. Time: 10 minutes Cook Time: 15 minutes*

15 oz. (5 pkgs.) chipped smoked ham
1 lb. cubed cheese (your choice)
5 boiled eggs, peeled and diced
1 small onion, finely chopped
⅓ cup Miracle Whip Free™
¾ cup fat free Thousand Island salad dressing
hamburger buns

Combine smoked ham, cubed cheese, boiled eggs, onion and Miracle Whip™ in a food processor. Process until well blended. Add Thousand Island dressing and mix well. Use an ice-cream scoop and put a scoop of meat on each bun. Wrap each bun in aluminum foil and bake at 400° for 15 minutes. Serve warm.

# BROWN SUGAR PIE

*Prep. Time: 10 minutes Cook Time: 45-50 minutes*

4 cups light brown sugar
¾ cup butter, melted
¾ cup milk
3 eggs
3 tablespoons flour
½ teaspoon salt
2 teaspoons vanilla
1 unbaked 9" pie shell

Combine the sugar, butter, milk and eggs together; mix well. Add the flour and salt to the sugar mixture. Stir in the vanilla. Pour into an unbaked 9-inch pie shell. Bake at 350° for 45-50 minutes.

# September 25

## LAMB, BEANS AND RICE

*Prep. Time: 15 minutes Cook Time: 1 hour 30 minutes*

2 lbs. lamb meat, cubed and fat removed
2 medium onions, finely chopped
1 stick butter
2 lbs. string beans or fresh green beans
2 teaspoons salt
½ teaspoon black pepper
1 quart tomato juice
1 cup water
cooked rice

In large skillet, melt butter. Add chopped lamb meat and onions. Cook until meat is brown and onions are transparent; about 10 minutes. Add green beans and remaining ingredients. Cover with a lid and cook over medium heat for about an hour and a half, until green beans are tender. Serve over hot cooked rice.

# DATE PUDDING

*Prep. Time: 5 minutes Cook Time: 45-50 minutes*

1 cup flour

1 cup sugar

1½ cups dates, chopped

½ cup nuts, chopped

½ teaspoon salt

3 teaspoons baking powder

½ cup milk

1 cup brown sugar, firmly packed

3 tablespoons butter

1½ cups boiling water

In a large bowl, mix together flour, sugar, dates, nuts, salt, baking powder and milk. Pour into a greased pan. In medium saucepan combine brown sugar, butter and water. Bring this to a boil and cook for 2-3 minutes. Pour syrup over batter. Bake at 350° for 45 to 50 minutes.

# September 26

## SOUTH OF THE BORDER CASSEROLE

*Prep. Time: 15 minutes Cook Time: 30-40 minutes*

1 lb. lean ground beef

1 large onion, chopped

1 clove garlic, minced

1-to-2 lbs. fresh tomatoes, skins removed

2 cups red kidney beans

1 can (15 oz.) chili con carne without beans

2 teaspoons salt

2 cups shredded cheddar cheese

flour tortillas

In a large skillet, crumble up ground beef and add onion and garlic. Cook over medium heat until meat is browned and onion is transparent. Drain off all grease. Cut skinned tomatoes into small wedges and add those to the skillet. Add beans and their liquid and the chili con carne. Sprinkle salt over all and mix well. Heat mixture to boiling. Meanwhile, in a greased 9x13 pan, layer tortillas, overlapping if necessary, to cover the bottom of the pan. Spread 2 cups of the skillet mixture over tortillas and top with a handful of shredded cheese. Put down another layer of tortillas and repeat procedure. Bake at 400° for 30 to 40 minutes.

# FRESH OKRA CORN MEAL MUFFINS

*Prep. Time: 15 minutes Cook Time: 25 minutes*

2 cups self-rising corn meal

1 tablespoon sugar

½ teaspoon salt

1½ cups milk

2 eggs

¼ cup oil

1 teaspoon Worcestershire sauce

2 cups thinly sliced fresh okra (about ½ lb.)

1 small onion, finely chopped

Combine corn meal, sugar and salt in a mixing bowl and create a well in the center. Combine milk, eggs, oil and Worcestershire sauce and pour into the well. Stir until moist. Grease muffin pans and place in a 400° oven for about 5 minutes. Fold in okra and onion and stir well. Quickly spoon batter into prepared pans, filling each muffin ⅔ full. Bake at 400° for about 20 minutes or until lightly browned. Remove from pans immediately.

## KID BREAK!

### Quick and Easy Clay-Dough

Mix 4 cups flours (may need up to a cup more) with one cup salt and 2 tablespoon cream or tartar. Boil 2 cups of water and add 3 tablespoons of baby oil and food coloring. Add liquid mixture to dry mixture and stir and knead until well mixed.

# September 27

*Make tonight another theme evening. Tell your family to do some research on the Wild, Wild West. Let your kids dress up in their finest cowboy duds and get ready to enjoy this real chuck wagon dinner!*

## RANGE STEW

*Prep. Time: 15 minutes Cook Time: 1 hour*

1 lb. ground beef
1 pkg. dry onion soup mix
1 cup water
1 cup ketchup
2 tablespoons prepared mustard
2 teaspoons vinegar
32 oz. pork and beans
1 can (16 oz.) kidney beans

Boil the ground beef in a large soup pan. Drain off water and crumble meat. Add all remaining ingredients and mix well. Pour into a casserole dish and cover with a lid. Bake at 375° for about 1 hour.

## MOCK APPLE PIE

*Prep. Time: 15 minutes Cook Time: about 50 minutes*

Pastry for 2 crusts (To fit 9-inch pie plate)
1 ¾ cups crushed Ritz™ crackers
2 cups water
2 cups sugar
2 teaspoons cream of tartar
2 tablespoons lemon juice
2 tablespoons butter
1 teaspoon ground cinnamon

Place one pie pastry in the bottom of a pie pan. Crush crackers and put in the bottom of the pie pastry shell. In a saucepan over high heat, combine water, sugar, cream of tartar and bring this mixture to a hard boil. Add lemon juice and ½ teaspoon cinnamon and reduce heat to low; let simmer for about 15 minutes. Pour syrup over crackers. Sprinkle remaining cinnamon over all.

Dot with pats of butter. Top pie with remaining pie-crust. Flute edges. Slit top crust to allow steam to escape. Bake at 425° for 30 to 35 minutes or until crust is crisp and golden. Cool completely before cutting.

# September 28

## TACO RING SPECIAL

*Prep. Time: 20 minutes Cook Time: 30 to 40 minutes*

1 ½ lbs. lean ground beef
1 medium onion, chopped
2 tubes refrigerator crescent rolls
2 cups taco-blend cheese (or may use plain cheddar cheese)
1 large green pepper, cut in half, seeds removed
1 jar salsa
2 cups fat free sour cream

Brown ground beef and onion in a large skillet. Drain off all grease when meat is done. Spray a pizza pan with vegetable spray and place crescent dough around the sides with the tips outward and pinched together. Spoon the ground beef around the inner edge of the crescent dough. Sprinkle cheese over meat. Bring tips of dough inward and tuck under in the center. Bake at 375° for 30 to 40 minutes. Fill one half of the green pepper with salsa and the other half with sour cream. Set green pepper halves in the center of the ring. Serve with tortilla chips.

# COOKIES OF THE MONTH

## GRANDMA'S COOKIES

½ cup shortening
1 cup brown sugar, firmly packed
1 egg, beaten
2 cups sifted flour
½ teaspoon salt
½ teaspoon baking soda
2 teaspoons baking powder
½ cup sour cream
½ cup seedless raisins
½ cup chopped nuts

Cream together shortening and sugar; add egg and raisins. Mix sifted flour, salt, soda, baking powder and add alternately with sour cream. Mix all ingredients to form dough. Drop by teaspoons onto a greased cookie sheet. Bake at 400° until done.

## POTATO CHIP COOKIES

1 cup shortening
1 cup sugar
1 cup brown sugar
2 eggs, well beaten
2 cups flour
½ teaspoon salt
1 teaspoon baking soda
2 cups crushed potato chips
1 cup nuts (optional)

Mix together shortening, sugars and eggs until creamed. Add salt and baking soda to flour and mix well. Add dry ingredients to the creamed mixture. Stir in potato chips and nuts. Drop by teaspoon on ungreased cookie sheet. Bake at 325° for 15 minutes.

## ICE CREAM COOKIES

1 lb. butter, softened
1 pt. vanilla ice cream, softened
4 cups flour
2 tablespoons sugar
1 teaspoon almond flavoring

Combine all ingredients and mix well. Roll into small balls and place on a greased cookie sheet, about 2 inches apart. Flatten and make a small dent in center of each. Fill each with ½ teaspoon jelly or jam. Bake at 350° for 10 minutes.

# September 29

## BACON SPAGHETTI

*Prep. Time: 15 minutes Cook Time: 30-45 minutes*

1 lb. bacon
1 large onion, chopped
1 small green pepper, chopped
2 cans (15 oz.) tomato sauce
1 cup water
1 teaspoon Worcestershire sauce
2 cups sliced mushrooms, optional
2 teaspoons salt
1 tablespoon Italian seasoning
2 teaspoons dried oregano
2 bay leaves
1 lb. thin spaghetti

Cook spaghetti according to package directions and then set aside. In a large skillet, fry bacon until crisp. Remove bacon and add onion and green pepper. Cook until tender. Drain off bacon grease. Pour tomato sauce and water into skillet. Add Worcestershire sauce, sliced mushrooms, salt, Italian seasoning, oregano and bay leaves. Lower heat and let simmer 30 to 45 minutes. (The longer this cooks, the thicker the sauce will get.) Add crumbled bacon to sauce and serve hot over cooked spaghetti pasta.

Serve with a tossed salad and bread sticks.

# September 30

## ROASTED GARLIC CHOPS

*Prep. Time: 10 minutes Cook Time: 45 minutes*

2 tablespoons oil
6-8 pork chops, trimmed of fat
1 clove garlic
1 teaspoon minced garlic
1 can cream of mushroom soup
1 teaspoon salt
¼ teaspoon coarse black pepper
¼ cup water

In a large skillet, heat oil. Peel garlic clove and rub fresh garlic on both sides of each pork chop. Fry each pork chop in hot oil just until lightly browned. Remove chops and place in a shallow baking or casserole dish. Combine soup, minced garlic, water, salt and pepper and pour over chops. Cover tightly with a lid or aluminum foil and bake at 350° for 45 minutes.

## SOUR CREAM ESCALLOPED POTATOES

*Prep. Time: 20 minutes Cook Time: 30-40 minutes*

8 medium potatoes
1 stick butter
1 pint fat free sour cream
1 cup seasoned croutons, crushed
1 tablespoon dried chives`
1 teaspoon salt
¼ teaspoon black pepper

Boil potatoes until tender; peel and slice. Melt butter in a small saucepan and then add sour cream, chives, salt and pepper. In a 1½ quart casserole dish put down a layer of potatoes and cover them with a layer of the sour cream mixture. Top with a thin layer of the crushed croutons. Repeat layering until all ingredients are used. Bake at 350° for 30 to 40 minutes.

Serve with fresh vegetables and dip.

October is known as the: National Dessert Month, National Pasta Month, National Pizza Month, National Popcorn Poppin' Month and National Seafood Month.

# October 1

*Today is "World Vegetarian Day." Try this "vegetarian" dinner on your family then sit back and count the number of compliments you get.*

## MEATLESS TACO SALAD

*Prep. Time: 15 minutes*

1 large can fat free refried beans
1 large jar taco sauce
3 ripe avocados
1 teaspoon lemon juice
1 (16 oz.) container fat free sour cream
4 medium tomatoes, sliced
1 head lettuce
1 bunch green onions, diced
1 pkg. taco seasoning mix
2 cups shredded cheddar cheese or taco-blend cheese
1 can sliced ripe (black) olives, optional

Mash refried beans in the bottom of a large cake pan. In a blender, combine peeled avocados with lemon juice, sour cream and taco seasoning mix. Spread over the refried beans. Add a layer of lettuce, broken into bite-sized pieces. Top lettuce with tomatoes, green onions, cheese and black olives. Refrigerate for at least an hour before serving so seasonings have time to blend. Serve with tortilla chips.

# October 2

## GRILLED PIZZA SANDWICHES

*Prep. Time: 10 minutes Cook Time: 5-10 minutes*

1 can or jar prepared pizza sauce
4 slices bread per serving (enough for 2 sandwiches)
1 pkg. pepperoni
2 cups shredded mozzarella cheese
garlic salt
butter

Generously butter one side of each slice of bread. On a hot griddle, lay four slices of buttered bread, buttered-side-down. In the center of each piece of bread, spread a tablespoon of pizza sauce and place 2-3 slices of pepperoni. Top with a little bit of shredded mozzarella cheese. Place another slice of bread on top, buttered side facing up. Grill over medium heat until bottom is lightly browned. Flip sandwiches over and grill until the second side is lightly browned. Serve immediately.

Serve with vanilla ice cream topped with Hot Fudge Sauce.

## HOT FUDGE SAUCE

*Prep. Time: 5 minutes Cook Time: 15-20 minutes*

½ stick butter
3 (1 oz. each) squares unsweetened chocolate
1 large can evaporated milk
1½ cups sugar
2 teaspoons vanilla

Melt butter and chocolate squares in a small saucepan over low heat. Stir often and be careful chocolate doesn't scorch. Add milk and continue stirring. Add sugar and vanilla, continue stirring and cook until thick. Serve over hand-dipped ice cream.

# October 3

## BACON ROLL-UPS

*Prep. Time: 20 minutes Cook Time: 35-45 minutes*

½ cup butter
1 cup water
2½ cups packaged herb sesame stuffing mix
2 eggs
1 lb. mild bulk sausage
1 lb. sliced bacon

Pour stuffing in a mixing bowl. Combine butter and water in a small saucepan and heat until butter melts. Pour into stuffing mix and stir well. Add eggs and raw sausage, blending thoroughly. Pinch off a small ball of stuffing mixture and roll into a small oblong shape, such as a pecan. Cut bacon slices into thirds. Wrap each piece of stuffing mixture with bacon and fasten with a round toothpick. Place in a shallow baking dish and bake at 400° for 35 to 40 minutes. Drain these on either paper towel or brown paper before serving.

## QUICK & EASY COBBLER

*Prep. Time: 10 minutes Cook Time: 1 hour*

2 cans pie filling (your choice)
1 box yellow cake mix
1 stick butter, melted

Butter the bottom of a small cake pan. Pour pie filling in and top with dry cake mix. Melt butter and drizzle melted butter over the cake mix. Bake at 350° for about an hour. Serve warm or cold.

# October 4

## TUNA CHOWDER

*Prep. Time: 10 minutes Cook Time: 20 minutes*

2 cans water-packed tuna, drained
2 medium onions, diced
6 medium potatoes, peeled and sliced
4 teaspoons salt
⅛ teaspoon pepper
3 cups water
1 quart skim milk
2 cups frozen corn, thawed
2 tablespoons butter
fresh dill springs

Drain liquid from tuna. Melt butter in a large soup pan and sauté onion until golden, stirring often. Add water, potatoes, salt and pepper and cover pan. Cook over medium high heat for about 15 minutes. When potatoes are tender, add milk, corn and flaked tuna. Cover and cook another 5 minutes until all is thoroughly heated. Serve with a sprig of fresh dill on top of each bowl.

## LORNE DOONE™ DESSERT

*Prep. Time: 10 minutes Cook Time: 25-30 minutes*

2 cups crushed Lorne Doone™ cookies
1 stick butter, melted
1 cup semi-sweet chocolate chips
1 cup butterscotch chips
½ cup flaked coconut
1 cup crushed nuts (pecans or walnuts)
1 can Eagle Brand™ Sweetened Condensed Milk

Grease a 9x13 pan or spray with a non-stick vegetable spray. Pour cookie crumbs in the pan and press down to form a crust. Drizzle the melted butter over the cookie crumbs. Sprinkle the chocolate chips and butterscotch chips over the crust. Add a layer of flaked coconut. Sprinkle on the chopped nuts. Drizzle the condensed milk over all of it. Bake at 325° for 25 to 30 minutes. Cut into small squares while still warm.

# October 5

## BAKED HAM & MACARONI

*Prep. Time:20 minutes Cook Time: 20-25 minutes*

5 cups cooked elbow macaroni (may use other
    pasta shapes if desired)

2 tablespoons butter

1 tablespoon dried minced onion

2 tablespoons flour

¼ teaspoon dry mustard

1 teaspoon salt

dash pepper

2½ cups skim milk

2 cups chopped ham

2 cups shredded cheddar cheese

In a double-boiler, melt the butter; add onion, flour, dry mustard, salt and pepper. Slowly stir in milk and cook until mixture is smooth and thickened. Add ham and 1½ cups cheese, continue stirring until cheese melts. Add cooked macaroni and stir until pasta is well coated. Pour entire mixture into a 1½ qt. casserole dish. Top with the remaining half cup of cheese. Bake at 400° for 20 to 25 minutes.

## STRAWBERRY BAVARIAN PIE

*Prep. Time: 45 minutes*

1 baked 9-inch pie shell

1 teaspoon unflavored gelatin

2 tablespoons cold water

2 cups skim milk

1 cup sugar

¼ cup flour

½ teaspoon salt

3 egg yolks

2 tablespoons butter

1 teaspoon vanilla

4 teaspoons cornstarch

1 box frozen sliced strawberries, thawed

Dissolve gelatin in cold water. Scald milk in a double-boiler. In a medium bowl, mix ½ cup sugar, flour and salt; then slowly stir in scalded milk. Mix well and return mixture to the top part of the double-boiler. Cook over direct heat, stirring constantly until mixture thickens. When mixture is thick enough to coat spoon, put the top of the double-boiler over the bottom part and cook for about 10 minutes over boiling water. In a small bowl, beat egg yolks and slowly add them to the double-boiler. Cook until mixture is thickened, about 5 minutes. Remove from heat and add butter and gelatin, stir until dissolved. Remove top pan from the bottom and let cool. When mixture is lukewarm, add vanilla and mix well. Pour into the baked pie shell and refrigerate until firm.

In a saucepan combine the remaining sugar with the cornstarch. Drain juice from strawberries and slowly stir strawberry juice in with the sugar and cornstarch. Reserve the berries. Cook juice over medium heat until thickened and transparent. Remove from heat and cool. When glaze is lukewarm, stir in berries. When pie is set, top with the strawberries and glaze. Refrigerate until ready to serve.

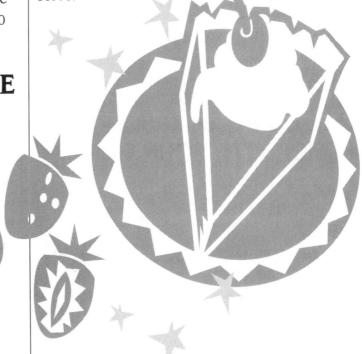

# October 6

*Today is "German-American" Day! For tonight's menu I asked my aunt, Anneliese Belzer, who was born and raised in Germany to share with me some authentic German recipes.*

## ROTKOHL MIT WEIN (RED CABBAGE & WINE)

*Prep. Time: 20 minutes Cook Time: 35-40 minutes*

1 head red cabbage (about 2 lbs.)
1 cup red wine
1/3 cup firmly packed brown sugar
1 teaspoon salt
dash cayenne pepper
4 Rome apples
1/4 cup apple cider vinegar
1/4 cup butter

Wash and remove the outer leaves from the head of cabbage. Quarter the head, discarding the core. Coarsely shred cabbage quarters and put it in a large heavy saucepan. Add wine, brown sugar, salt and cayenne pepper to cabbage. Wash, peel and quarter the apples. Discard the apple cores. Add the apple pieces to the saucepan. Cover with a tight fitting lid and cook over low heat for about 20-30 minutes or until cabbage is tender. When cabbage is tender, add the vinegar and butter. Toss well and serve when butter is melted.

## LAUCH IN RAHMASSE (LEEKS WITH SOUR CREAM)

*Prep. Time: 20 minutes Cook Time: 15-20 minutes*

8 large leeks
3 tablespoons butter
1/4 cup hot water
1/2 teaspoon salt
1/4 teaspoon Accent™
1 cup real sour cream
1 tablespoon flour
1/4 teaspoon Accent™
1/8 teaspoon cayenne pepper

Trim off roots and tough parts of leeks. Rinse and peel. Cut into 3/4-inch slices. In a large skillet, melt butter and add sliced leeks. Cook over medium heat for about 2 minutes then add 1/4 cup water, salt and 1/4 teaspoon Accent™. Cover skillet with a tight fitting lid and cook for 10 minutes or until leeks are tender. NOTE: There should be little to no water left in the skillet at the end of this cooking time.

Meanwhile blend together in a small mixing bowl the sour cream, flour, 1/4 teaspoon Accent™ and cayenne pepper. Push leeks to one side of the skillet and add the sour cream mixture. Stir the sour cream mixture constantly to avoid sticking. When sour cream mixture is heated through, begin stirring the leeks into the sour cream mixture. Continue stirring leeks and turning them over with a spoon for another 2-3 minutes until the sauce becomes smooth and thick. Serve immediately.

## SÜPS-SAURE ROTE RÜBEN (QUICK PICKLED BEETS)

*Prep. Time: 10 minutes Cook Time: 20 minutes*

1 lb. can small whole beets (about 2 cups drained)
2 medium onions, sliced
1 cup vinegar
1/2 cup sugar
1/2 teaspoon salt

Slice the beets very thinly and place into a medium-sized mixing bowl. Slice onions and add to beets; toss. In a small saucepan, mix together vinegar, sugar and salt. Bring vinegar mixture to a fast boil and then pour over the beets and onions. Set bowl in refrigerator and let chill for at least an hour before serving.

# COOKIES OF THE MONTH

## PUMPKIN COOKIES

1 stick butter, softened
1½ cup sugar
1 egg
1⅓ cups pumpkin
2¼ cups sifted flour
4 teaspoons baking powder
2 teaspoons pumpkin pie spice
1 cup raisins

Bring 2 cups of water to a boil and pour over the raisins. Let set and soak while you mix together the cookies. When ready to add to dough, drain off water and dry on several layers of paper towel.

Cream together butter and sugar. Add egg and pumpkin, beat well. Add spices to flour and sift flour into mixture in three installments; mixing well after each addition. Fold in raisins. Drop by teaspoon on greased cookie sheet. Bake at 375° for 15 minutes or until done.

## CINNAMON BOO-BOO COOKIES

1 stick butter
1½ cups sugar
1 egg
2¼ cups sifted flour
4 teaspoons baking powder
2 teaspoons cinnamon

Cream together butter and sugar; add egg. Add spices to flour and sift into creamed mixture in three installments; mixing well after each addition. Drop by teaspoon on to a greased cookie sheet. Bake at 375° for 15 minutes or until done.

## GRANDMA JAMES' SUGAR COOKIES

⅔ cup shortening
¾ cup sugar
½ teaspoon vanilla
1 egg
4 teaspoons milk
2 cups sifted flour
1½ teaspoons baking powder
¼ teaspoon salt

Thoroughly cream together shortening, sugar and vanilla. Add egg and beat until light and fluffy. Stir in milk. Sift together dry ingredients; blend into creamed mixture. Divide dough in half and wrap each part in waxed paper. Chill in refrigerator for 1 hour.

On lightly floured surface, roll one-half of the dough to ⅛ of an inch. Cut in desired shapes. Bake on greased cookie sheet at 375° for 6-8 minutes. Roll out second half and repeat procedure. Frost cookies with prepared frosting and sprinkle with colored sugars.

# SAUERBRATEN MIT NUDELN (MARINATED BEEF WITH NOODLES)

*Prep. Time: 4 days Cook Time: 3 ½ hours*

*NOTE: My Aunt sent me this authentic German recipe for Sauerbraten. If you want to fix it the way it is served in Germany, you need to plan ahead as it takes 4 days for marinating the beef.*

**4 lb. beef pot roast (or any 4 lb. piece of beef)**

**2 cups vinegar**

**2 cups water**

**1 large onion, sliced**

**¼ cup sugar**

**2 teaspoons salt**

**10 peppercorns**

**3 whole cloves**

**2 bay leaves**

**1 lemon**

**3 tablespoons plus ¼ cup butter**

**¼ cup flour**

**½ cup real sour cream**

**Prepared Parsley-Buttered Noodles**

Place meat in large bowl. In a saucepan combine vinegar, water, sliced onion, sugar, salt, peppercorns, cloves and bay leaves. Heat this until almost boiling. Pour over the meat and allow this to set at room temperature until completely cooled. Cut lemon in 1/4-inch slices and add slices around the meat. Cover and set in refrigerator. Every day for four days, turn the meat over once. On the fourth day, remove meat from marinade and place in a very large soup pan. Strain and reserve marinade.

Add 3 tablespoons butter to the soup pan with the meat. Over medium heat, brown all sides of the meat. Slowly add 2 cups of the reserved marinade (reserve the remaining marinade for gravy). Bring liquid to boiling. Reduce heat; cover pan with a tight fitting lid and simmer on low heat for 3 hours; or until meat is tender when pierced with a fork. Add more of the marinade if necessary to keep liquid around the meat. Liquid surrounding the meat should be simmering, but not boiling.

When meat is tender, remove meat and put it on a warm platter. Set in a warm oven to keep warm while you prepare gravy. For gravy, melt ¼ cup butter in the soup pan that you cooked the meat in. Blend in ¼ cup flour. Heat until the butter and flour mixture bubbles and is golden brown, stirring constantly. Remove pan from heat. Gradually add 3 cups of reserved marinade liquid. Stir until well mixed and replace pan over heat. Bring contents to a boil while stirring constantly. Cook until gravy thickens and then lower heat and cook for another 2 minutes. Remove pan from heat and whip gravy using a whisk beater. Add sour cream to gravy in 2 tablespoon increments. When the entire ½ cup sour cream has been added, return pan to low heat and cook for another 2 to 5 minutes, stirring constantly. Do not let gravy boil.

Serve meat and gravy with prepared Parsley-Buttered Noodles (see page 158)

# October 7

## SAVORY BAKED PORK CHOPS

*Prep. Time: 5 minutes Cook Time: 90 minutes*

**6 pork chops**

**2 large onions, sliced**

**¼ cup lemon juice**

**¼ cup Parmesan cheese**

**1 teaspoon salt**

**½ teaspoon dried savory**

Slice onions and place a layer of sliced onions in the bottom of a 9x13-inch pan. Arrange pork chops over onion slices. Drizzle lemon juice over chops. Combine Parmesan cheese, savory and salt and sprinkle over chops. Cover with a second layer of onion slices. Cover pan with aluminum foil and bake at 325° for 90 minutes.

# SAVORY RICE

*Prep. Time: 15 minutes Cook Time: 15 minutes*

1 tablespoon oil

1 tablespoon butter

6 green onions, chopped finely (including green tops)

1 clove garlic, minced

3 chicken-bouillon cubes dissolved in 3 cups hot water

3 cups uncooked instant rice

½ teaspoon salt

½ teaspoon Accent™

1 teaspoon paprika

2 tablespoons fresh chopped parsley or 1 table-spoon dried parsley

¼ teaspoon dried savory

Combine oil and butter in a small skillet. Heat until butter melts and add onions and garlic. Sauté until onions and garlic are golden. In a saucepan, bring bouillon water to a fast boil. Remove from heat and stir in salt, Accent™, paprika, parsley and savory. Add onion and garlic in oil. Stir in rice and cover with a tight fitting lid. Let pan set for about 15 minutes then fluff with a fork and serve.

Serve with cooked frozen peas.

# October 8

*Today begins a week long observance for National Pasta Week, so it's only fitting that tonight's dinner feature some pasta!*

## STUFFED PASTA SHELLS

*Prep. Time: 20 minutes Cook Time: 25 minutes*

1 box large pasta shells

1 teaspoon salt

1 tablespoon butter

1 quart jar prepared spaghetti sauce

2 lbs. ground beef

1 large onion, chopped fine

1 green pepper, chopped fine

3 cups shredded (mixed) cheddar and mozzarella cheese

In a large soup pan, cook pasta shells according to package directions. Add butter to pasta while cooking. When shells are cooked, drain and rinse in cold water. In a skillet, brown ground beef with chopped onions and green pepper. Add salt and stir often. When meat is cooked and vegetables are tender, drain off all grease and pat meat with an absorbent paper towel. Let meat cool. Add one cup mixed shredded cheese to the meat. Stuff each large pasta shell with the hamburger and cheese mixture. Lay open side down in a greased baking dish. Spoon spaghetti sauce over all filled shells. Bake at 350° for 20 minutes. Top shells with remaining shredded cheese and return to oven to bake for 5 more minutes.

Serve with tossed salads and garlic bread sticks.

## TIRAMISU TOFFEE DESSERT

*Prep. Time: 15 minutes*

1 (10 ¾ oz.) frozen pound cake, thawed and cut into 9 slices

¾ cup strong coffee

1 cup sugar

½ cup chocolate syrup

1 (8 oz.) pkg. cream cheese, softened

2 cups heavy whipping cream

4 bars Heath™ candy bars, crushed, or 1 cup crushed toffee candy pieces

Arrange cake slices on bottom of a rectangular baking dish, covering the bottom. Drizzle coffee over the cake. In mixing bowl, beat sugar, chocolate syrup and cream cheese together with an electric mixer set on medium-high speed. When cream cheese mixture is smooth, add chilled heavy whipping cream. Continue to beat on medium-high speed until light and fluffy. Spread over cake pieces. Sprinkle with the toffee candy. Cover and refrigerate for an hour to set dessert and blend flavors. Serve within 24 hours.

# October 9

## STUFFED PORK CHOPS

(see page 130)

## 5-STEP CORN CASSEROLE

*Prep. Time 5 minutes / Cook Time 45 min-1 hr.*

1 box Jiffy™ corn bread mix
1 can sweet kernel corn with liquid
1 can creamed style corn
1 cup sour cream
½ stick butter, melted

Combine all ingredients in casserole dish. Stir to blend well. Bake at 400° for 45 minutes or until lightly browned and a knife comes out clean when inserted in middle.

## PUMPKIN PIE DESSERT

*Prep. Time: 15 minutes Cook Time: 45 minutes*

1 pkg. yellow cake mix
½ cup melted butter
1 egg
1 small can pumpkin
2 teaspoons pumpkin pie spice
¼ cup sugar
2 eggs
⅔ cup milk
¼ cup sugar
2 teaspoons cinnamon
¼ cup butter (solid)

In a greased 9x13 cake pan, combine cake mix (minus 1 cup reserved for top) with ½ cup melted butter and an egg. Spread over the bottom of the pan and flatten into a crust. In a small mixing bowl, combine pumpkin, pumpkin pie spice, ¼ cup sugar, 2 eggs and ⅔ cup milk. Blend until smooth using the low setting of an electric mixer. Pour over the first layer. Combine the 1 cup reserved cake mix and add ¼ cup sugar, 2 teaspoons cinnamon and the ¼ cup cold butter. Using a fork, cut ingredients together until blended and crumbly. Sprinkle over pumpkin layer. Bake at 350° for 35-45 minutes or until a knife inserted in the center comes out clean. Serve with whipped topping or ice cream.

# October 10

## SWISS STEAK CASSEROLE

*Prep. Time: 15 minutes Cook Time: 90 minutes*

3 lb. round steak, 1/4-inch thick
½ cup flour
2 teaspoons salt
½ teaspoon coarse black pepper
¼ cup oil
2-3 onions, sliced
2 cans condensed tomato soup, undiluted
1 soup can filled with water
9 potatoes, peeled and quartered
6 carrots, peeled and quartered
2 cups frozen peas

Cut meat into 6-8 serving portions. Combine flour, salt and pepper on a sheet of waxed paper and dredge each piece of meat in the flour mixture, coating both sides. Use a meat mallet and pound each piece of meat until it is almost double in size. In a large skillet, heat oil and brown each side of meat. Remove meat and place in a large roasting pan. In remaining oil, sauté onion slices until just tender. Add soup and water. Arrange carrots, potatoes and peas around meat. Pour tomato and onion mixture over all. Cover with a lid and bake at 350° for 90 minutes.

## PUMPKIN BREAD

*Prep. Time: 15 minutes Cook Time: 1 hour or longer*

2 cups solid packed pumpkin

⅔ cup water

3¼ cups sugar

1 cup oil

4 eggs

3 ½ cups flour

1 tablespoon baking powder

2 teaspoons baking soda

2 ½ tablespoons pumpkin pie spice

½ teaspoon ground cloves

1 ½ teaspoons nutmeg

1 ½ tablespoons ground cinnamon

In a large mixing bowl, combine all ingredients and mix together with an electric mixer on the low setting. Pour batter into greased and floured loaf pans. Bake at 350° for 1 hour or until a knife inserted in the center comes out clean. Cool for 10-15 minutes before removing from pan.

# October 11

*Back on this day in 1987, the world's largest pizza was baked. It was cut into 94,248 slices! Tonight's version doesn't make quite that much.*

## PIZZA CRUST

*Prep. Time: 10 minutes*

1 pkg. active dry yeast, dissolved in 1 cup hot water

1 teaspoon sugar

1 teaspoon salt

1 tablespoon oil

2½ cups flour

To the dissolved yeast, add sugar, salt and oil. Stir by hand, gradually adding flour. Let dough rest for 5 minutes. Oil hands and spread dough on greased pizza pan. Bake plain pizza dough for 5 minutes at 400°. Remove from oven.

## PIZZA SAUCE

*Prep. Time: 5 minutes*

1 (8 oz.) can tomato sauce

2 teaspoons oregano

1½ teaspoon garlic powder

2 teaspoons Italian seasonings

Blend together sauce and seasonings. Spread over pizza crust. Top with your choice of fresh vegetables (onion, green pepper, mushrooms, etc.), meats and cheese. Bake at 400° for 30-35 minutes or until crust is lightly browned and cheese is bubbly.

# October 12

## SEAFOOD FANCY

*Prep. Time: 15 minutes Cook Time: 30 minutes*

2 green peppers, chopped

2 large onions, chopped

1 cup diced celery

2 cups lobster or shrimp

1 cup cooked crab

1 teaspoon salt

½ teaspoon pepper

1 teaspoon Worcestershire sauce

1 cup mayonnaise

2 cups buttered bread cubes

Combine all ingredients except bread cubes. Spread in a buttered casserole dish. Top with bread cubes and bake at 300° for 30 minutes.

# October 13

## CHICKEN WITH HERB STUFFING & MUSHROOM SAUCE

*Prep. Time: 25 minutes Cook Time: 1 hour*

6 whole chicken breasts, skin removed
½ cup flour
1 teaspoon salt
½ teaspoon paprika
½ teaspoon pepper
3 tablespoons butter, melted

Combine flour and seasoning in a paper bag; add chicken and shake to coat each piece. Set chicken in baking dish.

2 cups dry bread cubes
1 tablespoon chopped onion
1 teaspoon salt
½ teaspoon poultry seasoning
⅛ teaspoon pepper
2 tablespoons melted butter
¼ cup hot water

Mix bread cubes and onion with seasoning; add butter and hot water. Toss lightly. Stuff the cavity of each chicken breast with stuffing. Melt the 3 tablespoons of butter and with a pastry brush, spread melted butter over each piece of chicken. Bake at 325° for 45 minutes or until tender. When chicken is done, arrange pieces on platter and pour mushroom sauce over each piece.

## MUSHROOM SAUCE

*Prep. Time: 5 minutes Cook Time: 10-15 minutes*

½ pint fat free sour cream
1 can cream of mushroom soup
½ soup can water
2 teaspoons parsley flakes

In a small saucepan, combine sour cream, condensed soup and water. Heat over low heat, stirring constantly. Pour over hot chicken and garnish with parsley flakes.

Serve with your choice of vegetables.

# October 14

## OPEN-FACED MEATBALL SANDWICHES

*Prep. Time: 20 minutes Cook Time: 25-35 minutes*

2 lbs. lean ground beef
2 jars or cans prepared spaghetti sauce
6 slices "Texas Toast" bread
½ stick butter
1 teaspoon garlic powder
2 tablespoons Parmesan cheese
2 tablespoons Romano cheese
1 cup shredded mozzarella cheese
salt and pepper to taste

Form 1-2 inch meatballs from the ground beef and lay them on a large jelly-roll pan. Put pan in a preheated 400° oven. Bake meatballs for 25-30 minutes. Meanwhile, pour spaghetti sauce in a large soup pan and set over low heat, stirring occasionally. In a small bowl, combine softened butter with garlic powder. Spread over one side of each slice of "Texas Toast" (thick-sliced) bread. Top each slice of garlic-buttered bread with Parmesan and Romano cheeses. When meatballs are cooked, remove pan from oven and turn off oven. Immediately place Texas Toast (buttered side UP) directly on oven rack. Close oven door. Remove meatballs from pan and place them in the spaghetti sauce. Let meatballs and sauce simmer together for about 5 minutes while the bread is toasting.

On each plate, lay a piece of toasted garlic bread. With a large spoon, cover bread with meatballs and spaghetti sauce. Top each with a handful of Mozzarella cheese. Serve immediately.

## APPLE PIE PIZZA (DESSERT)

*Prep. Time: 10 minutes Cook Time: 20 minutes*

1 pizza crust (store bought, prepared from mix or homemade)
1 can apple pie filling
½ cup brown sugar
2 tablespoons flour
½ cup quick cooking oatmeal
2 tablespoons ground cinnamon
½ stick butter

Prepare pizza crust and bake at 350° for about 5 minutes. Remove from oven and spread apple pie filling over the crust. For the topping, combine brown sugar, oatmeal, cinnamon and cold butter and work until mixture is crumbly. Sprinkle over apples. Bake at 350° degrees for 20 minutes or until pizza crust is lightly browned and apples are bubbly.

# October 15

## CHICKEN SUPREME WITH MUSHROOM SAUCE

*Prep. Time: 20-30 minutes Cook Time: 45 minutes*

3 cups diced "white" cooked chicken
1 (8 oz.) pkg. lasagna noodles
1½ cups cottage cheese
1 cup shredded American cheese
½ cup Parmesan cheese
Mushroom sauce:
1 small onion, chopped fine
½ green pepper, chopped fine
3 tablespoons butter
1 can cream of chicken soup
⅓ cup skim milk
1 cup sliced mushrooms, canned or fresh
¼ cup pimentos, optional
½ teaspoon salt
¼ teaspoon pepper

Cook lasagna noodles until tender. Meanwhile, in skillet, melt butter and sauté onion and green pepper with mushrooms until almost tender. Add soup, milk and pimentos. When noodles are tender, drain and rinse in cold water. In a 9x13 greased pan, layer half of the noodles on the bottom. Pour half of the mushroom sauce over the layer of noodles. Next, layer half of the chicken, cottage cheese and American cheese over the sauce. Salt and pepper to taste. Top with another layer of noodles. Repeat layers. Bake at 350° for 45 minutes.

### KITCHEN TIP
Add a pat of butter to boiling water when cooking potatoes, vegetables, pasta or rice. This will keep the water from foaming up and boiling over.

# SUGAR PLUM PUDDING

*Prep. Time: 15 minutes Cook Time: 40 minutes or longer*

1 cup butter

1 ¾ cups sugar

3 eggs

2½ cups flour

1 teaspoon baking soda

1 tablespoon ground cinnamon

1½ tablespoons pumpkin pie spice

1¼ cups buttermilk

1¼ cups prunes, cooked with pits removed

GLAZE:

½ stick butter

¾ cup buttermilk

1½ cups sugar

2 teaspoons vanilla

Cream butter and sugar. Add eggs and mix thoroughly. Add dry ingredients alternately with buttermilk. Add prunes and mix slightly. Pour into a greased pan. Bake at 325° for about 40 minutes or until firm. Remove from oven and pour glaze over the top.

Glaze: Combine butter, buttermilk and sugar and bring to a fast boil. Add vanilla. Pour over hot pudding.

# October 16

## BEEF CORN PONE

*Prep. Time: 20 minutes Cook Time: 20 minutes*

1 lb. lean ground beef (or ground turkey)

1 medium onion, chopped finely

2 teaspoons chili powder

1 teaspoon Worcestershire sauce

2 cups pinto beans, drained

2 cups canned tomatoes

1 cup corn bread batter

In a large skillet, brown meat and onions. Drain off grease. Add seasonings and tomatoes. Cover and simmer over low heat for 10-15 minutes. Add beans. Pour meat mixture into a greased casserole dish. Top with the corn bread batter. Bake at 400° for 20 minutes or until corn bread is done.

# FRUIT DUMPLINGS

*Prep. Time: 20 minutes Cook Time: 20 minutes*

2 cups canned pie-filling fruit

1 rounded tablespoon butter

3 cups water

1 cup sugar

1 cup flour

½ cup sugar

⅛ teaspoon salt

½ teaspoon ground cinnamon

2 teaspoons baking powder

½ cup milk

Place canned fruit in a saucepan. Add rounded tablespoon of butter, water and 1 cup sugar. Bring to a boil. Meanwhile, in a mixing bowl combine flour, ½ cup sugar, salt, cinnamon and baking powder. Sift dry ingredients together then add ½ cup milk. Mix well and drop by spoonfuls over boiling fruit. When batter is all used, transfer fruit and dumplings to a greased casserole dish. Bake at 350° for about 20 minutes or until dumplings are lightly browned.

## KID BREAK!

### Kool-Aid™ Clay

1 cup flour

½ cup salt

3 tablespoons oil

small package unsweetened Kool-Aid™ *(the color of the clay will be determined by the color of the Kool-Aid™)*

Mix all ingredients. Add one cup boiling water, stir and knead dough until soft. Store in an airtight container. This should last between 2 and 3 weeks.

# October 17

*A good memory is great to have, but possessing the ability to forget is the true test of greatness.*

## SWEET & SASSY PORK CHOPS

*Prep. Time: 15 minutes Cook Time: 1 hour*

6 pork chops
1 large onion, sliced
2 lemons, sliced
1 cup brown sugar, firmly packed
1¼ cups ketchup
1 cup water
2 tablespoons butter or oil

Heat butter or oil in a large skillet. Brown both sides of each pork chop. Place in a single layer in a 9x13 baking pan. On top of each chop, place a slice of onion. On the onion, place a slice of lemon. Sprinkle brown sugar over each chop. Cover each chop with ketchup. Add a cup of water to the bottom of the pan. Cover pan with aluminum foil and bake at 325° for 1 hour.

## CORN & BROCCOLI

*Prep. Time: 10 minutes Cook Time: 15-20 minutes*

1 stick butter
2 cups sweet corn, drained
½ red bell pepper, chopped fine
½ green bell pepper, chopped fine
1 teaspoon salt
1 pkg. (10 oz.) frozen chopped broccoli, thawed and drained
1 teaspoon dried basil
½ teaspoon garlic powder
½ teaspoon coarse black pepper

In a heavy saucepan, melt butter. Add all ingredients and stir to blend. Cover with a tight fitting lid and cook over medium heat for 15-20 minutes, until vegetables are tender. Stir occasionally.

# October 18

## NOODLE HASH

*Prep. Time: 10 minutes Cook Time: 15 minutes*

1 lb. lean ground beef or turkey
1 small onion, chopped finely
½ green bell pepper, chopped finely
½ red bell pepper, chopped finely
1 can cream of mushroom soup
1 cup sliced mushrooms, fresh or canned & drained
2 cups cooked noodles
1 cup shredded cheese
1 small can tomato paste
salt and pepper to taste

In a large skillet, brown meat with onion and peppers. Drain off all grease. Add soup, tomato paste, cooked noodles, salt and pepper. Let simmer together for about 10 minutes, then pour into a greased casserole dish. Sprinkle with cheese and bake at 350° for 5 minutes.

## PINEAPPLE BANANA CAKE

*Prep. Time: 10 minutes Cook Time: 1 hour 20 minutes*

3 cups flour
1 teaspoon baking soda
2 teaspoons ground cinnamon
2 cups sugar
1 teaspoon salt
1½ cups oil
2 teaspoons vanilla
1 (8 oz.) can crushed pineapple and juice
3 eggs
3 bananas, diced
1 cup chopped nuts, optional

Combine all ingredients in a large mixing bowl. Pour batter into a greased and floured tube pan. Bake at 350° for 1 hour and 20 minutes or until cake tests done when a knife inserted in the center comes out clean.

# October 19

## ORIENTAL EXPRESS

*Prep. Time: 15 minutes Cook Time: 20-30 minutes*

1 lb. cooked chicken pieces
1 cup chopped celery
1 cup chopped onion
1 chopped green bell pepper
1 cup frozen peas, thawed
1 cup bean sprouts, drained
½ cup water chestnuts, chopped and drained
1 pkg. chicken Ramen™ noodles, crushed
1 cup uncooked instant rice
1 tablespoon soy sauce
2 tablespoons butter or oil

Heat butter or oil in a large skillet and sauté celery, onion and green pepper until tender. Drain off grease. Add 3 cups water and the chicken seasoning packet from the Ramen™ noodles and bring to a boil. Add all remaining ingredients. Pour into a casserole dish and bake at 350° for 20 to 30 minutes.

## NO BAKE HOMEMADE CHEESECAKE

*Prep. Time: 10 minutes*

1 graham cracker pie crust
1 (8 oz.) pkg. cream cheese, softened
⅓ cup sugar
1 cup light sour cream
2 teaspoons vanilla
3 cups extra creamy whipped topping

Beat cheese until smooth; gradually beat in sugar. Blend in sour cream and vanilla. Fold in whipped topping, blending well. Spoon into crust. Chill until set. Serve with fresh or canned fruit.

# October 20

## BREAKFAST PIZZA

*Prep. Time: 10 minutes Cook Time: 30 minutes*

1 pkg. refrigerated crescent rolls
1 pkg. (24 oz.) frozen hash browns
6 eggs, beaten well with ¼ cup milk
½ lb. bacon and/or sausage, cooked and crumbled
2 cups shredded Cheddar cheese

Spread crescent rolls out on a cookie sheet. Layer the rest of the ingredients on top. Bake at 350° for 30 minutes or until crust is light brown and cheese has melted.

## PEANUT BUTTER BANANA MUFFINS

*Prep. Time: 15 minutes Cook Time: 20 minutes*

1 cup flour
¾ cup quick oats
⅓ cup brown sugar, firmly packed
1 tablespoon baking powder
1 cup skim milk
½ cup low fat peanut butter
1 large or 2 small mashed ripe bananas
1 egg, beaten
2 tablespoons oil
1 teaspoon vanilla
Topping:
¼ cup quick oats
¼ cup flour
2 tablespoons butter, melted
2 tablespoons brown sugar, firmly packed

Heat oven to 375°. Grease or line 12 medium to large muffin cups. Combine flour, oats, brown sugar and baking powder. Whisk together milk, peanut butter, banana, egg, oil and vanilla; add to dry ingredients, mixing just until moistened. Fill muffin cups ¾ full. Combine topping ingredients and sprinkle evenly over batter of each muffin. Bake 16 to 20 minutes, or until golden brown. Serve warm from the oven.

# October 21

## TANGY CHICKEN WITH POTATOES

*Prep. Time: 15 minutes Cook Time: 75-90 minutes*

2 whole chickens, cut in pieces, skin removed

8 medium potatoes, peeled and quartered

3 tablespoons sugar

2 tablespoons sweet basil

6 bay leaves

½ teaspoon coarse black pepper

2 medium onions, sliced

2 cups chopped celery

1½ cups lemon juice

¼ cup olive oil

2 tablespoons oregano

½ teaspoon cinnamon

½ teaspoon ground red pepper

1 teaspoon garlic powder

1 teaspoon salt

Salt and pepper chicken pieces and place them in a large roasting pan. Set pan in hot oven (375 degrees) without lid for about 15 minutes. Remove pan and turn pieces over. Drain off all juices. Cover chicken with onion slices, celery and potatoes. Cover pan with lid and place in oven. Meanwhile, mix together in a large bowl, the lemon juice, olive oil, sugar, oregano, sweet basil, cinnamon, bay leaves, red pepper, garlic powder, black pepper and salt. Mix well to blend and then remove lid from roasting pan and pour over chicken. Replace lid on roaster pan and bake at 375° for 1 hour. When chicken is done, remove lid. Turn on broiler and lightly brown chicken before serving.

## SQUASH BAKE

*Prep. Time: 15 minutes Cook Time: 25 minutes*

2 cups cooked squash, drained (your choice: summer, zucchini, acorn, spaghetti, etc.)

2 cups chicken broth

small package Pepperidge Farm™ dressing (stuffing) mix

1 can cream of chicken soup

½ stick butter

1 medium onion, finely chopped

Mix together all ingredients. Be sure it is moist. Bake at 375° for 20-25 minutes. Lay slices of cheese on top and melt just before serving.

# October 22

## CORNED BEEF CASSEROLE

*Prep. Time: 15 minutes Cook Time: 1 hour*

1 (12 oz.) can corned beef

1 can cream of mushroom or potato soup

1 cup skim milk

2 cups cooked elbow macaroni

1 cup frozen peas, thawed

1 can sweet corn, drained

2 cups shredded cheddar cheese

1 small onion, finely chopped

½ cup buttered toast crumbs

Cook macaroni according to package directions. Set aside. Blend soup and milk. Add macaroni and stir well. Add corned beef, cheese, peas, corn and onions; mix thoroughly. Pour into lightly greased 9x13 baking pan. Sprinkle with buttered toast crumbs. Bake at 325° for 1 hour.

# CRANBERRY BREAD

*Prep. Time: 10 minutes Cook Time: 35 minutes or longer*

2¼ cup sugar
3 cups flour
1½ cups milk
1⅛ cups oil
1½ teaspoons salt
1½ teaspoons baking powder
1½ teaspoons vanilla
1½ teaspoons chopped almonds
3 eggs
1 cup chopped cranberries

Mix all ingredients together in a large mixing bowl. Beat at medium speed with an electric mixer for two full minutes. Pour into greased loaf pans. Bake at 350° for 35 minutes or until tops are split open and lightly browned.

# CRANBERRY BREAD ICING

1 teaspoon vanilla
½ cup butter, softened
2 cups powdered sugar
2 tablespoons milk

Combine all ingredients, adding more milk if mixture is too thick. This should be the consistency of a thick glaze. Pour over warm loaves of cranberry bread before slicing.

## KID BREAK!
### Candy Clay

⅓ cup soft oleo or butter
⅓ cup light corn syrup
1 teaspoon vanilla
½ teaspoon salt
1 lb. box powdered sugar

Mix all ingredients. Any color of food coloring may be added. Sculptures may be eaten when completed.

# October 23

## BROILED LAKE TROUT WITH ALMOND SAUCE

*Prep. Time: 5 minutes Cook Time: 20-25 minutes*

6 servings lake trout fillets
salt and pepper
water
1½ sticks butter
⅛ teaspoon pepper
½ teaspoon paprika
¼ cup minced lemon rind
juice of 1 lemon
½ cup toasted sliced almonds

Place fish in large skillet and add boiling salted water to cover fillets. Cook for 10-12 minutes. Remove fish and place on a broiler pan. Melt butter and brush butter over each fillet. Sprinkle with salt and pepper. Broil 5 minutes. Baste fillets again with butter. Sprinkle with paprika. Broil for 3-5 minutes longer. Add lemon rind, lemon juice and toasted almonds to remaining butter. Heat until bubbly and pour over fish before serving.

# COLE SLAW

*Prep. Time: 20 minutes*

1 head cabbage, shredded
2 carrots, shredded
½ cup plus 2 teaspoons sugar
1 cup vinegar
¾ cup oil
½ cup pineapple juice
1 teaspoon dry mustard
1 teaspoon celery seed
1 teaspoon salt

Combine shredded cabbage and carrots in a large bowl. Sprinkle 2 cups sugar over vegetables and set aside; do not stir. In a saucepan, combine all remaining ingredients and bring mixture to a boil. Pour over shredded cabbage and carrots while boiling hot. Stir well. Cover and refrigerate at least four hours before serving. This slaw's flavor improves as it ages.

# APPLE STRUDEL

*Prep. Time: 20 minutes Cook Time: 1 hour*

2 cups flour
½ teaspoon salt
2 tablespoons sugar
2 tablespoons baking powder
½ cup shortening (butter-flavored shortening works well)
⅔ cup milk
FILLING:
2 tablespoons butter, melted
½ cup sugar
3 cups chopped tart apples (Gala, Jonathon, Granny Smith, Northern Spy, etc.)
¼ cup brown sugar, firmly packed
1 tablespoon cinnamon
TOPPING:
1½ cups powdered sugar
1 teaspoon vanilla
1 tablespoon butter, melted
milk (enough to spread)

Combine the first five ingredients for dough. Stir until coarse. Add milk. Knead and roll into a rectangle, about the thickness of pie crust. Prepare the filling by combining the next five ingredients. Spread filling over the dough. Beginning at one end, roll up jelly-roll style and place on baking pan. Bake at 375° for 1 hour. While strudel is still baking, prepare the topping by combining all the remaining ingredients and having it ready to pour over the warm dessert as soon as it comes out of the oven. Slice and serve.

# October 24

## MEAT & POTATO CASSEROLE

*Prep. Time: 10-15 minutes Cook Time: 1 hour*

2 cups cooked cubed ham, beef, lamb or veal— your choice of one or more
1 small onion, finely chopped
1 teaspoon salt
¼ teaspoon pepper
6 medium potatoes, sliced with skin on
2 tablespoons flour
1 tall can Milnot™
2 cups shredded American or cheddar cheese

Combine meat, onion, salt and pepper. In a lightly greased casserole dish, put a layer of the meat mixture on the bottom. Add a layer of sliced potatoes. Repeat layers. Sprinkle flour over last layer of potatoes. Top with Milnot™. Cover casserole dish and bake at 350° for 45 minutes. Remove cover and sprinkle on cheese. Bake uncovered for 15 minutes longer and serve.

# BUTTERSCOTCH TORTE

*Prep. Time: 10 minutes Cook Time: 15 minutes*

1 cup flour
½ cup chopped pecans
1 cup powdered sugar
1 package instant butterscotch pudding
1 stick butter
1 pkg. (8 oz.) cream cheese
1½ cups milk
1 tub Cool Whip™

Mix flour, butter and chopped pecans like pie crust. Press in 11x7-inch pan. Bake at 375° for 15 minutes. Meanwhile, mix and beat together cream cheese, powdered sugar, and 1 cup Cool Whip™. Pour into cooled crust. Mix instant pudding with milk and beat for two minutes on high with an electric mixer. Pour pudding over the Cool Whip™.

Top with remaining Cool Whip™. Garnish with chopped pecans. Refrigerate until ready to serve.

# October 25

## CRISPY HERB CHICKEN

*Prep. Time: 10-15 minutes Cook Time: 1 hour*

2 whole chickens, cut up, skin removed
1 cup light sour cream
2 tablespoons lemon juice
2 tablespoons Worcestershire sauce
1 teaspoon celery salt
1 teaspoon paprika
1 teaspoon garlic powder
½ teaspoon salt
⅛ teaspoon pepper
1 pkg. herb seasoned stuffing mix, rolled to fine crumbs
2 tablespoons oil

Combine sour cream, lemon juice, Worcestershire sauce, celery salt, paprika, garlic powder, salt and pepper. Dip each piece of chicken into sour cream mixture and then roll in the crushed herb seasoned stuffing mix crumbs. Coat a large baking pan with the oil and lay coated chicken pieces on pan in a single layer. Bake at 375° for 1 hour or until chicken is tender.

## HASHBROWNS SUPREME

*Prep. Time: 10 minutes Cook Time: 45 minutes to 1 hour*

2 lbs. frozen shredded hash browns, thawed
½ stick butter, melted
1 teaspoon salt
¼ teaspoon pepper
dash garlic powder
1 medium onion, finely chopped
½ cup beef stock or canned broth
1 cup milk
2 cups shredded Colby cheese

In a large mixing bowl, combine the thawed hashbrowns, shredded cheese and chopped onion. In another bowl, combine milk, beef stock, half of the melted butter, garlic powder, salt and pepper; mix well. Pour this mixture over the hashbrowns and blend well. In a large oven-proof skillet, heat remaining melted butter, coating the bottom of skillet. When skillet is hot, pour hash browns in skillet and cook over medium-high heat for about 5 minutes, stirring occasionally. When all cheese is melted, remove the skillet from the stove top and put uncovered in a 375° oven. Bake until the top surface is dark brown, between 45 minutes to 1 hour.

NOTE: If you do not have an oven-proof skillet, spoon hashbrowns from skillet into a greased baking pan, 9x13 or smaller.

## TAPIOCA CITRUS SALAD

*Prep. Time: 10 minutes*

1 box mandarin orange gelatin
2 boxes tapioca pudding
1 can mandarin orange sections
1 can crushed pineapple
1 pkg. Dream Whip™, whipped according to package directions

Drain juice from fruit and add enough water to make 3 cups liquid. Pour liquid in a medium saucepan and add gelatin and pudding mixes. Heat, stirring often, and bring this to a boil. Remove from heat and let cool in refrigerator or cold pantry for about 30 minutes. Add fruit and Dream Whip™, stirring to mix well. Refrigerate until ready to serve.

# October 26

## MAZOTTA PORK CASSEROLE

*Prep. Time: 15 minutes Cook Time: 30 minutes*

1 lb. ground pork
1 pkg. wide noodles
2 onions, finely chopped
1½ teaspoons salt
1 teaspoon sugar
1 can tomato soup
1 small can mushroom pieces, drained
2 cups shredded American or cheddar cheese
½ cup water
¼ teaspoon pepper
1 can French-styled green beans, drained

In a large pan, cook noodles according to package directions. When noodles are tender, drain and rinse. In a skillet, brown pork and onion. When meat is cooked, drain off all grease. Add pork and onions to noodles. Add all remaining ingredients except for cheese. Mix well and place in a greased casserole dish. Sprinkle top with shredded cheese. Bake at 350° for 20-30 minutes.

## BAKED CHEESECAKE

*Prep. Time: 15 minutes Cook Time: 45 minutes*

3 pkgs. (8 oz.) cream cheese, softened
1¼ cups sugar
1 (8 oz.) container sour cream
1½ teaspoons vanilla
4 eggs
3 tablespoons sugar
graham cracker crust mix

Firmly press graham cracker crust to bottom and sides of 9x13 cake pan. In mixing bowl, combine cream cheese, eggs, 1¼ cups sugar and 1½ teaspoons vanilla. Beat on high speed with an electric mixer for 7 minutes. Pour mixture into graham cracker crust. Bake at 350° for 35 minutes. Remove from oven and increase oven temperature to 375°. In mixing bowl, combine sour cream, 3 tablespoons sugar and 1½ teaspoons vanilla. Beat on low speed until well blended. Pour onto hot cheesecake. Return pan to oven for 10 minutes, then turn off the oven. Let cake set in closed hot oven until completely cooled (this will prevent the top from cracking, so be sure not to open the oven door during this time). Top with your choice of canned pie filling.

# October 27

## PANTRY SHELF CASSEROLE

*Prep. Time: 25 minutes Cook Time: 1 hour*

2 lbs. lean ground beef or turkey
1 pkg. (8 oz.) shell macaroni
1 large onion, finely chopped
1 green pepper, finely chopped
2 cloves garlic, finely chopped
2 small cans tomato sauce
1 can whole-kernel corn, drained
1 can peas, drained
1 can sliced carrots, drained
1 tablespoon brown sugar
1 tablespoon Worcestershire sauce
1 tablespoon chili powder
1 teaspoon salt
¼ teaspoon pepper
1 cup shredded sharp cheddar cheese

Cook shells according to package directions. When tender, drain and rinse in cold water. Set aside. In large skillet, brown meat with onion, green pepper and garlic. When meat is cooked, drain off all grease. Add remaining ingredients, except cheese and canned vegetables, and simmer for about 15 minutes. Combine cooked pasta shells, sauce and canned vegetables and pour into a greased casserole dish or small roasting pan. Cover with a tight fitting lid and bake at 300° for about an hour. Right before serving, top casserole with shredded cheese and replace lid. Serve when cheese is melted.

# October 28

## WILD HERBED CHICKEN

*Prep. Time: 20 minutes Cook Time: 1½ hours*

2 chickens, cut up and skinned
½ cup olive oil
1 teaspoon salt
1 tablespoon oregano
2 teaspoons parsley flakes
1 teaspoon basil
½ teaspoon dill weed
½ teaspoon pepper
2 large sweet onions, sliced
2 cloves garlic, sliced
1 quart stewed tomatoes

Pour oil into a large glass baking dish. Add chicken. Combine spices and herbs in a small container and sprinkle mixture over each piece of chicken. Top meat with slices of onion. Pour stewed tomatoes over onions and chicken. Bake at 350° for an hour and a half.

## BROCCOLI AND RICE

*Prep. Time: 20 minutes Cook Time: 25 minutes*

2 cups cooked rice
1 pkg. frozen chopped broccoli
1 cup milk
2 eggs
2 tablespoons butter
2 tablespoons dried minced onion
½ teaspoon Worcestershire sauce
1 teaspoon salt
¼ teaspoon thyme
¼ teaspoon basil
¼ teaspoon parsley flakes
2 cups shredded American or cheddar cheese

Cook and drain broccoli. Combine broccoli and cooked rice. Add all remaining ingredients and mix well. Pour into a greased casserole dish. Bake at 350° for 20-25 minutes or until set.

# October 29

## SCALLOPED POTATOES WITH PORK CUTLETS

*Prep. Time: 15 minutes Cook Time: 1 hour*

6 lean pork cutlets
½ cup flour
1 teaspoon salt
¼ teaspoon pepper
6-8 potatoes, peeled and thinly sliced
1 small carton light sour cream
½ cup water
1 can cream of mushroom soup
2 tablespoons oil

Combine salt and pepper with flour. Dredge pork cutlets in flour, coating both sides. In a skillet with 2 tablespoons hot oil, brown both sides of meat. Place potatoes in baking dish. Combine the soup, water and sour cream. Pour over the potatoes. Lay meat over potatoes. Cover and bake at 300° for 1 hour or until potatoes are tender.

## SWISS VEGETABLES

*Prep. Time: 10 minutes Cook Time: 50-60 minutes*

1 (16 oz.) bag thawed broccoli, carrots and cauliflower combination, drained
1 can cream of mushroom soup
1 cup shredded Swiss cheese
⅓ cup light sour cream
1 can French-fried onions
¼ teaspoon black pepper

In a casserole dish, combine vegetables with ½ cup cheese, sour cream, pepper and ½ can onions. Bake, uncovered, at 300° for 40 minutes. Top with remaining cheese and onions. Return to oven and bake for another 15-20 minutes.

# PEANUT BUTTER APPLE CRISP

*Prep. Time: 15 minutes Cook Time: 35-45 minutes*

1 cup flour
1½ cups brown sugar, firmly packed
1 teaspoon ground cinnamon
¾ cup chunky or creamy low-fat peanut butter
⅓ cup butter
6-8 tart apples, cored and thinly sliced
1 teaspoon lemon rind
2 tablespoons lemon juice

Combine flour, brown sugar, and cinnamon. Cut peanut butter and butter into flour mixture using a knife until mixture resembles coarse crumbs. Arrange apple slices in a glass baking dish or cake pan. Sprinkle with lemon rind and lemon juice. Cover apple slices with crumb mixture. Bake at 350° for 35 to 45 minutes. Serve with a scoop of vanilla ice cream.

# October 30

## PIZZA BY THE FOOT

*Prep. Time: 15 minutes Cook Time: 20 minutes*

2 loaves French or Italian bread, sliced length-
    wise in half
1 can or jar prepared pizza sauce
pepperoni slices
chopped ham
3 cups shredded mozzarella cheese
1 cup shredded cheddar cheese
your choice of other toppings

Slice each loaf of bread in half lengthwise. Spread pizza sauce on both halves. Cover sauce with pepperoni slices and ham, along with your choice of any other toppings. Combine cheeses and top each half with a generous portion of cheese. Bake at 350° for 20 minutes or until bread toasts and cheese melts.

# October 31

## JAMBALAYA

*Prep. Time: 10 minutes Cook Time: 15-20 minutes*

1 lb. lean ground beef
1 medium onion, finely chopped
1 green pepper, finely chopped
1 can red kidney beans
1 can tomatoes
1 tablespoon chili powder
1 can whole kernel corn
cooked rice

Brown ground beef, onion and green pepper. Drain off all grease when meat is cooked. Add tomatoes, corn, beans and chili powder. Let simmer for 15 to 20 minutes. Serve over a bed of rice.

## SEASONED CORN BREAD

*Prep. Time: 15 minutes Cook Time: 45 minutes*

2 eggs
1 cup self-rising flour
¾ cup milk
1 can cream style corn
1 green pepper, finely chopped
1 onion, finely chopped
2 cups shredded cheddar cheese

Combine all ingredients and pour into a greased 12-inch skillet or a 12-inch cake pan. Bake at 350° for 45 minutes or until cornbread tests done when a knife inserted in the center comes out clean.

**HALLOWEEN SNACKING**
Pumpkin Seeds: Wash and drain the pumpkin seeds and pat dry with paper towels. Sauté about 2 cups of seeds with 2 tablespoons butter or 1½ tablespoon corn oil and 1 teaspoon salt in a large skillet for about 3 minutes. Bake at 250° on a cookie sheet for 30-45 minutes until they are light brown and roasted. Drain on a paper towel.

# November 1

*If your other theme evenings were successful, perhaps you're ready to try another. This time I've provided authentic recipes from France. Just for the fun of it, ask every one to dress up for dinner and let your children do the serving.*

## POTAGE ST. GERMAIN (GREEN PEA SOUP)

*Prep. Time: 15 minutes Cook Time: 2 hours*

2 cups quick-cooking green split peas
5 cups water
1 teaspoon salt
1 tablespoon butter
½ cup finely diced bacon (uncooked)
1 medium onion, minced
1 medium carrot, finely diced
2 leeks—tops only, snipped in strips
1 cup snipped fresh spinach
1 bay leaf
pinch thyme
1 cup frozen peas
1½ cups canned chicken broth
salt to taste
2 tablespoons butter
½ cup light or heavy cream

In a large soup pan, bring split peas, water and 1 teaspoon salt to a boil; reduce heat and cover pan with a lid. Let simmer for about an hour—until peas are soft, stirring occasionally. While split peas are cooking, in a skillet, melt 1 tablespoon butter. Add the bacon pieces and cook over medium heat. Add the onion and cook until tender. Add carrots, leek tops, spinach leaves, bay leaf and thyme. Sauté this combination for about 3-5 minutes, stirring often. Add skillet contents to the soup pan with the split peas and add 2 more cups water. Reduce heat to low and cover soup pan with a lid. Cook together for another hour or until all vegetables are tender.

When vegetables are cooked, remove pan from heat. Pour content of soup into a blender and puree vegetables. Return to the soup pan. Add chicken broth and bring soup back to a boil. Stir in sugar and salt to taste; plus 2 tablespoons butter and the cream. Serve at once, topped with a dab of sour cream and chopped nuts, if desired.

## AUBERGINES ALA TOULOUSAINE (EGGPLANT A LA TOULOUSE)

*Prep. Time: 40 minutes Cook Time: 50 minutes*

1 medium eggplant
¼ cup oil
3 large tomatoes, peeled
2 cups fresh bread cubes
2 tablespoons fresh snipped parsley
1 clove garlic, minced
1 tablespoon oil
¼ cup Parmesan cheese

Cut eggplant into ½-inch slices and remove outer skin. Place slices on a double layer of paper toweling. Sprinkle each slice generously with salt and let stand for about 30 minutes. After 30 minutes, blot dry with paper towels. Start heating oven to 400°. Sauté eggplant in ¼ cup oil until golden in color. Add more oil if needed. Cut tomatoes into ½-inch slices and sauté in same skillet. In a 10x6 baking dish, arrange eggplant and tomato slices in alternate layers (four in all), sprinkling each layer with salt and pepper. Combine bread cubes with parsley, garlic, 1 tablespoon oil and Parmesan cheese. Toss well and sprinkle over the top layer. Bake at 400° for 20 minutes or until bread cubes are toasted golden and eggplant is tender.

## CREME RENVERSEE AU CARAMEL (CARAMEL CUSTARD)

*Prep. Time: 20 minutes Cook Time: 25-30 minutes*

½ cup sugar
¼ cup boiling water
2 cups milk, hot
¼ teaspoon vanilla
3 eggs plus 2 egg yolks
½ cup sugar

Preheat oven to 350°. First, prepare caramel sauce by evenly spreading the ½ cup sugar over the bottom of a heavy skillet. Heat slowly over low heat until sugar melts and is golden in color. Very, very slowly stir in the ¼ cup boiling water 1 tablespoon at a time. Continue to heat syrup until slightly thickened and all sugar lumps are dissolved. Pour syrup in the bottom of 6 custard cups or a 1-quart mold. Set aside.

In a saucepan, scald milk and vanilla. In a separate bowl, combine eggs and egg yolks with ½ cup sugar and beat with a fork. While stirring with fork, slowly pour hot milk into eggs. Then pour mixture into custard cups or the mold. Place custard cups or mold in a shallow baking pan and pour in boiling water until you come to within 1-inch of the top of the custard cups. Bake custards 20 to 30 minutes or until a knife inserted in center comes out clean. Refrigerate until ready to serve. When it's time for dessert, un-mold custards and the caramel sauce will run down over them as a sauce. Garnish with toasted almonds, if desired.

---

### KITCHEN TIP
If you open a soda can and can't drink all of it, keep it fresh by tightly covering it with aluminum foil or use the 9-ounce plastic snap-on lids that are made for plastic cups.

---

# November 2

## CHICKEN CACCIATORE

*Prep. Time: 40 minutes Cook Time: 45 minutes*

2 fryer chickens, cut up
3 tablespoons olive oil, plus ½ cup
1 large onion, finely chopped
6 strips of bacon, chopped
1 clove garlic, minced
¼ teaspoon coarse black pepper
2½ teaspoons salt
½ teaspoon dried oregano
1 pint canned tomatoes
1 (6 oz.) can tomato paste
½ cup flour
½ cup olive oil
½ cup dry red wine
cooked rice

Heat 3 tablespoons olive oil in large skillet. Add onion and sauté until tender. Add bacon, garlic, pepper, salt and oregano and sauté for about 15 minutes, stirring often. Add canned tomatoes and tomato paste and continue simmering for another 20 minutes, stirring often. Meanwhile, dredge chicken pieces in flour and brown chicken on all sides in a large skillet with ½ cup olive oil. When chicken is browned, add pieces to the tomato sauce. Pour the red wine over all. Cover with a tight fitting lid and let cook over medium-low heat for 45 minutes or until chicken is tender and cooked through. Serve over a bed of rice.

## MARINATED BEAN SALAD

*Prep. Time: 10 minutes Marinating Time: 4 hours or longer*

1 can green beans, drained
1 can wax beans, drained
1 can red kidney beans, drained
1 can bean sprouts, drained
1 green pepper, sliced (remove core and seeds)

1 onion, diced

Dressing:

⅔ cup sugar

⅓ cup oil

¾ cup vinegar

1 teaspoon salt

pepper to taste

In a large bowl, combine all beans with green pepper and onion. Toss to mix well. In a separate container, combine all ingredients for the dressing, shake well. Pour over the beans and toss again. Cover with a sheet of plastic wrap and refrigerate for at least 4 hours before serving. Toss well just prior to serving.

## FLUFFER NUTTER PIE

*Prep. Time: 15 minutes*

½ cup peanut butter plus 2 tablespoons

½ cup powdered sugar

1 box instant vanilla pudding mix

1½ cups milk

2 tablespoons peanut butter

1 prepared 9-inch pie shell, baked

1 large jar Marshmallow Creme™

Combine ½ cup peanut butter and powdered sugar in a mixing bowl. Spread in the bottom of a baked pie shell. Prepare pudding mix with milk, and add 2 tablespoons peanut butter; mix well. Beat pudding on high with an electric mixer until thick. Pour over peanut butter in pie shell. Refrigerate until set. Right before serving, spread a layer of Marshmallow Creme™ over top. Cut and serve.

# November 3

## HOT CHICKEN SANDWICHES

*Prep. Time: 10 minutes Cook Time: 20 minutes*

1½ to 2 lbs. shaved smoked chicken breast (from the deli)

Texas-toast style bread

2 pkgs. chicken or turkey gravy mixes

2 cups water

In medium saucepan, prepare gravy mixes with water according to directions. Add turkey and cook together for about 10 minutes. For each serving, lay a piece of thick Texas Toast bread in the center of plate and ladle a spoonful of turkey and gravy over the bread. You may want to serve this with mashed potatoes.

Serve with a tossed salad.

# November 4

## LEMON-BUTTERED HALIBUT

*Prep. Time: 10 minutes Cook Time: 30 minutes*

3 lbs. halibut steak, 1-inch thick (or more, if desired)

¼ cup lemon juice

2 teaspoons grated onion

½ cup butter, melted

pepper to taste

paprika to taste

fresh lemon wedges as garnish

Preheat oven to 350°. Cut fish in serving size pieces. Sprinkle both sides with salt and pepper. Combine lemon juice, onion and melted butter. Dip fish pieces in lemon butter mixture and place on a greased baking pan. Pour any remaining lemon butter over fish. Sprinkle with pepper and paprika. Bake at 350° degrees for 25 to 30 minutes or until fish easily flakes when forked.

Serve with baked potatoes.

# SUCCOTASH

*Prep. Time: 10 minutes Cook Time: 20 minutes*

1 (10 oz.) pkg. frozen corn

1 (10 oz.) pkg. frozen peas and carrots

2 teaspoons salt

1 teaspoon sugar

½ teaspoon pepper

½ cup light cream

½ cup water

Combine all vegetables in a medium saucepan and add ½ cup water. Cover pan and cook for 15 minutes. Uncover and add remaining ingredients; stirring to blend well. Continue cooking for 5 more minutes then serve hot.

# PEANUT BUTTER LOVER'S SHAKE

*Prep. Time: 10 minutes*

vanilla ice cream or frozen yogurt

creamy peanut butter

milk

vanilla

For each blender mixture, combine 4 scoops vanilla ice cream, ¼ cup peanut butter, 2 cups milk and 1 teaspoon vanilla. Blend on a high setting. Pour shakes into serving glasses. Serve with a straw and spoon.

## KID BREAK!

According to Mr. Fred Rogers, play is work to a child. Take advantage of this concept to get your children to help you around the house. Conduct a "race" to see who can pick up the most trash from the yard or clutter from the family-room floor. Write odd jobs on slips of paper and let your kids draw a duty. Play some music and tell them they can only do that duty for the duration of the song, then they must stop. See how much they can get done in 3 to 4 minute spurts. If you make cleaning a game, they may even ask to do it again!

# November 5

## SMOKED SAUSAGE CASSEROLE

*Prep. Time: 5 minutes Cook Time: 30 minutes*

2 lbs. skinless smoked sausage, sliced

1 pkg. (8 oz.) pasta twists

1 can whole kernel sweet corn, drained

1 small green pepper, diced

2 tablespoon butter plus 1 teaspoon

½ teaspoon salt

¼ cup Parmesan cheese

2 cups cheddar cheese cubes

In large saucepan, cover uncooked pasta, sliced smoked sausage and diced green pepper with water. Add ½ teaspoon salt and 1 teaspoon butter. Bring to a boil and cook until pasta is tender. Drain. Add 2 tablespoons butter and stir to coat pasta. Add corn and both cheeses. Pour into a shallow baking dish and cover with a lid or aluminum foil. Bake at 325° for 20-30 minutes.

# PUMPKIN BREAD

*Prep. Time: 15 minutes Cook Time: 1 hour or longer*

2 cups pumpkin

⅔ cup water

3¼ cups sugar

½ cup oil

½ cup unsweetened applesauce

4 eggs

3 ½ cups flour

1 tablespoon baking powder

2 teaspoons baking soda

½ teaspoon salt

2 tablespoons pumpkin pie spice

½ teaspoon ground cloves

1 teaspoon nutmeg

1 tablespoon ground cinnamon

Combine all ingredients and mix well. Pour batter into greased and floured loaf pans. Bake at 350° for 1 hour or until a knife inserted in center of loaf comes out clean. Cool in pans 10 minutes before removing from pans.

# November 6

## SPLIT PEA SOUP

*Prep. Time: 15 minutes  / Cook Time: 1½ hours*

1-lb. bag dried split peas
¼ cup butter
1 lb. ham cubes
1 smoked ham hock (for seasoning)
1 large onion, finely chopped
7 cups water
1½ teaspoons salt
⅛ teaspoon pepper

Melt butter in bottom of soup pan. Add chopped onion and cook over medium heat for about 5 minutes. Add 7 cups water, split peas, ham cubes, ham hock and salt. Reduce heat to low and let simmer for an hour. When peas are tender, remove ham hock and ham cubes. Put soup through a food mill, processor or blender and puree. Return stock to soup pan. Add ham cubes back in. Taste and add seasonings (salt/pepper) to taste.

## PEANUT BREAD

*Prep. Time: 15 minutes Cook Time: 1 hour*

1½ cups flour
1 cup light brown sugar, firmly packed
½ teaspoon baking soda
½ cup Butter Crisco™ or other shortening
2 eggs
1¼ cups whole wheat flour
1 tablespoon baking powder
½ teaspoon salt
1 cup chopped salted peanuts
¾ cup milk

Combine flour, brown sugar, baking soda, shortening, eggs and whole wheat flour in a large mixing bowl. Stir in nuts. Add remaining ingredients and stir to mix well. Batter will be lumpy. Pour batter into a greased loaf pan and bake at 350° for an hour or until bread tests done. Let bread cool 10 minutes before removing from pan. Serve with peanut butter syrup spread.

## PEANUT BUTTER SYRUP SPREAD

*Prep. Time: 5 minutes*

1 cup smooth peanut butter
1½ cups light corn syrup

Combine both peanut butter and syrup in a small mixing bowl. Stir well until peanut butter has a thin, easily spreadable consistency. Add more syrup if spread is too thick; more peanut butter if mixture is not thin enough. This spread is good when served on vanilla ice cream, too.

# November 7

## BEEF SPANISH NOODLES

*Prep. Time: 20 minutes Cook Time: 20-30 minutes*

2 lbs. lean ground beef
1 green pepper, chopped
1 onion, finely chopped
1 teaspoon salt
1 pkg. (16 oz.) dry egg noodles, medium or
   wide width (uncooked)
1 quart tomato juice
½ teaspoon chili powder
2 teaspoons sugar

Brown meat with half the onion and half the green pepper. Drain off all grease. In a large casserole dish combine cooked meat with remaining green pepper and onion, salt, chili powder, sugar and tomato juice. Add the uncooked noodles. Add 1 to 1½ cups water, if needed, to

# COOKIES OF THE MONTH

## MASTER CUT-OUT COOKIES

²⁄₃ cup shortening

1¼ cups sugar

2 eggs

2 tablespoons milk

1 teaspoon vanilla

3 cups flour

1½ teaspoons salt

2 teaspoons baking powder

Cream together shortening and sugar; add eggs, milk and vanilla; mix well. Add salt and baking powder with flour and sift into creamed mixture. Mix well and chill dough. Roll thin and cut into desired shapes. Put on greased baking sheet. Bake at 350° until lightly browned. Decorate with prepared frosting and colored sugars.

## LOG COOKIES

2 sticks butter

1 cup graham cracker crumbs

1¹⁄₃ cups flaked coconut

½ cup chunky peanut butter

2²⁄₃ cups powdered sugar

1 teaspoon vanilla

1 cup finely chopped nuts

1 lb. chocolate coating

Melt butter. In separate bowl, combine all dry ingredients and stir well. Add peanut butter, coconut, nuts and vanilla to the dry ingredients. Pour melted butter over everything and mix well. Shape into 2-inch "log" shapes and let stand in the refrigerator for 30 minutes. Melt chocolate coating in a double boiler and dip each log in chocolate. Let set on waxed paper to harden.

## TEACHER'S OATMEAL COOKIES

2 sticks butter

1 cup sugar

1 cup brown sugar

2 eggs

1 teaspoon vanilla

2 cups flour

2½ cup quick cooking oatmeal

1 teaspoon baking soda

1 teaspoon baking powder

½ teaspoon salt

1 cup raisins

1 cup chopped nuts, if desired

Cream together the butter, sugars, eggs and vanilla. Add the flour, oats and remaining ingredients and mix well. Drop by teaspoon on a greased cookie sheet. Bake at 375° for 7 to 10 minutes or until lightly brown.

cover all ingredients. Cover with a tight fitting lid and bake at 350° for 20 to 30 minutes.

## PEANUT BUTTER CANDY PIE

*Prep. Time: 10 minutes Cook Time: 40-50 minutes*

1 prepared 9-inch pie shell, unbaked
3 eggs
1 cup light corn syrup
¼ teaspoon salt
½ cup sugar
1 teaspoon vanilla
½ cup smooth peanut butter
semi-sweet chocolate chips
angel flake coconut
chopped nuts

In mixing bowl, beat eggs for 2 minutes and then gradually beat in sugar. Add syrup, vanilla, salt and peanut butter and beat well on medium speed with an electric mixer. Pour into unbaked 9-inch pie shell and bake at 300° for 40 to 50 minutes, or until a knife inserted in the center comes out clean. Place circle of chocolate chips in center of pie and sprinkle remaining chips around outer edge next to crust. Do this while pie is still warm, so the chips can melt slightly. Fill in remainder of top with either coconut or chopped nuts or a mixture of both. Let cool completely before serving.

# November 8

## ZUCCHINI CHEESE SOUP

*Prep. Time: 20 minutes Cook Time: 20-30 minutes*

2 large zucchini
½ lb. bacon
1 onion, finely chopped
1 green pepper, finely chopped
2 cups water
2 teaspoons salt
½ stick butter
½ cup flour
3 ½ cups milk
1 teaspoon Worcestershire sauce
2 cups shredded cheddar cheese

Fry bacon until crisp. Remove and blot on paper towel. Measure 3 tablespoons bacon grease and discard the rest. In remaining 3 tablespoons grease, sauté onion and green pepper. Add zucchini, cut in quarter-inch slices, water, and 1 teaspoon salt. Cover pan and bring to a boil. Simmer for 5 minutes. In a medium saucepan, melt butter. Add flour and 1 teaspoon salt, stirring constantly to make a thin paste. Gradually add milk, very slowly, stirring constantly until all the milk has been added. Cook over medium heat, stirring occasionally, until thick (like a gravy). Add Worcestershire sauce and cheddar cheese. Add vegetables and mix well. Spoon into serving bowls and top each serving with crumbled bacon.

## HAM, BACON & SWISS CHEESE SANDWICHES

*Prep. Time: 10 minutes*

1 long loaf of French bread
Miracle Whip™ Free or prepared mustard
1 sweet onion, sliced
½ lb. bacon, fried crisp
Swiss cheese slices

½ lb. deli shaved smoked ham
2 large tomatoes, sliced
shredded lettuce

Slice loaf of French bread in half lengthwise. Spread Miracle Whip Free™ or mustard on both halves. On bottom half, layer ham, Swiss cheese, bacon slices, shredded lettuce, sweet onion and tomato slices. Put top half of loaf on and cut into serving-size chunks.

# November 9

## MEATBALL STEW

*Prep. Time: 20 minutes Cook Time: 30-45 minutes*

1½ lbs. lean ground beef or turkey
1 cup crushed saltine cracker crumbs
1 medium onion, finely chopped
1 egg, beaten
1 teaspoon salt
¼ teaspoon thyme
1 can tomato soup
1 quart beef broth
6 medium to large potatoes, peeled and chunked
5 carrots, chunked
1 can whole-kernel corn, drained
1 can green beans, drained

Combine meat with cracker crumbs, onion, egg, salt and thyme. Mix well and form into 1-inch balls. Place on a shallow baking pan or jelly roll pan and bake at 425° for 15 minutes. Meanwhile, combine tomato soup with beef broth in a soup pan. Add vegetables and cook over medium-high heat. When meatballs are cooked, remove from oven and transfer meatballs to the stew. Reduce heat to medium-low and let stew cook for 30 to 45 minutes or when vegetables are tender.

## CAKE DONUTS

*Prep. Time: 15 minutes Cook Time: 3-5 minutes each*

2 cups milk plus 1 tablespoon vinegar or 2 cups buttermilk
2 eggs
2½ cups sugar
¼ cup light sour cream
2 teaspoons baking soda
2 teaspoons baking powder
2 teaspoons ground cinnamon
8 to 10 cups flour, just enough so dough can be handled

Combine all ingredients and mix well. Roll out dough on a lightly floured surface until dough is ¼-inch thick. Use a donut cutter or the rim of a large glass to cut donuts. Poke hole in center if necessary. Fry in hot oil, turning once. Be careful not to get oil too hot because the insides of the donuts will remain doughy while the outsides will be dark brown. Ideally, you want the insides of the donuts to cook while the outside is browning lightly. Drain on paper towel or brown paper.

## GLAZE WITH POWDERED SUGAR ICING

3 cups confectioners' sugar
½ cup milk
1 teaspoon vanilla

Stir until powdered sugar dissolves. Pour over hot donuts. Add sprinkles to wet glaze if desired.

### Household Cleaner

1 pint rubbing alcohol
1 gallon water
1 tablespoon household ammonia
1 tablespoon dishwashing liquid

Combine all ingredients in a gallon jug and label it well. Use this mixture to clean windows, chrome, painted surfaces in the bath and kitchen, etc. Use crumpled newspapers to dry your windows for a streak-free shine!

# November 10

## GREEN BEAN & HAM CASSEROLE

*Prep. Time: 10 minutes Cook Time: 40-45 minutes*

1 quart canned green beans, drained

3 cups cooked rice

1 cup shredded cheddar cheese

½ cup milk

¼ cup water

2 cups chopped ham

1 can cream of mushroom soup

2 tablespoons dried minced onion

1 cup crushed corn flakes or potato chips

3 tablespoons butter

Combine all ingredients except for corn flakes in a greased casserole dish. Mix together. Sprinkle top with crushed corn flakes. Dot top of corn flakes with dabs of butter. Bake at 375° for 40 to 45 minutes.

## BERRY BREAD CAKE

*Prep. Time: 20 minutes Cook Time: 1 hour*

2 cups bread flour

1 teaspoon baking soda

1 teaspoon ground cinnamon

2 cups sugar

⅛ teaspoon salt

1 whole egg plus 1 egg yolk

1 cup strawberries or blueberries

½ cup water

½ cup butter

Sift dry ingredients together. In small saucepan, combine berries with 1 cup sugar and ½ cup water. Stir and cook over low heat until berries are hot and soft. Stir often to avoid fruit from sticking. Cream butter and 1 cup sugar together then add whole egg plus 1 egg yolk. Mix well. To creamed sugar mixture add dry ingredients alternately with fruit; mixing well after each addition. Pour into a greased loaf pan and bake at 350° for 1 hour or until a knife inserted in the center comes out clean. Slice and serve each slice buttered, like bread.

# November 11

## BACON QUICHE

*Prep. Time: 20 minutes Cook Time: 30 minutes*

½ lb. bacon

8 eggs

2 cups milk

1 cup Bisquick™ Mix

½ cup butter, melted

⅛ teaspoon pepper

½ teaspoon salt

2 cups shredded cheddar cheese

Fry bacon until crisp, remove from pan and drain on paper towel or brown paper. In mixing bowl, combine eggs, milk, baking mix, melted butter, pepper and salt. Beat on low speed with an electric mixer until well blended. Pour into a greased casserole or baking dish. Sprinkle with crumbled bacon and shredded cheese. Bake at 350° for 30 minutes or until a knife inserted in the center comes out clean.

## HONEY BRAN MUFFINS

*Prep. Time: 10 minutes Cook Time: 25 minutes*

2 cups bran cereal

1 cup whole wheat flour

½ teaspoon baking soda

1 teaspoon baking powder

½ teaspoon salt

1½ cups skim milk

1 cup honey

Combine all ingredients and mix well. Spoon batter into prepared muffin cups and bake at 400° for 25 minutes or until done. Serve with whipped honey-butter.

# November 12

## CHICKEN-MACARONI CASSEROLE

*Prep. Time: 20 minutes Cook Time: 45 minutes*

3 cups elbow macaroni

2-4 boneless, skinless chicken breasts

2 cups shredded cheddar cheese

2 cans cream of chicken soup

1 cup milk

1 pkg. frozen peas, thawed

3 tablespoons butter

1 onion, finely chopped

½ cup chopped celery

2 cups cubed American cheese

2 cups shredded cheddar cheese

In a medium saucepan, cook macaroni according to package directions. In a skillet, melt butter and brown chicken breasts on both sides. Set chicken aside and add soups, milk, peas, onion and celery to skillet. Mix well and heat to almost boiling. Cut chicken up in bite-sized pieces. In greased casserole dish or small roasting pan, combine macaroni, chicken and soup mixture. Add cubed American cheese. Mix well. Bake at 350° for 35 minutes. Top with shredded cheddar cheese and bake for 10 minutes longer.

## EXTRA RICH CHEESE CAKE

*Prep. Time: 15 minutes Cook Time: 1 hour*

1 pkg. cinnamon graham crackers, crushed

3 tablespoons melted butter

¾ cup sugar

3 pkgs. (8 oz.) cream cheese, softened

3 eggs

1 tablespoon plus 1 teaspoon vanilla

8 oz. container sour cream

Crush the crackers by placing them in a sealable plastic bag and rolling a can of pie filling over bag.

Or pound them, or step on them. Pour crumbs in the bottom of pan. Drizzle melted butter over cracker crumbs and then press with your fingers, flattening and making the crumbs into a crust. Bake crust for 10 minutes at 350° degrees. Meanwhile, in mixing bowl, combine softened creamed cheese and ¾ cup sugar and mix well. Add eggs and 1 teaspoon vanilla. Beat on low speed with an electric mixer until smooth. Spoon cream cheese mixture over crust and bake at 300° for 1 hour. Remove from oven and let set for 10 minutes. Next combine sour cream, 1 tablespoon sugar and 1 tablespoon vanilla and beat on low speed with mixer until well blended. Spread sour cream mixture over cheese cake. Refrigerate cheesecake for at least 3 hours before serving. Serve plain or with your choice of fresh fruit or canned pie filling.

# November 13

## PORK CHOPS WITH PEANUT BUTTER SAUCE

*Prep. Time: 15 minutes Cook Time: 90 minutes*

6 pork chops, trimmed of excess fat

1 onion, finely chopped

1 can cream of mushroom soup

¾ cup smooth peanut butter

2 cups water

3 tablespoons oil

Brown pork chops in hot oil. Remove and place in shallow baking dish. Spread chopped onions over chops. In skillet with hot oil, add peanut butter, soup and water. Stir until smooth, heating over medium heat. Bring sauce to a boil. Pour sauce over pork chops. Cover dish with a lid or aluminum foil and bake at 350° for about 90 minutes.

# SCALLOPED CORN

*Prep. Time: 10 minutes Cook Time: 90 minutes*

2 cans cream-style corn
4 large eggs
1 cup crushed saltine crackers
1 "corn-can" full of milk
½ teaspoon salt
¼ teaspoon pepper
½ teaspoon seasoned salt

In a deep casserole dish, beat eggs with a fork. Add the corn, crushed crackers and seasonings. Fill one empty corn can with milk and stir into corn mixture. Bake at 350º for 90 minutes or until firm.

# November 14

## HIGH SEAS CASSEROLE

*Prep. Time: 15 minutes Cook Time: 25 minutes*

1 can cream of celery soup
1 can cream of mushroom soup
1⅓ cups water
½ teaspoon salt
1 small onion, finely chopped or 1½ table-
    spoons dried minced onion
2 cups instant rice
1½ cups frozen peas, thawed
2 (7 oz.) cans tuna, drained and flaked
2 cups shredded cheddar cheese
pepper to taste

In a large casserole dish, combine soups, water, salt, onion, uncooked rice, peas and tuna. Mix together well. Add pepper to taste. Cover with tight-fitting lid and bake at 375º for 20 minutes. Add cheddar cheese to top of casserole and return to oven to bake 5 minutes longer.

# HOT FUDGE PUDDING CAKE

*Prep. Time: 10 minutes Cook Time: 45 minutes*

1 cup cake flour
2 teaspoons baking powder
¼ teaspoon salt
¾ cup sugar
2 tablespoons Nestle™ cocoa
½ cup milk
2 tablespoons butter, melted
1 cup brown sugar, firmly packed
¼ cup Nestle™ cocoa
1 ¾ cups water, boiling

Sift together flour, baking powder, salt, sugar and 2 tablespoons cocoa into a mixing bowl. Stir in milk and butter. Grease a 9x9 square pan. Pour batter in pan. In another bowl, combine brown sugar and ¼ cup cocoa. Sprinkle over the top of the batter. Gently pour boiling water over entire batter. Bake at 350º for 45 minutes. The chocolate sauce will settle on the bottom and the cake will rise to the top. Serve warm with whipped cream or ice cream.

# November 15

## NACHOS GRANDE

*Prep. Time: 15 minutes Cook Time: 20-25 minutes*

1 lb. lean ground beef or turkey
1 bunch green onions, chopped
1 bottle taco sauce (your choice of mild, me-
    dium or hot)
1 cup sliced ripe (black) olives, drained
1 can Nacho cheese soup
½ soup can of skim milk
1 cup light sour cream
3 large tomatoes, diced
1 large bag nacho chips

Cook meat in skillet until done. Drain off all grease. Add taco sauce and let simmer over low heat for about 5 minutes. Preheat oven to 400º.

Empty bag of nacho chips on to large platter, set aside. In small saucepan, combine nacho soup with milk. Stir often and cook until hot. Turn oven off. Set platter of chips in oven and close door. Let chips set in hot oven for 5 minutes. Remove platter of chips from oven. Spoon seasoned meat over chips. Pour cheese sauce over chips. Add chopped green onions, ripe olive slices and diced tomatoes. Top with dollops of sour cream. Serve immediately.

## FRESH APPLE CAKE

*Prep. Time: 20 minutes Cook Time: 1 hour*

2 cups sugar
1 cup shortening
2 eggs
4 cups chopped tart apples
2 cups flour
2 teaspoons baking soda
1 teaspoon salt
2 teaspoons vanilla
1 tablespoon ground cinnamon
SAUCE:
3 cups brown sugar, firmly packed
1 cup white corn syrup
½ cup butter
1 cup heavy cream
2 teaspoons vanilla

Cream sugar and shortening together, then add eggs and mix well. Add remaining ingredients for cake and mix well. Pour batter into a greased 9x13 cake pan. Bake at 350° for 1 hour. Top with sauce. While cake is baking, combine brown sugar, syrup and butter in a small saucepan. Bring to a boil over low heat, stirring constantly. When mixture begins to boil, remove pan from heat.

Cool slightly until cake is done. When cake tests done, add cream and vanilla to the sauce. Stir well and pour over the top of the cake.

# November 16

## CHICKEN GUMBO

*Prep. Time: 20 minutes Cook Time: 45 minutes*

2 cups uncooked chicken, deboned and diced
2 tablespoons butter
1 onion, finely chopped
2 stalks celery, finely chopped
6 cups chicken broth or stock
½ green pepper, finely chopped
1 can sweet corn, drained
1 can green beans, drained
1 teaspoon garlic powder
2 cups rice
2 teaspoons salt
½ teaspoon pepper
1 cup canned tomatoes (diced) with juice

In large soup pan, melt butter and sauté onion and celery for about 5 minutes. Add broth, chicken meat, green pepper, garlic powder, tomatoes, salt and pepper. Increase heat to medium and bring contents to boil. Add corn, green beans and rice. Reduce heat to medium low and let simmer for 45 minutes or until chicken meat is cooked through.

# November 17

For this theme dinner send your kids to the library in search of customs and history of Hungary. The authentic Hungarian recipes may take a bit longer to prepare, but consider all the time you'll save in not having to travel to Hungary!

## GULYÁS (HUNGARIAN GOULASH)

Prep. Time: 25-30 minutes Cook Time: 3 hours

1 lb. fresh tomatoes
⅓ cup butter
1 large onion, minced
2 lb. beef round steak, 1½ - inch thick
½ cup flour
1½ teaspoons paprika
1½ teaspoons salt
½ teaspoon pepper
1 cup water
1 teaspoon sugar

Bring a soup pan of water to a hard boil. Carefully drop fresh tomatoes into boiling water and let stand for 1 to 2 minutes. Drain off water. Remove tomato skins, seeds and core. Quarter tomatoes and set aside. Melt butter in skillet and sauté onion until golden. Cut steak into 1½ inch cubes; roll lightly in flour; then add to onion mixture. Brown meat on all sides, stirring constantly. Add paprika, salt, and pepper; stir well; add tomatoes and stir again. Cover and simmer slowly until meat is tender—about 1½ to 2 hours. Add water if mixture goes dry. When meat is tender, remove cover and continue simmering until goulash is slightly thickened. Add sugar and stir well. Serve hot.

## RAKOTT BURGONYA (LAYER POTATOES)

Prep. Time: 45 minutes Cook Time: 30 minutes

8 medium cooked potatoes, sliced thinly
1 cup sour cream
½ cup heavy cream
1½ teaspoons salt
3 hard-boiled eggs, sliced
1 cup finely diced, fully cooked ham
1 cup fresh bread crumbs
2 tablespoons butter
¼ teaspoon onion salt

Combine sour cream with heavy cream and salt in a small bowl. Beat well. In greased casserole dish, arrange one-third of the potato slices on bottom. Top with egg slices, then half of the cream mixture. Add another one-third of potato slices. Sprinkle ham over second layer of potato slices. Pour remaining cream over the ham. Top with remaining potato slices. In a separate container, toss bread crumbs with butter and onion salt and spread evenly over the top of the casserole dish. Bake at 350° for 30 minutes or until hot and bubbly.

Serve with a fresh, tossed green salad.

## KOSÁRKÁK (LITTLE BASKETS)

Prep. Time: 10 minutes Cook Time: 18-25 minutes

1 small pkg. (3 oz.) cream cheese, softened
¼ cup butter, softened
1 teaspoon sugar
¼ teaspoon salt
1 cup sifted flour
Filling:
3 egg whites
¼ teaspoon salt
½ teaspoon almond extract
½ cup sugar
⅓ cup pecans, finely chopped
⅓ cup semi-sweet chocolate chips, grated

Blend cream cheese with butter, salt and sugar; beat until smooth and creamy. Add flour, stirring until mixture is well-blended. In ungreased muffin tins, drop 1 scant tablespoon of dough in each. Press dough evenly against bottom and sides of muffin tins using your fingers. Prepare filling next.

In mixing bowl, beat egg whites until foamy; add salt and almond extract; continue beating until soft peaks form. Gradually add sugar and continue beating until stiff peaks form. Remove beaters and using a spoon, gently fold chopped pecans and grated chocolate into egg-white mixture. Fill each dough-lined muffin tin with filling. Bake at 400° for 18 to 22 minutes. Let pan cool 15 to 20 minutes before trying to remove"baskets."Carefully remove filled baskets from muffin pan and serve warm.

# November 18

## CHICKEN MARSELLAISE

*Prep. Time: 20 minutes Cook Time: 1 hour*

2 whole chickens, cut up
1½ cups Catalina Fat Free™ Salad Dressing
2 cans (16 oz.) tomatoes with juice
2 large onions, sliced
2 teaspoons salt
1 teaspoon celery seed
½ teaspoon pepper
3 tablespoons flour
1 cup chicken broth or stock

Arrange chicken pieces in large skillet. Pour 1 cup Catalina™ dressing over chicken and cook over low heat. Turn chicken as needed in order to brown chicken on all sides. When chicken is browned, add remaining Catalina™ along with tomatoes, onion, salt, celery seed and pepper. Cover skillet and cook chicken over medium-low heat for 45 minutes or until chicken tests done. When chicken is done, remove from skillet and arrange on serving platter. Gradually add flour to chicken broth and stir until dissolved. Pour broth into skillet's hot liquid and stir constantly, increasing the heat to medium-high. Cook until mixture forms a thick gravy sauce. Pour sauce over chicken and serve.

Serve with mashed potatoes and baked beans.

# November 19

## SAUSAGE PIZZA PASTA

*Prep. Time: 15 minutes Cook Time: 30 minutes*

1 lb. pork sausage
1 can or jar prepared pizza sauce
1 can sweet corn, drained
1 green pepper, diced
1 cup mushrooms, sliced
1 pkg. (8 oz.) pasta twists (or other desired shape)
¼ cup Parmesan cheese
1 cup shredded mozzarella cheese
1 cup shredded cheddar cheese

Cook pasta according to package directions. Brown sausage in skillet with onion and green pepper. Drain off all grease. Drain water from pasta and rinse cooked pasta in cold water. Drain again. Combine pasta and cooked sausage in a greased casserole dish. Add drained corn, mushrooms, Parmesan cheese and pizza sauce. Stir to mix well. Combine mozzarella and cheddar cheeses and spread over top of pasta. Bake, uncovered, at 350° for 30 minutes.

---

**FOOD FOR THOUGHT**
Monta Crane made an interesting remark. Think about this: "There are three ways to get something done. Do it yourself, hire someone, or forbid your kids to do it."

# BROWNIES A LA MODE

*Prep. Time: 10 minutes Cook Time: 25 minutes*

4 cups sugar
¾ cup heaping Nestle™ cocoa
8 eggs
4 teaspoons vanilla
3 cups flour
½ cup baby food plums
½ cup butter, melted

Combine all ingredients in large mixing bowl. Pour batter into a greased 9x13 pan. Bake at 350° for 20 to 25 minutes or until brownies test done. Chopped nuts may be added if desired. Serve with a big dip of vanilla ice cream or frozen yogurt on top.

# November 20

## GLAZED PORK ROAST

*Prep. Time: 15 minutes Cook Time: 2 hours*

3-5 lbs. pork roast, trimmed of visible fat
1 teaspoon dry mustard
1 teaspoon seasoned salt
¼ teaspoon black pepper
½ cup orange juice x 2
½ teaspoon ground cinnamon x 2
¼ cup honey x 2
¼ teaspoon ground cloves x 2
2 tablespoons brown sugar x 2
8 medium potatoes
2 onions, cut in wedges
4 carrots, cut in thirds

Combine dry mustard, seasoned salt and pepper. Rub this into the meat, coating all sides. Place in a roasting pan. In small container, combine orange juice, cinnamon, honey, ground cloves and brown sugar. Mix well and pour over meat. Cover pan with lid and bake at 325° for 20 minutes. Pull pan from oven and baste roast with pan juices. Repeat basting every 20 minutes up to 1 hour. Peel potatoes and arrange potatoes, onion wedges and carrots around roast. Mix up the second batch of glaze mixture and pour over meat and drizzle over vegetables. Increase oven temperature to 350° and cover pan with lid. Bake for 1 hour or until vegetables and roast are tender.

# SPICE CAKE

*Prep. Time: 10 minutes Cook Time: 90 minutes*

3 cups sugar
1½ cups milk with 2 tablespoons vinegar
  or 1½ cups buttermilk
3 cups flour
4 eggs
1 cup jam (apricot, grape, strawberry, peach, or blueberry)
¾ cup melted shortening
1 tablespoon ground cinnamon
1½ teaspoon ground cloves
1½ teaspoon allspice
½ teaspoon nutmeg
1 cup fig preserves
1½ cups chopped nuts

Cream together melted shortening with sugar and eggs. Add spices, flour and sour milk. Mix well, then add jam and fig preserves. Add chopped nuts and stir well. Generously grease a tube or bundt pan and pour batter in pan. Bake at 350° for 90 minutes or until a knife inserted in the center comes out clean. Let cake cool for 10 minutes before removing from pan. Pour cinnamon glaze over cake while it is still hot.

# CINNAMON GLAZE FOR SPICE CAKE

*Prep. Time: 1-2 minutes*

1½ cups confectioner's sugar
2 teaspoons cinnamon
½ teaspoon allspice
¼ cup milk
2 tablespoons butter, softened

Combine all ingredients in a small mixing bowl.

Beat with a fork until smooth and runny. If mixture is too thick to pour easily, add more milk a tablespoon at a time. If mixture appears too thin, add more powdered sugar. Pour over spice cake.

# November 21

## COUNTRY CASSEROLE

*Prep. Time: 20 minutes Cook Time: about 1 hour*

2½ cups cooked chicken, diced

½ lb. bacon

2 tablespoons flour

3 cups milk

1 can creamed-style sweet corn

1 can sweet peas, drained

1 can French-styled cut green beans, drained

1 stalk celery, finely diced

1 onion, finely chopped

2 teaspoons dried parsley flakes

2 teaspoons dried chopped chives

1 teaspoon black pepper

½ teaspoon dried sweet basil

1 tablespoon Worcestershire sauce

2 teaspoons salt

1 cup American cheese, cubed

1 cup cheddar cheese, cubed

Fry bacon until crisp. Drain bacon on paper towel or brown paper. Remove all but 3 tablespoons bacon grease from skillet. Add onion and celery and sauté until tender. Stir in flour and make a paste. Gradually stir in milk, stirring constantly. Turn heat up to medium and stir until a thick gravy forms. Add parsley, chives, pepper, basil, Worcestershire sauce, and salt to gravy and mix well. Remove pan from heat and set aside. In large casserole dish, combine chicken, creamed corn, peas, green beans and both types of cheese. Pour in seasoned gravy and stir to blend well. Crumble bacon and sprinkle over top of casserole. Bake at 350° for 35 minutes.

## COUNTRY BISCUITS

*Prep. Time: 15 minutes Cook Time: 10-12 minutes*

2 cups flour

1 tablespoon baking powder

¾ teaspoon salt

¼ cup shortening

¾ to 1 cup milk

2 teaspoons sugar

In a large bowl, combine flour, baking powder and salt. Using fork, cut shortening into flour mixture until it looks like coarse crumbs. Add milk and stir with fork until the dough leaves the sides of the bowl. Start with ¾ cup milk and add more milk a tablespoon at a time if needed. On a lightly floured surface, work dough until it is no longer sticky. Roll out until it is about ½ inch thick. Use the rim of a drinking glass and cut out biscuits. Place on a greased cookie sheet. Bake at 450° for 10 to 12 minutes or until lightly browned. Serve hot.

# November 22

## SUPER MOIST BAKED TURKEY

*Prep. Time: 15 minutes Cook Time: depends upon weight of turkey*

1 whole frozen turkey, thawed

salt

1 quart chicken broth

1 turkey-sized cooking bag

1 large roaster pan

3 stalks celery

2 large onions

Remove the neck and sweet breads from inside the turkey cavity. Generously rub salt on inside of bird and all over the outside. Prepare cooking bag according to directions. Put turkey in cooking bag. If you want to serve stuffing or dressing with your turkey, prepare that now and stuff the cavity with the stuffing. If you choose not to prepare stuffing, then insert celery stalks and onions inside turkey.

Pour chicken broth over turkey. Close cooking bag. Here's the secret to keeping your turkey moist: Turn the turkey breast-side DOWN and place in the roasting pan. This way, all the cooking juices will continually flow down through the white breast meat. By using a cooking bag, the entire bird will bake up moist and delicious. Bake turkey according to time recommendations on the packaging of the turkey.

# GLAZED PECAN SWEET POTATOES

*Prep. Time: 15 minutes Cook Time: 45 minutes*

4-6 sweet potatoes, boiled and quartered
1 cup brown sugar, firmly packed
½ cup chopped pecans
1 cup orange juice
½ stick butter
½ teaspoon salt
2 teaspoons ground cinnamon
½ teaspoon nutmeg

Put quartered sweet potatoes in a deep casserole dish. Combine brown sugar with chopped nuts, salt, cinnamon and nutmeg. Sprinkle sugar mixture over potatoes. Dot with pats of butter. Pour orange juice in bottom of dish. Cover with a lid and bake at 375° for 45 minutes or until potatoes are tender. Miniature marshmallows may be layered on top of potatoes if desired.

# CARROT RAISIN BREAD

*Prep. Time: 25 minutes Cook Time: 45-50 minutes*

1½ cups baby food carrots
1 cup raisins
1 cup chopped pecans
1 teaspoon vanilla
⅔ cup vegetable oil
1 cup sugar
2 eggs
1½ cups flour
1 teaspoon baking soda

½ teaspoon salt
2 teaspoons ground cinnamon
½ teaspoon nutmeg

Combine all ingredients in large mixing bowl. Pour batter into greased and floured loaf pans. Bake at 350° for 45 to 50 minutes.

# PUMPKIN PIE

*Prep. Time: 10 minutes Cook Time: about 1 hour*

1 unbaked 9-inch pie shell
1 cup sugar
1½ teaspoons cinnamon
½ teaspoon cloves
½ teaspoon allspice
¼ teaspoon nutmeg
½ teaspoon salt
½ teaspoon ginger
2 eggs
1½ cups canned pumpkin
1 tall can evaporated milk

Combine all ingredients (except pie shell) in large mixing bowl. Beat until smooth and then pour into unbaked pie shell. Bake at 400° for 15 minutes then reduce heat to 350° and finish baking—about 40 minutes longer. Pie is done when a knife inserted in the center comes out clean.

## KID BREAK!

Do your kids have puzzles with missing pieces? Don't throw them away! Instead, gather all the "broken" puzzles together and put on the table. Using a bottle of tacky glue, let your kids glue the pieces together over a 5x7 or 8x10 picture mat or frame. Use leftover pieces to form a wreath shape. When glue dries, let the kids paint the pieces with acrylic paints. Add decorative touches by gluing on rhinestones, beads, shells, sequins or buttons. Use the picture mats and frames for showing off your child's school picture. These make great gifts, too. Hang the wreaths on the Christmas tree or send to school for the teacher's gift.

# November 23

## TURKEY ENCHILADAS

*Prep. Time: 20-30 minutes Cook Time: 30-35 minutes*

2 cups cooked turkey, diced
2 cups shredded cheddar cheese
8 corn or flour tortillas
2 tablespoons butter
1 onion, finely chopped
¼ cup chopped green chilies
½ cup light sour cream
1 can cream of chicken soup
¼ cup oil
¼ cup milk

In saucepan, melt butter and sauté onion until tender. Add the chilies, sour cream and soup; mix well. Reserve ¾ cup of this sauce. To remaining sauce, add turkey and 1 cup cheese. In skillet, heat oil. Lightly fry tortillas and drain them on paper towel or brown paper. Fill each tortilla with turkey mixture and roll up, placing seam side down in an ungreased baking dish. Add milk to the ¾ cup reserved sauce and spoon over filled tortillas. Bake at 350° for 30 to 35 minutes. Sprinkle remaining cheese over hot tortillas just before serving.

### FOOD FOR THOUGHT

- The best time to give advice to your children is while they are still young enough to believe you know what you are talking about.
- She who is not healthy at 20, wealthy at 40, or wise at 60, will most likely never be healthy, wealthy or wise.
- A kitchen is the only place where tea is kept in a cocoa jar and labeled coffee.
- Food isn't the only thing that causes indigestion; you can also get it from eating crow and swallowing your pride.
- I thought I had it all together but I forgot where I put it.

## AMBROSIA

*Prep. Time: 20 minutes*

5 navel oranges, peeled and divided into sections
3 bananas, peeled and sliced
3 sweet apples, peeled and diced
1½ cups crushed pineapple in its own juice
2 cups coconut flakes
1 cup sugar

Combine all ingredients in a large bowl and mix well. Refrigerate until ready to serve. Serve with whipped cream if desired.

# November 24

## CREAM OF TUNA OVER TOAST

*Prep. Time: 20 minutes Cook Time: 25 minutes*

2 cans tuna, drained
1 can cream of chicken soup
1 can cream of mushroom soup
2 cups frozen peas, thawed
1½ cups milk
salt and pepper to taste
toast

In large saucepan, combine soups, milk, tuna and peas. Mix well and season with salt and pepper to taste. Heat over medium low heat until almost boiling. Spoon over toasted bread or baked biscuits.

## LEMON CUSTARD

*Prep. Time: 5 minutes Cook Time: 45 minutes*

1¼ cup sugar
3 tablespoons flour
½ teaspoon salt
4 eggs, separated
2 tablespoons butter, melted
⅓ cup lemon juice
1 cup milk

Beat egg whites until foamy. Set aside. Combine

sugar, flour and salt; add egg yolks and beat well. Stir in melted butter and lemon juice. Add milk slowly so it won't curdle. Fold in beaten egg whites. Put in baking dish and set dish in larger pan filled with cold water. Bake at 350° degrees for 40-45 minutes or until custard is set firm.

# November 25

## TURKEY ALMONDINE

*Prep. Time: 20 minutes Cook Time: 30 minutes*

3 cups cooked turkey, diced
1 pkg. frozen chopped broccoli, thawed
2 cans cream of chicken soup
1 cup real mayonnaise
1 teaspoon lemon juice
¼ teaspoon curry powder
2 cups shredded sharp colby cheese
1 cup dried bread crumbs
2 tablespoons butter, melted
1 cup toasted almond slices
cooked rice

Spread almond slices out evenly on a greased baking pan. Bake at 325° for 10 minutes, then turn off oven. In the bottom of a greased casserole dish, layer thawed broccoli. Spread diced turkey meat over broccoli. In blender on high speed, mix soup, mayonnaise, lemon juice and curry powder. Pour blender mixture over the turkey. Spread shredded colby cheese over the top of meat. Toss bread crumbs with butter and spread evenly over casserole. Sprinkle almond slices over the top and bake at 375° for 30 minutes. Serve over cooked rice.

## CRUNCHY PEANUT BUTTER CAKE

*Prep. Time: 10 minutes Cook Time: 40-50 minutes*

1 pkg. yellow cake mix with pudding included in mix
¾ cup brown sugar, firmly packed

1 ¼ cups chunky peanut butter
1 cup water
¼ cup oil
3 eggs
½ cup semi-sweet chocolate chips
½ cup peanut butter chips
½ cup chopped peanuts

Combine cake mix, brown sugar and peanut butter in mixing bowl. Beat on low speed with an electric mixer until crumbly. Reserve ½ cup peanut butter mixture; set aside. To remaining peanut butter mixture, add water, oil and eggs. Mix at low speed until moistened; then turn mixer to high speed and beat for a full 2 minutes. Fold in ¼ cup semi-sweet chocolate chips, ¼ cup peanut butter chips and ¼ cup chopped peanuts. Pour batter into a greased 9x13 cake pan. Combine remaining chocolate and peanut butter chips and nuts in with reserved peanut butter mixture. Spread evenly over top of cake. Bake at 350° for 40 to 50 minutes or until a knife inserted in the center comes out clean.

# November 26

## STUFFED TURKEY MANICOTTI

*Prep. Time: 30 minutes Cook Time: 30-35 minutes*

8 manicotti shells
1 lb. ground turkey
1 onion, finely chopped
1 clove garlic, minced
2 cans (6 oz.) tomato paste
2 cups water
2 tablespoons parsley flakes
1 ½ teaspoons salt
2 teaspoons oregano
1 tablespoon Italian seasoning
1 teaspoon basil
¼ teaspoon pepper
2 bay leaves
STUFFING:
1 lb. small curd cottage cheese

2 cups shredded mozzarella cheese

2 eggs

½ cup Parmesan cheese

2 tablespoons parsley flakes

1 tablespoon Italian seasoning

1 teaspoon sugar

½ teaspoon salt

⅛ teaspoon pepper

Cook manicotti shells as directed on package. Set aside. Brown meat in skillet with onion and garlic. Drain off all pan drippings when meat is cooked. Add tomato paste, water and seasonings. Simmer over medium low heat while preparing the filling. In mixing bowl, combine all "stuffing" ingredients and mix well. Rinse shells in cold water and fill with cheese mixture. Pour 2 cups of meat/sauce mixture in the bottom of a baking dish. Set filled manicotti shells seam side down on top of meat sauce. Top shells with remaining meat sauce. Cover pan with aluminum foil and bake at 350° for 30-35 minutes.

Serve with bread sticks and a tossed salad.

# November 27

## TURKEY CHOW MEIN

*Prep. Time: 20 minutes Cook Time: 25 minutes*

3 cups cooked turkey, diced

4 cups cooked rice

¼ cup soy sauce

⅛ teaspoon ground ginger

1 cup chopped celery

1 small can stems and pieces mushrooms, drained

1 can water chestnuts, drained and sliced

1 can been sprouts, drained

1 cup chicken broth

1 tablespoon cold water

2 teaspoons cornstarch

1 can or package chow mein noodles

In large skillet, combine turkey with chicken broth and all vegetables. Cook over medium heat, stirring constantly. Add soy sauce and ground ginger. In a separate container, combine cornstarch in cold water and stir until dissolved. Pour into skillet when contents are boiling hot. Continue stirring until liquid thickens and becomes more like a sauce. Add cooked rice and mix well. Serve immediately, sprinkling a handful of chow mein noodles over the top of each serving.

# November 28

## STEAK SUPREME

*Prep. Time: 15 minutes Cook Time: 1 hour 15 minutes*

1 round steak, cut in thin strips

3 tablespoons oil

1 large onion, sliced

1 large green pepper, sliced

2 cups whole fresh mushrooms

8 medium potatoes, peeled, quartered and sliced

1 teaspoon salt

1 teaspoon paprika

½ teaspoon onion salt

½ teaspoon garlic powder

2 tablespoons Italian salad dressing

Heat oil in skillet. Brown meat in hot oil, stirring often. Slice onions and green peppers; add to meat. Add Italian dressing. Cover and cook over medium low heat for about 30 minutes. Add potatoes and seasonings. Stir to blend seasonings evenly throughout. Cover and continue cooking for another 45 minutes or until potatoes are tender. Uncover pan and increase heat to brown potatoes during the last 10 minutes of cooking time.

Serve with green bean casserole (page 100).

# November 29

## BROILED HALIBUT

*Prep. Time: 15 minutes Cook Time: 10-15 minutes*

2 to 3 lbs. halibut fish fillets
2 large sweet onions, sliced
¼ cup butter
2 egg yolks
paprika to taste
salt to taste
2 tablespoons lemon juice
Tartar Sauce:
1 cup real mayonnaise
¼ cup sweet pickle relish
1 teaspoon fresh grated onion
1 teaspoon minced parsley

Melt butter in skillet. Separate onion rings and cook in hot butter, stirring often until golden. Mound cooked onion rings in center of broiling pan. Place fish fillets on top of onions. Combine egg yolks and lemon juice and beat well. Use a pastry brush and generously brush fillets with lemon egg mixture. Sprinkle salt and paprika over fillets according to your tastes. Broil for 10-12 minutes. Do not overcook! If fish doesn't flake when pierced with a fork after 12 minutes, then turn oven off and let fish set in hot oven for another 3 minutes. Check for doneness again. Serve with tartar sauce.

To make tartar sauce, combine all ingredients for sauce in small bowl and mix well.

## CREAMY COLESLAW

*Prep. Time: 10 minutes*

1 bag shredded cabbage for coleslaw
¼ cup minced onion
Sauce:
2½ cups Miracle Whip ™
¼ cup sugar
½ teaspoon celery seed
milk (use only enough to make a thick sauce)

Combine shredded cabbage coleslaw mix with onion; toss well. In a separate container, combine Miracle Whip™, sugar and celery seed. Begin adding milk a tablespoon at a time until you get a thick creamy sauce. Pour sauce over cabbage and mix well. Refrigerate for at least an hour before serving.

Serve with Hush Puppies (page 113).

# November 30

## ONE-PAN DINNER BAKE

*Prep. Time: 20 minutes Cook Time: 2 hours*

½ lb. bacon, cut in 2-inch strips
1 lb. lean ground beef or turkey
8 medium potatoes, sliced thin
2 cans French-styled green beans
2 cans cream of mushroom soup
1 soup can water
1 onion, sliced
1 large can French-fried onions
salt and pepper to taste

Partially cook bacon in skillet. Remove from skillet and place in a single layer across a 9x13 pan. Crumble raw meat over bacon. Sprinkle with salt and pepper. Layer slices of potatoes over meat. Sprinkle with salt and pepper. Combine water with both cans soup. Reserve 1½ cups diluted soup. Pour the rest over the potatoes. Lay separated slices of onion over potatoes. Cover pan with aluminum foil and bake at 375° for 1 hour 20 minutes. Remove foil and spread drained green beans over potatoes. Top with reserved diluted soup. Sprinkle French-fried onions over beans. Return pan, uncovered, to oven and bake for 30-40 minutes.

# December 1

## CHEESY CHILI DOGS

*Prep. Time: 15 minutes Cook Time: 20-25 minutes*

1 pkg. Hamburger Helper™ mix for Chili Tomato
1 pkg. hot dogs
½ lb. lean ground beef
chopped onion
shredded cheddar cheese

Prepare mix for Hamburger Helper™ according to package directions, except use only ½ pound of ground beef. Drain off grease. When it's time to add the macaroni, slice the hot dogs into ½-inch slices and add them, too. Stir to mix well and let simmer over medium low heat until liquid gets absorbed. Top with chopped onion and the cheddar cheese. Serve immediately.

Serve with fresh vegetables and your choice of dips (page 33).

Prepare Toasted Garlic Herb Sticks (page 18) to go along with the Cheesy Chili Dogs.

# December 2

## TURKEY POPPY SEED CASSEROLE

*Prep. Time: 10 minutes Cook Time: 20-30 minutes*

4 cups cooked turkey (or chicken), diced
2 cans cream of chicken soup
1 (16 oz.) container light sour cream
1 soup can milk
½ stick butter
1 sleeve of Ritz™ crackers
2 cups uncooked rice
1 tablespoon dried minced onion
1 green pepper, diced
poppy seed

In a large casserole dish, combine both cans soup, milk and sour cream. Stir. Add uncooked rice, turkey, minced onion and green pepper. Stir. Crush crackers into a fine powder and sprinkle over the top of the casserole. Drizzle melted butter over the cracker crumbs. Sprinkle poppy seed over the top. Cover and bake at 375° degrees for 20 to 25 minutes or until rice is cooked and casserole is bubbly.

Serve with Honey Bear Carrots (page 17).

# December 3

## POLISH SAUSAGE & KRAUT

*Prep. Time: 15 minutes Cook Time: 25 minutes*

2 lbs. polish sausage links, cut into pieces
1 can (1 lb.) sauerkraut
2 teaspoons caraway seeds
1 tablespoon brown sugar
8 to 10 small potatoes, peeled or use washed
    red potatoes with skins left on
water

In large soup pan, empty can of sauerkraut with juice in bottom. Sprinkle with caraway seeds and brown sugar. Stir to mix well. Add raw potatoes and pieces of polish sausage. Cover all with water and bring to a boil. Cook over medium high heat for about 25 minutes. Serve hot.

Serve with Seasoned Green Beans (see page 67).

# December 4

## VERMICELLI & VEGETABLE BAKE

*Prep. Time: 20 minutes Cook Time: 30-45 minutes*

1 (8 oz.) pkg. vermicelli
2 lbs. lean ground beef or ground turkey
2 large onions, chopped
1 tablespoon minced garlic
1 green pepper, diced
1 cup chopped celery
2 cups sliced fresh mushrooms
1 can creamed-style corn
2 cans tomato soup
3 soup cans water
2 teaspoons Italian seasoning
1 teaspoon oregano
1 teaspoon basil
1 teaspoon parsley flakes
salt and pepper to taste

Sauté meat with onions, green pepper, celery and garlic. Drain off all grease. Pour into a large casserole dish. Add mushrooms, corn, soup, seasonings and water. Mix well. Break vermicelli in pieces and stir into casserole. Cover dish and bake at 400° for 30 minutes or until Vermicelli is cooked and tender.

## BROWN SUGAR FUDGE CAKE

*Prep. Time: 15 minutes Cook Time: 30 minutes*

½ cup butter, softened
2¼ cups cake flour, sifted
1 teaspoon baking soda
1 teaspoon salt
2 cups light brown sugar, firmly packed
1 cup buttermilk (or use 1 cup milk with 1 tablespoon vinegar and let set for 3-5 minutes)
1 teaspoon vanilla

3 eggs
3 squares unsweetened chocolate, melted

Cream butter. Sift together flour, baking soda and salt and stir into butter. Add sugar, ⅔ cup buttermilk and vanilla. Beat on high speed with an electric mixer for 2 full minutes. Add remaining ⅓ cup buttermilk, eggs and cooled melted chocolate. Beat on high for 2 minutes longer. Pour into 2 greased and floured 8-or-9 inch round cake pans. Bake at 350° for 30 minutes or until knife inserted in center comes out clean. Remove cakes from pans and let cool before frosting.

## CHOCOLATE CREAM-CHEESE FROSTING

*Prep. Time: 5 minutes*

¼ cup butter, softened
1 pkg. (8 oz.) cream cheese, softened
3 squares unsweetened chocolate, melted
dash salt
3 cups sifted confectioner's sugar
⅓ cup heavy cream
1 teaspoon vanilla

Combine all ingredients in deep mixing bowl and beat on high speed with an electric mixer until smooth. (Note: left over icing goes great spread on graham crackers!)

# December 5

## SALMON CHOWDER

*Prep. Time: 20 min.  / Cook Time: 30 min.*

2 cans (7½ oz.) salmon, drained and bones removed
1 large yellow onion, chopped
2 stalks celery, chopped
1 small green bell pepper, seeds removed, chopped
1 clove garlic, minced

6-8 medium potatoes, peeled and cubed

3-4 carrots, sliced

2 cans creamed-style corn

1 teaspoon seasoned salt

¼ - ½ teaspoon black pepper

1 can (14½ oz.) chicken broth, divided

½ teaspoon dill weed

1 can (12 oz.) evaporated milk

In saucepan over low heat, combine ½ cup broth with chopped onion, celery, green pepper and minced garlic. Cook until vegetables are tender. Transfer to a large soup pan. Add remaining broth, potatoes, carrots, seasoned salt and dill. Cook over medium heat about 20 minutes or until potatoes and carrots are tender. Add evaporated milk, creamed corn and salmon. Season to taste. Heat thoroughly then serve.

# COOKIE SEASON

## GINGERBREAD COOKIES

*Prep. Time: 20 minutes Cook Time: 5-6 minutes per cookie sheet*

5 cups flour

1½ teaspoons baking soda

2 teaspoons ground ginger

2 teaspoons ground cinnamon

1 teaspoon ground cloves

1 cup Butter Crisco™ (or other shortening)

1 cup sugar

1 egg

1 cup molasses

2 tablespoons vinegar

Grease cookie sheets. Stir together flour, soda, spices, and ½ teaspoon salt. With an electric mixer set on medium speed, beat the shortening for at least 30 seconds. Add sugar and increase mixer speed to high, beating until fluffy. Add eggs, molasses and vinegar; beat well on high speed until batter is smooth and well blended. Add dry ingredients gradually, beating continually with mixer. When batter becomes too stiff for the mixer, remove beaters and stir by hand. Cover bowl and chill for 3 hours or overnight. After chilling the dough, divide in thirds. Refrigerate two-thirds while you work with one-third. On a lightly floured surface, roll out dough to ⅛-inch thickness. Use cookie cutters to cut out shapes. Place cut-outs on a greased cookie sheet about 1-inch apart. Be sure to make small openings in the top of each shape if you want to hang cookies as ornaments. Bake at 375° degrees for 5 to 6 minutes. Let cookies cool for about a minute before transferring them to a wire rack. This recipe will make about 60 cookies, depending upon the size of the cut-outs you use. Decorate cookies when they are completely cooled using icings in various colors.

# December 6

## TWICE-BAKED DOUBLE-STUFFED POTATOES

*Prep. Time: 20 minutes Cook Time: 15 to 30 minutes, varies according to amount cooked*

1 large baking potato per serving, scrubbed
½ lb. bacon, cut in half
½ cup milk
1 teaspoon salt
⅛ teaspoon pepper
2 teaspoons chopped chives
½ stick butter
½ teaspoon dry mustard
1 cup shredded cheddar cheese
1 cup light sour cream

Prick each potato with fork and wrap in a paper towel. Microwave each potato on high for 10 minutes. Turn over potatoes and continue cooking on high for another 5-8 minutes or until potato is soft to the touch. Wrap each cooked potato in aluminum foil and set aside to finish cooking. Place bacon strips on microwave roasting rack and microwave on high for 3 ½ to 7 minutes or until just done. Lay a piece of paper towel across top of bacon to prevent grease from splattering the inside of the microwave oven.

Unwrap each potato and slice the top off of each. Scoop out centers and place in medium bowl. Add milk, butter and seasonings to potato. Mash them with either a potato masher or beat on low speed with an electric mixer until smooth. Crumble bacon and add all but ⅓ to mashed potatoes. Stir to blend well. Dip mashed potatoes back into potato shells. Top with remaining crumbled bacon and shredded cheese. Place stuffed potatoes on serving plate and microwave on High for 3 to 5 minutes, rotating dish after half the time. Serve hot.

Serve with Cheesy Vegetable Medley (see page 180).

## FRESH GRAPE PIE

*Prep. Time: 20 minutes Cook Time: 40 minutes*

2 (9-inch) pie crust dough
5 cups red seedless grapes
1 tablespoon fresh lemon juice
1 cup sugar (more if needed)
3 tablespoons cornstarch
1 teaspoon ground cinnamon
½ teaspoon salt
2 tablespoons cold butter
milk and sugar for glaze

Line pie pan with one of the prepared pie crust dough, letting edges droop over the sides of the pan. Pulse grapes in blender in 3 to 4 batches to make them the consistency of being coarsely chopped. Transfer to colander. Drain off juice. Place grape pulp in large bowl. Add lemon juice. In another container, combine sugar, cornstarch, cinnamon and salt. Mix well and then pour on grapes. Stir well and then pour grapes into pie crust. Dot with pats of butter. Add other pie crust dough and flute edges to seal pie. Use a fork or knife and poke holes in the top crust to allow steam to escape. Brush with milk and sprinkle top crust with sugar. Bake at 425° for 40 minutes or until crust is brown and filling is bubbly.

# December 7

## BEEF ROAST & VEGETABLE SUPREME

*Prep. Time: 15 minutes Cook Time: 90 minutes*

1 3-to-5 lb. beef roast, trimmed of visible fat
1 can tomato soup
1 can cream of celery soup
1 can cream of mushroom soup
2 tablespoons Worcestershire sauce
1 tablespoon A-1™ Steak Sauce
1 large onion, sliced
8 medium potatoes, peeled
5 carrots, cut in thirds
2 teaspoons minced garlic
1 tablespoon rosemary
½ teaspoon sage
1 bunch fresh broccoli

Place roast in the center of a large roasting pan. Arrange peeled potatoes, cut carrots and fresh broccoli spears around meat. In a small mixing bowl, combine soups, Worcestershire sauce, steak sauce, minced garlic, rosemary and sage. Stir to mix well. Pour over meat and drizzle over vegetables. Arrange sliced onions over meat and vegetables. Cover and bake at 350º for 90 minutes or until meat is tender and cooked through when forked.

## PINEAPPLE-ZUCCHINI BREAD

*Prep. Time: 15 minutes Cook Time: 1 hour*

2 cups shredded or grated zucchini
1 cup crushed pineapple, drained
3 eggs
½ cup oil
½ cup unsweetened applesauce
2 cups sugar
2 teaspoons vanilla
3 cups flour
½ teaspoon baking soda
1 teaspoon salt
1 teaspoon baking powder
1 tablespoon ground cinnamon
chopped nuts, if desired

Combine eggs, oil, sugar, applesauce and vanilla and beat until thick and foamy; stir in zucchini and pineapple. Combine flour, baking soda, salt, baking powder, cinnamon and nuts. Sift dry ingredients into zucchini mixture and stir until just blended. Pour into two greased and floured loaf pans. Bake at 350º for 1 hour or until a knife inserted in center comes out clean.

# December 8

## TURKEY NOODLE BAKE

*Prep. Time: 15 minutes Cook Time: 45 minutes*

2-3 cups cooked turkey, diced
1 pkg. medium-wide egg noodles
1 medium zucchini, peeled, quartered and thinly sliced
1 cup mayonnaise
1 onion, chopped
1 green pepper, chopped
1 cup celery, chopped
1 carrot, sliced
1 cup American cheese cubes
2 cups shredded cheddar cheese
2 cans cream of celery soup
1 teaspoon celery seed
1 soup can milk

Cook noodles according to package directions until just slightly tender; drain. In a greased 9x13 pan, combine cooked noodles, meat, zucchini, onion, green pepper, celery, carrot and American cheese cubes; stir to mix well. In separate container combine mayonnaise with soup, celery seed and milk. Beat to stir well and pour over noodles and vegetables. Bake at 350º for 30 minutes. Top casserole with shredded cheese and bake for 15 minutes longer. Serve immediately.

# December 9

*While tonight's dinner is in the oven baking, you can work on completing your Christmas cards.*

## BEEF 'N' BARLEY CASSEROLE

Prep. Time: 20 minutes Cook Time: 90 minutes

5 cubed steaks, cut in bite-sized pieces
2 tablespoons oil
1 cup barley
2 cans (16 oz.) tomatoes with juice
¼ teaspoon thyme
¼ teaspoon marjoram
½ teaspoon sweet basil
¼ teaspoon cayenne pepper
¼ teaspoon oregano
½ teaspoon salt
⅛ teaspoon pepper
1 onion, finely chopped
1 cup celery, chopped
4 carrots, diced
1 cup shredded cheddar cheese

In a medium skillet, heat oil and sauté meat with onion, stirring often until meat is all browned. Drain meat and onion and put them in a deep casserole dish. Add tomatoes and seasonings and mix well. Stir in barley and carrots. Cover and bake at 350° for 1 hour 15 minutes. Remove lid and sprinkle shredded cheese over casserole. Return dish to oven, uncovered and bake for another 15 minutes. Serve immediately.

# December 10

## BAKED FISH WITH CREAMY CUCUMBER SAUCE

Prep. Time: 1 hour Cook Time: 30 minutes

1 lb. cucumbers, peeled, seeded, and sliced
1 tablespoon lemon juice
1 tablespoon chopped chives
1 tablespoon chopped dill or dill weed
¼ teaspoon salt
¼ teaspoon pepper
1 teaspoon paprika
⅓ cup light sour cream
1 cup plain yogurt
Fish fillets enough for each serving
1 fresh lemon
3 tablespoons butter, melted

First, prepare cucumbers and put them in a microwave-safe bowl. Microwave on high for 1 minute. Stir and cook for additional minute on high. Remove from microwave and rinse under cold water, draining well. Add the remaining ingredients (except fish, butter and lemon) to cucumbers and mix well. Refrigerate for 1 hour before serving.

Meanwhile, melt butter and add juice from lemon; stir well. With a pastry brush, baste fish fillets with lemon butter on both sides. Put in a shallow baking dish and bake at 350° for 30 minutes or until fish easily flakes when forked. Baste with lemon butter every 10 minutes or so. Serve hot with cold creamy cucumber sauce poured over fish.

Serve with baked potatoes and Spinach Salad (page 77).

# COOKIES OF THE MONTH

## PEPPERMINT PATTIE COOKIES

1 pkg. Devil's Food™ or chocolate mint cake
  mix
½ cup shortening
1 tablespoon water
2 eggs
powdered sugar
48 creme-filled mints
prepared frosting

Lightly grease cookie sheets. In large bowl, combine cake mix, shortening, water and eggs; mix well. Shape dough into 1-inch balls; roll in powdered sugar. Place 2-inches apart on greased cookie sheet. Bake at 375° for 7 to 10 minutes or until the edges are set. Remove from oven. Immediately place a creme-filled mint in center of each cookie, pressing down lightly. Remove from cookie sheets and cool completely. Decorate as desired with prepared frostings.

## LEMON CRINKLES

1 pkg. lemon cake mix
1 ¾ cups non-dairy whipped topping, frozen
3 tablespoons oil
1 egg, slightly beaten
sugar or colored sugars

In large bowl, combine cake mix, whipped topping, oil and egg; mix thoroughly. Cover and chill dough for 1 hour in the refrigerator.

Lightly grease cookie sheets. Shape dough into 1-inch balls and roll into sugar. Place balls 2-inches apart on greased cookie sheets. Bake at 350° for 10-12 minutes or until lightly golden around the edges. Allow cookies to cool for 1 minute before removing from cookie sheets.

## GOOF BALLS

1 can Eagle Brand™ milk
2 sticks butter
Rice Krispies™ cereal
54 caramels
large marshmallows

Melt butter, caramels and milk in double boiler, making sure butter is stirred throughout. Using a toothpick, dip a large marshmallow into the melted mixture, thoroughly coating it. Immediately roll the dipped marshmallow in the cereal. Set on waxed paper until cool.

# December 11

## CHICKEN WRAPS

*Prep. Time: 20-30 minutes Cook Time: 10-15 minutes*

12 (or more) iceberg lettuce leaves, washed, dried and chilled

¼ cup oil

3 cups cooked chicken breast, diced (may use canned, drained chicken if desired)

1 green or red bell pepper, diced

1 tablespoon sugar

1 teaspoon salt

⅛ teaspoon pepper

2 tablespoons soy sauce

2 tablespoons fresh minced ginger or ½ teaspoon ground ginger

¼ cup water

1 tablespoon lemon juice

1 bunch green onions, diced

1 cup chopped nuts

SAUCE:

¾ cup rice vinegar

2 tablespoons soy sauce

2 teaspoons sesame oil

4-5 drops hot sauce

Heat oil in large skillet and cook meat with chopped pepper, sugar, salt and pepper—stirring constantly until pepper pieces turn dark green. Add ginger, soy sauce, water and lemon juice; stir well and cook for 2-3 minutes over medium heat. Remove from heat and stir in chopped green onions and chopped nuts. For sauce, combine the vinegar, soy sauce, sesame oil and hot sauce. Blend well. Place a scoop of chicken mixture in chilled lettuce leaves and roll up, laying wraps seam side down on each plate. Pass the sauce separately for dipping.

---

CHRISTMAS CARD TRIVIA
Q. What is the average number of Christmas cards received by an American family over the holidays?
A. 26

# December 12

## TURKEY SOUP

*Prep. Time: 15 minutes Cook Time: 2 hours*

2 cups cooked turkey, cut in pieces (or use any remaining leftover turkey)

1 quart chicken broth

1 quart water

1 onion, chopped

2 cups celery, chopped

1 cup barley

2 carrots, sliced

2 cups frozen peas

1 can whole-kernel sweet corn, drained

1 tablespoon chicken bouillon

2 teaspoon salt

½ teaspoon pepper

1 teaspoon sweet basil

1 teaspoon Accent™

½ teaspoon thyme

1 tablespoon butter

In large soup pan, melt butter and cook onion and celery until tender. Add all remaining ingredients, stirring to blend well. Add more water if more liquid is needed. Cover pan and let cook over medium low heat for 1½ hours, stirring occasionally. Check doneness of barley and vegetables. If more cooking time is needed, increase heat to medium and cook uncovered for another 30 minutes.

Serve with corn bread cakes (page 9).

## BLESSINGS OF THE SEASON

Surely every child's favorite holiday is Christmas. In our home, we do lots of different activities during the Christmas season as well as some traditional favorites. One year the children voted to decorate the Christmas tree with only handmade ornaments. So we started out by making Gingerbread Cookies using this month's featured Gingerbread Cookie recipe. We used Christmas shaped cookie cutters to make the ornaments and then pierced the top of each by sticking a ball-point pen through. After the cookies were baked and iced, we cut various lengths of ribbon and tied them on to the tree.

Another activity I love is creating a "Blessings Door."The true meaning of Christmas is to celebrate the birth of our Lord. Sometimes with all the social pressures, it's easy to lose track of the real meaning of Christmas and instead get caught up in the commercialism. Children, especially, are prone to the "greedy gimmies" that attack during this season. To counter these "gimmies" I purchase several boxes of candy canes in various flavors and I tape candy canes on both the outside and inside of the front door. In order to take a candy cane off the door, each person (child and adult alike) must state something for which they are thankful. No repeats or copying of others' blessings is allowed, and only one candy cane per person per day is allotted.

Do you want to know what happens when you put up a "Blessings Door"? I was surprised to discover my kids brainstorming with their friends and other neighbors about what blessings they could give in order to take a candy cane. Their focus was on the blessings they already have instead of all the new stuff they didn't have. For a three week period, and this is the honest truth, I never heard anyone say they were thankful for that big expensive Christmas present they got last year. Instead, the blessings my kids and their friends were most thankful for included parents, teachers, warm homes, beds with blankets, having a telephone, knowing their grandparents, etc. What a neat way to celebrate the Christmas season. Being surrounded by others with a thankful heart really adds appreciation to the otherwise commercialized holiday.

# December 13

## HAM STEAKS

*Prep. Time: 5 minutes Cook Time: 15 minutes*

½ stick butter
6 ham steaks, cut at least ½-inch thick

Trim excess fat off of ham steaks. Melt butter in large skillet and brown ham steaks lightly on both sides. Put ham steaks and any remaining butter in a shallow baking dish and cover with aluminum foil and set in oven to keep warm until ready to serve.

## CHEESE GRITS

*Prep. Time: 10 minutes Cook Time: 30-40 minutes*

7 cups water
2 teaspoons salt
2 cups quick-cooking grits
⅓ cup chopped onion
small jar Cheese Whiz™
2 cups shredded cheddar cheese
4 eggs, beaten
1 stick butter
1 teaspoon Accent™
1 teaspoon garlic salt
dash cayenne red pepper
small can diced green chilies, drained

Cook grits according to package directions. Combine all remaining ingredients and mix well. Pour into a greased casserole dish and bake at 350° for 30 to 40 minutes.

# CHRISTMAS MUFFINS

*Prep. Time: 10 minutes Cook Time: 20-25 minutes*

1 egg

1 cup milk

¼ cup oil

2 cups flour

¼ cup sugar

3 teaspoons baking powder

1 teaspoon salt

½ cup candied mixed fruit (as used for fruitcakes)

Line muffin tin pan with paper muffin wrappers. Spray each wrapper with vegetable spray. In mixing bowl, beat egg with a fork. Stir in milk and oil. Add flour and remaining dry ingredients; mix well. Fold in fruit. Batter should be lumpy. Spoon batter into muffin papers until ⅔ full. Bake at 400° for 20 to 25 minutes. Serve warm.

# December 14

# LAYERED ONE DISH DINNER

*Prep. Time: 15 minutes Cook Time: 2 hours*

1½ lbs. lean beef stew meat

2 cups chopped celery

8 medium potatoes, peeled, quartered and thinly sliced

1 onion, chopped

4 carrots, quartered and diced

2 cans tomato soup

1 can cream of mushroom soup

2 cups water

2 teaspoons salt

½ teaspoon pepper

Cut each piece of meat into fourths. Layer diced meat in the bottom of a casserole dish. Add chopped onion over meat. Layer chopped celery, then potatoes, then diced carrots. In separate container, combine cans of soup, water, salt and pepper. Mix well and pour over casserole contents. Cover and bake at 350° for 2 hours.

# CINNAMON STREUSEL COFFEE CAKE

*Prep. Time: 15 minutes Cook Time: 20-25 minutes*

CAKE:

1 egg

¼ cup sugar

1 cup skim milk

2½ cups Bisquick™

2 tablespoons butter

STREUSEL:

1 cup brown sugar, firmly packed

2 tablespoons ground cinnamon

2 teaspoon nutmeg

¼ cup butter, melted

1 cup sugar

Combine ingredients for streusel mixture and set aside. Prepare coffee cake. Beat egg, sugar and milk on low speed with an electric mixer. Add Bisquick™ and melted butter and beat on low speed until well blended. Add half of streusel mixture to batter, stirring just until blended. Grease a bundt or tube pan. Sprinkle half of remaining streusel over bottom of pan. Pour in half of batter. Sprinkle remaining streusel mixture in the center of batter all the way around, creating an inner circle of streusel within batter. Pour remaining batter over top. Bake at 375° for 20 to 25 minutes or until a knife inserted comes out clean. Remove from pan and let cool before slicing.

# December 15

## CUBED PORK AND RICE

*Prep. Time: 10 minutes Cook Time: 1 hour*

6 pork cutlets
½ cup flour
1 teaspoon salt
⅛ teaspoon black pepper
½ cup butter, melted
3 cups instant rice, uncooked
1 pkg. Lipton™ dry onion soup mix
1 can cream of celery soup
1 can cream of mushroom soup
1½ cups milk
2 cups frozen baby peas, thawed

Combine flour, salt and pepper. Dredge pork cutlets in flour, coating both sides. Using a meat mallet, pound cutlets until almost doubled in size. Melt butter in skillet and brown both sides of the meat, then set meat aside on a platter to cool. In remaining hot butter, combine dry onion soup mix, celery soup, mushroom soup and milk. Stir to mix well and heat to almost boiling. Add uncooked rice and thawed baby peas. Cut pork cutlets into strips. Pour rice and peas mixture into a deep casserole dish and arrange strips of browned pork over top of casserole dish. Cover with foil and bake at 325° for an hour.

## SNOW ICE CREAM

*Prep. Time: 15 minutes*

1 egg
1 small can evaporated milk
1 teaspoon vanilla
½ cup sugar
1 to 2 cups milk
clean, white snow

Beat egg, evaporated milk and vanilla together. Add sugar and beat, then add milk. Add snow and stir, adding more snow until ice cream is of desired consistency. Serve immediately.

Note: A heavy snowfall helps make this recipe complete. Not available in all parts of the country.

# December 16

## GLAZED MEAT LOAVES

*Prep. Time: 20 minutes Cook Time: 1 hour*

1½ lbs. lean ground beef or turkey
1 cup crushed saltine cracker crumbs
1 large onion, finely chopped
½ green pepper, finely diced
1 tablespoon Worcestershire Sauce
¼ cup ketchup
1 teaspoon dry mustard
2 eggs
2 teaspoons salt
¼ teaspoon pepper
⅔ cup grape jelly
3 tablespoons prepared mustard
2 tablespoons honey

In large mixing bowl combine meat with cracker crumbs, chopped onion, diced green pepper, Worcestershire sauce, ketchup, dry mustard, eggs, salt and pepper. Mix well using both hands and kneading meat to blend ingredients. Form into 6 mini-meat loaves and place in a large roasting pan. Cover pan with lid and bake at 350° for 45 minutes. Remove pan from oven. In a small bowl, combine jelly, prepared mustard and honey. Spread over the top of each meat loaf. Replace lid and bake for 15 minutes longer.

Serve with Stuffed Potato Pepper (page 151) and Cooked Greens (page 173).

# CHRISTMAS PIE

*Prep. Time: 15 minutes Cook Time: 45 minutes*

1 unbaked 9-inch pie crust
1 cup sugar
½ cup butter
¼ cup milk
2 eggs, separated
½ cup chopped pecans
½ cup chopped dates
⅛ teaspoon salt
¼ cup chopped candied green cherries
¼ cup chopped candied red cherries

Cream sugar and butter together and gradually add milk. Beat on low speed with an electric mixer. Beat in egg yolks until creamy. Remove beaters and fold in dates, nuts and both kinds of chopped candied cherries. Clean beaters and in separate bowl, beat egg whites until stiff peaks form. Remove beaters and gently stir in salt and vanilla. Fold egg whites into fruit mixture and pour into an unbaked pie shell. Bake at 350° for 40-45 minutes. Serve with either whipped cream or ice cream. Decorate using whole candied cherries, dates and gum drops, if desired.

# December 17

## PIGS IN POTATOES

*Prep. Time: 20 minutes Cook Time: 45 minutes*

1 pkg. low-fat Smokie Links™
14 medium potatoes, peeled, quartered and sliced
½ cup milk
½ stick butter
2 teaspoons salt
¼ teaspoon pepper
1 teaspoon minced garlic
1 can shell-out green beans, drained
1 can waxed beans, drained
1 can black-eyed peas, drained
1 cup water with 1 tablespoon ham seasoning or bouillon dissolved
1 can tomato soup
2 tablespoons A-1™ Steak Sauce

In large soup pan, cover sliced potatoes with water. Add 1 teaspoon salt and minced garlic. Bring to a boil and cook until potatoes are tender and ready to mash. While potatoes are cooking, combine green beans, waxed beans and black-eyed peas in the bottom of a deep casserole dish. Dissolve ham seasoning (or bouillon) in 1 cup water and pour over beans. Add undiluted tomato soup and A-1™ sauce; stir to mix well. When potatoes are cooked, drain off all water. Add milk and butter and 1 teaspoon salt. Use a potato masher and mash potatoes until smooth and creamy (having potato lumps are okay). Slice Smokie™ links into 2-inch pieces and stir into mashed potatoes. Spoon potatoes over beans. Cover casserole dish with foil and bake at 350° for 20-25 minutes.

# RIBBON MOLD

*Prep. Time: 1 hour*

RASPBERRY LAYER:

1 cup boiling water
1 pkg. raspberry gelatin (small box)
1 pkg. (10 oz.) frozen raspberries

Pour boiling water on raspberry gelatin in large bowl. Stir until dissolved. Stir in frozen raspberries. Chill until slightly thickened, but not set. Pour into 8-cup mold or a 9x9x2-inch baking pan. Chill until firm.

ORANGE LAYER:

1 cup boiling water
1 pkg. orange gelatin (small box)
1 pkg. (3 oz.) cream cheese
1 can mandarin orange segments

Pour boiling water in orange gelatin. Stir until dissolved. Gradually stir in softened cream cheese. Chill until slightly thickened, but not set. Mix in orange segments with juice; pour evenly over raspberry layer. Chill until firm.

LIME LAYER:

1 cup boiling water
1 pkg. lime gelatin (small package)
1 can (8 ¼ oz.) crushed pineapple

Pour boiling water on lime gelatin. Stir until gelatin is dissolved. Stir in pineapple with juice. Chill until thickened slightly, but not set. Pour evenly on orange layer. Chill until firm. At serving time, unmold and cut into slices.

# December 18

## CHICKEN FETTUCCINE WITH GARLIC CHEESE SAUCE

*Prep. Time: 15 minutes Cook Time: 25 minutes*

1 pkg. fettuccine noodles
6 boneless, skinless chicken breasts
1 pkg. McCormick's™ Garlic Cheese pasta sauce blend
1 pkg. McCormick's™ Alfredo pasta sauce blend
2 cups milk
1 cup water
¼ cup butter

In medium saucepan, combine both pasta sauce mixes with milk and water. Add butter. Arrange chicken breasts in a shallow baking dish and pour 1 cup of the blended sauce over the chicken. Cover with aluminum foil and bake at 350° degrees for 20-25 minutes or until chicken is cooked through. Cook fettuccine noodles according to package directions. Drain and rinse in cold water. Pour warm cheese sauce over fettuccine noodles. Remove chicken from oven and serve a baked chicken breast on top of each serving of fettuccine.
Serve with Broccoli & Cauliflower Salad (page 87).

# December 19

## CRUNCHY BAKED FISH

*Prep. Time: 15 minutes Cook Time: 20 minutes*

2 lbs. haddock
    or other mild-flavored fish fillets, thawed
⅔ cup flour
½ teaspoon salt
⅛ teaspoon pepper
1 ½ cups crushed corn flakes
¼ cup Parmesan cheese

2 tablespoons Romano cheese

2 eggs

½ cup water

Combine flour, salt, pepper and both cheeses in shallow dish. Beat eggs in separate bowl and add water. Dip fish fillets in flour mixture, coating both sides, then dip in eggs. Next coat both sides of fish with corn flake crumbs. Arrange on a shallow baking dish that has been sprayed with non-fat vegetable spray. Bake at 400° for 15-20 minutes or until fish easily flakes when forked.

Serve with Homemade Potato Wedges. (see page 11.)

# KID BREAK!

**Treat your kids to some "Reindeer Pops"!** You'll need Tootsie Roll™ Pops (suckers), twist ties, tacky glue, white tissue paper, brown print fabric, brown chenille stem, ¼" wide red ribbon, pinking shears, masking tape, 1/4" black pompoms and 7mm wiggly eyes

Cut a 5-inch diameter circle out of the fabric with pinking shears. Fold circle into quarters and snip at the fold ⅛ of an inch from the point. Open flat and you'll have 2 holes located about ¼ of an inch apart. Cut the chenille stems into two pieces, one at 4 inches and the other at 1½ inches. Bend the 4-inch piece into a "U" shape and insert the ends in the two holes from the underside of the fabric. Tape the stem on to the fabric in the center. Place fabric on pop, secure with twist tie, then tie the ribbon on over that. Glue on eyes and a nose. Add the branches to each antler using the 1½ inch pieces of chenille stem.

# December 20

## BEEF SCALOPPINI

*Prep. Time: 20 minutes Cook Time: 45 minutes to 1 hour*

1 ½ to 2 lb. round steak, trim off excess fat

½ cup flour

2 teaspoons salt

1 tablespoon unseasoned meat tenderizer

¼ teaspoon pepper

¼ cup oil

½ cup beef broth

3 large tomatoes, chopped

1 teaspoon beef-flavored instant bouillon

4 cups fresh sliced mushrooms

1 onion, chopped

1 green pepper, sliced

1 garlic clove, minced

1 pkg. medium wide egg noodles

¼ cup Parmesan cheese

2-3 tablespoons butter

Trim excess fat off of meat. Using a meat mallet, beat meat until it is about ¼-inch thick. Cut into serving size pieces. Combine flour, meat tenderizer, salt and pepper. Dredge meat in flour mixture, coating both sides. Pound flour mixture into meat on both sides. Brown meat in hot oil for about 5 minutes (browning both sides). Stir in beef broth, tomatoes and beef bouillon. Cover; simmer for about 15 minutes. In another large skillet, melt butter. Sauté mushroom slices, onion, green pepper and garlic in butter until tender. Cook noodles according to package directions to desired level of doneness; drain and rinse in cold water. Add cooked vegetables to skillet with meat. Cover and let simmer for 10-15 minutes longer to blend flavors. Serve over cooked noodles. Sprinkle with Parmesan cheese if desired.

# PLUM PUDDING

*Prep. Time: 10 minutes Cook Time: 2 hours or more*

1 cup flour

¼ cup light brown sugar, firmly packed

2 teaspoons ground cinnamon

1 teaspoon baking powder

½ teaspoon allspice

½ teaspoon ground cloves

¼ teaspoon baking soda

½ cup milk

3 tablespoons oil

2 tablespoons molasses

1 egg

1 cup candied mixed fruit (such as used for fruit cakes)

½ cup raisins

½ cup chopped nuts

Sauce:

2 cups confectioner's sugar

½ cup butter, softened

1 tablespoon milk

2 teaspoons rum extract

1 teaspoon vanilla

Generously grease casserole dish. In mixing bowl, combine all ingredients except candied fruit, raisins and nuts. Stir batter until moistened. Fold in fruit, raisins and nuts. Pour into prepared casserole dish. Cover with tight fitting lid. Place casserole dish inside a large stock pan. Pour 3 to 4 inches of boiling water into stock pan. Cover stock pan with a lid and set pan over medium low heat. Add more water if necessary. Cook for 1½ to 2 hours or until pudding will spring back when touched. Prepare sauce by combining all sauce ingredients in small mixing bowl and beating on low speed with an electric mixer. Spoon sauce over each serving.

# December 21

## CANTONESE DINNER

*Prep. Time: 20 minutes Cook Time: 2 hours*

1½ to 2 lbs. pork steak, cut into strips, bones removed

2 tablespoons oil

1 onion, sliced

1 green pepper, sliced

1 cup fresh mushrooms, sliced

1 can (8 oz.) tomato sauce

¼ cup brown sugar

1½ tablespoons cider vinegar

2 teaspoons salt

2 teaspoons Worcestershire sauce

prepared rice

Brown strips of pork steak in hot oil and drain meat on paper towel or brown paper. In large casserole dish, combine all remaining ingredients with meat strips and stir to mix well. Seal dish with a tight-fitting lid and bake at 325° for 2 hours. Prepare rice about 15 minutes before serving.

# December 22

## CONTINENTAL CHICKEN

*Prep. Time: 15 minutes Cook Time: 2 hours*

1 pkg. (2¼ oz. or larger) dried beef

6 to 8 skinless, boneless chicken breasts

1 lb. turkey bacon

1 can cream of mushroom soup

1 can cream of chicken soup

½ cup sour cream

¼ cup flour

1 onion, chopped

1 cup celery, chopped

In the bottom of a greased casserole dish, arrange dried beef so ends overlap and the entire bottom of dish is covered. Cut each piece of chicken into fourths. Wrap each piece of chicken with a strip of turkey bacon. Lay each wrapped piece of meat on top of the dried beef. In another container, stir together soups, sour cream and flour. Pour over meat rolls. Sprinkle with chopped onion and celery, covering the top of the casserole dish. Put lid on casserole dish and bake at 350° for 2 hours. Serve over Buttered-Parsley Noodles (page 158).

# CHRISTMAS PUDDING

*Prep. Time: 20 minutes Cook Time: 30 minutes*

3 tablespoons butter

⅓ cup sugar

1 teaspoon vanilla

1 egg, separated

¼ cup chopped dates

¼ cup chopped candied cherries

¼ cup chopped pecans

2 cups finely crushed graham crackers

¼ teaspoon salt

1 teaspoon baking powder

½ cup milk

Sauce:

½ cup butter, softened

2 cups confectioner's sugar

1 egg, separated

1 teaspoon vanilla

Cream together butter with sugar and vanilla; add egg yolk and beat well. Stir in fruit and nuts. Mix cracker crumbs, salt and baking powder; add to creamed mixture alternately with milk. In small bowl, beat egg white on high setting with an electric mixer until stiff peaks form. Fold in stiff egg white with creamed mixture. Grease custard cups and fill each one ⅔ full. Cover cups with a sheet of waxed paper. Place custard cups in a pan of boiling water. Set pan in a 350° oven and bake for 30 minutes or until firm. Meanwhile, prepare sauce. Beat egg white until stiff peaks form. Set

aside. Combine remaining ingredients and mix well; fold in beaten stiff egg white. When pudding is firm, invert bowls onto a serving dish and spoon sauce over mounds of pudding. Serve warm.

# December 23

## FRENCH ONION SOUP

*Prep. Time: 15 minutes Cook Time: 40 minutes*

1 quart beef broth

2 teaspoons dry beef bouillon seasoning

4 large yellow onions, sliced thin

¼ cup butter

2 teaspoons salt

1 tablespoon sugar

2 tablespoons cornstarch

1 cup cold water

Parmesan cheese

In large skillet, melt butter and cook onions over medium heat until golden and tender. Add salt and sugar to onions. Transfer to a soup pan. Add beef broth and dry beef bouillon. Heat over medium heat until broth begins to boil. In cup of cold water, dissolve cornstarch and pour into boiling broth. Stir constantly until soup thickens to the consistency that you desire. Serve hot with your choice of sandwiches.

# December 24

## SWEET & TANGY HAM STEAKS

*Prep. Time: 15 minutes Cook Time: 30 minutes*

3/4-inch thick ham steaks, enough for each serving
2 cups sweet apple cider
1 cup maple syrup
1½ cup crushed cranberries
1 cup raisins
1 can pineapple chunks in its own juice
¼ cup orange juice
1 teaspoon ground cloves

Arrange ham steaks in a single layer in a jelly-roll pan. Combine remaining ingredients in mixing bowl and whisk to blend. Pour evenly over meat. Cover pan with aluminum foil and bake for 30 minutes at 375°.

Serve with Twice Baked Double-Stuffed Potatoes (page 238) and Corn Broccoli Bake (page 96). Sesame Bread Sticks (page 121) go well with this as well.

# December 25

## MARINATED HERBED TURKEY BREAST

*Prep. Time: 10 minutes Marinade Time: 4 hours Cook Time: 1½ hours*

1 frozen turkey breast, thawed
½ cup olive oil
1 tablespoon ReaLemon™
2 tablespoons dried minced onion
1 teaspoon minced garlic
1 teaspoon rosemary
1 teaspoon tarragon
1 teaspoon thyme
1 tablespoon salt
½ teaspoon pepper
1 teaspoon Accent™
¼ cup white wine

Shake all ingredients (except turkey) together in a jar. Pour over thawed turkey breast. Wrap meat in plastic wrap and refrigerate overnight or for at least 4 hours before baking. Remove plastic wrap from meat and place in roasting pan. Baste with marinade every 10-15 minutes while baking at 350° degrees for an hour and a half.

Serve with mashed potatoes.

## HERBED TOMATOES & ZUCCHINI

*Prep. Time: 10 minutes Cook Time: 10-15 minutes*

1 lb. zucchini, washed and cubed
4 large tomatoes, washed and cut in wedges
2 tablespoons olive oil
½ teaspoon dried basil
½ teaspoon salt
⅛ teaspoon pepper
½ teaspoon parsley flakes
2 large onions, sliced

In cake pan, combine cubed zucchini, wedges of tomato and rings of sliced onions. Combine olive oil and seasonings and shake well. Pour over vegetables, coating each evenly. Place pan under broiler and cook for 5 minutes. Remove and stir. Place pan under broiler and cook for another 5 minutes. Remove pan and stir. If vegetables are not yet to desired tenderness, replace pan under broiler and cook for an additional 5 minutes. Be sure to add herbed oil before each session of broiling.

# EGGNOG FREEZE

*Prep. Time: 15 minutes*

2 cups finely crushed sugar cookies
¼ cup butter, melted
¼ cup chopped pecans
1 pkg. (4-serving size) instant vanilla pudding
   mix
1½ cups dairy eggnog
1 cup heavy whipping cream

Combine cookie crumbs, butter and nuts; press 1½ cups into a 9x9 baking pan. Prepare pudding mix according to package directions, using the 1½ cups eggnog for the liquid. In small mixing bowl, beat heavy whipping cream on high with an electric mixer until soft peaks form. Fold whipped cream into pudding mixture. Turn pudding into pan with cookie crumb crust. Sprinkle remaining cookie crumbs on top. Cover with plastic wrap. Freeze for 6 hours. Let pan stand at room temperature for 15 minutes before cutting into serving pieces.

# December 26

## COFFEE STEW

*Prep. Time: 20 minutes  Cook Time: 1 hour or longer*

2 lbs. lean stew beef, cut in 1-inch cubes
2 teaspoons unseasoned meat tenderizer
1 teaspoon salt
¼ teaspoon pepper
1 teaspoon dried basil
3 cups water
2 cups prepared brewed coffee
1 medium to large onion, finely chopped
2 stalks celery, sliced
6 carrots, sliced
6-8 potatoes, peeled, quartered and sliced
1 pkg. (10-oz) frozen peas
1 can sweet corn, drained
2 cups tomato juice

2 teaspoons cornstarch
2 tablespoons parsley flakes

In medium saucepan, combine 1 cup water, meat tenderizer, stew meat and ½ of the chopped onion. Cover and cook over medium heat for 40 minutes. Meanwhile, prepare the rest of the stew. In large soup pan, pour 2 cups water and add remaining onion, sliced celery, carrots and potatoes, peas and corn. Pour in 1 cup coffee and 1 cup tomato juice. Add salt, pepper, basil and parsley flakes. Cook over medium heat, stirring often. When meat is cooked through and tender, pour contents of saucepan into the soup pan. Dissolve cornstarch in remaining cup of tomato juice. Pour into soup pan. Add remaining cup of coffee. If more liquid is needed, add water until all vegetables are covered. Continue cooking over medium heat until vegetables are tender, about 20 to 30 minutes.

Serve with Corn Bread (see page 15).

# KID BREAK!

### Clay Ornaments
⅓ cup water
½ cup salt
1 cup flour
food coloring
yarn or string
paint or varnish

Mix together water, salt and flour. Divide into sections. Add food coloring, if desired. Roll out on a floured board to about a ¼-inch thickness. Cut with cookie cutters. Use a pencil to put a hole in the top of each ornament, large enough to put yarn through for hanging. Place ornaments on baking sheet covered with foil. Bake at 275° for an hour. Let cool and then paint. When paint is dry, varnish the ornaments. Push yarn through the holes and hang.

# December 27

## HOT TURKEY SALAD

*Prep. Time: 25 minutes Cook Time: 10 minutes*

2-3 cups cooked turkey (or chicken), chopped
1 cup chopped celery
½ cup slivered almonds
1 cup Miracle Whip Free™
½ teaspoon salt
2 teaspoons chopped onion
3 hard boiled eggs, chopped
1 cup shredded cheddar cheese
2 cups crushed potato chips

In greased casserole dish, combine chopped turkey, celery, almonds, Miracle Whip™, salt, onion and chopped eggs. Blend well. Sprinkle crushed potato chips and shredded cheese over the top. Bake at 450° degrees for 10 minutes or until heated through.

Serve on homemade Whole Wheat Bread (page 54).

# December 28

## YAM & LINKS

*Prep. Time: 10 minutes Cook Time: about 30 minutes*

2 pkgs. (8 oz.) brown and serve sausage links
2 small pkgs. (3 oz.) orange gelatin
½ cup light brown sugar, firmly packed
¼ cup butter
2 teaspoons dried minced onion
3 teaspoons dry mustard
½ teaspoon salt
⅛ teaspoon pepper
2 cans yams, drained
1 can (1 lb. 4½ oz.) pineapple chunks, drained

In large skillet, brown sausage. Remove sausage and blot off grease on paper towel. In same skillet, sprinkle orange gelatin over pan drippings and add ¼ cup water. Stir to dissolve gelatin. Add brown sugar, butter, dry mustard, minced onion, salt and pepper. Heat over medium heat, stirring constantly until mixture begins to boil. Add yams and pineapple chunks. Reduce heat and simmer gently for 15 minutes, basting often with sauce. Add sausage, continue to cook, basting frequently for about 5 minutes longer.

# December 29

## MARINATED FLANK STEAK

*Prep. Time: 10 minutes Marinade Time: 3 to 24 hours Cook Time: 10-15 minutes*

2 lbs. flank steak
½ cup oil
½ cup dry white wine
½ cup lime juice
2 tablespoons sugar
2 teaspoons minced garlic
1 teaspoon salt
1 teaspoon dried marjoram, crushed
⅛ teaspoon pepper

With a sharp knife, score steak on both sides creating a diamond pattern. Place steak in a plastic bag and set in a shallow baking dish. For the marinade, combine the oil, wine, lime juice, sugar, minced garlic, salt, marjoram and pepper. Pour the marinade over the steak and close the bag. Refrigerate for 3 to 24 hours, turning occasionally. Before cooking, remove meat from marinade. Place meat on an unheated rack of a broiler pan. Broil 3 inches from the heat to desired doneness, turning once. Allow 8 to 10 minutes total time for medium rare. Sprinkle with salt and pepper.

Serve with Rice Pilaf (page 133) and your choice of vegetables.

# December 30

## BREAKFAST CASSEROLE (AND GREAT FOR DINNER!)

*Prep. Time: 15 minutes / Cook Time: 45 minutes*

1 lb. bulk ground sausage
8 eggs
1 pkg. frozen hashbrowns, thawed
2 cups shredded cheddar cheese
1 small onion, finely chopped
1 cup milk
½ teaspoon basil
½ teaspoon parsley
½ teaspoon chives
½ teaspoon coarse black pepper
½ stick butter

In a large skillet, melt butter. Evenly spread out hashbrowns and cook over medium heat until they begin to turn brown on the bottom. Transfer hashbrowns into deep casserole dish. In same skillet, cook sausage until done. Drain off grease. Crumble sausage over hashbrowns. In separate bowl, combine eggs with onion, milk and seasonings. Beat well and pour over meat and hashbrowns. Stir well to blend eggs and seasonings throughout hashbrowns. Bake, uncovered, at 400° for 35 minutes. Cover top with shredded cheese and continue baking for another 10 minutes. Serve when eggs are cooked firm and cheese is hot and bubbly.

# December 31

*Today is New Year's Eve. It's also "You're ALL DONE Day." Take the night off, go out and enjoy...or get carryout from your favorite restaurant. Toast the evening and reflect on the joy the past year has brought and the promise of the next— just a day away.*

*Make the most of your New Year's resolutions by*

- *putting each resolution in writing.*
- *assigning a time-line (how long it will take you to accomplish your goal) for each resolution.*
- *listing specific steps necessary for each resolution to be fulfilled.*
- *transferring each step and time-line to the upcoming calendar.*

*planning your work and working your plan!*

# INDEX

# Kid Breaks

# Kitchen Tips & Tricks

# Food For Thought

## SOURCES:

*Celebrate Today!* by John Kremer. Published by Open Horizons Publishing Company, 209 S. Main St., Fairfield, IA 52556-0205. c 1995 by John Kremer.

*What Counts: The Complete Harper's Index* edited by Charis Conn and Ilena Silverman. c 1991 by Harper's Magazine. Published by Henry Holt and Company, Inc., 115 West 18th St., New York, NY 10011.

WE CARE COOKBOOKS published by WWKI WE CARE, Inc., Kokomo, Indiana. Food for Thought excerpts used. WE CARE is a community-based fundraising organization to provide money to local charities that provide food, clothing, housing, etc., to people in need.